NAPOLEON

PORTRAIT
By David, December, 1797

NAPOLEON

Translated from the French by Hamish
Miles

With an Introduction by H.A.L. Fisher

Jacques Bainville

Simon Publications
2001

Copyright © 1932 by Jacques Bainville

First published in London by. J. Cape.

Library of Congress Control Number: 32035768

ISBN: 1-931541-79-5

Published by Simon Publications, P. O. Box 321, Safety
Harbor, FL 34695

CONTENTS

ILLUSTRATIONS

INTRODUCTION

LORD ACTON used to say of Napoleon that he was the best
known character in history, and when we consider the wealth
of letters and recorded conversations, of memoirs and official
documents, of long biographies and short monographs which
go to the making of any well constituted Napoleonic library,
we may concede at once that no life has been more fully
reported and discussed. Moreover the material is constantly
increasing in volume. There seems no end to the curiosity
which is excited by the meteoric career of the wonderful man
who, starting without advantage of wealth or station, raised
himself by sheer force of genius, and within very few years,
to be master of France and arbiter of Europe.

Yet it is one thing to have information about Napoleon,
and another thing to understand him. Sometimes those who
have read most, understand least. This cannot be said of
M. Jacques Bainville, whose brilliant volume on Napoleon is
now presented to English readers in the excellent version of
Mr. Hamish Miles. M. Bainville has not stinted his researches.
Certainly the present writer, who has devoted more time than
he cares to acknowledge to the study of Napoleonic literature,
is not the man to find chinks in the scholarly equipment of
this most atmospheric and erudite Frenchman. But what is
more remarkable than M. Bainville's acquisitions is the skill
with which, avoiding the most fascinating excursions in all
directions, he succeeds in concentrating every scattered ray
of light upon Napoleon the man, and the insight with which
he dissects the why and wherefore of his actions. In a word he
has painted a luminous, intelligible portrait, omitting no
essential trait, giving us the dark shadows as well as the high
lights and just so much of the background as is necessary to
set off the figure to advantage. It is not difficult to account
for M. Bainville's success. The author of an admirable short

3

history of France is already a past master of historical perspective. He knows what should be said and what may be left aside. He has the courage of his affirmations and the still rarer and higher courage of his exclusions. He can omit all the battle pieces. He can say nothing of strategy and tactics, little of diplomacy and administration. The enquirer who wants to learn why Marengo was won or why Waterloo was lost must go elsewhere for his information. M. Bainville is not concerned with Napoleon the soldier but with Napoleon the man. Then, our biographer has the valuable gift of detachment. Certainly he is a patriotic Frenchman who cares little for the figure which his hero may cut in the eyes of an Austrian, a Spaniard or an Englishman. But neither is he interested in awarding epithets of praise or blame. Perhaps he feels that a career crowded with burning activity and lived at the very heart and centre of the world's affairs must lend itself to every shade of moral approval or disapproval. Did not Napoleon himself say 'I have so often made mistakes that I do not blush for them'? M. Bainville, at any rate, is content to explain, leaving his readers to judge. It is a wise and conscientious method and sometimes most impressive, as in the exact and entirely judicial account of the circumstances which led up to the murder of the Duc d'Enghien. Finally he has two qualities, both necessary to the effective discharge of his heavy task, psychological insight and political grasp. How excellent, for instance, is that phrase 'an exalted coolness of mind' as a description of Napoleon's normal condition, and again how just is that other observation that 'Napoleon never knew whether he was moving because he could not know; and that was why he always went further!' And on the political side, the reader will admire the clever use of the Belgian *leitmotiv* recurring again and again through the swift narrative like the note of a funeral bell heard above howling winds, for we are never allowed to forget that the underlying fact of the European struggle was Napoleon's resolve to retain Belgium, and the untiring determination of England and her

Allies to wrest from him this, the first prize of revolutionary France, and the territory above all others which no child of the revolution could cede to an enemy and still continue to reign in Paris.

We cannot have everything in one volume. It is M. Bainville's role, as interpreter, to study the activity of Napoleon's will and to see the world as he saw it. Others saw and continue to see that world otherwise, thinking then, as they continue to think now, that this man was a standing menace to the well-being of Europe and that while he was prepared to take every kind of risk in war, he would at no time take any kind of risk for peace. Much may be said on these lines which falls outside M. Bainville's purview, for among the necessary omissions of this delightful book is the whole case for British and Coalition diplomacy in the Napoleonic age.

H. A. L. Fisher

PREFACE

So many books, essays, studies — not to mention memoirs — have been written about Napoleon, about matters concerning him directly or indirectly, and about the events with which his name is connected, that the zealous bibliographer Kircheisen was able to assemble nearly two hundred thousand entries. And we are not yet at the end. Archives are opening, and will continue to open. The memoirs of Queen Hortense, and those of Caulaincourt, have been recently published. Other eye-witnesses have left some which will be printed in their turn. And there has been no slowing-up in historical works. A fairly complete Napoleonic library should include about ten thousand volumes. For the bare essentials, at least five hundred are necessary.

It is not astonishing that a life which stands out so conspicuously from the common order should remain the object of this intense interest. The marvellous history of Napoleon Bonaparte, as a whole or in detail, will long be recounted. Standing clear from any foregone conclusions, we have attempted to write his natural history.

He himself used to say that *how?* and *why?* were such useful questions that they could not be used too often. We have used them on himself. And, by composing a continuous biography, leaving the main figure constantly before the reader's eyes, we have sought to proffer answers to the *hows* and *whys* that arise in the minds of all who have the inquiring taste for obtaining a clear reason for events. Napoleon used to say of Tacitus, in whom he saw only the greatest colour-painter of antiquity, that he 'did not convey the motives which impelled men to their actions'. Our wish is to understand and set forth the career of Napoleon Bonaparte, to establish its connecting links, to discover the 'motives' which 'impelled' him, the reasons which he may possibly have had for taking

7

one decision rather than another. We have tried to discern the general and particular causes of a fortune which has something prodigious in it, and of events which seem to have been fashioned by some Eastern story-teller.

In striving for comprehension of Napoleon, we abstain from any pre-established judgment, and, with especial care, from any explanation drawn from his character. The great weakness of such explanations is that they illuminate nothing, and that facts have to be adjusted to the conception which it is sought to impose on them. It is necessary, too, to be clear on the definition of a character, on the dominant trait or on the 'master faculty'.

For our own part, it is our aim that, when the reader closes this book, he may see the life of Napoleon with the unity and the breaks of unity which it contains, and then should form his own opinion of its central figure. And if every reader who has an opinion kept his own, our object, which is only one of comprehension, would be completely attained.

Comprehension is not easy. To tell the story at once accurately and succinctly is no less so. In everything connected with Napoleon, the extreme abundance of events compressed within a short period, the wealth of information and sources, the mingling of passions, all make the task particularly difficult. We have tried to keep always as close as possible to reality by checking the authorized testimonies one against the other, and by using the classic works, that is to say, those which are not only learned but well-considered.

Albert Sorel has thrown light upon the heights of the subject. The clarity of Thiers, in spite of the panegyrical tone that spoils many parts of his work, should not be under-rated: he had collected many oral traditions, seen many documents, and he wrote his history of the Empire after himself acquiring experience of affairs and government alongside men of the Empire. But there were things which Thiers did not know and could not know. When these were divulged, they invalidated several of his theses. To-day it is fashionable to minimize the work of Albert Sorel, and to set up against the German historian Fournier. The curious thing is that one cannot abandon Sorel without falling back into the decried groove of Thiers.

It is unnecessary to add that one cannot concern oneself with Napoleon without making use of the researches of Albert Vandal, Henry Houssaye, Chuquet, Frédéric Masson — rich in penetrating views amid a wealth of tiring detail — and of the book of M. Louis Madelin on Fouché, a book which is one of the keys to the reign, and of the same author's recent studies of the government of the Consulate and Empire. And I cannot conclude without thanking my friend M. Frédéric Delebecque, whose modesty is combined with a profound knowledge of the Napoleonic epoch. He has been good enough to read this work line by line, surveying it with scrupulous accuracy. I might say that he had been my conscience.

J. B.

CHRONOLOGICAL TABLE

Ætat		
–	1769	Napoleon Bonaparte born (August 15th)
10	1779	Enters school at Brienne
15–16	1784–5	Military School in Paris
18	1787	Lieutenant in Regiment of La Fère
20	1789	Beginning of FRENCH REVOLUTION
24	1793	Sardinian expedition (Maddalena) Lieut.-Colonel in Corsica Siege of Toulon (Decr.)
25	1794	General of artillery under Kellermann in Italy 9th of Thermidor (July 27th): Robespierre deposed Refuses service in Vendée; removed from active list; poverty in Paris
26	1795	DIRECTORY established on 5th of Fructidor (Aug. 22nd) 13th of Vendémiaire (Oct. 4th): Barras and Napoleon suppress royalist revolt in Paris. Promoted General again ('General Vendémiaire')
27	1796	Marries Josephine (March) Commander-in-chief in ITALY Montenotte (April 11th) Arcola (Nov. 15-17th)
28	1797	Rivoli (Jan. 14th) Negotiations at Leoben (April) Supports Directory against moderates and royalists, through Augereau, in *coup* of Fructidor (Sept.) Treaty of Campo Formio (Oct. 17th)

29	1798	EGYPTIAN EXPEDITION: leaves France, May 19th
		Malta (June 12th)
		Lands in Egypt (July 1st)
		Battle of Pyramids (July 21st)
		Battle of Nile (August 1st)
		Cairo (September)
30	1799	Siege of Acre (April)
		EUROPEAN COALITION against France (April)
		Return to France (August 22nd–October 8th)
		18th–19th of BRUMAIRE (Nov. 9th-10th): Council of Five Hundred deposed and CONSULATE established
		Provisional consulate (Nov. 11th)
		First Consul (December 29th)
31	1800	Division of France into Prefectures, etc. (February)
		Second campaign of ITALY
		Marengo (June 14th)
32	1801	Treaty of Lunéville (February 9th)
		Concordat with Pope Pius VII (July 15th)
33	1802	Peace of Amiens (March 27th)
		Amnesty to *émigrés* (April)
		Legion of Honour founded (May)
		Consul for life (August 2nd)
34	1803	The Civil Code issued (March 15th)
		War with England reopened (May 18th)
35	1804	Execution of Duc d'Enghien (March 21st)
		EMPIRE proclaimed (May 18th)
		Coronation (December 2nd)
36	1805	King of Italy (March 18th)
		Fresh coalition against France (August 5th)
		Trafalgar (October 21st)

CHRONOLOGICAL TABLE

36	1805	Austerlitz (December 2nd)
		Peace of Presburg (December 24th)
37	1806	Jena (October 14th)
38	1807	Eylau (February 7–8th)
		Friedland (June 14th)
		Treaty of TILSIT (July 7th)
		Decree of Milan regulating blockade (December 17th)
39	1808	Creation of new nobility (March 1st)
		Abdication of Charles IV of SPAIN: insurrection (May)
		Napoleon in Madrid (December 4th)
40	1809	England and Austria ally against France (April)
		Eckmühl (April 22nd)
		Essling (May 22nd)
		Wagram (July 5–6th)
41	1810	Marriage to Marie Louise of Austria (April 1st)
		Holland united with France (July 9th)
42	1811	King of Rome born (March 20th)
43	1812	War with RUSSIA (June 22nd)
		Moscow (September 14th)
		Passage of Beresina (November 26–28th)
44	1813	Alliance of Austria, Prussia and Russia (March)
		Lützen (May 2nd)
		Bautzen (May 19th)
		Wellington occupies Madrid (June 21st)
		Dresden (August 26–27th)
		Leipzig (October 18–19th)
45	1814	Campaign in France against invading Allies (February-March)
		Paris surrendered (March 31st)
		ABDICATION of Napoleon at Fontainebleau (April 14th)

45	1814	Louis XVIII arrives in Paris (May 3rd
		Napoleon lands on Elba (May 4th)
46	1815	Return from Elba (March 1st): the HUNDRED DAYS
		Reaches Paris (March 20th)
		Waterloo (June 18th)
		Final ABDICATION (June 22nd)
		Paris occupied by Allies (July 14th)
		Napoleon on the *Bellerophon* (July 15th)
		Arrival at St. Helena (October 17th)
51	1821	DEATH of Napoleon (May 5th)
–	1840	Remains buried at the Invalides, Paris (December 15th)

NAPOLEON

CHAPTER I

THE KING'S PUPIL

IN 1768 Louis XV annexed Corsica to the kingdom of France. How could he have suspected that, in the following year, the founder of a fourth dynasty would be born within this new acquisition? And what if the annexation had not taken place? There were many opposed to it in France, many who thought it a useless burden. Suppose that their voices had prevailed and the island had fallen into the hands of the English; or again, that Paoli had brought an independent Corsica into being. What would have been the lot of Napoleon?

An obscure life amid clannish feuds, with his worldly goods a few rows of olives, a meagre vineyard; perhaps some commonplace, respectable, administrative post, in the footsteps of his grandfather, Ramolino, inspector of roads and bridges under the Genoese republic. The English? It is doubtful whether they would have given this young Corsican a post. And to offer his sword to the service of a foreign power, Napoleon would still have required a military education. Where would he have got it? Had it not been for France, his genius would not have been revealed. This annexation was his first good fortune, for Corsica thus became part of a reasonably liberal and trusting nation, generous in opening her best schools to new-made Frenchmen. And then, just when the young man from Ajaccio was twenty years old, that same country was to be plunged into a vast confusion which offered unrivalled chances of fortune to men of parts.

The extraordinary man realized not only the element of the prodigious entering into his destiny, but also the concatenation of events required to raise him to Empire, and make an obscure lieutenant into the nephew of that king whose downfall he had witnessed on August 10th, 1792. On St.

Helena, once, he said that it would be a thousand years before the circumstances which had gathered round him recurred, picked out another man from the crowd, and raised him to such heights.

Of his beginnings he was not forgetful. They were not imposed by the nobility of his family, although this was quite authentic. Charles-Marie Bonaparte, his father, a lawyer of sorts, was a gentleman, poorly off and burdened with children. Napoleon was to be the Tom Thumb of this large brood. They scraped along at Ajaccio, with a little land and some expectations of a mulberry plantation, counting on an occasional gift and on the legacy of Uncle Lucien, the archdeacon, who had something put by. In 1776 Charles Bonaparte obtained a certificate to attest that his means were insufficient to educate his sons, and for his last journey but one to the mainland he borrowed twenty-five louis from the Governor, Beaumanoir, which were only repaid by the First Consul. Such was his starting-point.

Napoleon smiled at the fulsome genealogists who declared his forebears to have been rulers of Treviso and Bologna. But he was connected with the Bonapartes, or Buonapartes, richer in quarterings than in florins, who had long been known in Tuscany, and were in general noted for a taste for letters. Early in the sixteenth century one of them had settled at Ajaccio. The Bonapartes were notaries and suchlike, carrying on clerkly work in any case, and acquiring good repute but scant fortune. The Corsicans were neither boors, nor bourgeois, nor gentlefolk, and were almost untouched by feudal notions; there was a strong sense of equality amongst them, because their wealth was very modest, and that was why they delighted the heart of Rousseau. Charles Bonaparte, the hard-up attorney, only made use of his good birth after the annexation, when blue blood became a token for favours. One thing certain is that the connection between the Tuscan and Corsican branches of the family was still surviving at the end of the eighteenth century

Charles Bonaparte had breeding. Outstanding physique, quick intelligence, courage, and charm marked him out. At the age of eighteen he had married Letizia Ramolino, a girl of fourteen. She was beautiful, hardly educated, a powerful and even slightly virile woman, a true daughter of Western Corsica, that blend of Moors and Greeks and Phœnicians. Through her, perhaps, Napoleon inherited more from Carthage than from his father's Florence, and had in his veins some drops of the same blood as Hannibal's. Is anything more uncertain and indefinable than the transmissions of heredity?

Letizia was the daughter of a Corsican who held an official post under the Genoese administration. Her widowed mother had married a captain of the Genoese navy named Fesch, a native of Basel, father of the future Cardinal. The family had served the Genoese conquerors, and Charles was likewise to rally to the new regime and serve France.

In years to come, when Letizia was an Emperor's mother, people laughed at her avarice no less than at her outlandish speech. But she had known days when money was scarce, a brood of children to rear with one servant-girl, patched shoes, frugal ways. Corsica does not flow with milk and honey. An island proverb says that you eat there as best you can: 'if it doesn't kill you it will fatten you'; and she would often repeat the saying. She retained the habit of rising still hungry from table: so long had she had eight young mouths to fill — Joseph, Napoleon, Lucien, Elisa, Louis, Pauline, Caroline and Jerome! And with a fortune of a million provided for her, Madame Mère would excuse her stinginess in her Parisian palace, saying: 'But I've got seven or eight kings who'll fall back on me one of these days'.

The son of young and fruitful parents, Napoleon was born on August 15th, 1769, after Joseph, but really the fourth child, two others having died as infants. Begotten in battle and adventure, he was born into scheming and politics. His days within his mother's womb were as an image of his history.

Charles Bonaparte had fought for Corsica's freedom by Paoli's side. It was during the month after the renowned victory over the French at Borgo that Napoleon was conceived. But Paoli's raw troops had perforce to yield, and in May 1769, at Ponte Novo, came the collapse. Despite her pregnancy, Letizia had followed her husband. Everybody, even the women, sought refuge from the conquerors on the Monte Rotondo. Charles had issued a flaming appeal to Corsican youth for a mass levy, and was eager for further resistance. But it was a lost cause. Paoli had taken ship and abandoned the island. The Comte de Vaux granted the refugees pardon and a safe-conduct. They returned to Ajaccio, and there Letizia was delivered of a son.

Later she used to tell how, during that dramatic pregnancy, those rides by night, those days of alternating triumph and defeat, she could feel the child within her furiously stirring. So Napoleon knew the hazards of war, and went from an Austerlitz to a Waterloo, before ever he saw the light.

Meanwhile Charles Bonaparte had been thinking things over. Corsican freedom was a hopeless cause, and France held out the hand of reconciliation. To France he rallied; and rallied whole-heartedly, for henceforth the Bonapartes were always to belong to the French party. But he was resolved not to let his adherence go unrewarded. Paoli's lieutenant made approaches to the commander-in-chief. M. de Marbeuf welcomed the advances of this Corsican notable, and Charles became an untiring, a skilful, and a fortunate postulant for favours.

Thus, thanks to the kind protection of M. de Marbeuf, Charles Bonaparte became a representative of the nobility in the new Corsican assembly, and obtained educational grants for his offspring. To Marbeuf that Napoleon owed his entry to Brienne — another piece of good fortune in his life. He did not regret that rout at Ponte Novo which made him a Frenchman.

It is best to admit that Napoleon's childhood was not a

sequence of prodigies. He was a turbulent, self-willed little boy, who liked playing at soldiers and was quick at figures: an ordinary little Corsican, half a peasant, living with zest, yet meditative, and drunk with the heady magic of his isle. The tales of the fighting in the *maquis*, local politics, the feuds of Ajaccio's factions, his father's share therein, financial straits, the famous mulberries, fruitful chiefly in disappointments — all these fell upon a burning imagination, and have their share in his first shapings, especially if we remember the characteristic trait in Napoleon which comes only second to his inborn gift for command — his memory, almost infallible, and at the service of an intelligence which turned everything to good use.

Still, alongside the little French boys whose companion he was soon to be, Napoleon was an uncouth child. At the age of nine he hardly spoke except in his Corsican dialect, and was a foreigner when he was taken to the mainland. Charles Bonaparte had attained his goal. Thanks to Marbeuf, the grants were obtained. Napoleon was to be an officer, Joseph a priest. They embarked on December 15th, 1778, and on his way to Versailles, whither he was bound as representative of the island nobility, their father left the two boys at the college of Autun.

France did things well. She undertook the free education of these sons of the rebel Paoli's lieutenant, with the children of poor gentlemen of good birth; and thus, between the ages of nine and seventeen, Napoleon was to lose touch with his native island, to which he returned only in September, 1786. As a 'King's pupil', he received a French upbringing in French surroundings, alongside of well-born lads from every province in the kingdom. He was reared in official institutions, the first directed by religious, the second by soldiers: in fact, he was made familiar with the traditions of the older France.

But no house is so well screened that the air of the time does not enter it, and at Brienne, as at the military school in

Paris, Napoleon was to breathe the air of the eighteenth century. Were not the Minim Fathers themselves unwittingly imbued with that spirit? They did not make a truly practising Catholic of their pupil, and their religion was fairly worldly. Of a man who had never made his first communion, the Emperor was to say: 'Something was lacking in his education'. His own first communion he made like a well-brought-up boy. But the outward observances of the faith were always to astonish him, and he let out the remark: 'I thought men really were more advanced'. In short, it gave him the wherewithal to plan the Concordat, and not much else.

The uprooted islander thus transplanted, then, was to absorb French ideas despite himself, at the same time reacting against them. One of his teachers already discerned his 'volcanic' temperament (defining his style as like 'granite warmed by a volcano'), and within him there was preparing a potent mixture which had its bearings on the future; nor did that particular blend repeat itself, for the same surrounding influences produced no result on the soft nature of his brother Joseph.

Charles Bonaparte left his sons at the college at Autun, Joseph to study the humanities, Napoleon to learn French. Within four months the latter was fit to enter the royal military school at Brienne. When the brothers parted, it is said, Joseph was in tears, but Napoleon's eyes were almost dry. And he strove to conceal his single tear, which, said the Abbé Simon, one of his masters, betrayed more real grief than a noisy lamentation. The Abbé judged accurately. Character and will were made manifest by the boy's self-restraint.

At Brienne Napoleon received, 'at the expense of His Majesty', a very careful education and a serious course of studies. Saint Germain, the War Minister, an admirer of Frederick II who wished to remodel the French army on Prussian lines, himself drafted the programme. Well-informed officers were to be trained, capable of mixing in good society and of making the uniform honourable in every respect. The school was controlled by religious, with lay masters collaborating, and private tutors for mathematics. Some Latin was taught, and German also, a language regarded as indispensable to soldiers, but in which Napoleon was never any more at home than he was in the tongue of Cicero. The polite accomplishments, music and dancing, were not neglected. In fine, it was a well-rounded course of teaching, which, though it had flaws, had no more than systems of later invention from which it did not greatly differ.

The important point is that this teaching was designed to mould French officers, and Napoleon absorbed it from his tenth year along with other boys, from Brittany, Lorraine and Provence, whose parents like his own had proved their title to nobility. Of this he was to retain indelible impressions which enabled him, first and foremost, to understand France and speak to France. 'I belong to Champagne more than to Corsica,' he said at St. Helena, scanning his past, 'for I was reared at Brienne from the age of nine.' Heredity cannot be overlooked, but education may be said to correct it or give it orientation. To explain the whole of Napoleon by his Italian origins, as Taine followed Stendhal in doing, is too simple. Or rather, explanations of that kind are insufficient. What likelihood was there that, in the dawn of the nineteenth century, the heart of the French people would be conquered by a *condottiere* of the Quattrocento, a Castruccio Castracani? For the 'magic' of Napoleon's name is one of the most astounding phenomena of his history, and Frenchmen have never been known to put themselves in the hands of any man who was not, to some extent at least, of their own land.

True, at Brienne the boy Bonaparte showed himself fiercely Corsican, and republican too. Paoli was his hero. How could the schoolboy appreciate the political suppleness employed by his father to make the brothers the King's pupils? He was a solitary in this unfamiliar setting he had been flung into, and a victim of the merciless age which made fun of his name, his accent, his oddity. This stiffened the lad's natural pride. He was taunted with being a Corsican. He boasted of his Corsican blood. But after all, whatever his pride and courage, too much could not be expected of his nine years. Anyone who has known the stresses of boarding-school life will realize what he must have suffered. Far from his family, uprooted from his soil, he was an exile. Even the climate was unfriendly; the stinting of sun and light is in itself a cruelty to the Southerner. If school be the training-ground of life, those years at Brienne were hard for Napoleon.

From his boyish writings there survive some touching lines inspired by a then-famous poem, *Les Jardins*, in which a Tahitian comes with transports of joy upon a tree of his native land. In that humble savage Napoleon recognized himself. He sought refuge in the vision of his island of orange-scented springtimes, and felt more Corsican than he would have felt at Ajaccio. His remark to his schoolmaster Bourrienne, later his secretary — 'I shall do all the harm I can to your Frenchmen!' — was the cry of a child vexed by the petty tyrannies of school. At Brienne he certainly acquired a passionate love of his island, which, as it turned out, was a very fleeting love. But at heart his memories of school were not too bad. Otherwise, why should he later have heaped favours on his former masters and schoolfellows, even on the school porter, who was given a post at Malmaison? His exact memory forgot nobody, but he harboured no grudges; and in the long run, like everybody else, he came to believe that schooldays were the 'good old days'. As Emperor in 1805, he was to stop in the old buildings on his way through Brienne, recalling former times. And he was to return again in 1814, to fight, shortly before the end.

Like other men too, he had his hours of amusement and his friendships. He was not perhaps so friendly with Bourrienne as the latter claimed; nevertheless it was Bourrienne whom the First Consul chose when he needed a secretary. And he had other ties of companionship. At first the self-contained little Corsican had been held odd and surly, but in time he was respected for his character, by masters and pupils alike. He was cheered by the school one winter's day when he directed operations, according to the rules of war, in a celebrated snowball-fight. He even had the joy of seeing his bastions and ramparts admired by the townsmen of Brienne, although, like the others, he had been through only an elementary course of fortification. But he profited by everything.

Everything that he did not reject. For he was not 'a good scholar'. Like most schoolboys who have later made·their mark in life, he liked being free from the time-table. He learned for himself, not for examinations. He rebelled against Latin and grammar as useless subjects, and read greedily during his spare time, preferably books of geography and history. His boyhood, one may say, was one prolonged reading, and from it he retained a rich harvest of ideas and notions. His imagination was enriched, and he also acquired a faculty for expression. Indeed, as we shall see, up to his twentieth year, and beyond it, he was at least as much a man of letters as a soldier.

Napoleon had been at Brienne for five years without a glimpse of his family when his father, on his way to Saint-Cyr with Elisa, came to see him. Charles had worries both of purse and health, and his children were growing up. Joseph showed no taste for the priesthood and clamoured to enter the army, to the distress of the family, and Napoleon himself intervened, declaring that he could see no military aptitude in his elder brother. This capriciousness disturbed the calculations of his parents, who counted on the advantages attached to the priesthood and on his becoming ultimately the archdeacon uncle of the family, a providence for nephews-to-be. Then there was Lucien, now of an age to go to school, who was sent to Brienne as a paying pupil, as the regulations did not allow two brothers to hold bursaries at the same time. The hopes of the father, tormented now by a presentiment of his coming end, were centred on Napoleon, whose energy, intelligence, precocious common sense, and nascent power of command were obvious to him.

But, good pupil though he was, Napoleon had not yet been nominated for the Paris school. There was even an interlude when he was put down for the Navy by the inspector-general of military academies, and was tempted by the sailor's life, which the successes of Suffren and Grasse had made popular. His mother, however, alarmed by the perils of the sea, diverted him from this scheme, and in any case a new inspector-general, Reynaud de Monts, decided, at the passing-out examination, that Napoleon Bonaparte could not be entered for the Navy.

He had to wait one more year. It is doubtful whether this pupil at Brienne had any fixed idea as to which branch of the service he would enter, when de Monts nominated him for entrance to the corps of gentleman cadets at the great Military School of Paris, marking his name 'artillery'. His high marks in mathematics had earned him this choice. His Corsican origins had not proved detrimental. The inspector had judged only by aptitude and merit.

Under Louis XVI the artillery was, as it had been for generations, the intelligent branch of the Army. (Was it not so even before the invention of gunpowder? Amongst the Romans the *cataphractae* formed a corps of scientific combatants.) And on the eve of the Revolution the French artillery was generally held to be the finest in Europe. Under Gribeauval's command it had made even further progress; Napoleon would have excellent masters to learn from. It should be remembered, as Napoleon himself remembered, that he sprang from the royal army of France and owed whatever he knew to that army. His commission as gentleman-cadet was signed by the Marshal de Ségur on October

22nd, 1784, and sixteen years later the First Consul granted a pension to this old soldier of the monarchy, receiving him with full military honours at the Tuileries. It was, as it were, a salute to the Army of the old regime.

Under Louis XV there had been an attempt to make the Military School a model establishment. The buildings themselves, designed by Gabriel, are still amongst the finest in Paris. It was all in the grand manner, and Bonaparte, leaving a provincial institution which had offered no great change from his Corsican simplicity, was astonished by the magnificence. He is even said to have found the expenses excessive, and certainly, being early accustomed to count his pence, he always remained economical. But from this school where things were done almost too well, he perhaps received his first awareness that France was a very great country.

Here too he had as his fellow-pupils young men of good family, some of them bearing names such as Montmorency-Laval, Fleury, and Juigné. For the most part the youths who were then at the Royal Military School of Paris were to become *émigrés* and many of them refused to the last to serve the usurper, although he reopened the doors both of France and the Army to them. But the fact remains that, even more than at Brienne, Bonaparte was here in close contact with the French aristocracy. Momentary reactions may perhaps have stimulated the republican sentiments of the needy young Corsican, but perhaps these contacts also gave him the idea of founding a nobility in his turn.

At the Military School he made a friend — young de Mazis, who was to be an *émigré*; and an enemy — Phélipeaux. With Phélipeaux, a youth from the Vendée, he exchanged kicks under the table during lessons. He was to find him again at the siege of Acre. Otherwise his career at the Military School was not noteworthy. His masters discerned in him intelligence and spirit, and some of them in years to come boasted of having perceived his genius. But so slight was his reputation as a brilliant pupil that the German master was astonished to hear that the boy whom he found so dense excelled in mathematics.

During the year at the Military School, in February 1785, Charles Bonaparte died, from that cancer of the stomach which was also to carry off the prisoner of St. Helena. Charles Bonaparte was not yet thirty-nine. He had come over to Montpellier to consult the physicians of the famous medical school there, and Joseph and the seminarist Fesch were with him. If they are to be believed, the dying man prophesied that Napoleon would conquer Europe. Meanwhile, he counted on his second son as the real eldest son who should control the family in distress, and counted also on the pay of the future officer to keep the wolf from the door of the fatherless family.

Napoleon was not present at the deathbed, nor at the funeral. He wrote a letter to his mother in a very fine style; it had been revised by the masters of the School, for the King's officers were taught to express themselves with nobility. Between its rather emphatic lines one may detect the new, but to a young man exalting, sentiment of a great responsibility. And in years to come he spoke but seldom of the father he had known so little. But one day at St. Helena, looking back over his life, and exclaiming, as he always did, on the extraordinary network of circumstances which made it up, he said that none of it would have come to pass if his father had not died before the Revolution came. And true enough, Charles Bonaparte would certainly have represented the Corsican nobility in the States General. In the Constituent Assembly his opinion would have brought him amongst the moderates. He would have shared the fate of the La Fayettes and Lameths, with the choice of the guillotine cr exile. And whatever Napoleon's personal views, he would have been cramped and compromised by those of his father. Pondering these chances that control a man's whole life, the Emperor added: 'And that would have meant the upsetting and ruin of my whole career'.

Meanwhile, his father's death made it all the more urgent for him to secure the rank and pay of an officer. In September 1785, examined by the famous Laplace, he passed forty-second out of fifty-eight. This was a handsome success, if one remembers that he had had only one year's preparation, and that most of those placed above him on the list came from the excellent school of artillery at Metz. He became a lieutenant straight away, without being a cadet-officer first. Still, notwithstanding his sixteen years, he was not the youngest of his year, and his enemy Phélipeaux was one grade above him. All the same, although it was well enough in such circumstances to be forty-second, he had not been first, or second. And the famous Laplace, who was one day to be his Minister of the Interior, did not exclaim in admiration before Bonaparte at the blackboard.

'I was an officer at sixteen, for a fortnight.' That remark, consigned to the pages of a memento of youthful days entitled 'Epochs of My Life', betokens a justifiable self-satisfaction. They would be proud of him at home, at Ajaccio. And the future was assured. The young man had a position, and pay — though modest. It was high time. The vineyard at Milelli, the goats of Bocagnan, the mulberry plantation — a disastrous speculation — would not suffice to provide for all these brothers and sisters. One of the boys, at least, had got clear, and Letizia felt relieved.

CHAPTER II

THE ARTILLERY UNIFORM

HE was appointed to the regiment known as that of La Fère, and was sent to the garrison he desired. Valence is in the South, on the way to Corsica, and as the regiment provided two companies for the island, Napoleon had hopes of being sent to his native land. There was still home-sickness in his heart, and he lived there in imagination. Imagination and literature, indeed, gave him an idea of Corsica so much embellished that the reality was to prove a disappointment. Really, he knew the island which he left at the age of nine through the works of men whom one day he would term ideologues. He saw it inwardly through the eyes of Rousseau, who never set foot on it, and pictures it as an ideal republic, a land of free and equal men living according to Nature.

This boy officer was an intellectual. His friend de Mazis was scornful of books and had his mind full of women and love-making, and the adolescent Bonaparte was a dreamer too. But what interested him in Rousseau was the *Social Contract* and not the *Nouvelle Héloïse*. He probed the theories of natural rights and constitutions. He plunged deeper than ever into books, and was already tormented by the demon of writing. He was to write better and better, even when he laid aside his rather slow-moving pen and took to dictating his correspondence and memoirs. He was a man of letters, like others of his family, as his Italian ancestor Jacopo had been with his story of the sack of Rome, and as Joseph, Lucien, and Louis were all of them to be.

His reading lists, his note-books and first scribblings survive. It is surprising how little they contain of the art of war. Bonaparte learned his soldiering from day to day and at first hand, and his gift for assimilation allowed him to profit from that teaching. Returning to his modest rented room, he read unceasingly, but his reading might have been that of a student of political science.

After correcting the Prince-Primate on the date of the Golden Bull at Erfurt, the Emperor was to remark with just pride that, when he 'had the honour of being a second-lieutenant in the artillery', he had devoured the bookseller's library, overlooking nothing, 'not even subjects which were unconnected with my status'. His sustaining love for Corsica during those studious years at Valence made him meditate a history of his island, to be dedicated to another ideologue whom he greatly admired, the Abbé Raynal. But his widening curiosity passed to the study of men, countries, societies, governments, religions and laws, moving instinctively towards greatness and universality. A day was to come when the path of power stood open to a soldier, and on that day it was the prodigiously varied store of his reading which set him head and shoulders above his rivals.

It remained for him to become a soldier. He had passed through military schools, but they were really ordinary educational institutions. Like his comrades, he went through the usual procedure, an ordinary gunner to begin with, then corporal, then sergeant, mounting guard and taking weekly turns of duty. Not for three years did he reach full officer's rank. In the Army of the old regime things were taken seriously, and the young aristocrats had all to pass through the ranks. An excellent schooling it was. Bonaparte was always to know what the rank-and-file were like. He knew what the private soldier thought, what he liked, what to say to him and how to say it.

In January 1786, donning that blue uniform with red facings which he always felt to be the most handsome in the world, he at length took up his duties as officer, and enjoyed the first delights of wearing the epaulettes. Valence had a small provincial society of its own, which was open to him and his fellow-officers. He did not live entirely a hermit's life. For all his awkwardness, unruliness and studious zeal, he appreciated the welcome of an agreeable lady, Mme. du Colombier, and with her daughter he had a shy, tentative love-affair. Yes, he went off eating cherries with her, as Jean-Jacques with Mlle. Galley. Even with Mlle. Caroline he was unwittingly bookish!

He wore the artilleryman's uniform, but he had still to learn the science of artillery. Nothing does him more credit than the evidence of his gratitude towards his superiors and instructors. The artillery, he told Las Cases, when he entered it, was 'the finest in Europe, its composition unequalled . . . It was a branch with a family feeling of its own, its heads full of paternal feeling, the bravest and worthiest men in the world, pure as gold'.

In 1786 the little second-lieutenant, aged sixteen and a half, was barely initiated into ballistics, tactics, and strategy. He was most at home in his humble room, beside his books and inkstand. He was penniless, and found his enjoyment in ideas. His hand itched to write, and he flung on to paper a declamatory appeal to the heroes of Corsican liberty. Arguing on the fate of his native land, he declared its right to shake off the French yoke. And another time he was meditating in romantic vein: 'Always alone in the midst of mankind, I return to dream by myself and yield to the glowing current of my melancholy. Whither did it turn to-day? Towards death'. The voice was René's or Werther's. At that same moment a second-lieutenant in the regiment of Navarre, young Chateaubriand, might well have composed the same lament.

But whence came his desire for metaphorical death? Because of the woes and subjection of Corsica. During his first leave he would visit his island, the theme of his literary exercises and his daily thoughts. 'What shall I behold in my country? My compatriots in chains, trembling as they kiss the oppressor's hand?' And at last, on September 1st, he left for Ajaccio, calculating with precision that he would 'arrive on his native soil seven years and nine months after his departure, at the age of seventeen years and one month'. He would discover his own land. And what he took with him, along with the uniform he was so proud of displaying there, was a trunk full of books. But what books there were! Rousseau, of course, and historians and philosophers, Tacitus and Montaigne, Plato, Montesquieu and Livy. Poets too, Corneille, Racine, Voltaire, 'whom we declaimed every day', as his brother Joseph afterwards recounted. Of military books, not one. The god of war was still in limbo. In any case, he was on holiday.

He made his holiday last for twenty months, giving excuses of health and family affairs in turn to obtain extensions of leave. More than a year and a half: a long time in a brief and headlong life in which time was to be so precious. But when he reached Corsica he made the disquieting discovery that he had forgotten the dialect so completely that he had to set about learning it again. Seven years of France had left their imprint. He was rather less Corsican than he had imagined, despite his passionate zeal to become so.

But this long sojourn restored him to contact with his soil, for which he had the most stubborn love. He was still projecting a history of the island, and collected documents and first-hand evidence. But his days in Ajaccio were grievously taken up with his family concerns, financial troubles, that heartbreaking mulberry plantation which went from bad to worse, and the health of his aged uncle the archdeacon. When his leave was up, the *History of Corsica* still remained a mere project.

Nevertheless, 'M. Napoléon de Buonaparte, second-lieutenant of the regiment of La Fère' did plenty of writing — of petitions; he had become a suppliant like his father. Letizia pressed him to intervene with functionaries and ministers. She herself had vainly sent in claim after claim, piling up supporting statements of fact, signed 'widow of Buonaparte', in the hope of obtaining the payment promised for her brood.

If anything was to come of it, he must do as his father did, make his claim at first-hand and apply direct to Versailles. Napoleon made the journey. And there he was in Paris, with a light purse, but for the first time free, and almost grown-up, in the city of which he had caught hardly a glimpse from the Military School.

He called at the offices of the comptroller-general, waited in ante-rooms, had audience of the minister, Mgr. Loménie de Brienne, the prelate friend of the philosophers; and then the youthful subaltern explored Paris. One November evening he was passing through the arcades of the Palais Royal when he met 'a person of the sex'. He found in her 'an air which accorded perfectly with the attraction of her person . . . Her shyness emboldened me and I spoke to her'. This was how the future husband of an Archduchess first became acquainted with the other sex. Returning to his modest lodging, he set down — he always felt the urge to write — an account of this encounter, a curious story which might, this time, be taken as something escaped from the pages of Restif de la Bretonne. At the Hôtel de Cherbourg he also penned a parallel between the love of glory, as the distinguishing mark of monarchy, and the love of country, which belongs only to republics, as witness Sparta and Corsica. And Corsica cropped up again when he sketched a letter from the ex-King Theodore to Lord Walpole, invoking the loyalty of England. Theodore was the king whom Candide encountered in the Venetian inn. But our writer was not jesting. There was pathos in his Theodore, and the nobleman was magnanimous. Walpole rescued Theodore from his London garret and gave him an allowance of £3000 . . . In 1815 England was less generous towards the fallen Napoleon.

The future Emperor returned with little to show. At Ajaccio he found 'Madame Mère' more needy than ever, for his journey to Paris had been costly. She had no servant then, and asked Joseph, who had gone to Pisa to seek his diploma as Doctor of Law, to bring back a woman 'to do our plain cooking'. Visiting Bastia, Napoleon met his fellow-officers of the garrison and dined with them, surprising them by his 'dry and solemn turn of mind' and his 'magisterial tone'. He scandalized them with doctrines which we should nowadays call autonomist or separatist, and when an officer asked him whether he would go as far as to draw his sword on a representative of the king whose uniform he wore, Bonaparte was vexed and did not answer. He was upset, perhaps, at having departed from his usual reserve, for he was as prudent in speech as he was exalted when the pen was between his fingers.

In June 1788 he had at length to rejoin his corps. His garrison was at Auxonne in Burgundy, seat of an artillery school commanded by Baron du Teil. Here Bonaparte stayed until September 1789. The results were fruitful, for whilst France was entering upon revolution and duty obliged the young lieutenant to repress the widespread outbreaks of rioting, this period was genuinely formative to him not only as an artilleryman but as a soldier. His chief, General du Teil, had soldiering in his blood and enjoyed his duties as an instructor. He liked kindling a young intelligence, and picked out Bonaparte to go through a staff course with him. At Auxonne the young officer learned not only his principles of gunnery, general and detailed, but also his first ideas of tactics. And even more, he was initiated into the art of war and was imbued with the ideas which he was later to put into practice.

When he had attained supreme power, Bonaparte said to Roederer: 'I always find things to learn'. And we have already noted his wonderful aptitude for retaining and making use of whatever his mind absorbed. Now, the period of his intellectual formation was that during which a new doctrine was taking shape in the thinking minds of the French Army. Just as there was a revival of military studies after 1870, so the Seven Years War had made it needful to discard the old systems. Rosbach had produced the same result as

Sedan. Defeat is often a stimulus. And although, being accustomed to look at only one thing at a time, we tend to regard France in the years just before 1789 as entirely given over to political quarrels, nevertheless, as the storm approached, a generation of officers had been labouring, pondering, and living in a fever of ideas. These soldier writers had provided an inspiration and system for the wars that were to come. Their works were read and commented upon in military circles. Bonaparte was familiar with the books of du Teil (his chief's brother), of Bourcet, of Guibert. All these authors went further than Frederick II. Taking account of the possibilities of modern war equipment, they worked out new rules which would have been beyond the purview of the Prussian king. Frederick's campaigns were already dated. Guibert and du Teil were teaching new modes of warfare.

In their manuals and treatises are to be found the principles applied by the conqueror in so many battles. They contain the germ of Napoleonic strategy. Bonaparte's intelligence was impressed by certain clear and straightforward counsels: to have a numerical superiority at a given point and to concentrate effort; always to keep one's strength intact by a liaison between every part of one's army; to surprise the enemy by swiftness of movement — 'fighting with your legs', the old soldier was to call it. These points he applied, developed, put into words, translated into action, in such a way that he made them his own and amply entitled to his name. But it was a heritage, and a French heritage. In the words of Captain Colin: 'The military generation which preceded and instructed him can only have inspired him with the burning desire to realize that ideal of offensive and vigorous warfare which they felt certain of attaining'.

The theorists of the new system of combat were expectant of a man who would put it into practice. Guibert, in his *Essai Général de Tactique*, had prophesied his coming: 'Then a man will arise, hitherto perhaps left obscurely in the crowd, a man who has not made a name by words or writings, who has pondered silently, who has perhaps been ignorant of his talent, becoming aware of it only in exercising it, and a man who has studied very little. This man will seize hold of opinions, of circumstances, of fortune, and of the great theorist he will say what the practical architect said to the Athenians of the orator architect: "What my rival has told you, I shall carry out for you".'

Prophecies only go half-way. Guibert did not foresee the day when this coming man would command a vast army, and that his task would be, not the leading of a few divisions across the Italian plains, but the handling of huge masses, the waging of the battles of nations. The face of war would change. Guibert's method would no longer suffice, Napoleonic strategy would be upset. On that day, although he declared that nothing was impossible, Napoleon would feel the difficulty of refashioning himself anew.

His months at Auxonne, then, were a time of work and study. He profited by everything. One day he was put under arrest: 'a lucky accident', says his admirer Roederer. For the room in which he was confined for twenty-four hours contained only one book — the *Institutes* of Justinian. He devoured the dusty folio. And nearly fifteen years later, during the preparation of the Code, he astonished the State Council by quoting Roman statutes. From a chance reading he had retained enough to put him at his ease with experienced jurists.

Great events were needed for these stores of knowledge to be serviceable, for the reader of the *Digest* to become the supreme legislator. They were approaching. From Auxonne it was that Bonaparte witnessed the beginnings of the Revolution, in a spirit which it is important to examine and define, for herein lies another explanation, and not the least significant, of his career.

Ranged nowadays in its appropriate category of political events, the Revolution is being stripped of its legend. Its development has been repeated elsewhere, and its pathology has proved to be not exceptional. It began with mob outbreaks which preceded and followed the taking of the Bastille. Such disorders occurred in the Burgundian region where Bonaparte's regiment was stationed, and he took part as a soldier in the suppressions. Despatched with his company in April, 1789, to Seurre, where trouble had broken out, he displayed an energetic mien, and scattered a mob assembly by giving a loud order to load, and shouting to the crowd: 'Let all honest men go home! I fire only on rascals!' At Auxonne he witnessed grave scenes. On July 15th the populace broke into the octroi offices, smashing everything and tearing up records: for, as Carnot later remarked, the deepest reason for revolution is hatred of taxes. In the following month came a fresh symptom of decomposition: the sequence of military sedition began. The La Fère regiment followed suit, called on the colonel to hand over the regimental funds, and the mutineers were victorious.

Lieutenant Bonaparte viewed these events as a foreigner in French pay. As a soldier under discipline he would not hesitate to fire, if so ordered, on the rising. He had no liking for mutinies or insurrection. But he regarded it all as someone who at heart did not belong to the country. His reading, doubtless, had inclined him towards the new ideas; and some of his companions had likewise been influenced towards dreaming of the regeneration of France. His own calculations were for the liberation of Corsica. Others held royalist views. Where would he have acquired these? When the hour struck, there was nothing to tie this recently naturalized citizen to the past. But although he might not like the old regime, he did not hate it either. His was a privileged, almost unique position, which would later enable him in complete freedom of mind to keep part of the Revolution and to re-establish some of the institutions it upset, to enlist in his service émigrés as well as regicides. Having neither regrets nor enmity for the sinking monarchy, he felt no duty towards it or towards the Republic. In the drama which was being played in France he was a spectator, pending his role of arbiter.

What, then, was Bonaparte doing whilst the Revolution was opening in Paris? Writing, always writing. He had submitted his *History of Corsica*, in epistolary form, to Father Dupuy, one of his old masters at Brienne, and on July 15th, 1789, received his first comments and corrections of style. The absorbed young author was not troubled by the news from Paris as the philosopher Kant is said to have been. The fall of the old fortress is not mentioned in the lieutenant's papers, any more than it was in the journal of Louis XVI.

What was more important in the orientation of his life was the fact of his absence from France during the greater part of the real Revolutionary period, the period of enthusiasm. He was in Corsica from September 1789 until the end of January 1791, again from October 1791 to April 1792, finally from October 1792 till June 1793. Episodes of the French Revolution he saw, but he did not live it; he breathed its passions only from afar, neither engaged in it nor compromised by it. He would enter it, but not until it was accomplished. In head as in heart he was as free towards the Republic as towards the fallen monarchy.

Did he set off on that second leave in Corsica with thoughts of being another Paoli? Precocious as he was, he was nevertheless in the age of disinterested idealism. And for great ambition he was similarly too young. Here again he was helped by age, dates, and the harmonious blend of circumstance. Had he been older, higher in rank, more conspicuous, he would perhaps have intrigued in his own country and obtained a deputy's seat in the Revolutionary assemblies. Once again his destiny would have turned, his career would have been spoilt.

But disillusion awaited him on landing. Was this the ideal republic of his dreams and of the ideologues? The citizens of the New Sparta were far from sharing his zeal for the liberating Revolution. Clans and factions rent the island asunder. He found himself in collision with conservatives and reactionaries, distrustful of, or even rejecting, the ideas of Paris, and things were still worse when the religious question entered in. The consequence proved decisive for this novice in politics. Having espoused the Revolutionary cause in the interest of Corsica, he could not combat the counter-revolution in his island without unwittingly enlisting on the French side. He landed at Ajaccio with autonomist sentiments, believing in the Revolution because the Revolution would free the island from tyranny, but this doctrine put him on the side of the unionists, that is to say, of France. On that side he remained. In the end he parted company with even Paoli, because his god and hero, whom the Assembly had ingenuously allowed to return to Corsica, wished to hand over the island to England, holding that the Frenchman, whether he wear the tricolor or the white cockade, is always the enemy.

So the outcome of Napoleon's successive sojourns in Corsica was chiefly a series of mortifications. But he learned there something of men and politics, intrigue and action. Dabbling in departmental elections and in local risings against the French administration, he grew accustomed to bold strokes, to plotting, to contempt for legality, acquiring precocious experience and continually shedding illusions about mankind. The flame of enthusiasm still burned within him when he composed his open letter to Buttafuoco, heaping insults upon this deputy who treacherously strove to set the Assembly against the heroic Paoli. The municipality of Ajaccio granted the honours of publication to this vengeful letter, and the indefatigible scribbler had the joy of seeing himself in print. But Paoli was chilly in his reception of the pamphlet, and Bonaparte left for France with his enthusiasm clouded by this slight rebuff. Despite his devotion, he was suspect to the Paoli faction; his uniform made him too French for their taste.

Rejoining his regiment, he was promoted to the rank of first-lieutenant and sent to Valence. He had brought his brother Louis from Corsica and was supervising his studies. And he resumed his garrison life, which was more austere than ever because his pay had now to suffice for two.

Reading, always reading, and zealous scribbling. Was this young man a soldier, a man of letters, or a politician? In 1791, after composing electoral professions of faith for his brother Joseph, he competed for a prize awarded by the Academy of Lyons. There were 12,000 *livres* to be won, no trifle in his present penury, with a young brother to keep. The subject set was as remote from artillery as from the bickerings of Corsica: '*What Truths and Sentiments had best be Inculcated in Men for their Happiness.*' And on this theme he embroidered forty pages, not devoid of talent, nor even of a certain poetry, and certainly not free from inflation. Bonaparte did not win the prize, but he wrote his essay with satisfaction to himself. He prepared it with a collection, in a special note-book, of expressions inducing the fine style he sought to attain. In a word, he was not far from seeing himself as an author.

Then he began to rub off his rough edges. He civilized himself. The excitement of Ajaccio had improved him, and at Valence he was found to have changed for the better, being sociable, much more cheerful, though perhaps a shade too republican. Having tasted politics, he enrolled in the society of the Friends of the Constitution, and even spoke there, without noticing that the more his interest developed in events in France, the further he moved away from his other country.

He was thus harmonizing many varied roles of his life — officer and gentleman, Corsican, philosopher, writer and club orator, when the events of Varennes took place. The departure of Louis XVI, and his humiliating return to Paris, foreshadowed the overthrow of the monarchy. This was the meaning understood by officers from the new oath required of them, much more serious than the other, as it had to be written and given to the Assembly alone. Many officers refused, regarding themselves as being in honour bound to the King. These officers were to go into exile, and Napoleon, who had known their conscientious scruples, was indulgent towards these *émigrés*. Others gave their oath, either because they were first and foremost soldiers and rejoiced in their profession, or because it was repugnant to them to leave France, or because they had no resources beyond their pay. General du Teil, for instance, consented to serve the Revolution although he had no love for it. He was poorly rewarded, for he was shot in 1794.

And why should Bonaparte have hesitated? He had no ties with the Bourbons or the monarchy. He might have served the Grand Turk as readily as the Revolution — a step which later, at a moment of difficulty, he did contemplate. And at the moment he did not realize that the process of emigration amongst the officers, by starving the proper establishments, gave him opportunities of advancement, just as the march of events was giving soldiers opportunities to become conspicuous.

To carve out a career in France, to make his adherence to the new regime profitable, he must conquer his infatuation for Corsica, that enchantress to whom he kept obstinately returning. It was his good fortune that his charmer herself rebuffed him. For there are men who owe their freedom and their fortune to some youthful disappointment, some salutary reverse in love.

CHAPTER III

UNGRATEFUL COUNTRY

In the month of September 1791 France was on the brink of the elections, and men felt that the new Legislative Assembly would not be long in declaring war. Nevertheless, Bonaparte once more requested and, thanks to General du Teil, obtained leave of absence. It is astonishing that so intelligent a youth should not have guessed how very easy promotion in the Army would soon become. Hoche, Marceau, and even his old tutor Pichegru, were commanding armies well before he was. He was late in the race because he had himself appointed adjutant-major of a battalion of volunteer national guards in Corsica, a rank no higher than a captain's in the regular forces. Not only did he thus waste time, but being marked as absent at the moment of a strict examination into the activities of officers who had become *émigrés*, he scored a bad mark in his official records. His island still lured him. He did not see that he was wasting his days there.

To secure his election as lieutenant-colonel of the national guard, Napoleon had to intrigue more elaborately than to become Emperor, and he spent part of his uncle Lucien's heritage on the task. He did not even hesitate to keep one elector captive in order to make sure of him at the polling. It would be an exaggeration to see in this a preface to the 18th of Brumaire; but Napoleon's election was certainly secured by surprise and violence, and he made mortal enemies in the rival clan, that of Pozzo di Borgo and Peraldi. The interest of Bonaparte's Corsican adventures lies in their showing how petty and pointless were the quarrels and schemes in which he would have spent himself, had not his fortunate star expelled him by the hand of Paoli.

April, 1792, was the month which hurled France into a

43

war that was to last for twenty years, and after uprooting the old monarchy, overturned the Republic and raised up an imperial throne only to upset that in its turn. How was Napoleon Bonaparte then occupied? With an exploit in the streets of Ajaccio. On Easter Day the pious populace, instigated by their priests and monks against the civil constitution of the clergy, attacked the volunteer guard, and Bonaparte retorted with volleys of musket-fire and stern measures which earned him a truly Corsican hatred in his native town, where he then had the reputation of a St. Bartholomew's butcher. Colonel Maillard, commanding the regular forces, intervened, but Bonaparte refused to obey, being anxious to get possession of the citadel, which was the plan of the Paolists from end to end of the island with a view to proclaiming independence. Although he was a French officer, he even tried to undermine the rank and file. He lost his scruples. Oblivious of his note-books and literary essays, he ceased to declaim against faction, ambition and conquest.

The skirmish went against him, and left him in bad odour with his own compatriots, as also with the French government. He realized that Corsica was not to be counted upon. Only in France had he any social standing. Absence from his regiment exposed him to the danger of being cashiered and included in the list of *émigrés*. In May, in order to regularize his position with the military authorities, he went to Paris.

France, and the capital, he found in a state of 'combustion'. The word is his own. His already practised eye discerned that the Revolution was heading for disaster, and he was an eye-witness of riots far graver than those of Ajaccio. On June 20th, he watched the invasion of the Tuileries. On August 10th he witnessed the capture of the palace 'by the vilest dregs'. Every time he was indignant that there was not a better resistance against the 'most abject elements' in the populace, and was struck by this inconceivable weakness. In later years he remarked that Louis XVI, during those fatal days, had really a greater number of defenders behind him than the Convention on the 13th of Vendémiaire. After the massacre of the Swiss Guard he ventured into the Tuileries, and even helped to save one of these luckless men. The soldier in him was reviving; his training began to show again. His natural bent was not that of a *sans-culotte*.

But he was prudent enough not to assume the airs of an aristocrat. Like all his family, he dropped his 'de'. He watched events primarily as an observant inquirer, detachedly interested in foreseeing their course. Remaining in touch with the Corsican deputies, he obtained, on their recommendation, his restoration to the Army. A breach of discipline being at that moment less grave than the crime of counter-revolution, the report on the Ajaccio rising had no sequel. He was preparing at last to return to a regiment with the rank of captain, and, as hostilities had begun with Austria and Prussia, to take part in the campaign, when suddenly his ideas changed.

The downfall of Louis XVI, the abolition of the monarchy, the vexatious opening of the war, all convinced him that the 'combustion' would result in a vast anarchy in which France would crumble away. Corsican independence would then come naturally. Caught up again by his old dream, he wanted to be there to see the great day dawn and take his place in the liberated country. The necessity for escorting his sister home from Saint-Cyr, and the insecurity of Paris (it is supposed that he kept in hiding with Elisa during the September massacres), gave him a fresh excuse for going back. Captain Bonaparte was waiting for a boat at Marseilles when the guns were thundering at Valmy. He seemed to be stubbornly turning his back on fortune.

In Corsica he was immediately drenched in bitterness. An idea had been put to the Revolutionary government which they had considered admirable — that of conquering Sardinia. Bonaparte, with his battalion of national guards, took part in the expedition, which was to start by occupying the Maddalena islets opposite Bonifacio. When the Revolution was at its climax, when it had hurled the head of Louis XVI as a challenge to Europe and was entering on war with England and Spain, Bonaparte's ambition was to distinguish himself by the conquest of a fishermen's shelter.

He had no fondness for recalling his last stay on his native soil. The Maddalena expedition was not so much as a disaster; it was merely shameful. Paoli, put in command of the Corsican battalion because he was a hero of liberty and a martyr of despotism, began to behave suspiciously. He did not favour an attack on Sardinia, viewing the Sardinians as brothers, and the least that can be said is that he did not put his heart into it. On the other hand, the sailors of the Republic who transported the troops and were to support them on disembarking, were drawn from the scum of the ports. At the first shots from the opposing forts they cried 'Treason!' and mutinied. The Corsian volunteers had already landed. Seeing their supporting frigate disappearing, they were seized with panic in their turn. They had to get off again quickly, so quickly that Bonaparte, with fury in his heart, had to abandon his three pieces of artillery. And this lamentable start nearly became something worse, for on the return to Bonifacio the seamen of the Republic came near to murdering the young lieutenant-colonel.

His cup of disillusion was not yet filled. Paoli was now to turn his back on this Revolution which was not giving Corsica her freedom. He resumed his hostility to France. Bonaparte was treated by his hero with coldness, and then with suspicion. Henceforth it was enmity, an enmity which spread to the whole French party. Disturbed by the reports sent to it, the Convention despatched to the island three commissioners who were to supervise the old leader.

They made cautious attempts to avoid civil war and arrange a settlement, when suddenly there arrived from Paris an order for the arrest of Paoli, who had been denounced to the Convention as an English agent and traitor. A Corsican uprising was now a certainty. But whence came this stroke? Its author boasted of it in a letter to his brothers. It was the third of the Bonapartes, Lucien, little Lucien (only eighteen at that time), who, at the Jacobins' club in Toulon, had accused Paoli of being a foe to liberty. And the Convention answered the club's appeal without delay. Lucien, active and inventive, but troublesome and turbulent, would more than once prove to be the *enfant terrible* of the family.

The vendetta between Paoli and the Bonapartes had now begun. Napoleon realized that his only course was to leave Ajaccio. Trying to reach the commissioners at Bastia he was caught by Paolist peasants, but he escaped, and after hiding in a relative's house, succeeded in the end in rallying the French squadron which was vainly trying to recapture insurgent Ajaccio. He and all his kin were denounced as enemies of Corsica. At Corte the Paolist chief condemned the Bonapartes, 'born in the slime of despotism', to 'perpetual execration and infamy', bringing up against them the loyalty of their father, the patronage of Marbeuf, and the royal scholarships.

Letizia fled with her younger children. It was high time. The house at Ajaccio was sacked, and even it is said, burnt down. Fleeing into the mountain scrub, as in the days of Monte Rotondo, Letizia was wandering on the coastline when Napoleon and Joseph, on board a French ship, rescued her with her children. On June 3rd the family took refuge at Calvi.

The Corsican dream was shattered. Before long the Paolists had handed over the island to the English. And twenty-one years later — so prodigiously short is this prodigiously crowded history — Bonaparte was to meet his enemy Pozzo di Borgo again, lusting to strike the last blow against him in 1814. But the force of events, whatever his own will, flung Napoleon back towards France, as had been written from the day when his father took him to the college at Autun. In that country where hitherto he had felt himself a foreigner, he now had no further career before him, and not even means of subsistence.

At the end of June the family landed on the mainland. They lodged at first in Toulon, but had to leave there for Marseilles. They were no longer poor, they were in dire need. They became friendly with a cloth merchant, Clary by name, and Joseph married one of his daughters. Napoleon would gladly have married the other. According to a story which is rather too good and belongs really to legend, the Marseilles tradesman declared that 'one Bonaparte is enough in a family'. All that is known for certain is that Napoleon had leanings towards Eugénie Désirée, who stood for simple happiness in his eyes, too simple, maybe, for he chose the brilliant Josephine in preference to her. But, still the man of letters, he confided this love story to paper and made a short romance of it: *Clisson et Eugénie.* Mlle. Clary married Bernadotte and became Queen of Sweden, whilst her sister Marie Julie, Joseph's wife, was to be Queen of Naples and then of Spain. But who suspected in those days that everything, every marvel, would become possible?

At the end of June, 1793, the Bonaparte family were in grave distress. Napoleon was lagging behind in his promotion, still a subaltern officer, and would have gravely compromised his career and wasted his time in Corsica if he had not gained the patronage of the deputy Saliceti. For merit did not suffice. Politics also must aid his success, and the taking of risks at a moment when the heads of the ablest men were in peril and nobody could be sure of the morrow.

But what was that risk when compared with the blind alley which his life had nearly taken? 'Since then,' he used to say, 'great concerns have not allowed me to think often of Corsica.' It was a petty stage, and he would have had only a small role. With no qualms he had shaken the dust of his ungrateful country from his shoes. Towards his compatriots he had even harboured rancour, or at least mistrust. He has been painted as an islander and a clansman because he raised

LETIZIA BONAPARTE
Statue by Canova (Museum at Naples)

up his brothers and sisters. He never surrounded himself with Corsicans, although, as he said, he had 'about eighty cousins or kinsmen'. And he was careful to avoid the appearance of being escorted by the tribe, for that, he added, 'would have been much disliked by the French'.

And if he now thought but little of Corsica and kept his cousins at arm's length, Corsica in her turn was slow to take little Bonaparte seriously, or that family of his, whom they had known at close quarters, and as fugitives too. Miot de Melito, who was governing the island at the time of the plebiscite on the life Consulate, noted that 'if all the departments of France had been animated by the same spirit as those of Golo or Liamone, Bonaparte's rapid rise would perhaps have met with more obstacles'.

But his reverse at Ajaccio was a deliverance. Corsica herself had cured Bonaparte of the sentimental, literary moodiness which pervaded his early youth. All unwittingly he was saying farewell to Rousseau and Raynal, to ideology, to the romance of Revolution, when he turned his back on Paoli. He believed no more in the goodness of human nature. Perhaps he did not need that ordeal in order to stiffen himself, but he did stiffen himself. Even his style changed, to the taut and nervous. Bonaparte had emerged from the age of sentiment. The skin of youthfulness was sloughed.

CHAPTER IV

LIGHTNING FLASHES

WHEN Bonaparte returned to the army, still a captain, after this long and sterile Corsican interlude, it was to find a state of civil war. The South had risen against the Convention. Posted to a company of artillery doing garrison duty at Nice, he there carried out his humble functions, General du Teil, brother of his former patron at Auxonne, detailing him to serve with the coastal batteries. The captain built reverberatory furnaces, a new invention for casting the cannonballs destined 'to blow up the vessels of the despots'. This was the style of writing he then used; and indeed it was both usual and prudent to write thus in 1793. From this he went on to Avignon to organize the convoys of the army of Italy, a kind of wagoner's job. But he found Avignon occupied by the Marseilles federalists and had to await the recapture of the town before he could carry out his mission.

Occupied with these obscure tasks, he began to feel restless. Was he going to be overlooked, forgotten in subaltern posts? He must attract attention. Cooling his heels with the Avignon convoys, he sent in a request to the 'citizen minister' to be attached to the Army of the Rhine. And with the same pen he composed the dialogue entitled *Le Souper de Beaucaire*.

This short work, even if it were not the production of a future Emperor, shows an unmistakable talent. Its conciseness attains to real strength. Its arguments, political and military, press forward in orderly array to prove the futility of the insurrection in the Midi, that it will certainly be overcome, that it has neither the means nor, more especially, the inspiration which sustained the formidable opposition of the Vendée. For *Le Souper de Beaucaire* is a topical pamphlet.

Its author understands propaganda. With cool and balanced mind he analyses a situation, whilst at the same time he is upholding the policy of the Terrorist government. He showed the Marseilles federalists that the Girondin cause is doomed in advance, abandoned by the 'genius of the Republic'. The Convention would win because it could command trained troops, and the rich city of Marseilles would be ruined by terrible reprisals. Reason, therefore, commanded the instant cessation of a vain resistance. And all this was set forth in authoritative but polished style, the writer steering clear of insults and Revolutionary jargon, affecting impartiality and a consideration of nothing but plain facts. Nothing could be more welcome to the representatives of the people in charge of the suppression of the federalist movement in the South.

Poor though he was, Bonaparte paid for the printing of this pamphlet from his own pocket. It was a shrewd calculation. The work was intended not so much to convince the insurgents, as to draw attention to the author. By good fortune it happened that Bonaparte's former ally in Corsica, Saliceti, was one of the Convention's commissioners with the army of Carteaux, engaged on the stifling of the rebellion in the Midi. After reducing Avignon, Nice and Marseilles, Carteaux had laid siege to Toulon, where the insurgents had called on English assistance. Returning to Nice with his convoy, the young captain halted at Bausset's headquarters to visit his compatriot Saliceti. And by another stroke of luck it happened that Dommartin, commanding the artillery, had just been seriously wounded. Saliceti proposed that his place should be taken by 'Citizen Bonaparte, a trained captain', and Gasparin, the other representative, acquiesced. The convoys set off for Nice as best they could. At last the captain had an active post.

We should not exaggerate the impression made by his military talents. Legend laid her hand later, but late enough, on the great Napoleon at the siege of Toulon. The most remarkable feature of his share in the operations could then be neither known nor appreciated, and even his greatest admirers seem barely to have noticed it.

Eleven years later, the young Prince of Baden remarked that there was nothing to see at Mayence, and the Emperor replied sharply that he was wrong. At his age, said Napoleon, whenever he had to spend any time in a town, he made a point of examining its fortifications, and that was what he had done at Toulon when he walked about there as a young officer whilst waiting for the boat to Corsica. 'Who has told you that you may not have to lay siege to Mayence some day? Did I know then that I would have to capture Toulon?'

There we have one of Napoleon's secrets, one of the justifications of his prodigious fortune. Swiftness of conception, sureness of glance, he possessed: but they were fostered by study. If, on his way to embark there in years gone by, he had not, as always and everywhere, learned something, would he have known where he ought to launch an attack on Toulon when he joined its besieging force? Instead of idling in a café, he had studied the topography and examined the defensive system, with his ever insatiable curiosity and craving for knowledge. Similarly, in the guard-room, he had read the *Institutes* of Justinian, never suspecting that he would one day preside over a State Council in the preparation of the Code. Again, in his cheap lodgings, he had made notes on the Swiss Constitution with no glimmering of his mediation in the Helvetian Confederation. Every page of his history teaches the advantage of knowledge, as in the fable of La Fontaine.

Thus it was, not intuitively but by reason, that when Bonaparte took over his post he instantly pointed to the Fort of l'Eguillette, and declared that Toulon was there. For over a month Carteaux blocked the young officer's plan. But Saliceti and Gasparin obtained the retirement of Carteaux, calling attention to 'Buona Parte, as the only artillery officer competent to plan these operations'. Doppet, formerly a doctor, was no more valuable to the Convention, and he in turn was succeeded by Dugommier.

This officer had more experience of war, but was hesitating to adopt Bonaparte's ideas when support came to the latter from another quarter. The besieging forces had been increased, and their artillery was entrusted to General du Teil, with Bonaparte as his second in command. But du Teil was to see the situation in the same light. To every real soldier it was plain that to capture Toulon it was necessary first of all to dominate the harbour. If Bonaparte was distinguished by anything, it was by the clarity of his ideas, the precision of his exposition, the sense of sequence with which he asserted the essentials of success.

The ageing du Teil was tired and gave Bonaparte a free hand. He had succeeded in convincing Dugommier, whose plan, almost wholly inspired by Bonaparte's, was approved by the Council of War. And this, so far as it is possible to determine, was the part played by the second in command of the siege artillery. It should be added that he suffered in person. Twice during the attacks he was wounded. He himself served the cannon, and it has always been admitted that he caught the itch, from which he suffered so long, in handling a ramrod abandoned by a disabled gunner.

In the end, L'Eguillette fell on December 17th, 1793, and everything came to pass as he had foreseen. The English and Spanish vessels, in peril of being set on fire by fireballs, made for the open sea and left the rebel town to the vengeance of the Convention.

Bonaparte was rewarded with promotion to the rank of general of brigade, at the request of Saliceti and the younger Robespierre, who was present at the event. This recommendation from the brother of Maximilien proved harmful to Bonaparte after Thermidor, but he also became acquainted with another Convention leader, Barras, who was likewise a commissioner in the Midi. He had been doubtful of the possibility of capturing Toulon, and the name of Bonaparte was impressed on his mind. He remembered it again at the time of Vendémiaire, in circumstances which were altogether decisive in Napoleon's career.

The new-made general's reputation was still known only to a few. But he made friendships, with Junot and Marmont, and with Muiron, the man nearest his heart, who was to die shielding him at Arcola. But his name had as yet made little general impact. In those days of the Terror men had so many dramas to watch! When Junot told his family that he had been chosen as aide-de-camp by Bonaparte, his father said to him: 'Why have you left your regiment? Who on earth is this General Bonaparte? Nobody's ever heard of him!' In Bonaparte's career Toulon is no more than a good start, but one made in an episode of civil war, which had gravely inconvenient implications. By the close of 1793, in any case, the chances and changes of war were in full swing. There was nothing extraordinary in promotion like his. Generals abounded, and famous ones too. In a word, Bonaparte had not yet emerged from obscurity; his services had been acknowledged, but nobody attributed the victory to him. And he himself had sufficient self-control not to let this first success go to his head. He may have caught glimpses of advancement, but he did not imagine he had won the crown of Charlemagne. Ambition was stirring within him, an ambition different from that of being a Corsican notable, but, as he said to Las Cases, 'It did not go very far, and I was a long way from regarding myself an outstanding man'.

He was right to be modest. Other obstacles lay ahead, for these were difficult times, and one day's gain became the morrow's stumbling-block. At Toulon Bonaparte had made useful acquaintances, but he had also made dangerous ones. He had thrown in his lot with the Terrorists. He was to do so still more: more perhaps than he could have wished, for Thermidor was drawing near, and Thermidor found him linked with Augustin Robespierre, who had commended him to his terrible elder brother as a man 'of transcendent merit'. This tribute was as deadly after the reaction of Thermidor as the name of Girondin or Federalist had been before. Napoleon was very discreet concerning this period in his life, during which, after one smile, fortune ceased to be kind to him. The day came when he was accused by the Jacobins of having one of the forts of Marseilles leagued with the enemies of the Republic. And General Bonaparte was summoned to the bar of the Convention. To avoid this fatal journey he had to procure certificates of loyal citizenship, which before long would turn against him and be used to prove his complicity with the men of blood.

Extricated from this vexatious affair, he was appointed to command the artillery of the Army of Italy in March 1794. This was his first appearance on one of the scenes of foreign wars, and he attracted attention. From the date of his arrival at headquarters the plans were almost certainly drawn up by him. His presence can be felt in the sequence of operations. At Saorge and on the Roya he tested his military talents, ripened his strategic principles, and formed the general conception of his coming Italian campaign. It is none the less true that he did not invent everything, and that most of the ideas which he applied on a larger scale two years later were already awaiting him there. The idea of conquering Italy to feed the armies there and obtain money for the Republic, was already in the mind of the Convention, and the people's representative Simond had already, before the famous proclamation, spoken of 'the rich granaries of Lombardy'. Simond himself was only repeating what the French *chargés d'affaires* at Genoa and Rome and Florence had been writing for months, painting the riches of Italy as an easy prey when the Republic was in such dire need of money. As for attacking Austria through Lombardy and taking the Germanic Empire from the rear, this had already been suggested by the generals of the monarchy, before the Revolution; Catinat, Villars and Maillebois had come before Bonaparte, and Charles VIII and Francis I had trod the path on which the Republic in its turn was starting.

Yet these first days in Italy, so fruitful for the young general preparing his shattering campaign of 1796, came near to being his undoing. At Saorge and on the Roya he was all unwittingly running other dangers than those of the firing-line. He was becoming involved in the formidable quarrels which were setting the men of the Revolution at one another's throats.

At General Dumerbion's headquarters he again came across Saliceti and the younger Robespierre. He found himself at once in sympathy with them. The representatives of the people were for offensive measures, and offensives were his business, both by temperament and by doctrine. But the moment when he was sketching a plan of offensive was just the moment when the Committee of Public Safety were divided amongst themselves on the conduct of the war and on general political considerations. Carnot, notably, joined the opposition to the dictator Maximilien Robespierre, who dropped his former pacifism to urge an uncompromising warfare on all the fronts, whilst his colleague showed alarm at the spread of hostilities. This clash ended on the 9th of Thermidor.

On the day of Maximilien's fall, Augustin Robespierre was in Paris. He had left the army in order to obtain a vigorous prosecution of the campaign on lines agreed to in concert with Bonaparte. Augustin perished with his brother, and next day the Committee of Public Safety ordered the halting of the offensive in Italy and the limitation of operations to a defence of conquered territory.

It is hard to say how far Bonaparte's Jacobinism was sincere, and harder still to know whether he joined hands with Augustin through sympathy or for interested motives. He kept silence about his relations with the Robespierre brothers. His authoritative temper, perhaps, made him appreciative of the Robespierre dictatorship, apart from the guillotine. 'Prolixity in the correspondence and orders of a government is a sign of its inertia; laconic government is the only possible government.' This maxim, which might be one of the Emperor's, is Saint-Just's, and points to certain affinities. In any case, he was to remain a Jacobin for a long time yet, with shades of distinction perhaps, but always careful not to be abandoned by the 'genius of the Revoluton'.

In times of revolution, one day's gain is the next day's loss. Bonaparte was on the winning side only to become immediately one of the losers. He was more deeply involved with the Robespierres than he might have wished when the 9th of Thermidor struck, and the Terror left its mark. The new masters of the hour had to be placated; scapegoats were sought, a frenzy of zeal was displayed, names were denounced. Bonaparte had a fine opportunity of gauging human coward-ice, when Albitte, Laporte, and even his protector Saliceti, hastened to disown the 'plan-maker' of Robespierre and Ricord. The scare made him suspect to them; they had very nearly been compromised. Yesterday's collaborators were now merely 'intriguers and hypocrites' who had 'tricked' them. This Bonaparte was 'one of their men'. He must be a traitor. A mission of investigation with which he had been entrusted by Ricord became a dark plot in their eyes, linked up with the conspiracy of the faction lately stifled by the Convention. Eleven days after the 9th of Thermidor, by their orders, the general of artillery was put under arrest.

He was soon released, protesting against an absurd accusation, and with his protests backed by those of his friends, notably Junot and Marmont. He was released, first from lack of proof. And then the enemy, observing the hesita-tions of the French, took fresh heart and became threatening. Bonaparte was set free, and his command given back to him because nobody could be found to take his place. He advised that the attack should be forestalled, and on September 21st, the Austrians were beaten at Cairo. The victory was blank in results. But in these operations, heralding more startling

victories, Bonaparte was turning to account the experience
he had gained on the terrain, and could discern the lines of
a wider and more complete plan, which he would carry out
when he in his turn became commander-in-chief and when
he had had time to mature.

For notwithstanding his recent services, he had not got rid
of the suspicion which had been thrown on him at the time of
Thermidor. Moreover, the offensive was definitely abandoned. Bonaparte was thrown back into obscure employment, organizing coastal defence. Paris was suspicious of
the officers of the Army of Italy, who were reputed to be
tainted with Jacobinism, and they were scattered amongst
different corps. In March, 1795, Bonaparte was recalled
from the Italian front, and posted to the Army of the West,
that is to say, to the repression of the Vendée.

He refused. Did he find it repugnant to fight against
Frenchmen? Was it a deep calculation for manipulating the
future? After all, he had waged war at Toulon, and would
soon be bombarding Royalists on the steps of Saint-Roch.
Marceau, Kléber and Hoche fought against the Vendeans
without tarnishing their names, even showing that military
leaders were more humane than civilians and that ferocity
dwelt elsewhere than in armies. But Bonaparte had no fancy
to be removed from Italy. He did not like a small stage,
and in Italy there were great things to be done. Nor was
he pleased to learn, on arriving at Paris, that he was destined
for an infantry brigade. He was an artillery officer, and
thought he would fail. After a heated argument with the
Commissioner of Public Safety, Bonaparte was struck off the
Army list for refusal to proceed to his post.

The refusal did not straighten out his affairs; it seemed
absurd; and it cost him some very unpleasant days. He took
an obstinate pride in his act of disobedience. But he had no
resources to fall back upon, and his enforced unemployment
came at a bad time. The *assignat* was then falling in value,
and the cost of living rose from week to week. Friends and

relatives had scant resources. The Bonaparte family had to give each other help. Joseph, whose marriage with the cloth-merchant's daughter brought him some money, did what he could for his brothers and sisters. The faithful Junot received small sums from his parents, which he risked at the gambling-table, sharing his gains with his chief. Poverty he had already known, but there were now days when dire necessity was at Bonaparte's elbow.

His aspect during this calamitous period of his life was a sorry one. He was deplorably thin, his skin was yellow, his hair unkempt, his wardrobe threadbare. He was of average height (hardly more than five foot five) but his lack of flesh made him look small, just as he did later when he became stout. With him there trailed round a couple of aides-de-camp, or rather acolytes, Junot and Marmont, who were no more impressive than their general. One day as they paced the boulevard Junot confided in Bonaparte that he loved his sister, Pauline, and her brother argued with him: 'You have nothing. She has nothing. What does that add up to? Nothing.' There was no glimpse as yet of duchies, principalities, thrones. . . .

He spent his days in paying calls and keeping up his connections, cultivating that pseudo-society of which Barras was the ornament, and prowling round the War Ministry in search of a job. For he was not a beaten man. His mind was at work, and he made 'endless projects every night when going to sleep'. Some of these he submitted to the section of the Committee of Public Safety supervising plans of campaign, and as they showed his knowledge of Italy, where operations under Kellermann were none too happy, he was attached to the topographical branch. He was consulted as the specialist on the Italian front. But just then he learned that the Sultan was requesting artillery officers from the Republic. The East, where things are done not only on the grand, but on the grandiose, scale tempted him. The idea that English power could be dealt a blow there was already

59

in the air — and besides, a foreign mission is well paid. Twice Bonaparte put forward his name as an organizer of the Turkish army. He was appointed, and was on the point of leaving, even of taking some of his family to Constantinople, when a countermanding order intervened. One member of the Committee pointed out that the presence of General Bonaparte was more useful to the topographical branch. And had it not been for this obscure Jean Debry, Bonaparte would have missed the first great opportunity of his life, the one which determined the rest. In the same way, one of his historians has rightly remarked, Cromwell was kept back in England when he was about to embark for America.

Pending the opportunity, those months of August and September, 1795, were among the most uncertain of all the months of Napoleon's life, one day utterly black, the next full of hope. 'If things go on like this,' he wrote to Joseph, 'it will end in my no longer stepping aside when a carriage drives past'. And in another letter, a month later: 'I can see nothing but pleasantness in the future'. But meanwhile, in the Committee of Public Safety, Letourneur had been going through the files of the Jacobin officers, in league with Robespierre, and on September 15th he gave orders that 'Brigade General Bonaparte, formerly attached for duty to the Committee, be struck from the list of employed generals, in view of his refusal to proceed to the post assigned to him'.

Tugged this way and that, the unhappy government of the day was in a state of growing incoherence. Within six months the cashiered general was to receive a high command, because, before three weeks had passed, he had saved the Republic.

CHAPTER V

INTRODUCTION TO FORTUNE

In October 1795 there came to pass two events which, in conjunction, were to make an emperor. Unless one keeps a firm hold on this chain, the career of Napoleon is inexplicable. For the fact of his having in him the stuff of a dictator, enough and to spare, was not in itself sufficient: 'circumstances', as he himself said, were also essential. And at this point we reach the circumstances which made dictatorship necessary, and enabled Bonaparte to seize it after circumstances had given him the chance of emerging from the obscurity of the crowd.

Whilst he was vegetating in Paris, changes had come about in the Republic. The Conventionals had just set up a new Constitution. The rule of a single assembly had brought about the tyranny of Robespierre, and this had had to be broken. The concentration of power in the Committee of Public Safety was only an expedient during a time of crisis. The establishment of a regular government could no longer be dispensed with; but the danger lay in making something which, by too close a kinship with parliamentary monarchy, would obliterate the Revolution. In that event the men who had compromised themselves during the days of Terror, those who had been lastingly branded by regicide, the touchstone of Revolutionary sincerity, would be threatened, and their works likewise. The Convention adopted a regime, that of the Directory, arranged in such a way that it secured its own survival. And the safeguard whereby the future was supposed to be arranged was to prove fatal to the Republican regime. We are at the point of junction.

In place of one single assembly, the Constitution of the Year III of the Revolution created two: the Council of the

Five Hundred as a lower house, with the Council of Ancients as a kind of senate. The consitutional law further arranged that one-third of the legislative body should be renewable every year, it being understood that the two first thirds should be obligatorily chosen from members of the Convention. This ensured against one immediate risk, that of elections of the Right. It was essential that the reaction should not go beyond the bounds assigned to it by the Thermidorians. The Directory was planned to perpetuate a government of the Left, faithful to the spirit of the Revolution.

On the other hand, the re-establishment of an executive power was determined upon. But to avoid any semblance of a reversion to royalty, this executive power was to have five heads. Furthermore, the five Directors were to be elected by the Councils, and would be renewable in yearly rotation. Still further, they would be chosen at first from the regicides; and its absence from the written constitutional law made this secret clause not the least important.

Thus the doors were closed against the moderates and the Royalists. The first elections could hold no surprises. But thereafter these safeguards would no longer be effective. There could be no further certainty regarding the composition of the Councils, and these bodies themselves would no longer necessarily choose the Directors from the 'approved' men; in fact, it could be foreseen that the old Conventionals, by virtue of the kind of divine right which they attributed to the Revolution, would refuse to bow if the majority swung over to the Right. In that event force alone would decide. The country would then enter the period of *coups d'état*, in which the Republicans themselves would take the initiative and give the signal.

Meanwhile, since the 9th of Thermidor and the measure taken against the extreme demagogues, the Revolution had lost its mainspring, its instrument of attack and defence. The insurrectional Commune had been outlawed at the same time as Robespierre. And now the federates, the insurgents, the street Megaeras, the men with pikes and red caps, were no longer virtuous patriots, but 'anarchists' and 'bandits', against whom the men of Thermidor had twice defended themselves by the means which governments must employ. Louis XVI, although accused by the revolutionaries of bringing troops into action, had never done so. It was now the Convention who used them against the risings. By the 12th of Germinal Pichegru had been given the command of the sections. On the 1st of Prairial the insurrection broke out again, more severely, and the Convention did not hesitate to call upon the troops of the line. On that day one of the first detachments to come to the aid of the Assembly was led by a young officer, a soldier of fortune, son of an innkeeper, who was to reappear on the stage of the 18th of Brumaire. His name was Murat. He was to have a kingdom.

Nor was this all. After each of these clashes, the Thermidorians had dealt blows at Jacobinism, condemning to death or deportation the popular representatives allied with the factions. The Revolution thus deprived itself of the elements which had been its salt. But when at last it was flooded by the reaction to which the way was being opened, as also when there was a question of expelling the Councils by a majority of the Right, the Revolution was to find it impossible any longer to count upon the sans-culottes. Organized force was to be its forced resort. From whichever side it was threatened, the Revolution had henceforth to rely on military support; and this delivered it into the hands of soldiers.

In this way the Convention had paved the way for the appeal to the soldiers in internal affairs. And, as if the legacy of a regime accustomed to the intervention of bayonets in politics were not enough, it also bequeathed heavy burdens in foreign affairs to this weak and divided government, fated to days of tempest.

On October 1st, 1795, shortly before separating, the Convention dictated its true testament. It voted the annexation of Belgium, which meant the annexation of the left bank of the Rhine. The decision was one of supreme gravity, and a redoubtable pledge for the future. The invasion of Belgium by the Revolution made England the Revolution's enemy. And England was not to make peace so long as the French were on Belgian soil, any more than she did so long as it was held by the Germans.

Few indeed were those who saw the consequences. Only a handful in the Convention raised their voices against this annexation, which was bound to drive the enemy powers to extremities. Harcourt and Lesage pointed out that Europe would not pass over their extension of French territory, urging that the absorption of Belgium by right of conquest presupposed that the French people would always be in a state of unvarying superiority, that Austria would be permanently prostrate, that England would abandon the Continent to France. The annexationists retorted that the Republic would not have peace so long as England did not admit defeat. To defeat England, she must be weakened. To England and her trade, the absorption of Belgium would be a blow to force her to surrender. For fifteen years Napoleon was to strive for nothing else than this surrender of England; and it was the motive behind every one of his annexations.

Carnot was the most fervid defender of this thesis. In the style of the moment, he translated it into imagery: 'Cut the leopard's claws!' And he added an argument which was decisive for the Convention. He told his colleagues that they must safeguard the prizes of the battles waged by the Revolution. 'Otherwise,' he declared, 'I venture to say, you may very well be asked: "But what has come out of all these victories and sacrifices?" Only the evils of the Revolution would be visible, and you would have nothing to show in return, nothing but liberty.' And Carnot could foresee that to many men liberty would be a scant reward: 'an imaginary boon' he said.

Thus, the Revolution could not renounce its conquests

without destroying itself. Renunciation meant summoning back the Bourbons. That was the meaning of the refusal which Napoleon, barely twenty years later, was to give to the Allies when they offered peace on condition that France should withdraw within her old frontiers. The dying Revolution chained its heirs to war everlasting. Either England must be beaten, or the Revolution must be. Napoleon would try to bring England to her knees by the continental blockade, and the continental blockade would lead him into undertaking the subjection of the whole of Europe. This was to be one more legacy of the Revolution. Already a decree of October 1793 had prohibited merchandise of British origin, and Klootz had declared that this measure must be imposed on neutrals in order that 'Carthage should be destroyed'. In 1796 the same prohibition was renewed. The Emperor invented neither the policy nor the system. But the Emperor was to be indispensable for their continuance.

Let us summarize these indispensable explanations. By leaving a disputed and debilitated power, and by bequeathing to that power the huge task of conquering England and Europe, the Convention twice over opened the door to the dictatorship of a soldier. By a series of *coups d'état* at home, and by an unending war abroad, it paved the way for a general. But how did Bonaparte's destiny become linked up with that combination of causes? How came it that these fruits ripened for him and not for another? We left him when his star, after a momentary gleam, seemed extinguished. We must take up the thread of events again.

The man who, within twenty years, was to end with grandiose disaster on a Belgian plain, no doubt paid as little heed on October 1st, 1795, to the absorption of Belgium as did his contemporaries and his historians. Interest at that moment was centred elsewhere. While the Convention deliberated neutral frontiers and imagined that it had finally reconstituted the Gauls, Paris was still in ferment. In one year the counter-Revolution had made great strides amongst that bourgeoisie which had hailed 1789 as the dawn. Nearly every group was protesting against the decrees limiting the choice of the electors and violating the sovereignty of the people by allotting two-thirds of the seats in the new assemblies to the members of the Convention. And when the Convention found that it was threatened, no longer by the *sans-culottes*, but by the reaction, it realized also that 'the thunderbolt of Revolution had been quenched in its hands'. Hesitating before vigorous repression which might revive terrorism, and so supply the Right with a disturbing argument on the eve of the elections, it let matters drift, and put up with the challenges of the groups in the belief that the provinces and the Army would prove more docile than Paris. But when it was learned that the Army and the provinces had accepted the decrees, Paris rebelled.

Once again, as on the 1st of Prairial, General Menou was the defender of the Convention. This time he was faced by the sound groups with which he had shielded the Convention four months earlier, whilst the Jacobins whom he crushed were now offering them their aid. Menou lost his sense of direction. He had seen the guillotine at close quarters under the Terror, and his sympathies veered naturally towards his former allies whom now he had to oppose. Furthermore, his somewhat loose instructions reflected the Thermidorian perplexities. To avoid bloodshed, Menou, on the night of the 12th of Vendémiaire (October 4th) made a truce with Delalot, the energetic bourgeois at the head of the Le Pelletier group. The rumour ran through Paris that the Convention's defender had capitulated, and the insurrection uttered cries of victory.

And here we hail the rising star of Bonaparte. If Menou had been stronger or Delalot less firm, the opportunity would have passed. A young officer emerged from the shadows, thanks to the conversation between two obscure men one evening, in a room of the old convent of the Filles Saint-Thomas, on the spot where the Bourse now stands.

Thus it was that the upheaval of Vendémiaire launched Bonaparte and his future across space.

The retired general was spending the evening with a friend quite close to that spot, at the Théâtre Feydeau, when there occurred the incident which was to count in his career far more than Saorge or the fort of L'Eguillette. The Convention, in permanent session, turned to Barras, and appointed him to command the army of the interior. Bonaparte had frequently seen this influential deputy in Paris, and had even visited him at Chaillot that very morning. Barras was distrustful of his own military talents, but valued those of the young officer whose debut he had seen at Toulon. He asked to have General Bonaparte as his adjutant. The Assembly consented, granting whatever he wanted. The peril was pressing. Action must be speedy, and Barras himself perhaps did not know how well he had picked his man. The appointments were made on the night of the 12th-13th Vendémiaire, and Bonaparte made his dispositions at once. They were so well conceived and expeditiously carried out that everything was ended at six o'clock in the evening. The Parc des Sablons contained artillery, and it was essential that the insurgents should not have these in their hands. Before dawn the cannon had been seized by Murat under Bonaparte's directions; the insurgents were attacked with grape-shot in front of the church of Saint-Roch and their survivors scattered. Three or four hundred were killed, and the hopes of the counter-Revolution wiped out.

So Bonaparte, who had so lately refused a post in the Vendée, had not hesitated in Paris to fire on moderates and Royalists. True, he did so without passion, acting as if indifferent to these disputes. But the soldier of fortune did not miss the excellent opportunity. Besides, he was at one with the Army itself, which was the camp of the Revolution. He would be 'General Vendémiaire' not only to the soldiery but to the politicians. At last his name was on all men's lips. Five days after the event, Fréron was citing him with eulogy in his report; and Fain noted in his *Manuscrit de l'an III:* 'People wonder where he comes from, what he was, what previous services recommended him. Nobody can answer, except his former general, Carteaux, and the Representatives who were at the siege of Toulon or on the line of the Var.' His popularity was born.

But one thing which Bonaparte neither felt nor calculated, so natural was the position to him, was that he was dominating a debate which he ended by letting the guns speak out. Everything came to him at once. His rank was restored to him and he had money in his pockets. He sent some to his mother: 'the family lacks for nothing', he wrote to Joseph. Then, when Barras withdrew from the military command, it was Bonaparte who succeeded him. Further, he was launched into politics, pursuing a policy which was already his own. His task was repression, the disarming of the insurgents, the pursuit of the guilty. After the grapeshot he used conciliation, bearing these shattered reactionaries no grudge of his own. Thus it was that he enjoyed telling an anecdote which became a pleasing adornment of his legend. During the last days of October, he said, he was called upon by a young man of good appearance who asked permission to keep the sword of his father, General de Beauharnais, guillotined under the Terror. According to his own account, Bonaparte gave Eugène a kindly reception. He was already enjoying the potency of that smile of his, one of his great instruments of action, by which he could charm where he wished, or 'overwhelm'. A few days later the mother came to express her gratitude at his headquarters in the Rue des Capucines. Eugène had told her with enthusiasm about the young general who had heard his plea as a gentleman and soldier, and something was pushing her towards this hero of the day, who might be a useful man to know. She was not mistaken. In that office of military police the crown of an Empress lay awaiting for Madame Beauharnais.

She was still a fairly young woman, a Creole of dangerous

beauty, of outstanding elegance, and combining the non-chalance of the Indies with the manners and bearing of the old regime. The blend had a quick appeal for the former gentleman-cadet who had been touched by the rather mincing charm of the merchant Clary's daughter. The widow of the Vicomte de Beauharnais, president of the Constituent Assembly, commander-in-chief of the Rhine Army, had suppressed the *de* of her name, as the son of the Corsican gentleman had likewise done, but she was a lady of quality. Penniless, yes; a life of adventures and lovers; Bonaparte did not look at that too closely. He returned the call at the Rue Chantereine, and went back there every day. He liked Josephine, he liked her seriously. Instantly she had caught him, and instantly, with love, he desired marriage. His career promised well. He felt that he had the means to marry the woman of his taste, and she, that he was as good as anyone else. At least six years older than this impetuous Corsican lover of twenty-six, Josephine regarded him as ' queer'. She drifted easily into accepting his love. Bonaparte did not propose marriage, he begged it on his knees. He was caught by his heart, and by his vanity a little, the lieutenant in love with a lady of fashion. 'In his own mind,' said Marmont, 'he was taking a longer stride in the social order than when, fifteen years later, he shared his bed with the daughter of the Caesars.' He himself told Gourgaud that Barras advised him to marry Josephine. She belonged 'to the old and the new regimes', which would give the young general a surer footing and would 'make him more French'. Has it ever been noticed that Bonaparte never seems to have thought of finding a wife in Corsica?

Josephine accepted, and lied about her age before the civil official who celebrated the marriage on March 9th, 1796. Her connections in the Republican aristocracy were her dowry. Bonaparte brought a fairer portion, but his mistress had taken no mean part in procuring it. A week before their liaison was legitimized, a decree of the Directory had appointed him commander-in-chief of the Army in Italy.

Those past four months had not been entirely taken up with love-making. Vendémiaire let him show the heads of the Republic that they could trust him. Street warfare, yes; but he could wage another sort. The cannonade in the Rue Saint-Honoré was only an incident that put his foot in the stirrup. He still cherished his idea, the same idea, of the war in Italy. If there was any place where he could put his conceptions of warfare into practice, it was Italy. He wanted the command of the Army. He asked for it as the reward for his saving of the Republic. From the end of October he worked to obtain these wages from the Directory, and worked with zeal no less than with patient subtlety. He had ambition, but he was dexterous, persuasive, and devoid of arrogance. There were still so many mediocre men ahead of him!

On Barras, who could refuse Josephine nothing, he could count. Everything depended on Carnot. And nearly every day, after discussing daily business, the commander of the army of the interior talked to the Director about Italy and displayed to advantage his first-hand knowledge. Cold and distrustful as he was, Carnot liked listening to his 'little captain', whom he had known since Toulon. One day there came bad news from Scherer, who held the Italian command. 'If I were there,' exclaimed Bonaparte, 'the Austrians would soon be showing their heels!' — 'You shall go!' said Carnot. Whereupon Bonaparte adroitly assumed modesty, proffering the objections that would be raised against him, especially his youth. And then, himself again, he told Carnot to have complete confidence: 'I'm quite sure of the job,' he said. Carnot-Feulins tried to warn his brother against this 'adventurer' whose ambition would sow trouble in the Republic. But Bonaparte was familiar with the Italian front; and had he not been the saviour of the Republic? Why pass over his services? And under the Empire, standing aside until the invasion, the representative of the Republic militant could say to himself that the staunchest Republicans had held the despot on their knees. They had fondled him and fed him and warmed him. Carnot made the excuse that he had wanted to make Bonaparte the Washington of France. At other times he gloomily assured himself that in a victorious general ambition can be unfailingly foreseen. But Carnot, first and foremost, made the rule of a soldier inevitable by committing France, through the annexation of Belgium, to a war without end.

CHAPTER VI

'THE FAIR LAND OF ITALY'

HE was not yet twenty-seven. Foreign courts hardly took him seriously. Their agents reported the new general in Italy as a 'Corsican terrorist', a commander with no war experience, and no more formidable than his predecessor, Scherer. He was the ill-kempt commander of a ragged soldiery whom he himself called 'brigands', thirty thousand men keeping body and soul together by looting, and faced by the armies of Piedmont and Austria. The coalition felt no anxiety.

But the youthful general brought with him a plan of campaign, which at first he followed in the spirit of discipline. He had no thoughts as yet of spreading his own wings. It was success that gave him assurance, and only gradually did he shake free from his instructions. In so doing he was to make himself independent of Paris and become a power, and when the Republic grew jealous of the victorious general, it was too late. Before the Consulate, there was to be the pro-Consulate of Italy. What Gaul had been to Caesar, Italy was to Bonaparte.

From the very start he showed himself a master mind, sizing up situations at a glance, and controlling them. He had the military genius and the political sense. He grasped the diversity of Italy, which would offer a new problem with each of his victories, and he disconcerted the enemy by an art of fighting as bold and original as his art of negotiating was subtle. His conquest of a whole country with a handful of men was a masterpiece of intelligence. And that is why his contemporaries, barely grasping the process, saw in it something supernatural.

When he arrived he found a decrepit and grudging army,

Republican and Jacobin, as in 1794; he had to command 'free men', real *sans-culottes*, no respecters of persons. Who was this little general, this weed of a fellow from the Paris offices? 'An intriguer', was the judgment of the battalion commander Suchet, a future Marshal of the Empire. His age, his build, his lack of presence, his Corsican accent — everything was against him with these veterans 'who had grown hoary in battle . . . I had to act with *éclat* to win the trust and affection of the common soldier: I did so'. Augereau, Serurier, Berthier, Masséna — his seniors who had become his subordinate officers — soon felt that here they had a leader. To the common soldier, he knew how to speak. It is probable that Bonaparte at a later stage, when he had acquired the heroic Roman style, refashioned the famous proclamation: 'Soldiers! You are ragged, you are starving . . . I wish to lead you into the world's most fertile plains. Rich provinces, great towns, will be in your power. There you shall find honour, glory, and riches'. It is the amplification of the more modest text, the only authentic one extant. And the soldier laughed at first about those fertile fields which the new general promised him, asking for 'boots to get down to them with'. All that was artistically worked up, embellished by success and by time. But it remains true that from the first moment General Bonaparte gave that hopeless and derelict army a tone of triumph.

Stendhal also was perhaps embellishing when he spoke of the sense of quickening which still, after long years, came to those who had taken part in that galloping foray. The memory survived of a marvellous adventure, a surging of youth, with the fascination which 'the fair land of Italy' has always held for Frenchmen, a romantic episode in which 'such great things were done with scant means' that nothing seemed impossible. As death drew near, that was the period of his life which the Emperor delighted to recall. 'I was young, like yourself,' he was to say to the doctor Antommarchi. 'I had your vivacity, your ardour, and I could feel my

73

own strength; I burned to be in the lists.' That descent into the land of sunshine and art retained the chivalrous spell that it had held in the days of Charles VIII and Francis I. It was a real renaissance. And besides, that glorious warfare had its complement of love.

Bonaparte was still infatuated with Josephine. We have his ardent letters, attesting to longer intimacy than his two days of marriage would have allowed. And we see his senses ablaze, a 'scorched soul', and one devoured by jealousy . . . No unwarranted jealousy: for Josephine, in Paris, was finding her distractions. She feigned pregnancy to avoid having to join him, and her lies, though sometimes he forced himself to be blind to them, drove him to despair. The Directorate feared that the young general might be distracted by the presence of his wife, and they kept her behind, a willing victim. Not until his battles made a stir was she to perceive that this little Bonaparte was somebody. There was something a little ludicrous about Bonaparte in the exaltation of his passion for his faithless spouse, and the 'old moustachios' thought him too free in displaying the portrait of his beloved whilst disdaining the beauties of Milan who offered themselves to the liberator.

But what matter? Beautified by time, the romance of Bonaparte and Josephine provides the Italian campaign with an accompaniment of love. Already the picture of a woman, of sensibility, a core of sorrow within the gleam of fame, were beginning to shape the cloud of legend around his face and accoutrements. Those love-letters of his, ablaze with passion, often with rage, and haunted by the idea of death, make a strange contrast with the jubilation of victory which he raised into poetry by a romantic backward glance after action; and a still stranger contrast with that 'transcendent faculty of geometry' which he applied to the arts of war.

Nor was that all. The politician was coming to light. With a maturity beyond his years, he controlled himself in the hour of triumph, realizing that with so small an army as his every victory brought its own problem, inasmuch as every step he took forward left in his rear populations of whom he could not be sure. One rash step would undo the work of his campaigns. The map of Italy was as much divided as its opinions; there were not only the Austrians, but two kings, Republics, Grand Dukes, and in Rome, the Pope. They must not be brought to close their ranks against him. And then, alongside the great soldier, a skilful politician was revealed.

Bonaparte (for some days he had ceased finally to sign his name as 'Buonaparte') opened his offensive on April 9th, 1796, confronted, as in 1794, by the Piedmontese and the Austrians. By the 14th, after the battles of Montenotte, Millesimo and the fight of Dego, he had separated them. On the 17th, from the heights of Montezzemolo, the French looked down upon the plains: 'Hannibal crossed the Alps', said Bonaparte, addressing himself to the soldiers' understanding; 'but we have outflanked them'. Within two weeks the way to Piedmont and the way to Lombardy had been opened, and King Victor Amadeus requested an armistice, which Bonaparte granted.

Here came the first independent action taken by the young general. His orders did not admit powers to sign an armistice. Bonaparte went beyond them. His victories, the flags and the gold which he sent back from Italy, were to obliterate the memory of his disobedience. The Directorate were in need of a success and of money; and Bonaparte, knowing them at close quarters, despised them as a government. Saliceti, whom he knew even better, he put in blinkers by giving him the handling of the funds of the war-chest. He was beginning to take the measure of men, and to treat them according to their merit. . . .

It was a sound decision. The commander-in-chief's instructions left him a free choice on one point. According to circumstances, he was to carry the Revolution into Piedmont and dethrone the King of Sardinia, or else cajole the Piedmontese into an 'advantageous alliance'. His main task must be to expel the Austrians from Italy, and he went straight for the essential. He would not vanquish Austria with 30,000 men, and impose French principles on the Italians against their will. He stuck to the simpler and more practical of the two plans.

Provided that the army of Italy was freed from one adversary, King Victor Amadeus could remain on his throne; and this 'prentice diplomat could inspire at once reassurance and fear. In a few days the armistice was concluded, and signed at Cherasco, with sound safeguards and lines of communication. Before April was out, Piedmont had left the field. Within a few hours the Duke of Parma submitted in alarm, bringing two million francs, provisions, and works of art. Bonaparte had gone beyond his powers, but the Directory did not breathe a word. The cartloads of money left them marvelling, and they hardly raised an eyebrow at the proclamations of the general to the Italians, in which he promised them, with liberty, respect for their religion. But it was a novelty, and the herald of others to come.

These precautions taken, Bonaparte turned against the Austrians with the same swiftness, the same calculated boldness, the same good fortune, and the same preliminary conquest of his own troops, who were wondering whether their general was not going too fast. On May 10th the extraordinarily bold stroke of Lodi gave him the total confidence of his men. It was after this battle that his veterans gave him that title of 'the Little Corporal' which was later to be so helpful to his popularity. It was after that day also, on his own admission, that for the first time he had presentiments of his future. 'I saw the world in flight beneath me as if I were borne up on the winds,' he told Gourgaud. And even on St. Helena he was to feel again the intoxication of the first rays of glory, when it became clear to him that he was entitled, like others, more perhaps than others, to lay claim to all.

And how could he have escaped that conviction? He had beaten renowned generals, he was master of a Lombardy freed from the Austrians, and Milan acclaimed him as her liberator. Italy was his conquest, and he would have no other hands laid upon it. The Directory, alarmed at last by this too-victorious general, ordered him to hand over Milan to Kellermann and to advance on Rome and Naples. But wisely he was suspicious of this venture, which Championnet was soon to undertake, and ingratiatingly but firmly, Bonaparte replied that they must choose between Kellermann and himself — between Valmy and Lodi. It was a test of strength. And again he won. It was the end of his respect for the Directory. He had become sure of his own indispensability, and for the moment that was all he needed.

For he had no projects. Now, as throughout his career, his course was determined by circumstance. The Directory had its plan. This consisted in compelling Austria to make peace, and to recognize the annexation of Belgium by France, with the restoration of Lombardy to the Emperor as a counterpart. It would be still better if Austria were further to allow France to join up the left bank of the Rhine. In fine, the general was not only to beat the Imperial armies, but was to establish himself as strongly as possible in Italy so that the bartering should seem important at the court of Vienna. With this Bonaparte's mission widened its scope. He became at once an administrator, a diplomat, and a warrior, exercising all the functions of the head of a state.

What a school of governance that was! Amongst these conglomerate Italian states there had to be incessant, ever-shifting negotiations. After Lodi, when he reached the line of the Adige, Central Italy submitted to the conqueror. Parma and Modena were at his discretion. The Grand Duke of Tuscany received him warmly at Florence, eagerly paying the customary tribute of money and works of art. The Pope despatched an ambassador to request an armistice. The Venetian Republic entered into preliminary discussions.

The King of Naples followed suit. Meanwhile, he had to lay siege to Mantua, held by a strong Austrian garrison, recapture Pavia from insurrectionists, stamp out other rebel risings in the country districts; and just then, news came that Austria was putting a new army in the field, under the command of an energetic leader, the old Marshal Wurmser.

Overnight the negotiations with the Pope, Naples and Venice, were broken off. The French army was seriously threatened, and Austria had summoned to her aid her Hungarians, her Croats, her motley of races. The French advance posts were swept away, the road to Milan cut, the line of the Adige was nearly forced — and then Italy would have been lost. It was the first time that Bonaparte had known danger, and he took the measure of the peril. He experienced 'that self-distrust which the beginner always knows, however great he may be supposed to be'. He laid before Masséna and Augereau his idea, which would save everything or lose everything: to raise the Siege of Mantua, concentrate all his forces, and attack each of Wurmser's armies before they were able to unite. If these operations failed, Italy could only be evacuated . . . At Lonato on August 3rd, at Castiglione on the 5th, they succeeded. But the shattered Austrian forces came together again and in September the struggle re-opened. After Roveredo Bonaparte penetrated into the Trentino in pursuit of Wurmser. In this bold campaign, an amazing man-hunt, Bonaparte just failed to hold his adversary, who returned to the plain and was compelled to shut himself up in Mantua.

These impetuous battles and prodigious recoveries of strength all went to magnify the political character who was coming into being with the proconsul of Italy. Contrast carried the process further. Bonaparte stood victorious at Milan, Modena, Bologna, Ferrara and Verona, and meanwhile Moreau was being forced to retreat on the Rhone after Jourdan's defeat at the hands of the Archduke Charles. The dream of a converging march upon Vienna faded. All hopes centred on Bonaparte, who now stood alone against the weight of Austrian might.

The Directory understood the risks. Weariness, too, was beginning to spread within France. For the elections it would be useful to claim that negotiations for an honourable peace had been tried. Pitt was in a similar frame of mind, and Lord Malmesbury came to Paris for conversations. But the Republic would not bow its head to England. In the very presence of this ambassador, and 'to force the British Government to sincere negotiation', a law was promulgated forbidding the sale and use of British merchandise throughout the Republic. This was the continuation of a Revolutionary idea which ultimately expanded into the continental blockade. Napoleon likewise, the successor of the Convention and the Directory, was to believe that to force Great Britain's hand in negotiation it sufficed to strike at her trade and her merchants.

The conversations broke down on the question of Belgium, and were brought to an end on December 21st. A week later Pitt announced in Parliament that England would never consent to a union of Belgium with France. This meant war for an indefinite period. The Republic would need a soldier with the habit of victory. And there was only one such, the man who was then still safeguarding the unique asset, the only negotiable currency the Republic held — Italy. And this fact was soon to make the young general, already master of the war, into the master of the peace.

Three more campaigns were needed before the Court of Vienna would agree to negotiate. In November 1796 Bonaparte was still faced by the continuance of Austria's 'magnificent defence'. Another, perhaps the best, of her marshals, Alvinzi, entered from the Tyrol to free Wurmser in Mantua. Bonaparte had a difficult hand to play, but he won it by his inventive genius, his swift manœuvring, and also by a freer expenditure than ever of his person, despite the fact that he was so feverish and exhausted and thin that he was supposed to be the victim of some gnawing poison — a recurrence of the itch of Toulon. He could hardly stand upright that day at the famous Bridge of Arcola, when the general commanding had to dash forward, standard in hand, setting the example and repeating the crossing of the Bridge of Lodi. Lannes was wounded, Muiron killed, shielding him with their bodies. He himself fell in the marsh, which protected him from the grapeshot, and was dragged away by his brother Louis and Marmont just in time not to be captured. Finally, after three fierce days, Alvinzi was beaten, but he escaped. But the retreat of that formidable army, whose advent had alarmed the bravest, restored to the French 'confidence and the sense of victory'.

In January 1797, the adversaries opened a sixth campaign. Alvinzi was again beaten at Rivoli, and his right-hand man, Provera, surrendered at La Favorita. This time Wurmser, still blockaded, could only surrender, and Bonaparte granted honourable terms to the aged soldier. His refusal to be present at the surrender struck men's imaginations even more than if the illustrious generalissimo had been obliged to hand over his sword to a conqueror in his twenties.

For Bonaparte had no mind to strut before the footlights. He knew that his position was still difficult, that Austria was not yet conquered, that Italy would turn against him at his first check. And the Directory, with its ill-conceived orders which had to be shelved, made his task no easier. They actively distrusted Bonaparte, but they could not dispense with him. They could not even refuse him their thanks and eulogies, for he was the only man who won battles and advanced the hope of a longed-for peace. The Directory had roused Bonaparte's contempt even before they asked his help and protection in Fructidor — and before they opened his path to power in Brumaire.

Daily experience for almost a year in Italy had convinced Bonaparte that the government of the Republic understood nothing at all of Italian affairs. They understood nothing because they were puffed up with dogma and doctrine. Bonaparte knew what systems and principles are worth. As a youth he had believed in them, and he still held to the path of the Revolution. But there are men, and there are things. He himself was rising above sentiments and fanaticisms, to judge them and make use of them. They were forces to be reckoned with, which he used, or neutralized by setting them against each other. To the Italians he was already what he was later to be to the French — a judge and conciliator, set above party — and he was so in a more difficult situation, inasmuch as France was one, with a centre in Paris, whereas Italy was a headless body with scattered limbs. But Bonaparte's reading and knowledge of history carried him through the Italian morass. Without it he would hardly have struck unaided on the idea of founding the two republics on either side of the Po. Nor could he have negotiated as he did with the Pope himself.

To pacify the Italian Catholics, their monks and clergy, Bonaparte needed the spiritual sovereign, although from the temporal sovereign he had demanded his millions and his paintings. He handled the Supreme Pontiff with tact, and handled religion likewise, and at the same time took precautions not to offend his republican-minded soldiers. On occasion, he even threatened the Cardinal Archbishop of Ferrara with shooting. He was equally careful to avoid injury to the Catholic faith and to the Republican faith, though himself bound scarcely at all by either. A policy shaped by circumstance was taking form in his mind.

He developed and enlarged it, in his anxiety to ensure tranquillity in his rear and to avoid insurrection. Peace parleys were resumed with the Holy See at Tollentino. Had he hearkened to the instructions of the Directory, the conqueror of Rivoli would have gone right to Rome to destroy 'the Roman cult', and 'fanaticism', and 'the Inquisition'. One order of his would have sufficed to upset and totally ruin the Papal power. That order he did not give. On the contrary, he even dared to proclaim himself to the devout populations as the 'protector of religion'. And with a gesture of dexterous generosity he refrained from persecution of the French *émigré* priests who had taken refuge on Papal soil. The policy he was applying to Italy seemed to be already taking shape in his mind for France.

Did his brother Joseph exaggerate when he said that the proclamations of Bonaparte in Italy 'were a clear indication that if he attained power, he would set up a government which would not be Republican'? Miot de Melito, the diplomatic agent of the Republic in Tuscany, noted that in the victor of Lodi he saw a man very far removed from Republican ideas and forms; but he added, notably: 'I recognized in his taut yet flowing style, uneven and incorrect though it is, and in the nature of his questions to me, a man unlike other men. I was struck by the depth of the military and political opinions he showed, a depth which I had not seen in any of the correspondences which I had hitherto had with the generals of our army in Italy.'

So far, these were only outlines of the future. Italy held other triumphs for her conqueror. In France, circumstances were working in his favour. A new date of crisis loomed ahead of the Directory, whilst Bonaparte would be the Republic's only victorious general. Moreau and Jourdan had been forced completely out of Germany. Hoche was soon to die. All eyes were fixed on General Bonaparte. His name, scoffed at a year before, was now speeding from mouth to mouth. And Frenchmen were beginning to tell one another that if any man could give them the natural frontiers, and rest and glory and peace, or, in other terms, could conclude the Revolution — this was the man.

CHAPTER VII

MASTER OF THE PEACE

HISTORIANS of Bonaparte who allow too much space to the descriptions of his campaigns do not assist understanding. That dazzling fame of arms thrusts the rest into a kind of half light. Napoleon was a virtuoso in strategy, who acquired a gradual certainty over his instrument and over himself. But military art was not everything to him; it was a means. Yet in Italy his deeds of war count more than elsewhere in explaining his fortune. They made him famous; and then, by the intelligence with which he wedded them to politics, they very quickly made him more than a victorious general. Simultaneously watching the enemy, Italy, France, attentive to happenings in Paris, quick to seize the shifting of popular opinion, and to reckon the alternating or parallel forces of the two currents of warlike revolution and pacific reaction, Bonaparte is seen rising step by step to a role greater than that of proconsul, influencing the progress of events, modelling them himself, and forming from them his resolve really to become the man of whom it was being said that he obtained everything that was wanted, and was a universal conciliator. We must, therefore, follow him in the marches and countermarches whereby he overwhelmed the Austrians, and in the results which he won from his successes.

Austria, then, was the Empire, and the Empire was Germany. A vanquished Austria left no important foe in Europe. And now a Republican general who, eighteen months before, had been tramping the streets of Paris, was going to negotiate with the Germanic Caesar.

The Aulic Council of Vienna had but one soldier to set against him, but he was the most illustrious of all — the Archduke Charles, who had thwarted the hope of a con-

verging French advance upon Vienna. When he turned to
face the Archduke, Bonaparte asked Paris in vain for the
offensive to be resumed in Bavaria. But nothing was done
by the powerless and irresolute Directory. In this last
Italian campaign Bonaparte was left to his own resources.
He would, then, be sharing success with nobody. All that
happened was that his insistence brought him strong reinforcements from the Rhine army, which, for the first time,
gave him numerical equality with the enemy, and hastened
his progress to the end.

That seventh campaign was merely one long forward
march, and the withering of the Archduke's laurels. Within
three weeks the Austrians were pushed back across the
Brenner, Germany was invaded, and the way to Vienna lay
open. The Imperial family hid their valuables and prepared
for flight. A little five-year-old girl was sent away into
Hungary, to be safe from these dreadful Jacobin soldiers.
She was called the Archduchess Marie Louise.

But the conqueror did not push through to Vienna. He had
still to fear an insurrection in his rear. And it came, in the
'Vespers of Verona'. Yet, despite his increasingly urgent
advice, the Rhine army received no forward orders. On
April 2nd, 1797, Vienna decided on peace negotiations, and
the victorious general entered upon preliminary discussions.

He decided to do so for both military and political reasons
. . . at another of those junctions of events which he knew
how to gauge so accurately. The imminent elections in
France were certain to bring a swing to the Right, which
meant a majority for the moderates, liberals, and monarchists, in favour of peace. Once in power, they would remove
this Jacobin soldier from his command. But if he became the
man of the approaching peace, he would be immune from
attack.

The elections for the Councils took place on April 10th, and
produced a reactionary majority for the partisans of peace.
On the 18th, at Leoben, Bonaparte signed the preliminaries

of peace with Austria, without waiting for the arrival of the government's emissary bearing authority to negotiate. It is hard not to see a connexion between these two events. But the signatures were exchanged just when Hoche, now commanding the army of Sambre-et-Meuse, had at last crossed the Rhine. His offensive and the consequent armistice made the Austrian plenipotentiaries at Leoben still more accommodating. Hoche helped to strengthen his rival in fame, and he never again found a chance to outstrip him.

Nevertheless, Bonaparte came forward now as the pacific warrior, and literary images did not fail him. In Paris, Josephine and a few friends, who were already fostering his fame, were ordering prints showing the general of the Army of Italy at the tomb of Virgil and crowned with the same laurels. To the Archduke Charles he wrote: 'Have we not slain men enough, and done damage enough to suffering humanity? For my own part, if the overtures which I have the honour to make to you can save the life of single man, I shall deem myself more proud of the civic wreath that I should feel I had merited, than of the melancholy glory that springs from military triumphs'. Fine words in the ears of the new parliamentary majority, and for those whom he called the 'Paris ninnies'!

It was a subtle game that Bonaparte played, and won, at Leoben — to be the man of the peace, without standing for the old boundaries. And the skill and success of his negotiations preserved his own proconsulate in Italy. Indeed, after the preliminaries at Leoben, and pending the final peace, he was practically the sovereign ruler of Italy. He dictated his law to Genoa, to the Pope, and to the King of Naples, and was Protector of the new Republics. The King of Sardinia was his auxiliary. He ruled, and reigned. For the Republics of his creation were so only in name. Everything passed through him. 'Unity of military, diplomatic and financial ideas is necessary,' he had boldly written to Paris.

This single command was now a fact. It was in his own hands, and the Government left it there because Bonaparte, until the peace at least, remained the indispensable man in Italy. The proconsulate was a sketch for the Consulate.

And it was his apprenticeship in monarchy. At the castle of Mombello, near Milan, he lead a princely life, and Josephine was all but a queen. He had his court, and court festivities. Foreign diplomats surrounded him, and the poets and writers of Italy lauded the saviour, the liberator, the man of Providence. The whole picture would be transferred to Paris three years later. One thing serves to measure the distance so far traversed, and how much of the path remains before real greatness is reached. General Bonaparte had raised his family from want. Already his fame was darting rays on his brothers, bringing them honours and profits. Joseph was elected a deputy in Corsica, which was now French again, and appointed a resident agent of the Republic in Parma. Lucien too was preparing his candidature. General Bonaparte was also able to give his sisters dowries. The plain Elisa married Bacciochi, who being a Corsican was poor, but of noble blood. He had to prevent the beautiful Pauline from making a compromising marriage with Fréron, the former Terrorist. She was given General Leclerc, a soldier of sound worth, and the marriage even took place in church. Mombello had its chapel, and the chaplain was allowed to remain. No, these unions were not yet princely. But how long was it since the Bonaparte girls were eating off pewter plates in a garret in Marseilles?

During those three months at Mombello, Bonaparte followed events in Paris closely, and his dominant and natural preoccupation was to know what would be done with him and what would happen to his command. If he toyed sometimes, as others did, with the notion that he might well one day be ruler of France, he must first maintain himself in Italy. He saw very well that there, for the moment, his strength lay.

And if he did not like 'those Directory barristers', if he had not won his victories 'to puff up a Carnot or a Barras', nor even to consolidate a Republic ('What an idea! A republic of thirty million men, with our morals and our vices!'), if he had ceased to be a Republican in feeling and in theory, he still remained as Clarke had defined him in his report, 'the man of the Republic'. And indeed, when the moderates and royalists and 'Clichyans' were gaining preponderance in Paris, Bonaparte sent his aide-de-camp Lavalette to promise 'his support to the section of the Directory which best preserved the colours of the Revolution'. From that line of conduct he was never to depart. He preferred anything to the role of Monk.

But on the subject of peace he was hesitant. Peace was 'not in his interest', although his end of hostilities had given him much prestige after Leoben. But it was difficult for him to break down the peace. A delicate choice . . . Once peace was concluded, he would have to renounce 'this power and high place' in which he had been placed by his victories. There would be nothing for it but to go and 'pay court to the barristers at the Luxembourg'. And he confided in Miot: 'I should not want to leave the Army of Italy except to play a role in France resembling that which I am playing here, and the time has not yet come . . . Peace may be necessary to satisfy these Paris ninnies, and if it has to be made, it is for me to make it. If I left the merit of that to another, that boon would set him higher in public esteem than all my victories.'

These arguments were to regulate his policy, a real balancing policy, up to the signature of the treaty of Campo Formio; and as regards his career and the future, his line of conduct was flawless. Just then, the breach between the Thermidorians of the Left and the new majority of the Councils had opened. Bonaparte sides quite openly with the Left. His message to the Army of Italy on July 14th, was a manifesto of loyal Republicanism: 'Let us vow war, vow on our flags, war against the foes of the Republic and the Constitution of the Year III'. It was the signal for flaming manifestos in the best Republican style, provoked by the commanding officers under his instructions, whereby the Army of Italy placed itself at the disposition of the Government of the Republic.

But Bonaparte was careful not to intervene himself. If the royalists and moderates won the day, he would perhaps take a few divisions to march on Paris. But he was more subtle in his calculations than Hoche, who had just burnt his fingers by clumsy haste. Comparing himself with that rival of his, whose memory always haunted him, Napoleon told Gourgaud: 'My own ambition was cooler; I wanted no risks. I always said to myself, Now then, let things take their course — let's see all that's going to happen . . .' By bringing one of his divisions to Paris, ostensibly for the Irish expedition, Hoche compromised himself, and had to return to the Sambre-et-Meuse Army, where he died two months later. His death rid Bonaparte of the only soldier who might one day have been capable of barring his path.

He did not need that example to play his hand more skilfully. From Paris came word of a severe, revolutionary purging of the Directory and Councils, whilst Bonaparte was sailing with Josephine on Lake Maggiore. Slowly he pushed forward the conversations with Austria for a definite peace, seemingly detached from events in France. But under cover of forwarding the addresses from the Army of Italy, he had despatched Augereau to the three Directors who were preparing the blow. Augereau's Jacobin turbulence was a nuisance at Mombello, and he was a useful tool for this task, a 'rascally adventurer' not subtle enough to realize that his general was sending him to soil his hands in a secret service job. Bonaparte was careful not to act himself. But the preparation was his work. He handed over the papers found at Venice which revealed the dealings of Pichegru with the Prince de Condé, and put one of his subordinates at the disposal of the men of the Left. According to Carnot he even informed certain moderates in the Councils that he had been subjected to 'irresistible pressure'. He was covered on every side.

In a few hours Augereau had done everything. The suspects indicated by the three Directors of the Left wing were arrested; Carnot was warned in time to flee; some fifty members of the Councils were deported to Guiana without trial. The Republic was saved. But at what a price! It was now more dependent than ever on the Army. The appeal to the soldier was becoming the rule.

But it had not escaped Bonaparte's perspicacity that one of the sacrificed Directors, Barthélemy, had owed his election to his diplomatic negotiation of the peace with Prussia and the peace with Spain. This was the circumstance which had brought him into favour with the reactionary majority of the Councils, now decimated and terrorized into impotence. So it was of some use to be the man of peace? Was it as useful a tool for popularity as victories in the field? Here was a role to undertake. Bonaparte was careful not to seize it, and thus completed the manœuvre that he had sketched with the preliminaries of Leoben.

A curious and significant thing was then seen — the warrior more pacific than the 'barristers'. The staunch old Convention men of the Directory wanted all the conquests, and refused to make any concessions to Austria. The events of the 18th of Fructidor had intoxicated them, and the 'genius of the Revolution' inspired them. They wanted Belgium, and all the left bank of the Rhine, and Italy liberated to the very toe and heel of the boot; and they were already casting eyes on Turkey and Egypt. If Austria refused, hostilities would be resumed, the Hapsburgs would be dethroned and the Republic proclaimed in Vienna. Bonaparte opposed these wild ideas, threatening the Government with his resignation. Once again the god of war was appearing as the moderating force. And he found an auxiliary in

Talleyrand, who had become Foreign Minister and was a buffer between the bellicose Directors and the 'pacifying general', whose ideas he understood and whose future destiny he discerned. The element of the old regime in the former Bishop of Autun was obscurely attractive to Bonaparte, and from that time their relationship dated.

The peace was thus at once glorious and reasonable. Bonaparte was courteous in his dealings with the Austrian delegates. Once he lost his self-control with Cobenzl, whose rigidity outwore his patience, and with a carelessly abrupt gesture he knocked over some porcelain. Whence arose a famous legend to which Napoleon himself gave written form in his memoirs, because it formed part of his epic paraphernalia along with the grey overcoat, the little hat and a few other accessories. But he embraced Cobenzl after signing the treaty of Campo Formio on October 17th, 1797, a deal which shared Italy with Austria. The Emperor renounced Belgium, an outlying possession which was no sore bereavement and was never claimed again by Vienna, even in 1815. Belgium was the concern of the French and the English. As for the left bank of the Rhine, that was only secretly promised to the Republic, and subject to the acquiescence of the Germanic states, which would entail the convocation of the Congress of Rastadt.

All in all — and this is of great importance for future events — the relatively moderate peace of Campo Formio determined neither the natural frontiers nor the status of Europe. England had no part in it. That settlement would be revocable so long as England's name were not put to it, and she would agree to it only by compulsion. Until then, wars would be endlessly engendered. Austria knew that, and was only seeking to gain time and harbour her strength. To her, this was a breathing space. Longer perhaps than she supposed. Seventeen years. In the eyes of history, that is not much.

For we are still very close to the circumstances which have

already transformed Bonaparte from a nobody into a famous and important man; but we are only seventeen years from his fall, and power is not yet in his grasp.

He had no lack of desire to seize it. But how was he to do so? The idea of marching on Paris with his troops was childish. No, to raise him to mastery, events and circumstances not yet in existence were needed. The *coup* of Fructidor and the treaty of Campo Formio had consolidated the Republic, and its government was suspicious of this 'peace-making general' who was receiving too many Parisian plaudits, although, on the other hand, the true patriots accused him of having concluded an incomplete peace. And nine days after the exchange of signatures with Cobenzl, the Directory carried out their scheme of separating Bonaparte from 'his army', and from Italy, where he was 'a sovereign rather than an army commander'. He must either bow, or cross the Rubicon.

Bonaparte bowed. Grudgingly, it is true. At Turin, on his way back, he told Miot that he was no longer capable of obedience: 'I have tasted supremacy, and I can no longer renounce it'. Then he threw out various projects — for leaving France, for distinguishing himself by 'some extraordinary expedition which should augment his fame'. That was all very risky: but no more so than making a peace which ended his task in Italy, or resuming hostilities, with that donkey Augereau replacing Hoche on the Rhine, and with ten million doubtful Italians in his rear.

The Directory were in no hurry to see him again. They appointed him to the command of the army which was to invade England and dictate the final peace in London — a chimera which returned periodically, and would return again. But this expedition was in great need of organization. It was not to be hurried. Above all, the Directory did not wish to see the proconsul appearing too soon in Paris, straight from his conquests and with all the glory of his pacific victories about him. So they conceived the idea that the negotiator of Campo Formio might be to some extent forgotten if he went on to the Congress of Rastadt.

They did not know that, for Bonaparte, nothing was a loss of time. They themselves were not only completing his education as a statesman, but introducing him to Europe. He had already introduced himself to Austria, to the Pope, to the kings and republics of Italy. At Rastadt, brief though his stay was, he did the same with the whole of Germany; and so immediate and conspicuous was his success at this Congress, that once again the Directory took fright. Uncertain where they would best like to see him, they recalled him to Paris before he had enhanced his renown by obtaining from the Empire the surrender of the left bank of the Rhine.

Obtaining it was nothing. It had to be kept safe and held with the rest. And so, with every step, the 'genius' of the Revolution made ever more necessary the thing which it held in dread and horror — the government of a soldier.

CHAPTER VIII

ROUTE FROM THE PYRAMIDS TO THE LUXEMBOURG

HE would have been an able man who divined what Bonaparte's thoughts were on his return to Paris in December 1797, after twenty-one months' absence. General Bonaparte was an enigma. Solemnly welcomed by the Directory, he was led to the 'Altar of the Fatherland' by Talleyrand, who now celebrated only secular masses. Gravely he listened to the 'Hymn to Liberty' sung by the pupils of the Conservatoire. Then, to the congratulation of the Directors, the proconsul of Italy replied with short, vague phrases, and general maxims which could bear whatever interpretation his listeners might prefer. He was the hero of Arcola, or the peacemaker of Campo Formio — at choice. He was the man who stopped the war, or the man who waged it to give the Republic for ever those frontiers which 'nature herself had laid down', just as he was the man who prolonged, or who concluded, the Revolution.

His dress and demeanour were correspondingly equivocal. To a meeting of the Court of Appeal held in his honour, he went escorted by a single aide-de-camp, both in civilian attire. He was elected to the mathematical section of the Institute. He did not miss a meeting, charming scientists, men of letters, and the 'ideologists', and for official ceremonies the academic uniform became his favourite. Soldier, diplomat, scholar, legislator — he was all of these at once, as he had been at his court of Mombello. The renown of arms seemed to be what he prized least. It seemed to cling to him incidentally.

This was not so much an affectation, nor even perhaps

design, as a sense of superiority. Towards the 'barristers' of the Directory he was neither servile nor arrogant, but rather calmly and secretly disdainful. He sought the favours of none. Hoche had intrigued with Barras. Joubert was hand-in-glove with Sieyès. Pichegru, and perhaps Moreau, had royalist connections, as Augereau had Jacobin. Bonaparte stood alone. He was himself. He was above faction, whether inside or outside the Revolution, a man with neither rancour nor love. It was his natural position. It might be said that he had held it ever since he first set foot in France and went to Brienne: a position of indifference, of insularity, a position of great strength which was entirely his own, that of an arbiter, already almost a sovereign's. On January 21st, 1798, took place the annual celebration of the death of Louis XVI. Bonaparte would have been conspicuous had he refrained from attending this Revolutionary ceremony; but he declined to go in his capacity as general, and went inconspicuously among the ranks of his colleagues in the Institute. He could not approve of regicide. 'This business of celebrating the death of a man,' he said, 'could never be the act of a government, but only of a faction.' It was a memory which sundered Frenchmen when they sorely needed unifying. In fine, it was not national. Already his thoughts turned to reconciliation, to that merging of the new France with the old which was to be the spirit of his Consulate.

But he set aside the temptation to conquer power. He was the man who is always teaching himself, whose eye can make a sure survey. The impression he had received in Italy of the moral and political state of France was confirmed by observation. 'If he had attempted a seizure of power by violence,' said Marmont, 'nine tenths of the citizens would have deserted him.' To be the syndic of the malcontents, there must needs be discontent. To succeed, he must also find the points where ideas clashed and where interests could be reconciled. In short, he must not mistake the moment, and he must strike with precision. 'Time is man's great art,' he wrote later to his brother Joseph. 'The Gallic temperament is ill accustomed to that great calculation of time; yet it is solely in virtue of this that I have succeeded in everything I have done.'

When 1798 opened, the Directory, notwithstanding Fructidor, was still fairly moderate and was not seriously alarmed. Any possible coup would have to be dealt in the direction of a counter-revolution, and would have to rely on the reactionary elements; and this was totally repugnant to Bonaparte. These elements were the faction favouring 'the old frontiers', whereas the great mass of Frenchmen was overjoyed by the supposed acquisition of the 'natural frontiers', and was determined to shatter the last enemy power which obstinately refused to recognize these boundaries. Coburg was beaten. Public opinion now demanded the overturning of Pitt and 'perfidious Albion', not that of the Directory.

In any case, Bonaparte had long known that the Government mistrusted him and spied upon him, and that there were jealousies directed against him in the Army. He knew also that one popular renown is supplanted by another: 'if they saw me thrice at the theatre, they wouldn't look at me again. . .' He might almost have read the letters written at that moment by Mallet du Pan, the princes' secret intelligence officer: 'This sulphur-headed Scaramouche has only had a success of curiosity. He is finished.' According to the Prussian minister Sandoz, the Parisians were beginning to murmur: 'What is he doing here? Why hasn't he landed in England yet?' And Bonaparte himself was saying: 'If I stop much longer without doing anything, I am lost.' He was afraid of being forgotten, as he had been in those not-so-distant days when he was in charge of the convoys from Avignon to Nice. He regretted Italy. He felt a need to do something, and something no less great.

But if Bonaparte felt that his fame was at a discount, the Directory still felt it to be excessive and 'inopportune'. To keep him safely away from Paris, the best way was to give him a task of such importance that neither he nor the public could complain of any lack of fairness. The Government entrusted him with the 'Army of England'.

It was no new idea to dispose of the English by invading their island. The Revolution had had it in mind long before the camp of Boulogne. Hoche had wasted a year in organizing his chimerical Irish expedition. In less than three weeks, after a tour of inspection to Calais and Ostend, and on the report of Desaix from Brittany, Bonaparte realized the futility of this vast project, for the success of which the first condition was lacking — a fleet capable of standing up to the English navy. For the moment his conclusions were negative, and he dropped the plan, as well as the title of commander-in-chief of the Army of England. A ridiculous title. But at least he had not assumed it himself. He even claimed, talking at St. Helena with O'Meara, that it was a mere diversion intended to trick the English, the Egyptian expedition having already been decided upon by the Directory.

Here was the moment to make actual the idea which had long been occupying him, which almost led him into the service of the Turks, which he had continuously studied in detail since his return from Italy. The fascination of the East had held him since his first reading. Junot used to tell his wife how, in their days of sorry idleness in Paris, Bonaparte used to talk about the East, and Egypt, Mount Lebanon and the Druses. There was a touch of literature and fantasy — Antony and Cleopatra, the *Arabian Nights* — added to an idea which was not at all new, and had already had its partisans during Anglo-French wars before the Revolution: to strike at the 'tyrants of the seas' through the roadway to the East, by seizing the key of Suez, and to stretch a hand towards Tippoo Sahib in India. Since the resumption of war with England, Magallon, the French consul in Alexandria, had urged the Revolutionary Government to take possession of Egypt. But the man bold and adventurous enough to do so had not appeared. The reports however were in the ministry. Talleyrand asked for more. When Bonaparte, following Hoche in dropping the plan of invading the British Isles, talked of attacking England and her Indian trade through Egypt and Persia, it came as no surprise to the Directory.

And his proposal was greeted with an eagerness in which there was but a very small element of desire to get rid of a troublesome soldier. Indeed, there was a risk of magnifying his importance by sending him away; and Bonaparte, for his part, was perhaps less concerned with enhancing his fame by a striking campaign, than with installing himself in a proconsulate of the East to take the place of that of Italy. No government, however detestable, ventures 40,000 men and its last fleet in order to rid itself of an ambitious general. The Directory had other reasons for deciding on the conquest of Egypt.

No more extravagant or adventurous enterprise, not even the expedition to Russia, was undertaken by Napoleon when he had become absolute master. All the remote chimeras in which neither space nor difficulties count, all the gigantic schemes, prospects of Constantinople, dividings and barterings — all formed part already of the Directory's heritage, just as the Directory itself had received it through the Committee of Public Safety from the first Pyrrhus, Brissot, who had dreams of throwing all Europe, all the world, into a vast melting-pot. The Revolution was now in pursuit of an ever-receding peace. Albert Sorel shows clearly how the Egyptian expedition appeared to supposedly reasonable men as the means of a general pacification through the dismembering of the Ottoman Empire. One detail suffices to show how drunken with ideas of force men had become. The Egyptian expedition was financed by the treasure — thirty million francs — lately extorted by Brune from the 'Bernese aristocracy', and this act of brigandage, destined to provide fodder for war, was perpetrated in the name of the Republic and of Liberty. The flood-tide of violence had set in before Napoleon's Empire.

When things went badly with the expedition, Bonaparte was not reluctant to let it be thought that he had been 'deported' to Egypt with his soldiers — a grievance in storage against the Directory. And the Directory declared that the factious general had forced their hands. The truth is that, although both sides had their hidden motives, they were agreed in believing in success, agreed in risking this chance of bringing England to her knees.

How small a chance that was! There had to be a surprise crossing, not of the Channel to dictate peace in London, but of the whole length of the Mediterranean. That was accomplished, by an almost inconceivable prodigy of luck. In spite of all precautions to cloak preparations and destinations, the English were informed. Nelson hurried south with his finest vessels. Bonaparte, on board the *Orient*, weighed with Admiral Brueys the risks of an encounter; they were heavy. There was nothing to be done but go ahead.

They set sail on May 19th, 1798. On the way, Malta was taken, in accordance with official advice to seize this strategic point of the Mediterranean. It would also be a work of Revolutionary piety to liberate the island from the famous Order, the institution of another age. If the Knights of Malta had remained behind their walls, the siege would have dragged on. Their rashness shortened everything. A few days sufficed Bonaparte to organize the Republic's new conquest. On June 19th, the fleet was headed for Alexandria.

Nelson sought them feverishly, but missed them everywhere. He reached Malta too late, and the French escaped him by chance at Candia. He spread all sail for Alexandria, and that haste was again unfortunate for him. He could not find the French squadron, supposed it was heading for Syria, left port to intercept it, and crossed its course within a few miles during the night. If dawn had come, or if Nelson had held a slightly different course, the later disaster off Aboukir, the Battle of the Nile, would have occurred before the army had landed.

This good fortune, not his last, enhanced belief in Bonaparte's 'star'. He made good use of that belief, though he hardly shared it. We are too ready to believe, from our knowledge of the sequel, that Bonaparte read the future as an open book. His certainties were no more than other men's. The naval disaster at Aboukir, the reverse at Acre, would have been warning enough that his star was not infallible. But this fantastic expedition, which, against all reason, he turned to his advantage, gave new force to that impression amongst Frenchmen that to this hero of past exploits all things were possible, That impression became stronger as men were able to measure the prodigious rise of the general, and of those who in his train became kings and princes, when improbabilities vanished because everything was true.

Supreme power was one of these possibilities. With every stage of his progress towards the crown, we can see why, if it were going to anyone, it would go to Napoleon. It was always he who had the widest horizon and the largest view. He left for Egypt with soldiers, and also with scholars, artists, engineers, naturalists, jurists, all the elements wherewith to build up an administration and found a state, to disclose what sleeps beneath the soil of the Pharaohs, to estimate the riches of the country, to prepare for the piercing of the Isthmus of Suez. He even took a poet to sing his exploits, Parseval-Grandmaison by name. It was the fault of the age, not of Bonaparte, that he did not find a better.

In Egypt as in Italy he had ideas of government; he was creative. He was to prove the founder of modern Egypt, first in freeing it from the oppression of the Mamelukes, rather as he had liberated Lombardy from the Austrians, and then in leaving upon it a Western and French imprint of a kind which the Egyptians were capable of receiving, and so exactly proportioned that the mark has endured. He had already a studious knowledge of Islam. He could talk with Moslems and understand them. He was interested in their religion, their history, their morality. He conversed with their priests, and showed respect for their persons and their beliefs. As First Consul he was to tell Roederer: 'It was by making myself Catholic that I ended the war in the Vendée; by making myself a Moslem that I established myself in Egypt; by becoming Ultramontane that I won sympathy in Italy. If I were ruling a people of Jews, I should rebuild the Temple of Solomon.' After Bonaparte, his successor Kléber, a fine soldier but only a soldier, was to seem harsh and aloof. He was murdered, whilst 'Sultan Bonaparte' was respected. Even the revolt of Cairo, an accident of fanaticism, had not perturbed him. He made examples, and terrible ones. But he continued to link up the Crescent and the Cap of Liberty, the Rights of Man and the Koran: which, all in all, was the formula that he came to apply in France by the 'fusion'.

Once again, on the banks of the Nile, he was a sovereign, an enlightened and reforming despot, as he had been at Mombello; completely at home on these confines of Africa and Asia, using picturesque language to reanimate his quickly disillusioned troops, who were often driven to suicide by fatigue, unwonted sufferings, a barbarous enemy, ophthalmia and the plague. In his career as commander, Egypt was to him what Atala was in the career of Chateaubriand. And from the valley of the Nile Bonaparte brought back, along with originalities to impress the 'ninnies' of Paris, along with the Turkish sabre fastened to his greatcoat, turns of speech and thought and a decorative element which were clamped on to his legend like the sphinxes on the tables and armchairs of the Empire style.

In his innermost heart he brought back something else from this new experience. 'I am especially disgusted with Rousseau since seeing the Orient,' he said. 'The uncivilized man is a dog.' What name would he give to the civilized woman with neither loyalty nor faith? There was bitterness in that remark. It was in Egypt that Bonaparte learned that Josephine was betraying him, and bringing ridicule upon the hero who, not so long ago, had marched to the conquest of Italy marking each of his victories with a love-letter. The sour taste of treason was in his mouth. 'I have bitter domestic griefs,' he wrote to Joseph, 'for the veil is quite lifted.' And like a romantic René or Manfred, he added: 'I need solitude and isolation. Grandeur wearies me, sentiment has dried up, glory is dulled. At twenty-nine I have drained all the cup.' But not to such a point that nature and will and ambition did not rise in protest. He thought he was suffering: he was only vexed. In fact, Josephine's faithlessness gave him freedom. He took a mistress, the wife of one of his officers. In his misanthropy he became something of the Pasha.

But he would hear less patiently than ever about the natural goodness of mankind. Not on that principle did he base his system of government. For in Egypt he governed, and organized, and legislated. He surrounded himself with the provisional, the fragile, the precarious — as would be his destiny to the last. Only after the event did he represent his sojourn on the Nile as a waiting position. There as elsewhere he gave himself up entirely to what he did at the actual moment, and ready at a moment's notice to turn in a fresh direction.

A month after the landing at Alexandria, when the Mamelukes had been broken and their remnants chased into the desert, came the disaster which had been miraculously averted ever since the departure from Toulon. On August 1st Nelson attacked and destroyed the French fleet off Aboukir. Only a few frigates were spared from the general destruction, and Admiral Brueys himself went down with the *Orient*. It was a memorable naval defeat, a collapse which Trafalgar was to complete. From that day the army was cut off from France, blockaded in Egypt without hope of return, for the Republic had lost its last squadron. The impression caused by the catastrophe was immense. England was unmistakably ruler of the seas. She no longer had any difficulty in uniting Europe against the conquering Revolution.

But it is striking to note how little this disaster affected Bonaparte. His expedition had no more ships? It would do without them. It could not count on supplies from abroad? It would be organized to live on the occupied country and to produce necessities on the spot. The commander-in-chief was not disturbed for a moment. Difficulties seemed to stimulate him. A week after the fatal news he was founding the Institute of Egypt, just as he signed the statute regulating the actors of the Théâtre Français at Moscow. Throughout 1798, and until March 1799, he was engaged in pacifying and administering his conquest as though he would be staying there for ever.

But another danger threatened. The Turks, instigated by England and Russia, were advancing from Syria to recapture Egypt. Instantly Bonaparte decided to advance to meet them. It was a flight forwards; and it was also the grandiose plan which he had expounded to Junot as they paced the Paris boulevards. Once master of Syria, he would raise the Christians of Lebanon, rally the Druses, and then his army, with these strong auxiliaries, would open the way to Constantinople, and march from there on Vienna — unless, renewing the exploits of Alexander, he turned towards India to join hands with Tippoo Sahib and expel the English.

But although the campaign of Syria had the same boldness and logic that took Napoleon to Moscow to try to break the English ring, it was to fail. True, the Turks were beaten at Mount Tabor and they abandoned the invasion of Egypt. But Bonaparte was checked before Acre, where, hampered by lack of heavy artillery, he decided to raise the siege after two months of vain efforts.

The painful memory left within him by the siege of Acre was a proof that the Egyptian venture was no diversion in his mind, but an important enterprise capable of vast development. 'My projects and my dreams, all — yes, England destroyed them all,' he said later. He still thought of it on St. Helena. His whole life, one might think, had gone wrong at Acre. And yet that Syrian campaign, admirably staged, really proved advantageous to his legend. In the Holy Land he dropped his Moslem disguise. He appeared as a Christian, almost a Crusader, and showed his emotion at Nazareth. And the abundant atrocities and scenes of horror (such as the visit to the plague-stricken of Jaffa) received the artist's touch which transfigured them for popular consumption. Even the failure at Acre took on an epic air, by virtue of the desert retreat, when the commander-in-chief left his horse to the wounded and marched on foot, just as he carried a staff on the return from Moscow. And just as he was to withdraw silently from the Grand Army, so now he was not long in leaving Egypt, a venture with no issue now before it but capitulation.

He returned first to dispose of the Turks who had landed at Aboukir itself, veiling with a land victory the name of a crushing naval defeat. July 1799 was at an end. Since leaving Toulon, fourteen months ago, Bonaparte had received only scanty news from France. After the restoration of the fort of Aboukir there came into his hands a whole package of newspapers from Europe. Roused at midnight, Bonaparte immediately read through the gazettes. He learned that the general war had broken out again, that the armies of the Republic were everywhere withdrawing, that Scherer had been beaten on the Adige and that Italy was lost, that Jourdan, likewise defeated in the Black Forest, had recrossed the Rhine. Next morning he summoned Rear-Admiral Ganteaume and was closeted with him for two hours. His decision was taken. He would return.

Had he any thoughts of assuming power? Not until he landed in France was he to know the real state of the country or be informed of the chances that now offered for a *coup d'état*. Not until he came near Paris would he know that at least one member of the Directory was thinking of a soldier as saviour of the Republic and the Revolution. He did not know, for the despatch had not yet reached him, that the Directory had already recalled him, but he had a presentiment that he would be needed to restore the military situation, and that in that the pre-eminent role was awaiting him. The rest he would perhaps have. But the obvious thing was that the Egyptian chapter was closed. His Eastern proconsulate had given him even more self-confidence than his reign in Italy. He had governed two countries already. The idea of ruling France, at thirty years of age, no longer alarmed him. The 'great ambition' which came to him after Lodi had opened out wider after the Pyramids.

But he had to get back. And first of all he must leave the Army of Egypt to its hopeless conquest, and arrange this desertion in secret, so as not to offend the rank-and-file or demoralize the leaders to whom command would be delegated. Also, this departure must be made honourable, if not glorious, in the eyes of Frenchmen themselves. Lastly, fortune must be kind enough to allow the frigate *La Muiron* and her three escorting vessels to slip through the watching English fleet. The return voyage was as hazardous as the outward. Luck willed that it should end as fortunately. But Bonaparte was risking his all. If he remained bottled up in Egypt his career was ended. He trusted in his star. Faithfully it led him straight to France. And the incredible, unhoped-for elements in the success of this boldness obliterated the resentful feelings caused by the desertion of his comrades-in-arms, left by their chief to an approaching surrender. That audacious cruise across the whole length of the Mediterranean, over seas dotted with English sails and foes itching for so brilliant a prize, had in it an insolent good fortune which amazed, which by its own force made men hail a decree of destiny.

Bonaparte risked not returning at all. He also risked returning too late. At that moment, Sieyès in the Luxembourg was meditating a *coup d'état*, 'seeking a sword', not thinking of the leader of the far-off Egyptian adventure. He thought of Joubert.

It happened that Joubert, courted and even espoused by the men who felt the need of a soldier to save and consolidate the Republic, and sent by them to Italy, on to the stage where the other had won his glory, was killed at Novi. His death on August 12th had gravely discomfited his supporters when, seven weeks later, Bonaparte appeared. He was unscathed — by bullets, by pestilence, by the waves. Joubert had followed Hoche. Who could now be preferred to him, or set against him, amongst the Republican soldiers? If he had other points of superiority over his rivals, he had also the chief one — he was alive.

CHAPTER IX

BRUMAIRE

BONAPARTE had been absent from France from May 19th, 1798, until October 9th, 1799. During these seventeen months the causes working to make a dictatorship necessary had not ceased to be increasingly active. Since the annexation of Belgium, the Revolution had no longer been mistress of her destiny.

Henceforth we have the situation which was to be repeated right on to 1814, until France returned to within her old boundaries. England would doggedly knit coalitions of which she was the soul and the money-chest; France would exhaust herself in breaking them; and they would become larger, stronger and more united in proportion to the forward moves of France into Europe. 'If I had been beaten at Marengo,' said Napoleon to his St. Helena companions, 'you would have had then the whole of 1814 and of 1815.' That was perfectly true.

The disaster to the French fleet at Aboukir had been the signal in Europe for a resumption of hostilities. Nelson ruled the Mediterranean, Bonaparte was trapped in Egypt. English diplomacy was everywhere active and Nelson induced the King of Naples to take up arms. As soon as war was declared by the Neapolitan government, the French hurried against these opponents, routed their army, and entered Naples itself. The Bourbons fled to Sicily. The Parthenopæn Republic was established.

In 1799 there were also seen the beginnings of a movement which within a few years would assume larger dimensions — the revolt of the peoples against the conquering Revolution, the turning of the ideas of liberty and nationality against those who had been propagating them throughout the world. It·has been said too often that the signal for these national risings was given by the Spanish peasantry in 1808. The Calabrian peasants and the *lazzaroni* of Naples were first in the field. Albert Sorel has well described the stupefaction of the French Republican soldiery before this phenomenon; the cause of the kings was transformed into that of the peoples, as strange a prodigy as a river flowing backwards to its source. Before long this popular frenzy brought about the retreat from Naples, and the crash. And it was not long before the Russians under Suvarof, emerging from their steppes with their ikons, debouched upon Italy to drive forth the French, whilst Hungarian Hussars murdered two Republican plenipotentiaries at the gates of Rastadt, where the interminable Congress had just dissolved. Swiss, Dutchmen, and Belgians rose too — and it was to preserve Belgium that this exhausting war was sustained! At the same time the Vendée took up arms once more.

The peril had been the same in 1793, though less grave. It would be the same, but graver, in 1813, and 1814. Why did the Directory escape it in 1799? Because, as in 1793, the coalition powers did not wage war to the uttermost, being divided in interests and having other ends before them. The rivalries of Austria and Russia in the Near East checked their offensive. Masséna profited by that slowing-up to beat Suvarof at Zurich, and almost at the same time Brune had the luck to beat the English and Russian forces landed in Holland. This time again France was saved from invasion. Italy was lost, but the 'natural frontiers' were preserved.

This was the moment when Bonaparte reached the end of his adventurous crossing of the Mediterranean. On October 1st, having escaped the English by a series of miracles, the *Muiron* reached Ajaccio. There Bonaparte learned the latest news. He realized that Brune and Masséna were filching his chances. He believed that general acclamation would put him in command of the armies of the Republic to repulse the enemy. But the invasion was stemmed. He was arriving too late.

No matter. He hurried on. When the way was clear the *Muiron* set sail, and never again was Bonaparte to see Ajaccio. On October 8th he was in sight of the Provençal coast. Once again he slipped clear of the English squadron cruising to capture him. On the 9th he landed near Fréjus, in the bay of Saint-Raphaël.

Then came a revelation. During his absence his popularity had grown beyond all his hopes. Hardly had his frigates approached the shore when the Provençal population hastened to acclaim the general, clambering on board to see him at closer quarters. Again, luck. This point of arrival freed him from the quarantine which a spiteful administration might possibly have inflicted on him as he was coming from a country where plague was raging. Already the cries he heard, the gladness of which he saw so much evidence, assured him that he was expected. The hour might have gone by when a great captain was needed to beat the enemy, but a soldier, a leader, was still needed to save the Republic and the State.

But he did not yet know all. As he approached Paris he learned something new and definite which gave his fortune a fresh aspect. He had caught glimpses of power, and desired it, like others, without finding the means of attaining it; now power was offering itself to him. Not only was the fruit ripe, but the means of plucking it were being brought to him. A *coup d'état* was implicit in the nature of the situation. The 'how' showed itself spontaneously to Bonaparte. His brother Joseph hurried to meet him and informed him of the actual position of the ideas and projects of Sieyès, who had been crippled by the death of Joubert. To become master in France, Bonaparte would not have to inflame troops or the mob, a chancy and adventurous procedure in which he had no trust. The *coup d'état* in preparation, which lacked only an executant, would not compromise him with the royalists, nor leave him under control of military influences. It would be organized from the interior by civilians, Republicans, with the caution of a Revolutionary who was one of the 'pure' men of the early days of '89, and a regicide too. This *coup d'état* would be still faithful to the 'genius of the Republic', in the direct line of the Revolution, and thereby hardly illegal at all — just such a *coup*, in fact, as might be conceived, desired, even approved, by the general of Vendémiaire and Fructidor.

It remains to be understood why, within the Republic itself, and at the head of the State, there were men of influence and weight who had come to believe that the only hope of safety lay in the appeal to the soldier, and why Sieyès, the man of endless constitutions, was seeking 'a sword' as Diogenes sought 'a man'.

The fact is that the system of government set up in 1795 could last no longer. Augereau might have purged the Councils at Fructidor, but in the following year it had been necessary to begin again and quash new elections hostile to the Directors in control. It was the fundamental vice of a regime based on the popular will, violating the popular as soon as it opposed the unexpressed, but not the least powerful, article of the Constitution: that is, as soon as it tended to remove power from the former Conventionals, the Thermidorians of the Left. In May, 1798 (22nd of Floréal), accordingly, came a fresh abuse of authority, whilst the external war was being resumed. With that came a revival of Jacobin spirit. The Right parties abstained from voting in the May elections of 1799; they were disheartened and intimidated. The 'patriots', with all their exaltation and exaggeration, reappeared in the Council, claiming and imposing a return to terrorist methods because the country was in dire peril. Rigorous measures followed, at the cost this time of the bourgeois classes. The forced loan alarmed the mass of well-to-do people, but was far from curing the increasing weakness of the national finances. There was a sense of insecurity and anxiety everywhere, and day after day came news of military disaster. Meanwhile, returning from a diplomatic mission to Berlin, Sieyès was elected a Director in place of Rewbell. Quite rightly, he had never liked the Constitution of the Year III, which was not of his making. He saw the Republic and the Revolution plunging to ruin, and this great disorder, intensified by military reverses, could only end in the restoration of the Bourbons. This regicide ex-priest was perhaps the most conscious and clear-sighted of the Revolutionaries. The machinery must be changed, at any cost, or catastrophe would be at hand.

He was now on the spot. Silently he set to work and began to weave his conspiracy to save the Republic. His first task was to make sure of having with him the executive power, that five-headed authority. The Directors had purged the Councils. He would reverse the process and purge the Directory. On 30th of Prairial (18th June, 1799) he carried out his first *coup d'état*, the preliminary to the other. Having allied the former Gironde element with the extreme Left in the Councils, Sieyès got rid of three of his colleagues, retaining Barras, and brought into the Directory Roger Ducos, his confidant and accomplice, and two Jacobins of the strict observance, Gohier and General Moulin. When the day came, it would only be a question of shaking off these figure-heads. Sieyès had tricked the extreme Left, his ally of a day, and he disarmed them by closing the Manège, where the Jacobin Club had resumed its meetings. The preliminaries of the crowning stroke were accomplished. General Bonaparte found the machinery of the 18th of Brumaire already started.

He also found France ready to yield to it. All the way from Fréjus to Paris, there was no mistaking what he saw and heard. His fingers could feel the anarchy. The carriages with his baggage were pillaged near Aix by brigands, 'French Bedouins', as they were termed by his mameluke Roustan, whom he had brought from Egypt to adorn his train and lend it a gleam of the Orient. The need for order and authority could be felt everywhere. And it crystallized round the person of General Bonaparte. His welcome at Lyons was significant, so warm indeed that he resolved for the future to avoid compromising ovations.

It was important, indeed, not to spoil an admirable state of affairs. There was nothing mysterious in this lightning popularity. Instinctively the French were seeking a leader, just as Sieyès was deliberately seeking an executant. And there was no other leader than himself: certainly none with such a blend of the essentials. The country's aspirations were vague and contradictory. Men were weary of the confusions sprung of the Revolution, but the mass were resolved to preserve the results of the Revolution — equality, and national wealth. Men were tired of war, but would not renounce the 'natural frontiers'. And Bonaparte's reputations were ready-made. He achieved victories that brought with them peace. He had no truck with reaction, and indeed used grape-shot if necessary, and his speech excluded any suspicion of feudal spirit, but he did not wound sentiments or beliefs, and persecuted neither persons nor interests. And there, if he reaped after sowing, he had sowed unintentionally, for the deep, innate, fundamental reason that these passions, Revolutionary or counter-Revolutionary, which sundered true-born Frenchmen, were not shared by him. He had never been able to feel them as Frenchmen did.

By the very fact of his remoteness, away in Egypt, Bonaparte had made himself desired, and nobody had come forward to play the role of saviour. Besides, how could the fact be overlooked that victory, in Bonaparte's absence, deserted the French camp? And as the Government is always blamed for every evil, this Government was duly blamed for having 'deported' him to Egypt; he became a victim as well as a hero.

Meanwhile preparations had gone so far forward that everything was staged and carried out in less than a month. Bonaparte had returned just in time to take up the tasks left by Joubert's death, tasks which Moreau, forewarned already, hesitated to undertake. Later Moreau regretted it. But he was irresolute by nature, and a bad starter. When Bonaparte's return became known in Paris, he told Sieyès: 'That's your man. He will do your job much better than I could.' One sincere Republican, Baudin, deputy for the Ardennes died of joy that same day. To him, as to the patriots of Fréjus who had boarded the *Muiron* with cheers for the Republic, Bonaparte's arrival meant the salvation of the Revolution. There was a similar feeling amongst the Royalists. Never had the regime been so near to collapse. But they now felt that, for years ahead, there was no possibility of a restoration.

And it was just against a return of the Bourbons that the Republicans wished, in the first place, to forearm themselves. The 18th of Brumaire had the same motives behind it as Fructidor. The dictatorship of a soldier was the risk which these Republicans ran by their operation. They consented to run that risk rather than incur the danger of a counter-revolution, just as they were to see a Napoleonic monarchy and the foundation of a fourth dynasty as the surest rampart against the Bourbons. And when we see what became of the regicides after 1815, when they tasted in exile the miseries of the *émigrés*, it is comprehensible that they should have preferred anything to that, and placed a sword, even a throne if need be, between the Bourbons and themselves.

But the instinct of self-preservation was not the only one active. Sincere Republicans saw the necessity of concentrating the waning strength of the executive power, and for that reason the plan of Sieyès allowed for the five heads of the Directory to become the three heads of the Consulate. Furthermore, common sense declared the impossibility of resisting Europe in the midst of convulsion and anarchy. The Convention had recognized that, and organized the Terror. The Terrorist regime was now a thing hateful to Frenchmen. It was essential to refashion an authority which had not a Gorgon's head.

JOSEPHINE FORGIVEN

The reinforcement of the executive, then, the goal of the new *coup d'état* in preparation, was both a reasoned and a reasonable idea. Furthermore, all the intelligence and ideology represented in the Republic was on the side of Sieyès. And as the need was felt for a leader to continue the war for the natural frontiers under good conditions, it was likewise consistent with the situation that this leader should be a soldier. If the Revolution was to end with a Caesar, it was lucky to find ready at its hand the very soldier who, with a minimum of caste spirit, was penetrating enough to assure the pre-eminence of the civil element in his government, and so avoid opening an era of proclamations of Imperators in the camp.

Five-and-twenty days, no more, passed between Bonaparte's return home to the Rue Chantereine, and the evening when he emerged, already a Caesar, from the Orangery of Saint-Cloud. From his brothers, who hated her, he had had detailed information about the habits and delinquencies and debts of Josephine. The guilty and anxious woman wished to state her case and win a pardon. But Bonaparte was resolved to sweep his house clean. He was tired of sharing with this Monsieur Charles, of being a tricked husband. The coming master of France had not yet moved far from his bohemian setting, from the demi-monde where he had found his companion.

But Josephine had her pardon, as soon as she reached the Rue Chantereine after missing him at Lyons. He forgave because she had not lost all power over his heart or his senses. He forgave because, when he shut his door without consenting to see her, she was clever enough to send her children, Eugène and Hortense, to beg his forgiveness through the door, confident that this theatrical touch would soften him. He forgave because a divorce would be an ill-timed scandal. And finally, he forgave because, on reflection, it looked as if Josephine would be a useful ally to him. He reckoned wisely. Josephine, as usual, kept on friendly terms

113

with the holders of authority. Barras, her old protector, was still her friend. She knew Gohier, the head of the Directory, and through him was on a friendly footing with Moulin. So that Bonaparte, during those first days, and thanks partly to Josephine, found himself on very good terms with the three directors who were to be edged out, expelled, and exiled.

In this way, to the last, he was to put people off the scent. That was also the reason why nobody bothered him to account for himself, although he was living in Paris in circumstances which were to all respects ill-defined, for he had abandoned the Army of Egypt, and, ever since landing at Fréjus, had treated all military regulations or orders with disdain, feigning ignorance of their existence or their applicability to himself. Besides, who would venture to touch General Bonaparte? His renown was his best shield, and his behaviour kept it from making him suspect, for he affected to shun rather than to seek any ovations. He was impenetrable, and discouraged neither parties nor persons; yet he did not compromise himself either with the Jacobins of the Manège, or with the Barras element from the Directory, or with the moderates. Sieyès himself was a shade too reactionary for Bonaparte's taste. As for the Royalists, they were mistaken in their illusions. He would make use of them, but never help them.

Fundamentally his judgment of the state of France was sound. The element to be captured was the Third Estate — the class which had already sustained Henry IV after the League, and Louis XIV after the Fronde, that solid mass which, as Cardinal de Retz said, is null at the start and in the middle of great crises, but weighs the most at the end. The nearest approach to the Third Estate was the moderates, who were likewise powerless by themselves, and that was the reason why Sieyès, their leader, was in need of a sword. But the General was reluctant to appear to be offering himself to Sieyès, just as Sieyès did not wish to seem to be inviting the General. Each declined to take the first step, so as to retain liberty of action. A vexing game. Sieyès complained of this young man who ought to be shot for abandoning his army on the banks of the Nile. Bonaparte retorted that Sieyès had betrayed France in the Berlin negotiations.

Meanwhile precious time was being lost. The Council of Five Hundred divined the danger, and showed an inclination to withdraw some of its most unpopular decrees. A semblance of relaxing and appeasement would content the public and mollify feeling. The iron must be struck while it was hot, and direct contact must instantly be made between the man who had conceived and prepared the *coup d'état* and the man capable of executing it, natural collaborators who would each bring an indispensable element to the success of the operation.

Hitherto they had merely caught sight of each other at official ceremonies. It was Talleyrand who brought them together. Not until the 2nd of Brumaire (October 24th) did Bonaparte decide to pay Sieyès, at his request, the visit which he had himself vainly awaited at the Rue Chantereine. With Talleyrand there was also Fouché — types of men as indispensable for the plot in the background of its workings as Sieyès and Bonaparte were for its foreground. The ex-Oratorian and ex-Bishop have been termed his evil geniuses, and he has been held wrong in not dispensing with them. But nothing would have been possible without Sieyès, Fouché and Talleyrand — his 'three-card hand of priests' — who brought him not only their ability and intelligence, but also the caution of men all interested in preventing a counter-revolution.

Here then was a *coup d'état* presenting itself in the most favourable conditions. It was being engineered within by Sieyès and Ducos, two of the heads of the very authority which it sought to overturn. Of the two Assemblies, one, the Council of the Ancients, was an accomplice, and the other, the Five Hundred, was being manipulated by Lucien Bonaparte, who, young though he was, had made sufficient stir to secure the presidency. Finally, public opinion was sympathetic. Even in the Faubourg Saint-Antoine no rising need be feared. And yet this *coup d'état* was within an inch of being a failure.

It was to some extent Bonaparte's fault. But when the stroke was actually won, it was he who had calculated best. He had been dogged in his determination to give the operation a civilian character, as free from the military hand as possible, and without the use of violence. On the eve of Saint-Cloud he refused to listen to Sieyès and Fouché, who favoured preventive arrests amongst the deputies known in advance to be ardent opponents. Rash as that refusal may have been, it gave him the advantage of making his regime accessible to the purest Revolutionaries and not opening him to the reproach of the 'crime' of the 18th of Brumaire, as his nephew was later to be reproached with the 'crime' of December 2nd, 1851. He risked difficulties, but fundamentally he was right, because after that 'day', one more in the long series of Revolutionary 'days', he secured one of the results that were in his mind. He was not to be a dependent of the barracks, as he would have been if he had owed his rise to power only to the Army.

The danger, in fact, was that his example would serve to enable others to launch against himself the same blow that he was about to deal the Directory. Bonaparte was well aware that, however great his superiority over all other military leaders, the fact would not prevent them from saying to themselves: 'Why not I?' Whilst Fouché and Sieyès had their eye on the parliamentary opposition, Bonaparte, knowing his own *milieu*, informed about the plot only such officers as he could be sure of. With the others he was more than circumspect. On the eve, and on the day, of Saint-Cloud, the men whom he had specially watched, because he regarded them as the most suspect, were General Bernadotte, General Jourdan, and General Augereau.

It was not hypocrisy that made him write to Talleyrand two years earlier: 'What a disaster it is, for a nation of thirty million living in the eighteenth century, to be forced to have recourse to bayonets to save the country!' Bonaparte would have preferred to dispense entirely with the bayonets. His future power would only be the stronger for it. There his vision was accurate, but in practice he went beyond moderation. His desire, as a true son of his century, would have been to triumph by the pure force of Reason. In that he was more of an ideologist than the ideologists who surrounded him, adopted him, and made his *coup d'état* a kind of conspiracy of the Institute. For he had not omitted to let himself be seen again at the academic sessions. If he had his spurred and booted bodyguards, Murat, Berthier and Marmont by name, he had also a whole escort of intellectuals, men of letters, scientists, jurists, philosophers, a throng of belated Encyclopædists, the famous Cabanis himself, representative of the whole struggle against 'superstition' and 'abuses'. Voltaire, the advocate of enlightened despotism, would have been with that philosophical procession which went to Auteuil on the eve of the 18th of Brumaire, led by the General, to call upon Madame Helvétius, the widow of the author of *De l'Esprit*.

Now that the ice was broken, Sieyès and Bonaparte met and worked in concert. They counted on handling the national representation with even less violence than Fructidor had subjected it to. To alter the Constitution they planned to obtain the vote of both Assemblies whilst pushing respect for parliamentary forms as far as possible. The majority of the Council of Ancients was secured, and it only remained to leave the Five Hundred incapable of resistance. Force would be used only if it were indispensable, as a heroic remedy and a last resort.

The plan, then, presented grave risks, but it was hardly possible to imagine any very different one. We must set aside the accepted idea of an 18th of Brumaire with Bonaparte expelling the representatives of the people with his grenadiers. In the first place, he had no grenadiers of his own. The body of men to whom that name was applied was actually the guard of the Directory and the Councils, the remnant of the French Guards of sorry memory, and some gendarmes of the Convention. If these men, police rather than soldiers, were anybody's pretorians, they were the pretorians of the Republic. The Paris garrison was much easier to carry along. The rank-and-file fighting man, who had often served under Bonaparte, was like the rest of France. He complained of everything, the distress everywhere, the defeats, his tatters, his arrears of pay, his rations and tobacco, and laid the blame for all these woes on these 'lawyers of the Directory'.

Everything conspired to complicate an operation which looks simple at a distance. When Bonaparte, on his return from Paris, asked: 'Do you think the affair is possible?' Roederer, one of the intellectual aristocracy surrounding and instigating him, answered: 'It is three-quarters done.' True, the last quarter was the hardest, and remained very risky.

Despite the precautions of the arch-conspirators, suspicions of something began to arise. Of the five Directors, three had to be jettisoned, and of these Barras was little to be feared. At no price must the others be put on the alert. Josephine came in useful here, and undertook to keep the blinkers on Gohier, who was smitten by her charms. She pushed her astute audacity to the point of asking the poor man to luncheon on the very day — the 18th of Brumaire, November 9th, 1799 — for which the *coup* was fixed. The evening before, Bonaparte was dining at the Ministry of Justice with Cambacérès, who was not in the plot. Three days previously, he had attended — but without eating, for fear of poison — a banquet given by the Councils in honour of himself and of Moreau. Everything went forward right inside official society.

And the scenario imagined by Sieyès was also official.

The operation was to be carried out, in two days, in Parliament and with Parliament, according to Parliamentary procedure. On the pretext of an anarchist conspiracy unearthed in Paris, the Ancients were to be convoked for an extraordinary session, at an hour which, for the season, was very early. The conspirators had their accomplices skilfully posted in this assembly, and for further security, the suspect members were 'forgotten' in the nocturnal despatch of the summoning messages. The Ancients, after hearing a report on the imminence of the danger, would vote without debate for a transference of the legislature to a point outside Paris, as the Constitution authorized them. The spot chosen was Saint-Cloud. The execution of this decree, the security of the Councils, and the maintenance of public order, would be entrusted to General Bonaparte, who was to be appointed to the command of the troops of the Paris garrison. This done, Bonaparte, with armed force at his disposal, would obliterate the three unwanted Directors. Gohier, fooled to the last, and Moulin, blind until it was too late, would be tethered in the Luxembourg until they resigned office, under the guard of Moreau, who was content with this inglorious role of gaoler for the executive power. As for Barras, likewise tricked — for he had been encouraged to believe that he was 'in it' — Talleyrand made himself responsible for getting him out of the way. He would be urgently invited to proceed under escort of a few dragoons to his property of Grosbois.

As Sieyès saw it, the transference of the legislature to Saint-Cloud would have the advantage of isolating the Council of Five Hundred, which would more easily be induced to vote for the new Constitution when once it felt itself outside Paris and surrounded by troops. It would have been far better to rush matters before the Left wing of the Five Hundred had time, before the second day, to recover its breath. But they wished to do everything in the name of the Constitution, which they proposed to destroy in due parliamentary form, affecting to treat the legislative power as respectfully as they handled the executive power cavalierly. The splitting of the manœuvre into two days' operation had the further drawback of bringing Bonaparte into contact with the Assemblies, and on that unfamiliar terrain he acted with a clumsiness which very nearly spoilt everything.

The first part of the programme went off superbly. On the morning of the 18th of Brumaire, at the Rue Chantereine, surrounded by his faithful aides-de-camp, the commander of the armed force was very lively, completely master of himself, and charming in his greetings to the officers of the Paris garrison, who were now under his orders and were vaguely realizing what was required of them. But there were a few stubborn men, such as Lefebvre, the husband of 'Madame Sans-Gêne'. Bonaparte took him apart, stormed, and convinced him, and behold! — Lefebvre was ready to 'pitch these damned lawyers into the river'. Crossing Paris on horseback with his staff, Bonaparte was cheered by the passers-by. When he entered the Council of Ancients to take the oath, he was less at his ease. He spoke too long and lost the thread of his speech. The president had to come to his aid to adjourn the session to the following day, at Saint-Cloud. Bonaparte made amends as he came out, when he saw Bottot, the emissary of Barras, and called to this figure-head scapegoat: 'What have you done with the France I left so glorious? What have you done with the hundred thousand Frenchmen who were my companions in glory? They are dead.' The Directory was put on its trial, and it was excellent propaganda, supported by posters and scattered leaflets in a sympathetic and passive Paris. Meanwhile Lucien was presiding over the meeting of the Five Hundred called to hear the reading of the decree, and gagged any questioning voices. He too arranged for a meeting next day, out at Saint-Cloud, and his intervention would be still more useful. The day of the 18th had passed off successfully, but the main task had still to be gone through.

And how were the Councils to be deceived? They must be blind not to see what was in preparation. Paris suspected already. There were foes of the Republic, men who had never forgiven the Terror, who felt their necks none too safe, and now were promising themselves a visit to Saint-Cloud to see with their own eyes the strangling of the beast. The machinery was obvious. Of the anarchist plot, pretext of the whole affair, there was no sign anywhere. Both presidents had invoked standing orders to silence those deputies who demanded further information and proofs. But the morrow? The fear of that morrow disturbed several associates of the conspiracy. Some took fright. These twenty-four hours of reflection went for nought. They were also twenty-four hours of parleying, coming and going, intrigues. And although Bonaparte still refused preventive arrests, he was not without fears. He slept with a pistol within reach. Sieyès himself had a carriage in waiting, ready for flight in case of accident.

Again, there were not only men who were carrying out the *coup d'état,* and men opposed to it. There were others who wondered what would happen if the scheme broke down, who feared especially the consequences of a failure, a redoubling of confusions. The Minister of Justice, Cambacérès, hastened to arrange a combination intended to replace that of Sieyès and Bonaparte if the need arose. Napoleon's contemporaries were far from unanimity in a belief in his star. He was always to have men, close at hand, who were struck more by the fragility than by the glitter of his power, and who did not forget the element of uncertainty in the 18th of Brumaire.

More exactly, the 19th of Brumaire. For it was on the 19th that things nearly went askew. Success hung by a thread. In reality Bonaparte owed it to his brother Lucien. He was not meant for turmoils of this sort. Contact with crowds always filled him with a nervous repulsion. He was used to command, and as soon as he was not acting by his sole prestige, he lost grip.

The deputies of both Assemblies may be pictured arriving at Saint-Cloud, for the most part ignorant of what they would do there and of what would be asked of them. The session was supposed to be opened immediately, and things carried through at rattling pace. The meeting rooms improvised in the Orangery were not ready. Workmen were still hammering. Wearing their uniforms, the Ancients and the Five Hundred mingled on the terrace, exchanging views, and the display of military around them would suffice to persuade the most trusting that a forcible *coup* was in preparation. Excitement rose, and the awkward delay gave a bad start to the afternoon. When benches and platforms were at last ready and the debate opened, the Jacobins took the offensive In both Assemblies the supporters of Sieyès were bewildered and began to waver. The moderates were intimidated by the wild men, and were not far from dropping a plan which, on the scene of action, began to appear in its true colours as a loosely stitched affair, full of gaps, with too much left to chance. Sieyès and Bonaparte perceived that a revolution, even a parliamentary one, is not so easily carried through with well-bred conservatives, pacific intellectuals and sound cabinet men; in Vandal's phrase, 'the Institute was beginning to bungle its *coup d'état*'.

Then Bonaparte decided to step in and hasten on the lagging climax. Already it was being rumoured in Paris that the affair was taking a wrong turn. One more hesitation and all would be lost. It was the moment to stake all for all.

The Councils had just been told of the resignation of the five Directors. This part at least of the plot had been well handled. Kept under Moreau's eye, Gohier and Moulin were in no position to offer any denial. The executive did not exist. Now was the time to bring the necessary pressure to bear on both Assemblies and to secure the voting of a new Constitution; and Bonaparte still fancied that to decide the Parliamentarians it would be enough to show himself to them.

He appeared first before the Ancients, whose majority was

still well-disposed. He was admitted and listened to. But, even more nervous than on the previous day, he spoke in a voice that did not carry well, and his words were clipped and almost incoherent. Bonaparte was a writer, not an orator. Eloquence, especially of the parliamentary order, was not one of the strings on his lyre. Irritated by his own impotence, he became excited and threatening, and left behind him a stormy hall and his friends in consternation. Thence he passed on to the Five Hundred. They had already heard of his abrupt offensiveness to the other legislators, and his appearance raised a clamour. A general violating the zone of Law! The deputies rose in tumult, and jostled round him, catching him by the collar with shouts of 'Down with the dictator!' — 'Down with the tyrant!' — and with the much more alarming cry 'Outlaw him!' His escort had to hurry in from the doorway, plunge into the confusion, and tear him away from the furious men who were throttling him. They brought him out pale and trembling, almost swooning, in one of those nervous collapses to which he was always to be subject, together with that loathing of crowds and tumult, that dread of civil war which he would know again in 1814 and 1815, and which were to lead him to an unresisting acceptance of abdication.

It was a disaster. Nothing now remained but the last resort of force. Revived from his faint, but still agitated, in contrast to the perfect coolness of Sieyès, Bonaparte came out to harangue the troops, and rode down between the ranks sitting limply in the saddle, calling out that they had tried to assassinate him. His face, it is said, was bleeding from scratches which he had inflicted on himself in his nervous agitation. But these cursed grenadiers remained unresponsive to this piece of stagecraft, wondering whether they should obey the supreme commander, or the Councils whose guard they were and on whom they depended. In short, they did not know whether they ought to arrest this factious general or follow him and expel the Five Hundred.

Lucien saved the whole situation. At least, he contrived the climax that saved it. Not succeeding in making himself heard over the tumult in the Assembly, he left the chair for the speakers' stand to defend his brother. A few minutes would be gained. He was struggling to delay the vote which would· outlaw his brother, when amid din and fisticuffs, he found with splendid coolness a means of warning the conspirators outside. At any price, by any device, the session must be closed within the next ten minutes. Bonaparte, calm again, understood. Ten men and a captain entered the hall, brought down Lucien from the stand, and led him out to the courtyard in front of the troops. The tables were now turned. Here was the president of the Five Hundred, himself accusing the deputies of disturbing the deliberations and terrorizing the Council. They were no longer the representatives of the people, but 'representatives of the dagger', brigands in revolt against the Law.

The Law — that magic word with which the parties had played in turn for ten years — swept all before it. The last scruples vanished. The grenadiers gave way. Murat took their head, and the hall was invaded and the deputies were thrust out pell-mell just as darkness was falling.

It was not at all the end that Bonaparte would have wished. The invocation of legality as personified by Lucien had been a fake, almost a comedy. The parliamentary *coup* had taken on every appearance of a military one. The public did not look very closely at it, and the news, immediately announced by the agency of Fouché in the theatres of Paris, was received with acclamation. The Minister of Police, however, deemed it useful to speak of 'counter-revolutionary manœuvres', and of an attempted assassination of Bonaparte, prevented by 'the genius of the Republic'. The story of the attempted assassination, vouched for by the torn sleeve of a grenadier, was much exploited for several days.

In fine, then, the operation of the 19th of Brumaire was troublesome. It was not a Rubicon crossed at one leap. The obstacles which Bonaparte encountered, the thwartings of his original scheme, his movements of anguish, showed him, as they showed Fouché, the advisability of accord with the 'genius of the Republic'. Before leaving Saint-Cloud, they assembled as many as possible of the fugitive legislators: thirty, say some; fifty or more, say others. By candlelight Lucien made this remnant of the Five Hundred vote for the setting-up of three Consuls as approved by the docile Ancients. They voted for this, and added congratulatory speeches. The men of Brumaire were just as fully convinced that they were preserving and continuing the Revolution, as the men of Thermidor had been. Nor were they wrong. They had carried out their intention well. But — always for the safeguarding of the Revolution, always for its preservation — they would go forward to government by one man alone, and forward again to the Empire.

CHAPTER X

THE FIRST OF THE THREE

IT is instructive to wonder what would have happened if the 18th of Brumaire had failed. The confusion would have been enormous, and complicated by military sedition and the rivalries of generals, on lines which are familiar to us in, say, Mexico. The army had become compromised in politics before the day of Saint-Cloud. And Bonaparte, being not only the most intelligent of soldiers but something more than a soldier, was to close the era of *coups d'état.* He was to stifle the powerful caste of pretorians. 'It is not as a general,' he said, 'that I rule, but because the nation believes that I have the civil qualities that fit one for ruling.' And his government was to be that of a soldier, but not of soldiers. Bonaparte now would be above, not amongst, them. They would all depend on him, and none could outstrip him. His first service to the State was to ban the politics of the general staff, and make the great leaders revert to discipline and toe the line.

On St. Helena Napoleon said that, far from being his own master, he had always obeyed circumstance. During the Consulate, he said, 'my real friends, warm supporters, used sometimes to ask me, with the best intentions and for their own guidance, what goal I planned to reach; and I always answered that I simply did not know. This left them impressed, perhaps discontented, but I was telling them the truth. Later, when I was Emperor, there was less familiarity, but many faces seemed still to be asking me that same question, and I could only have met it with the same reply'.

That was true, and accurate. Bonaparte never knew whither

he was moving, because he could not know; and that was why he always went further on.

And if authority became fixed in one man, that did not happen in one day. Not all Bonaparte's ambition and will, even after Brumaire, could have availed, had they not been headed with the stream. Single-handed power resulted from a necessity, from the same need that had already engendered the Directory, a simplified successor to that cumbrous Committee of Public Safety which had had as many as sixteen members. The five-headed executive power had shown its dangerous inadequacy, and now the Republic was reverting, as it were, to the triumvirate of Robespierre, Couthon and Saint-Just, with the three Consuls. Successive stages would bring them to one single person, by prolongations of the mandate — ten years, then the life Consulate, finally the hereditary monarchy — always, and without any paradox, directed to enable the men of the Revolution to save the Revolution itself, with its civil consequences and its territorial conquests above all else. Napoleon was carried to the imperial throne by the currents which had borne the Republic along ever since it had become a conquering force. He was not yet there.

In November 1799 men did not see beyond an improved Republic, 'regenerated' by constitutional changes. And although the presence of the youthful general in the government improvised at Saint-Cloud was of unmistakable importance, he was only one of three, and alongside a great Republican pontiff. The Constitution which Sieyès had been meditating for months on end, and which was to crown his career as a legislator, was the accidental cause of Bonaparte's being able to take the leading place without having further recourse to force.

The new provisional government comprised the two Directors who had prepared the *coup d'état*, together with the general who had been needed to carry it out. It was not a noisy government. It was modest, even shrinking. It affected to be a continuation of its forerunner and to regard the Councils as still in existence. It confined its activity to a revocation of the vexatious laws, the law of the hostages and the progressive taxes or forced loan, which the Councils themselves had felt to be unpopular and were inclined to abrogate. Bonaparte went in person to free the hostages at the Temple. The Ministry of the Interior was given to the learned Laplace, a sop to the intellectuals of Brumaire. And to make for equality among the three Consuls, it was agreed that each would preside in daily turns — which produced a certain coldness between Sieyès and Bonaparte. To settle matters the intervention of Talleyrand was necessary, and in this way he recovered the portfolio of Foreign Affairs. Before long, as the effaced figure of Roger Ducos counted for little or nothing, it was Bonaparte who, by common consent, took administrative charge, whilst Sieyès put the finishing touches to his Constitution.

Men have smiled at that masterpiece of the tireless constitution-maker, supposedly slashed across by a few words of Bonaparte's. But the truth was rather different. The essential idea of Sieyès was the same as that of the Year III. Brumaire, a continuation of Thermidor, sought to perpetuate the remnant of the Convention, shielded from Royalist or Jacobin enterprises. And there, at least, the system of Sieyès had something of genius in its very simplicity. The Directory had quashed elections hostile to itself. Sieyès abolished election. The people would henceforth only choose 'eligibles'. The pre-revolutionary regime had the Notables, and this one was to have its 'lists of notability'. Whereupon a Senate, its core composed of old Convention members, would choose from the 'national list' the members of the other two Assemblies. These were, the Tribunat, charged with discussion of laws prepared by the Council of State, and the Corps Législatif, charged with voting them without a word. But the sovereignty of the people, the public and parliamentary liberties, everything, in fact, which marked and made the Republic, were abolished by Sieyès. In its mechanism, its 'clockwork', the authoritarian Empire would establish itself unaided. The great promulgator of Law had opened the door to what was later styled despotism.

But all this, which Bonaparte had only to preserve and continue, still did not make him supreme in power. Sieyès had thought that he was forearmed against a dictatorship. On the apex of his 'pyramid', he placed a great Elector entrusted with the naming of two Consuls, one of peace, the other of war, one for internal, the other for external, affairs. If this great Elector caused anxiety, the Senate was enabled to 'absorb' him into its bosom, in other words, to strip him of power. When they came to discuss the Constitution, Bonaparte accepted everything, except the Elector, which was all the easier for him to do because Sieyès, to overcome his distaste, offered him the place which he had at first reserved for himself, or, it is said, for either a foreign prince or a prince of the Orleans line. It was a rash offer, which would prove his own undoing and spoil his design — a First Consul. Circumstances helped the young general. But what art he showed in grasping every circumstance, in instantly seeing the weak points, and manipulating the subtle old politicians!

Bonaparte, then, was reluctant to become the Elector, 'the fleshless shadow of a *fainéant* king', and preferred to be 'nothing at all rather than a laughing-stock'; and the supreme personage of the State as imagined by Sieyès proved alarming to the Republicans. He seemed to them the equivalent of a king: a president on the lines of the United States president, he seemed too much like that already. Bonaparte used this scare to abolish the Elector. Laying the Sieyès plan before the legislative committees drawn from the Councils, he entrusted Daunou, the chief author of the Constitution of the Year III, with the project of preparing an alternative. Daunou followed the original idea of Brumaire by suggesting the supplanting of the five Directors by three Consuls, to be appointed for ten years, with supremacy for one of the three. Thus, from the notion of the Elector, there emerged a First Consul. And this, of course, would be Bonaparte, as it was to him that the highest rank had previously been offered. So the Sieyès Constitution, having already abolished the elective system, was now further provided with a real head by the initiative of a Republican, a former member of the Convention. The choice of General Bonaparte was even approved as well by the two legislative committees drawn from the remnants of the Ancients and the Five Hundred, the representatives therefore of the tradition of the Revolutionary Assemblies.

If the authority emanating from the person of the young general — let us remember that he was just over thirty — secured its mastery over the men of Brumaire, it was thus, and not otherwise, that he attained supremacy in the State. He reached it by his sure-eyed judgment and decisive handling of circumstances. Republicans called him to that position. He came to it by ways of at least equal legality as those who had taken advantage of the *coup* of Fructidor. And fortuitously the Sieyès constitution gave him notable help in placing the governing power completely in his hands. Sieyès effaced himself at the price of a comfortable pension, whilst Roger Ducos modestly disappeared. All that Bonaparte had now to do was to make a free choice of his colleagues, the Second and Third Consuls.

Judiciously he picked men who were at once decorative and docile, a selection that was full of good sense and pointed towards a definite policy. There was first Cambacérès, the neutral Minister of Justice of Brumaire, a man of good family, an official under Louis XVI, the brother of a bishop. He had sided with the Revolution and presided over the Committee of Public Safety, a man always prudent, opportunist, and moderate — a born dignitary, of whom it was said that he was 'the man most fitted to lend gravity to baseness'. And someone was also needed who, without having a reactionary reputation, was still less clearly marked than

Cambacérès, and would provide a link with the old regime. For a 'fusion' was already in the First Consul's mind. After careful search and inquiries, he appointed Lebrun.

The Third Consul was in his sixties, and represented a current, a tradition of the monarchy. He had been secretary to the chancellor Maupeou, whose ordinances he had drawn up at the time of the 'revolution' attempted by that minister when, with Louis XVI's support, he had sought to break the Parlements as obstacles to reform. A continuation and completion of the 'revolution' of Maupeou would probably have averted another, and these matters had not been forgotten even thirty years later. By design or by chance, the choice of Lebrun was emblematic. Had not Frenchmen in 1789 really mistaken their real desires? Had it not been authority rather than liberty, with equality first, that they wanted?

In any case, that was what they accepted at the close of 1799. Shortly before the 18th of Brumaire it had been said by Portalis, a man of sense: 'But I think it can be said that the mass of men are tired of choosing and deliberating.' As indeed they were, to the point of letting everything go, and after ten years of voting on everything and electing for everything, they lost with no regrets, and, so to speak, without thinking, the right to vote, allowing that right to be replaced by another innovation of Sieyès, the ratifying plebiscite. The result of that plebiscite was assured in advance and would express public assent, but less forcibly perhaps than it expressed the absence of any protest against the Consular regime. For, amongst the crowd at any rate, there was no serious voice of protest. And what would the crowd have complained of? They were not even astonished. Was not everything going on as before, and for the better? Was not the new Constitution the work, barely touched up by Bonaparte, of the same Sieyès who had interpreted the great aspiration of the Third Estate in 1789? The fact that Frenchmen accepted the elimination of intermediary bodies, accepted the two elements of administration and administered, is explicable only by their emergence from years of misery and anarchy, or by their sense of relief at the rebirth of a power which was vigorous without being one of blood or persecution. Their conformity had something deeper in it. It was perhaps Bonaparte who had fulfilled the wishes of the States General, and realized in spirit the *cahiers* of 1789.

On the other hand, too, the intellectuals who had supported the Brumaire revolution were weary of the caprices of the mass. This *coup* had been that of the Institut, which Bonaparte still attended, even making the author of the *Mécanique Céleste* his Minister of the Interior. Cabanis, spokesman of eighteenth-century philosophy, said with pride of the new Constitution: 'The ignorant class will no longer influence either the legislation or the government; everything is done for the people, in the name of the people, and nothing is done by it or under its unreflecting dictation.' Nevertheless, the ignorant class knew pretty well what it wanted. It wanted at last 'to enjoy the Revolution', a materialist translation of the ideologues' notion of 'rectifying without abjuring the eighteenth century'.

The Constitution of the Year VIII was promulgated on December 14th, 1799, hardly more than a month after the day of Saint-Cloud. The three Consuls took up their duties on December 25th. The Convention, as perpetuated in the Assemblies of the Directory, solemnly and officially transmitted power to General Bonaparte and his two colleagues. There was a transition, not a rupture. And the proclamaton announcing that the final Consulate had succeeded the provisional Consulate was sincere when it claimed: 'Citizens! The Revolution is now based solidly on the principles of its inception!' When it added: 'It is concluded', they were merely surrendering to a general illusion, and no new one. How often had men said that it had touched its limit? Louis XVI himself had believed it when the president of the Constituent Assembly told him so.

But the end of the Revolution, as then desired, depended on peace, and peace with the natural frontiers. That desire for peace had helped to prompt Brumaire, as it was also an element in Bonaparte's popularity. But the war still went on, and that factor is to be borne in mind if the sequence of events is to be understood. Although he was the head of a civil government, the First Consul would also be a war leader.

France flattered herself in 1800 that this would not be for long. One last effort would bring repose. Instinctively men said that this last effort called for a vigorous government, and for an internal, national reconciliation no less than for the suppression of anarchy. The union of Frenchmen amongst themselves could be left to no hands better than Bonaparte's. Such a programme was in his thoughts, because it was from the first implicit in the nature of a man who, as we have seen, was foreign to factions, foreign in the strongest and even the strictest sense of the word. Doubtless a definitive peace was a will-o'-the-wisp. Disappointment would come but slowly, because the mass of men saw, in the master whom they accepted, the man who pledged the foundation of the Revolution 'solid on the principles of its inception'. Not even the final invasion of France was to make the masses forget what they had expected from their head. On the return from Elba, they renewed their credit for the man who, as Emperor, had remained the General of Vendémiaire, saviour of the Revolution. As Chaptal remarked, conscription and the requisitions ought to have made him hated by the rural population. But he 'reassured them against the restoration of tithes, feudal rights, the restitution of émigrés' property'. Such was the aspect of the First Consul. In these respects the Emperor did not belie him. Even when he ceased to be the 'man of the Republic', he would remain true to the genius of the Revolution.

His present task was to put on its feet a stricken country which, once the winter was past, would have to sustain a war again. And here we must pick up the thread, and bear in mind that at Bergen and Zurich, Brune and Masséna had merely stemmed the invasion. Hostilities would reopen with the spring. Meanwhile, the failures of the Directory, causes and justifications of Brumaire, had not been solely military and diplomatic. They had left their mark on the general political picture. And this enabled Bonaparte to show his superiority. His general conception of the government was that which the situation demanded. As proconsul in Italy, he had realized that to occupy a foreign country with a few divisions of troops it was essential to handle carefully the feelings and interests of the population. Similarly he saw that, to oblige Europe to recognize the natural frontiers — which could clearly be done only by force of arms, unity and organization were essential within France. She needed all her strength, as she needed all Frenchmen; it was urgent 'to rally, to unite the different parties which had divided the nation, in order to enable her to present a solid front against her foes'. It came about then, to the enduring glory of the Consulate, that Bonaparte, with simple and sensible ideas, aiming at a very definite goal, and with an imminent campaign in sight, did everything that would satisfy the French in their most varied aspirations. He gave them order, prosperity, laws, finances, security for the morrow — everything that they had lacked for ten years past. He put an end to rifts, religious persecutions, class conflicts. In short, from a more or less accidental idea, though one in close accord with actual circumstance, Bonaparte gradually contrived a system of government for which, as the details of his development have shown us, he was more suited and better trained than anybody.

Four and a half months of crushing toil, in every field of administration and politics, during which he ceaselessly instructed himself about all that he did not yet know, placed Bonaparte in a position to achieve his new victories. Everything turned on the forced and inevitable resumption of a war which, it was imagined, would at last be the war of liberation. For, brilliant as that dawn of the Consulate seems at a distance, the situation which had brought the fall of the Directory still survived, with all its dangers. The Austrian army under Melas, was moving in Italy, and from early in March had been operating against the French army, whose command had been given to Masséna. But the conqueror of Zurich was soon obliged to take refuge in Genoa, whilst his lieutenant Suchet was driven back to the Var and the enemy violated French territory. In other words, the invasion so barely averted when winter set in, was still threatening.

The first essential before the foreign war was resumed was to put an end to internal war. This was one of the government's first actions. The rising of the Vendée in 1793 had come as a surprise to the Convention. The Republic believed it was making the happiness of the French people, and of all peoples. That a part of France should remain blind to the boons of the Revolution was a disconcerting phenomenon. But if the Convention drove the West into rebellion, they did so unwittingly. The Directory had not that excuse. It could not be ignorant that Jacobin methods, levies of men, and religious persecution would rekindle the Vendée insurrection, as they had raised one in Belgium. Just when the war of conquest was being pushed to its farthest, the Directory had deliberately planted this dagger in its own back. The pacification of the Vendée was one of the First Consul's earliest concerns.

He gave the insurgents ten days to submit, and entered into parleys with the leaders. He showed his esteem for their character and their dashing bravery, and appealed to their national temperament, giving them to believe, if need be, that he would not be opposed to a return of the Bourbons. At the same time he recalled the Abbé Bernier, an influential figure in the West who had taken refuge in Switzerland, giving him assurances of liberty of worship and promising that the

Catholic countries would keep their 'non-juring' priests. The reopening of churches, and other signs of a revival of faith to which he closed his eyes, lent weight to his words. It was a foreshadowing of the Concordat. The suppression of the Revolutionary festivals, that of January 21st especially, was another sort of pledge. The First Consul had shot down the Royalist opposition in Vendémiaire and crippled it by Fructidor; he was now disarming it by wise acts and fair words. If he did not repeal the laws against the *émigrés*, which would have alarmed the classes who had acquired confiscated property, if he did not annul the proscriptions of Fructidor, which would have perturbed the Republicans, he granted individual pardons which made many people dependent on him. There too, he invented nothing. It had already been Fouché's method at the Ministry of Police before Brumaire.

In this way he mollified, if he did not finally quench, the great rising of the West. Some of its leaders were won over by his greeting and his language. But one intransigent, Frotté, betrayed and captured, was sent before a firing-party; implacable hatreds were to spring from that. Another, the famous Georges Cadoudal, was secretly admired by Bonaparte, who wished to see him and conquer him. After the interview Georges said he had longed to throttle the little man. He gave a dogged No to everything, and they parted for a fight to the death. One of the two was to die in it. But if the Chouan, a man of a kind no less prodigious than the other, risked his head in full awareness, he did not suspect what consequences would come from his aiming at the head of Bonaparte. The Royalists whom the First Consul failed to rally to his side regarded him, rightly as it turned out, as the last obstacle against a restoration which the death-agonies of the Directory had brought within measurable distances. They would want to kill him, and they would fail. And their plots, by a strange recoil, would help to make an emperor.

To follow chronologically the activities of the First Consul during these four months of reconstruction would require a whole book. Everything had to be refashioned. It was not a question of a few decrees, a few laws. Merely to restore some administrative and financial order, it proved necessary to start everything afresh from the bottom, because the system was inherently bad. Sometimes, before trusted men, Bonaparte allowed glimpses of his inmost thoughts. They must 'get out of this republican rut'.

Finance? To wage war, said a captain of long ago, three things are necessary: first, money; second, money; and third, money. The Directory had waged war without money, by squeezing the conquered countries. But there were few left, and Italy, which had yielded so many millions, was lost. The penury of the treasury was extreme. To get through the first days, it had been necessary to raise loans from the bankers, who would however advance money to this provisional government only on condition that the forced loan was abolished. These expedients could not go on. In short, the finances had to be reconstructed, like the rest of the State, as the Directory had reached the last stages of insolvency. Bonaparte fell back upon a man whom nowadays we should style an expert. This was Gaudin, an official of the old regime who had been in the administrative service ever since the last year of the reign of Louis XV.

We who have seen for ourselves how panic is converted into confidence, are less astonished at the financial recovery that was brought to pass under the First Consul. His part was to reassure the owning classes, and to 'stop the rot'. He also listened to the experts who advised the creation of the Bank of France and a return to the indirect taxation abolished by the Revolution. The end of the *gabelle* and the *aides* had been greeted with enthusiasm. And here were the '*droits réunis*', the same taxes consolidated under other names. But the main thing was to provide the Treasury with resources to continue the great external enterprises. And a restoration of order in the finances, a healthy currency, and the prompt payment of government dividends, were all benefits of the Consulate.

Ten years of Revolution, years when the whole administration had been on an elective basis, had left a moral confusion and a dilapidated structure. Everything, everywhere, had to be refashioned, from roads to law-courts. It was extraordinary that a country so ravaged could so long have carried on a war on several fronts, not to mention a civil war. The richness and vitality of France had made this possible, but it could not last. It was the last gasp, as Bonaparte very well saw.

From his starting-point — to fit France for a victorious struggle for the natural frontiers and for peace — flowed a whole system of government. His eclecticism was shown by a choice of men as well as of means. He adopted another idea of Sieyès when he placed the Departments under direct delegates of power, styled Prefects — the fashion was for Roman titles, like his own. But the creation of these functionaries was inspired by the 'intendants' of monarchical days; a few realized that this was in fact obliterating the Republican regime. These Prefects, as also the new magistrates and members of the State Council, were chosen by Bonaparte from all the weakening and dissolving parties. His administrative structure was 'salted' with Jacobins and Royalists and Girondins. 'I like honest men of any colour', he said; and he mixed the colours designedly. He had no prejudices. He was alone in not being able to have prejudices, and that was already a sovereign's position, not only an arbiter's.

The assemblage of institutions styled 'of the Year VIII', the essential arrangement of which still endures, dates from this. Bonaparte had not given them long study; he did not carry plans with him for years like Sieyès. But quite naturally he had met the desires of the mass of men, and found the thread of conciliation without any attempt to construct for time everlasting. It was perhaps hardly any exaggeration to say that he did not see much beyond the next spring campaign.

His work was not inspired by this or that principle of social reform. It was a work to meet the needs of the moment. It put an end to a glaring material anarchy, from which Frenchmen had suffered more than enough. It preserved the general ideas and results of the Revolution, inscribed in the Civil Code. The 'genius' of the Revolution was still respected, coloured mainly by the passion for equality by which the body of the laws was permeated. A very simple, even summary, system — order in the street, rights of inheritance and of property, office open to all, freedom to go to Mass for those who wished it, no government by nobles or by priests. Thus, far better than the revolutionary convulsions and the theatrical dramas of the Convention, better than the muddle of the Directory, the Napoleonic formula satisfied the aspirations of '89, apart from the fact that since '89 there had taken place the sales of public property. The purchasers of that were anxious to consolidate their property, as also to be protected against counter-claims, just as amongst the high political staff the regicides dreaded the reprisals of a counter-revolutionary government. To all, the Consulate brought guarantees.

Such were the strongest props of Bonaparte's power. Another of his controlling ideas was that of reconciliation, or rather, as he called it, 'fusion' — the collaboration of Frenchmen. From the camp of counter-revolution this brought over to him those who had suffered from persecution and exile. Here Josephine was useful to him by her early aristocratic connections. And his uncle Fesch as well. Everything has its use. To be the nephew of an ecclesiastic, before long of a bishop, was no bad thing for the First Consul. Moreover, he flattered the national taste for glory, as he flattered the hope for peace, that ever-promised but ever-deferred hope. He even lent prestige to authority, yet another necessity which he had divined. Perhaps his most remarkable action at this time, within the first weeks of the Consulate, on February 19th, 1800, was to leave the Luxembourg and instal himself, with his two colleagues, in the Palace of the Tuileries — although there was a nuance distinguishing the Tuileries from Versailles, in which he could never bring himself to reside. By moving into the palace of the Kings, was not Bonaparte making it plain to the Bourbons that, whatever might befall, their return was impossible, and that he was not disposed, as so many royalists liked to believe he was, to play the role of General Monk?

He was not Monk, the restorer of the Stuarts, but Washington. The founder of the American Republic had lately died. The Consular government had organized a commemorative service in his honour, and delivered a eulogy as that of an exemplar. The name of Washington hovered over Bonaparte, when, acclaimed by some, quizzed by others, he left to take over the Tuileries, with a procession to which the persisting penury of the Treasury allowed but little pomp.

The remarks he made when alone with his intimates are amongst the most famous, and the most revelatory, of those which are quoted of him. Nothing escaped this singularly mature young man, who occasionally, when he had time to spare, could stand aside and survey his own life, his destiny, his self. Roederer, struck by the forlorn air of these rooms so redolent of the past, said to him: 'This is very gloomy, General!' And he replied: 'Yes — and so is glory.' The parvenu was outdone by the man of letters, the poet with perception.

His deepest thought, his political ideas, were always expressed before his secretary: 'Bourrienne, it isn't everything to be in the Tuileries. The thing is to stay there.' To stay there, to carry on this prodigious adventure, the incredible career of a Corsican cadet who at thirty was head of the French State — this was already Bonaparte's preoccupation. It would not leave him, even at the peak of his power. He would retain that acute awareness of how brittle and precarious his power was. He had too much penetration not to realize that, even now, anything which had come about from a series of fortunate events could easily be undone by some abrupt accident, a well-staged conspiracy, or a military reverse such as even a genius cannot avoid. These dangers were close about him. The sight of them did not perturb him; but they were clear enough never to let him be dazzled by his soaring fortune, his dizzy rise.

CHAPTER XI

THE POINTED PISTOL

THREE days before his death, Napoleon in delirium lived once more through the day of Marengo, if a traditional story is to be believed. They heard him utter the name of Desaix; and then he cried: 'Ah! Victory is ours!' A decisive victory in his career. What was Marengo? A Waterloo with a happy ending, with Desaix as a Grouchy who arrived in time. On June 14th, 1800, Napoleon staked his fortune, and won. On June 18th, 1815, he staked again, and lost. Had the Austrians been the victors at Marengo, as they thought they were until Desaix turned the tables, the Consulate would very probably have been a brief episode, lasting only ten weeks longer than the Hundred Days.

Before that battle Bonaparte had told his soldiers: 'The result of your efforts will be — unclouded glory, and a solid peace.' Before concentrating the reserves, he had asked for recruits for 'concluding the war of the Revolution'. It was the wish, and the illusion, of Frenchmen, and was shared by their leader. Bonaparte was a prisoner of that programme of peace with the natural frontiers. At the end of December 1799 he had written to the King of England and the Emperor offering peace, a peace as conceived by the French nation. The response was negative. Neither Britain nor Vienna was disposed to yield. It was manifest proof that conquests made by the sword would have to be kept by the sword. And, as Cambacérès fairly and illuminatingly remarked, it was 'for Belgium' that they would again be fighting at Marengo.

The preservation of conquests — that was what was expected of Bonaparte. It would always be expected of him. France would allow him to 'carry forward' his account right up to 1814 — and even renewed that credit in 1815. He must not be beaten. Otherwise he would be put 'into liquidation'. As soon as there were doubts of his success and defeat seemed a possibility, the liquidators grew restive and showed themselves. Even as early as the spring of 1800 they were not unknown.

His services in the restoration of order were not yet sufficiently tested by time, nor were they yet so closely associated with his personal action, to serve him as a shield and protection. The suddenness of his rise had quickened jealousies, in military even more than in civil circles, but it was too recent, and too many men had become popular for a day, for his pre-eminence to appear final and permanent. Yet Bonaparte did not raise his voice louder than circumstances allowed. It was not only that he handled everybody with care; it was not only that the 18th of Brumaire, which was contrived at once for and against the Revolution, left everybody with his own hopes; but nobody in either camp supposed that this young general, for all his talents, authority and prestige, must surely bury invincible Liberty or prevent the inevitable return of the Bourbons, any more than it was admitted abroad that, despite his Italian victories or his Egyptian fantasia, he was capable of defeating the armies and fleets and generals of the whole of Europe. How could France possibly win in such a contest! And this incredulity found expression at Berlin, where the First Consul, continuing the diplomacy of the Revolution, tried to make an alliance which was to have been completed by one with Russia, but from which Prussia stood aside.

Similarly, in France, after the first shock of Brumaire and the glowing dawn of the Consulate, men began to collect their wits, and it seemed that there had not been such great changes after all. The parties stood where they were. Neither Royalists nor Jacobins disarmed. They were in agreement to wait. In the spring Austria was resuming hostilities; everybody knew, and Bonaparte better than anyone, that a reverse would put an end to the new regime. He himself might die in battle like Joubert, or succumb to illness and fatigue like

Hoche; and it was observed that he had never looked so shrunken or so yellow, for he was cruelly overworked. Therefore, why upset him? He would perhaps vanish unaided. And so the first six months of the Consulate were fairly quiet. The attempted blows against him would not begin until after Marengo.

Nevertheless, even among his partisans and his close adherents, minds were occupied by the problem of his end or his fall. There were those, like Fouché and Talleyrand, who had enlisted with him at Saint-Cloud in order to save what could be saved of the Revolution, and their own persons in particular. There were others, like Carnot, who yielded to the event, and who, without abjuring the Republic, wanted to see it shielded from anarchy as well as from royalism, by Bonaparte if need be, but who remained opposed to a dictatorship. There were also his brothers, Joseph and Lucien, anxious for their own fate and quickened by ambition, imbued with the dynastic spirit before there was a dynasty. 'Bonaparte's fortune would have been far happier if he had had no family', Stendhal has said. The family, so long a burden on Bonaparte's back, was now becoming a heavy care, a nest of intrigue added to the intrigues outside.

In so far as he was partly the master of France, it was by virtue of his own prestige rather than of the Constitution. By its terms he was not entitled, he seemed even to be refused the right, to command the armies. Respecting this 'constitutional truth', he had to be content to 'accompany' the army of Italy, of which Berthier was the nominal head. And whilst Berthier completed the preparations for the campaign at Dijon, Bonaparte remained in Paris, prolonging a sojourn demanded by 'the still precarious situation at home'. Meanwhile, a Minister of War was required. Who was chosen? Carnot, to satisfy the Republicans. They had still to be given their sops. And likewise, the still more formidable military leaders. With Moreau, strong in the devotion of his Rhine army, the First Consul used diplomacy. He left him with the main theatre of operations. To defeat Austria, she must be struck within her own frontiers, and when Napoleon was his own master it was not through Italy that he opened the way to Vienna. But in 1800 he was obliged to respect Moreau's rights. And when Moreau, in the manner of the Directory generals (Bonaparte's own manner three years earlier), answered distasteful orders with a threat of resignation, the First Consul hastened to placate him, and it was by flattery rather than commands that he managed to bring their plans of campaign more or less into line.

Bonaparte, then, stood in need of some victorious and dazzling stroke which would impress men's imaginations. He said as much to Volney: 'I act only on the imagination of the nation; when that tool fails me, I shall be nothing.' For the First Consul the outcome of this campaign would have to be all or nothing. But, as at Waterloo, his intense consciousness of something enormous being at stake, for his country as well as for himself, may perhaps have robbed him of part of his faculties, and intimidated his genius on the critical day. Splendid narrations, repeatedly touched up, have portrayed that campaign, the crossing of the Saint Bernard, the breakthrough into Italy. Its general conception was large and splendid. In detail it was twice on the brink of failure. At the outset, the fort of Bard suddenly appeared as an unforeseen obstacle, and for a moment seemed unsurmountable. Appropriate anecdotes effaced these faulty reckonings, and painting immortalized the gaunt and thoughtful Cæsar crossing the Alps like Hannibal. Coming down to the plains, the liberation of Milan revived the miracles of 1796; flowers, songs, the resurrection of the Cisalpine Republic revived the heroic days. The Austrians were outflanked. But when they confronted him, Bonaparte missed his major principle. He all but lost the battle, possibly because he was thinking too much of what would happen in Paris if he lost it.

At three o'clock, Bonaparte was beaten and Melas was already sending word of his victory to Vienna. At five o'clock everything was changed by the arrival of Desaix, who was shot dead almost at once. He could not dispute the honours of the day with the First Consul, who was not grudging with his funeral tributes to this dead hero. Bonaparte's star was lavish with boons! On that same day, Kléber was assassinated in Cairo, whence he would have returned raising an accusing finger. Suppose that Marengo had been a defeat, whilst the Egyptian expedition was ending in capitulation, what would have remained of the 18th of Brumaire? Nobody would have been willing to believe in the great captain. A German historian has sternly remarked that he would have been 'the laughing-stock of Europe'.

Paris meanwhile was alarmed. News came of a lost battle, and a general killed. There were endless confabulations amongst the two Consuls in Paris, the ministers and politicians and the men of Brumaire. It seemed so natural that this new regime should perforce be as transient as its forerunners. But by whom was it to be replaced? Some, to retain the lustre of a name, thought of Joseph Bonaparte, or rather, Joseph suggested himself. As the eldest, the head of the family, he thought it quite natural that the place should revert to him, and therein lay the source of his coming difficulties with his brother. Others thought of Carnot, or La Fayette, in order to use the Bonapartist formula, with an added touch of Washington, for leverage towards the Left. Fouché and Talleyrand schemed for a triumvirate in which they would associate an 'accommodating colleague', the senator Clément de Ris, the same who, ere long, was to be removed and shut up in the mysterious circumstances, never unravelled, from which Balzac fashioned *Une Ténébreuse Affaire*. In fine, men spoke and acted as if the succession to the First Consul lay open. The certainty of his being alive and that defeat had been changed to victory cut short all these arrangements. But Bonaparte was aware of them, made anxious haste to sign an armistice honourable to Melas, and returned to Paris. On July 2nd he was back.

Back, with a heart grown old, he said – as if he did not know enough about men already. And with a bitter heart, with a distrust that was never to leave him. He had seen the gulf open beneath his feet. He knew that he could never count on anybody, not even on his brothers, and on his brother soldiers still less. The generals? Not one of them, he told Chaptal, 'did not think that he had as full rights as I had'. Several of them, in the Rueil conspiracy, planned to propose to him a sort of cutting-up of France, each of the great military leaders being given appanages like his own. 'I am forced to be very stern with these men.' And with a clear vision of his own end, he added: 'If I met with a great check, they would be the first to quit me.'

But he returned a conqueror, resolved on extracting the full rewards of victory. First and foremost he must be the sole master of the army. His main fear was not from the civilians but from the soldiers. In that sense he was an anti-militarist. The army was not the ruling force; he was ruler, and they must obey him. In the Napoleonic system, in the establishment of his authority, this was the least visible and the least comprehended aspect. Into his policy it gives perhaps the most penetrating view. It accounts for the suspicion in which he held so many of his generals, his frequent brutality towards them, and the blows, as abrupt and overwhelming as the favours, which he dealt out to them. It was important on the other hand to give both officers and men the conviction, stimulating at once to zeal and obedience, that their fortune depended on him alone. For this reason, immediately after Marengo, he made himself the dispenser of rewards, pending the conferring of dignities and ranks. Planning the Legion of Honour, he began by distributing swords of honour, the warrants of which he signed without the collaboration of his two colleagues, and having the blades inscribed: 'Battle commanded by the First Consul in person.' Then, to preside over the Council of State, he donned the uniform which formerly he had affected not to wear when it was essential that no cry of dictatorship by the sword should be raised. But that uniform was always to be sober and severe, with a touch of disdain and menace for the men with gold and plumes. He insisted at the Council of State that it was not as a general that he ruled. But his first task, and not the easiest of his reign, was to rule, sometimes to checkmate, the generals. He would make himself the idol of the soldier, the god of the regimental officer, so as to be more sure of the high officers, formerly his superiors or his equals, emerging like himself from the Revolution. Without this precaution, his reign would not have come, or else it would have been more brief.

For every campaign, every war, brought new plots of Marengo or Rueil into being. Every great battle would expose Bonaparte, as he knew, to the double danger of Marengo. What, then, was the main interest of the First Consul on his triumphal return from Italy? Peace, without a doubt. This time his prestige, enhanced by the unhoped-for victory, really placed power in his hands. To feel himself more sure therein, he must be protected from those hazards of the battle-field which, as he knew better than anyone, are ever entailed by the shifting fortune of arms.

A pacific Napoleon — the joined words clash strangely. Nevertheless, peace, renewed from Campo Formio, was the great result which he sought. To the Consulate it would give that splendour, gleaming across the century, which would make it a brief Golden Age, one of those moments in French History — Henry IV after the fury of the League, Louis XIV after the confusions of the Fronde — when the people have loved the government that allowed them to breathe. Peace, a glorious peace, with Austria, then with England, and internal peace, achieved by the Concordat, were to be the fruits of Marengo. And because the masses felt this in the air, Bonaparte's popularity waxed greater, taking on a quality unknown before. For ten years, since the famous festival of the Federation, no rejoicings had been so whole-hearted and national as those which met the return of

the First Consul. Vanquished, he would have been buried·
Victor, he was worshipped. Hyde de Neuville was to express
what was happening, in a menacing form: 'Power became
incorporated in himself.' Whence the temptation to strike
at his person. The Revolution could now be killed in a single
man, and, for the Republicans, dictatorship likewise. The
task was simplified. Murder was being hatched in the shadows, and, with it, its uncalculated outcome — the hereditary
Empire. Every fresh success of Bonaparte now would exasperate his adversaries, and furnish them with fresh reasons
and means for attacking his person, until their very fury,
which he escaped, brought the throne nearer and nearer to him.

From Italy he had returned with a hardly veiled anger with
the Republicans who had thought to supplant him. This
rancour led him into mistaking the feelings of the royalists.
Resuming his system of 'fusion', he weighed down the scales
on the side of the Right, and the Jacobins seemed to him his
only foes. In his advances towards the Pope, he had gone
even further in Italy than he had in 1797. After Marengo he
attended a Te Deum in the cathedral of Milan, where, perhaps, the crown of Charlemagne appeared to him, if we do
not force the meaning of a part of the victory despatch. The
man who loved the sound of the bells, like the clock-towers of
his childhood, had no distaste for the rites of the Church,
and he was eager to make a speedy end of the religious
quarrels in France, to complete the internal peace by legal-
izing public worship in the churches, which already had been
spontaneously reopening their doors, to rob, in his own
favour, the Bourbon cause of its strength of Catholic sentiment,
whilst still ensuring control of the French clergy. Nothing
remained but to force the acceptance of the idea of the Concordat by those ideologues, heirs of the eighteenth century
philosophers, and by the atheistic soldiers, with their profound scorn of the priesthood, who made a point of keeping
their helmets on their heads when they entered a sanctuary.

The war with Austria, however, was not over. The peace

negotiations had broken down. The Austrian delegate was disowned by the court of Vienna, and hostilities must be resumed. This time Bonaparte did not leave Paris. The Italian operations were entrusted to Brune. In Germany the command still belonged to Moreau. And here the thread of events joins up with the happenings yet to come, and the simple chronology is explanatory.

On September 1st, 1800, the Austrian armistice was broken off. On the 7th Bonaparte's reply to Louis XVIII destroyed the illusion of the Royalists who saw in him a new Monk. On October 10th came the Jacobin attempt on the First Consul's life at the Opéra. On November 5th Lucien was disgraced. On December 3rd Moreau won the brilliant victory of Hohenlinden. On December 24th (3rd of Nivôse) came the attempted assassination in the Rue Saint-Nicaise. These dates are all linked, heralding and determining the future.

The taste for authority was developing in Bonaparte. Upheld by popular favour, resolved to remain master, he had lately said nothing when a tribune had styled him 'the fortnight's idol'. But now the opposition of the Tribunat, which was making serious use of the right to criticism and free speech, seemed insulting, and contrary to that discipline without which the country would never recover its strength. He laid prudence aside. Words escaped him, perhaps of set purpose, directed against the anarchists and terrorists. As for the Royalists, he intended to use them, but had less intention than ever of working for them. Baudot, a proud Republican, one of those rare beings who were to accept nothing from the Empire, accused him of having given special welcome to the absolutists and 'ultras' amongst the *émigrés*, those most ready to accept a despotic power, whilst he set aside the constitutional and liberal monarchists. The rumour ran that the First Consul proposed to restore a royal regime, in exchange for a consolidation of his own position, either by his appointment as a supreme officer of the crown, or by a sovereignty in Italy. He let them think and say what they pleased. Twice he left unanswered the direct messages from Louis XVIII asking for the restoration of his throne. Three months after the second, as if he had awaited the consecration of Marengo to address the heir of the ancient kingship of France, the reply came. It rang out proudly: 'You ought not to desire your return to France: you would have to march over a hundred thousand corpses.' But a door was left open: 'I am not insensible to the sufferings of your family. I shall contribute gladly to the pleasure and tranquillity of your retirement.' Louis XVIII had sounded Bonaparte's intentions, and he in his turn had sounded those of the claimant, with the idea perhaps that the head of the House of France would renounce his rights and leave no further obstacle to a 'change of dynasty'. But Bonaparte was wrong about Louis XVIII, at least as much as Louis XVIII had been mistaken about Bonaparte.

Only, from that day on, the Royalists became mortal enemies of the First Consul. Vows were taken against him by men of extraordinary boldness and perseverance, moulded in the merciless struggles of the Chouans. He did not suspect it. He fancied his danger came from the Jacobins. Were they not seeking a fifth attempt on his life? The plots of Arena, Ceracchi and Topino-Lebrun strengthened his conviction that he must root out the breed.

But every attempt revived the underlying thought of the Marengo conspiracies. Dagger or pistol might find its mark, but who would succeed General Bonaparte? There, by chance or design, the Constitution was dumb. And that silence, that 'void in the social pact', stimulated the murderers, as the death of this man would throw everything into the melting-pot. The idea then began to take shape that the eventual successor ought to be named in advance, named by Bonaparte himself, in order to discourage the murderers. And this idea, rising and widening, leading quickly to the hereditary system, was far from attractive to Bonaparte. He was scarcely tempted by the crown of Charlemagne or the foundation of a fourth dynasty, if he had thought of either. It may be said that at this moment, and for some months yet, he was strongly opposed to the establishment of any royalist form in his favour, because he was reluctant, above all else, to have talk of his succession. Bequeath his power? To whom? Heredity did not matter to him. He had no child, and Josephine had small chance of giving him one, notwithstanding the counsels of Dr. Corvisart and the waters of Plombières. Would he have a substitute and rival trailing his shadow, when he had already had to efface Sieyès? The mere announcement of a name would revive those rivalries he dreaded, and put a weapon in the hands of his foes, who were capable still of stirring great forces by shouting about ambition and monarchy. His brothers would have liked to force his hand, themselves pushed on by the men of Brumaire, anxious about the future. At this moment Lucien indulged in one of the scandals he was accustomed to make use of. As Minister of the Interior, since Laplace had been sent back to his celestial mechanics, Lucien, without the knowledge of the First Consul, distributed officially through the Prefects a pamphlet, *Cæsar, Cromwell and Bonaparte,* which asked with brutal directness the question, 'Where are his heirs?' It was a personal challenge to the First Consul. His brothers were thinking not of him, but of themselves. They coveted his heritage, and their greed and impatience put Bonaparte on his guard, and also threatened to spoil everything by spreading alarm amongst the Republicans. Sharp action was necessary. Lucien was publicly disavowed and disgraced, and sent from his Ministry to the Embassy in Madrid. For a time Bonaparte was freed from this bogy of the succession. But he had not finished with his brothers, that restless, exigent family for whom he never did enough, amongst whom he never found anyone quite to be trusted, one jealous and headstrong, another lazy, a third sick, neurotic and anxious. Yet it was to this third, Louis, his little *protégé,* that Napoleon's thoughts would perhaps most readily turn, if he found himself at last unable to resist the pressure of those who were tortured by uncertainty for the morrow. This secret Josephine divined; imperceptibly she encouraged the project, in order to get her enemies Lucien and Joseph out of the way, and to avert the threat of a divorce should Napoleon become anxious for an heir of his own body. Josephine fancied she had triumphed with the marriage of her young brother-in-law to her daughter Hortense, a marriage which, as she thought, would avert her own repudiation. Cæsar did not yet wear the crown, but domestic intrigues and palace rivalries were pressing all around him.

Meanwhile the war continued, and the enigmatic Moreau gathered laurels in Germany as fair as those of Bonaparte himself. Was not the victor of Hohenlinden entitled to claim equality and say, 'Why not I?' 'Why not he?' echoed all the elements that hated the First Consul. Moreau was surrounded, enticed, flattered through his jealousy and his pride. Nevertheless it was Bonaparte who plucked the fruits of Moreau's victory. Austria decided to negotiate. Cobenzl arrived in Paris at the same time as the Papal Envoy, Monseigneur Spina. The hour of peace was approaching, the general peace, the great peace at home and abroad, the great dream, the triumph of the Consulate. Resistance to that triumph, which would be crowned by the coming Concordat, must be speedy. Bonaparte must be got rid of, quickly, at any price. Three weeks after Hohenlinden, he escaped only by chance the explosion of an infernal machine laid one evening where he was to pass.

The attempt of the 3rd of Nivôse was within a few seconds of success. If it had succeeded, it would have altered the course of history. Even its failure had an influence on events. The plots directed against the First Consul became an element in his policy. Either they would strike him down at some street corner, or they would raise him to Empire.

The universal congratulations on his escape in the Rue Saint-Nicaise, their form, the addresses of the assemblies, the joy of the crowds, all showed him that his person was precious, all authorized him to take measures, which, in other days, would have been viewed as murderous to liberty. Sincere or not, his first thought was that the criminals could only be terrorists. A royalist attempt would upset his policy of fusion. He refused to believe in that; a Jacobin attempt suited him, as conforming to his system of the moment. It was a good pretext for annihilating the last remains of the violent factions, but a 'purging' like that of Robespierre when he sent the '*exagérés*' to the guillotine, that of the Convention when they condemned the accomplices of the 1st of Prairial, that of the Directory when they shot Babeuf. At bottom, it was the progressive obliteration of the active Republicans which had made possible the return to order; and there too Bonaparte was carrying on rather than innovating. When their small number had disappeared, no counter-attack from the extreme Jacobins need be feared. There would be royalist plots, military plots, domestic palace plots. There would be no further Republican conspiracies. For 'days' and insurrections a new generation would be required, which did not arise until 1830.

One hundred and thirty suspects, hardly any of whom reappeared, were the ransom of the infernal machine. When Fouché held the real culprits, Saint-Rejan and Carbon, when it was known that the attempt of Nivôse was the work of 'Chouans', it was too late. There was no pardon for the proscribed Jacobins because their proscription had been really desired. By a subtle precaution they had not been condemned for participation in the affair of the Rue Saint-Nicaise, but dealt with under a measure of public safety. The First Consul turned everything to his advantage: public anger, the annihilation of the intransigent Revolutionaries, and the indication that he had implacable enemies among the royalists. Nor was that all. The very difficulty of making a law to meet special circumstances placed in his hands a ruler's instrument of incomparable convenience.

LEAP FROG

An English Cartoon of 1803

OUTCOME OF A PLOT

If the deportation of the 'remains of Robespierre', as they were called, might meet with opposition, it was in the two assemblies responsible for the manufacture of laws. The Tribunat was hostile, the Corps Législatif unfriendly. Talleyrand suggested the idea of appealing to the Senate, a small, docile, tractable, conservative body, whose deliberations had the advantage of not being public. The method of appeal to the Senate, then invented, became a method of government with unmatched suppleness. It would serve for everything, like a magic formula. On the grounds that it would 'preserve' the Constitution, the Senate was asked to modify it. The system of Sieyès was so perfect that it could even obliterate itself. It contained everything needful to pass by 'imperceptible gradations' from the Republic to absolute monarchy. It would remain so until the day when, untying itself and dissolving itself, this same Senate, having become indispensable by services rendered without reckoning the cost, found itself alone upright amid the general ruin. On that day a supreme *senatus consultum* would pronounce the forfeiture of the master raised up by its own complaisance.

A few days after these stern measures against the terrorists, the Minister of Police furnished proofs that the real authors of the attempt on the 3rd of Nivôse were Chouans. No doubt Fouché knew it from the start. But the blow had been struck against the conspirators of the Left, while the First Consul appeared beset by invisible and ever-returning enemies, his person threatened every moment, and his government consequently 'at the mercy of a pistol-shot', just at the moment when this regime of reconstruction seemed to be giving France even more than it had promised. Bonaparte became the more valuable in proportion as his existence became more fragile. In this way, having won prestige by his victories and power by fortunate circumstances, the anxiety felt for his life matured an authority in his hands which could not be shared. Henceforward the secret spring of his incredible rise to the throne lay in that phrase, that fear, which spread

155

throughout France, and was made all too actual by the infernal machine of the Rue Saint-Nicaise — 'they'll end by assassinating him'. Returned *émigrés*, with everything to fear from a reversion to Jacobinism after the disappearance of their protector; compromised revolutionaries apprehensive of the Bourbons' return; the intermediate mass who desired neither revolution nor reaction — 'on all sides men were alarmed at the idea of seeing the First Consul perish'. Like a favouring wind, this alarm bore him towards supremacy, and everything attempted against him helped him on. Through his enemies he prospered.

CHAPTER XII

THE ILLUSION OF AMIENS

THE years 1801 and 1802, and the beginning of 1803, were the months of fortune for Bonaparte. The First Consul was not exempt from grave cares. But France had 'yielded to the most dazzling dreams', thinking she had reached port, dropped her anchor, and found peace.

Punctually the First Consul brought what he had promised to this country which, though weary of war, would be content only with honourable peace. And in applauding him, France applauded herself for having chosen so well and having trusted the man who fulfilled her desires. Peace at home and abroad, greatness, prosperity, and repose. There was the reward of long efforts, the end of a nightmare. The sense of happiness was almost inexpressible for a people who had lived in convulsion for ten years. They did not know what a halt was. But they relished the prize to such a point that, to recover the delights of the Consulate, that fleeting paradise, the dream they had touched with their fingers, they would be ready to wage war again for another ten years.

The treaty of Lunéville was the treaty of Campo Formio renewed, confirmed, and consolidated. The conquests of the Revolution were recognized by Austria, beaten at Marengo and Hohenlinden. She made a separate peace, not waiting for England. The second coalition was broken. And Austria was the German Empire, her head the Germanic Cæsar. A great tide of history and secular memories surged up to the heads of Frenchmen. Austria, the old enemy, was with one stroke abandoning Belgium, Luxemburg, the left bank of the Rhine, to the Republic. The treaty was dated February 9th, 1801. On March 16th, there were Prefects in the Departments of the Roer, the Sarre, Rhin-et-Moselle, and Mont-Tonnerre.

And there was more. Natural frontiers needed a protecting glacis. Austria recognized the French protectorate over the Batavian, Helvetic, Cisalpine and Ligurian Republics; she bowed to the occupation of Piedmont; and she accepted French arbitrament for a reshaping of the Germanic states which was to mean the end of the Holy Roman Empire. It was vast — intoxicating — too beautiful.

Too beautiful, because Austria could not sign such a peace in full sincerity, leaving part of Germany and part of Italy under French domination or influence. She was not so utterly vanquished that she could not have come to terms with Bonaparte and retained Venice and the line of the Adige. Fundamentally, the treaty of Lunéville was merely one more arrangement. As such, it would have real validity only if England agreed to it. But then that would be the real peace, in a Europe permanently content with its lot, with the old conflicts uprooted, as its frontiers would be in conformity with the desires of France, desires which Frenchmen confused with reason. 'To end the war,' Albert Sorel said, 'was in Bonaparte's eyes an operation allied in kind to concluding the Revolution.' And indeed it seemed the same, and was thus understood by everybody, from the First Consul to the humblest owner of national property, from the rulers of the Bank of France, the custodians of the restored currency, to the village priest who had seen the advent of the Concordat. To organize Europe, to give Europe statute and law, was merely the equivalent of the Civil Code.

So Bonaparte stood as the great pacifier. Nothing was lacking for the further soaring of his popularity but peace with England, and that was drawing near.

It has been said that Napoleon never believed in it, and recognized that it would be no more than a truce. But there are plenty of signs to the contrary. It is proof enough that for this peace he made the most careful preparations, and sought the means of giving it solid strength. To make it solid, it was essential that it should not come merely from reciprocal weariness. His intention was to treat with England on a footing of equality, after convincing her that it was in her interest to negotiate: for were not the French people masters of the continent, of the great rivers and their estuaries, and so the counterpart of the mistress of the seas? Austria's separate peace had been a hard blow to Pitt's policy. With Austria out of the contest, it was French policy to have as many allies and supports in Europe as possible. Over England was always suspended the threat — and she did not take it lightly — of an army landing on her shores. Efforts were made to alarm her commercial interests by the closing of all the European ports. And Spain was approached, as she had been by the Convention, to induce her to detach Portugal from the English. Nor must the Bay of Naples serve as an anchorage for Nelson; and King Ferdinand of Naples yielded. The Prussian alliance was sought, as it had been since 1795, but with a new hope, almost a certainty, of obtaining it. For, this time, the pursuit of peace opened up a chance which the Revolution had not given, that of an alliance with the Russia of Paul I. If the King of Prussia did not ally himself with a good grace, the Tsar would ally him by force.

In Bonaparte's calculations with regard to England, Russia was an important factor. But what was more frail and deceptive than the Russian alliance? That he had still to learn. At this moment it depended on the life of a Tsar, just as the Consular regime did on his own life. Leaning on Russian support, Bonaparte even spoke of a gigantic project for an attack on India from the rear, which was to strike terror into the City of London. The First Consul had to renounce both his threat to India and his approaches to Prussia. At Alexandria Kléber's successor, Menou, had just capitulated; and England could now be sure that the French would not become masters of the Mediterranean. Nelson's guns at Copenhagen shattered the League of Neutrals. The Spaniards were easy-going in securing Portugal. The English cabinet, no longer animated by Pitt's ardour, was now awaiting a tolerably good position, no more, to begin negotiations. They held these events sufficiently minimized the blow of Austria's defection, and resolved to discuss terms.

Few treaties of peace have been greeted with more popular enthusiasm and confidence than that of Amiens. When Colonel Lauriston, in October 1801, brought back the ratification of the preliminaries to London, the crowd took the horses from his carriage and dragged it through the streets in their joy. The First Consul was fully alive to this longing of the peoples, and knew that this peace was not only useful but a kind of consecration of himself; and until the final signature on March 25th, 1802, he showed his impatient anxiety lest England should draw back and change her mind. And was it not indeed incredible that she should be thus resigned, for the first time in five centuries, to see France reaching out into Flanders and along the Rhine, to the very mouth of the famous river, and even beyond? It made the First Consul look even greater than Louis XIV himself. History could show no peace comparable with that of Amiens, the triumph of the Revolution militant, which brought the power of France and the glory of Bonaparte to the apogee.

It was he who gave reality to all the hopes of the nation. As the general conciliator, he was giving peace at home, union abroad, prosperity with greatness. And thereby he was irresistible, with the masses beside him, upholding him and shielding him from criticism and objection, the unique man, whose place none could take without throwing back all the apparent gains into the melting-pot. And there, too, were the origins of the magical potency of his name.

It was the same potency that the name of Henri IV had had. And the Concordat was the First Consul's Edict of Nantes. He alone, the universal pacificator, was capable of giving also religious peace, the great idea which he had been cherishing since his first Italian campaign. For although the churches had been reopened for worship, and the long-silent bells had begun to ring once more (and, listening at Malmaison to those of Rueil, he remarked how their music moved him by the memories of childhood they evoked), it still remained to set the position of Catholicism on a regular footing. Henri IV had abjured his own religion to adopt that of the majority of Frenchmen, but not without encountering resistance when he granted toleration for Protestants as well. Similarly the First Consul met with opposition to his Concordat, political and national though the conception was, since it was rallying the Church to the 'modern France', to the government of Brumaire, to all the elements — and they were far from insignificant — deriving from the Revolution that entered into the new regime. But he obtained another result. He severed the bonds of the Church with the Bourbons by enforcing in conjunction with Rome, the resignation of all the legitimate Bishops dating from the monarchy, as also of the constitutional Bishops of the schism. This did not prevent the First Consul from desiring afterwards that bishop-rics should be given without distinction to royalist or constitutional bishops. His constant concern with 'fusion' was a blend of utility and indifference, of scorn for men and esteem for their services.

Nowhere, perhaps, so clearly as in the Concordat can we see his bent for speaking divers tongues, for assuming successive attitudes according to the men he is addressing and the circumstances of the moment, for giving himself over, successively or even simultaneously, to different aspects of matters in hand. He varied because he was supple. That suppleness enabled him to impose his will and attain his ends. In catching the passing wind he excelled, like that other lover of glory, the author of *Le Génie du Christianisme*, the Vicomte de Chateaubriand. Both of these men felt that fashion was turning to religion, and they made religion fashionable.

Bonaparte was not a believer, either now or later. He was too deeply imbued with the eighteenth-century spirit. Fundamentally, it might be said, he was a 'deist with an involuntary respect and a predilection for Catholicism'. That was all; but it was enough for the needs of the day. To the atheistic ideologues, he pointed to the stars and asked: 'Who made all these?' To the politicians he made out that the problem was one of 'giving a framework to spiritual things', and of utilizing the force of religious ideas and institutions for the good of the State. But when he addressed the Pope, or the Cardinal Secretary of State Consalvi, or the Cardinal Legate Caprara, he spoke as the head of the French State, often menacing, imposing terms, maintaining the prerogatives of the Gallican Church. As Minister of Public Worship he chose a Catholic, a man of the old regime, Portalis, who restored to Napoleon's correspondence with the Bishops those suave and decorative forms of which the old royal *aumônerie* held the secret. But Portalis was chosen for his docility and submissiveness, and in exquisite terms he recalled the clergy to the duties of subjects towards the prince.

For already, in the mind of this young Corsican who had barely and but distantly seen the last days of monarchical France, the idea of re-welding the chain of time was taking shape. It was the idea of André Chénier translated into actual politics, the greatest of his audacities. To make a fresh start in history, on new foundations, was doubtless an ambition; but it was not within the grasp of the vulgar, because it was the conception of an intellectual, a brain standing alongside of history and with a sense of historic greatness. These bold strokes of the mind he had already practised with his books, at Valence, in Mlle Bou's modest furnished room. He was the 'poet in action' whom Chateaubriand was to hail, and because he was a poet who acted, greatness was natural to him. Nothing astonished him, nothing intimidated him, nothing made him ridiculous. To deliver the panegyric of the Concordat, to hear himself compared with Pepin and Charlemagne, he chose the Cardinal Archbishop de Boisgelin, the same prelate who, twenty-eight years before, had delivered the coronation sermon of Louis XVI. And Josephine, who had been through a civil marriage with Barras as a witness, received a chaplet from Pope Pius VII — pending much more.

Thoughts were already turning to coronations during that Te Deum in Notre-Dame at Easter, 1802. But mention of crowns was banned. Not that Bonaparte was displeased at being thus divined by the soothsayers, nor did he see a trap in these allusions. But at that moment he saw the trap elsewhere. His sentiments had not altered. Anything that roused the problem of the succession annoyed him, and those who thought about it he could not regard as his friends. Absolute power, complete power — yes: but for himself. What could it matter to him to have his power made hereditary? For what heir? Hereditary had no reason to tempt him; indeed, by increasing the similarity to the old monarchy, it could only rouse objections and obstacles. After the installation in the Tuileries, the Te Deum in Notre-Dame came as another proof of the First Consul's popularity, and of the resistance which might be encountered not only by his ascent towards the supreme power but by the policy of pacification which was bearing him thither. Bonaparte was well aware that in the Council of State, that precious core of his government, the reading of the Concordat had been coldly received, that there had even been laughter at certain religious turns of expression. 'The Concordat? One of the most difficult things I ever did,' he said. And the coronation would not be any less difficult.

It was very dexterous to make use of circumstances and celebrate the peace with England at the same time as the peace with the Church. It was the triumphal chariot which would bring the laggards and opponents and malcontents to the steps of the altar. And the chariot was no mere image. For the procession to Notre-Dame the state coaches of Louis XVI were refurbished. And on that day Paris again saw liveries: green and gold — the future livery of the Imperial House — the whole display of court pomp already, and with it a revival of court etiquette.

The reply of General Delmas, when the First Consul asked him what he thought of the ceremony, has remained famous. It has received more than one application in history: 'A fine mummery! It only lacked the million men who died to abolish all that!' replied the soldier of the Revolution. And the army was murmuring. Lannes was among the grumblers; and Augereau and Bernadotte, the latter almost of the Consular family, as he had married the other Mlle Clary and was thus the brother-in-law of Joseph. To assassinate the First Consul during the 'fine mummery' and to march the army of the West to Paris under Bernadotte, was the plan behind that military conspiracy which linked up the Rennes plot — the latter consisting essentially of an exploitation of the Republican feelings of the troops, to the point of spreading a rumour, on the day of the Te Deum, that the flags were to be blessed by priests. On the actual day, the picked troops devoted to the Consul, his pretorians, cowed the conspirators and brought the plan to nought. Joseph, fully informed by Bernadotte, declined the place by his brother's side which Napoleon offered him, and only went to Notre-Dame inconspicuously mingling, far from the target, with the State Councillors. The blow failed, and the affair was hushed up. But the First Consul was convinced by the episode that if power was coming to him in the natural course of events, his foes would be the more relentless as they saw 'usurpation advancing with long strides'.

The reason that decided the 'usurpation' is not to be sought in the mob feeling that authorized, even compelled, him to make himself more than Consul, any more than it is to be found in a devouring ambition. He made a reckoning. The authority given to him by the Constitution of the Year VIII was insufficient, fragile, and precarious. Bonaparte was concerned with stability — the outcome for which he strove to the very last, until everything abandoned him and the sceptre fell from his hands. The ten years granted by Brumaire were too short. What would happen at their end, even before they ended? The nearer their term came, the stronger would be the opposition whose hatred he had just been tasting. Everything – even concern for his personal future – advised him not to await that delay and to consolidate a still revocable authority by institutions that ensured durability.

For, great though it was, that authority of his was still shapeless. Bonaparte had, within the country, the prestige of a sovereign. How swift had been his rise from the first days of the Consulate, when his entourage still had a tinge of the bohemia and demi-monde from which the First Consul and his wife, and the Consular family, had sprung! And when Bonaparte pardoned Josephine on his return from Egypt, he had not been mistaken. She had been useful to him. They were well-assorted, in that he had the gift and the impulse for command, whilst she had the art and the impulse for attracting; and this had made their rise swifter and the transitions smoother. Josephine, of whom Metternich said that she was 'endowed with social tact', had been a far from negligible ally. But she herself, discovering at last that this little husband of hers, who at first had been so lightly treated, was a unique being, began to feel alarm at the heights to which they were being lifted. Within their intimacy there were banned subjects, and silences. The problem of inheritance was fatal to them both: to Bonaparte, who still would have nothing to do with it; and to Josephine, who was too much of a woman not to feel that, when the day came and he accepted it, he would desire the son she could not give him. Meanwhile Joseph and Lucien regarded themselves as princes of the blood, natural heirs to the future monarchy towards which they pressed, Joseph secretly, Lucien impetuously. Thus Bonaparte found himself beset in his plans by domestic and family intrigues which, by their thwarting complications, added bitter cares to the resistance still set up by the last Republicans.

It would be erroneous to imagine the First Consul, in the apotheosis of peace and national reconciliation, marching forward to Empire without concealment. His mind was made up to escape from the Republican 'rut', but he still practised deceits with the Republic. The plan of his friends, those of the Brumaire men who saw in a monarchy of Bonaparte's the natural conclusion and the necessary guarantee for the outcome of these two years, was not to wait for the Treaty of Amiens to be forgotten, but to propose a national reward for the First Consul. The Senate should declare a wish that would be agreeable to him. Bonaparte, as if fearful of betraying his ambition, expressed no desire and wrapped his thought in vague phrases. For all its eagerness and docility, the Senate, being asked for nothing, gave little. They merely prolonged the functions of the First Consul for ten years. It was essentially a disappointment to Bonaparte, and also a warning that supreme power would not come to him by its own accord, he must find or create the opportunity of seizing it.

And meanwhile, in shadow and silence, the foes of a personal power transformed into monarchy did not remain inactive. There were those, Fouché at their head, who did not want to see the old regime under a new label, and those who had not wished to upset the Bourbons just to have them replaced by the Bonaparte family. And, day by day, the system of fusion was bringing back the past little by little. The royalists were returning in large numbers, under terms of an amnesty, and the Catholic hierarchy had been re-established. The men of 1793 saw reaction on every hand. And it was true that already, in his own heart and really without knowing it, Bonaparte was acquiring a liking for these gentlemen who had preserved the usages of Versailles: M. de Narbonne pleased him by handing him a letter laid upon his hat. It was being noticed that 'manners were a good recommendation with Napoleon'. And he was no less appreciative of habitual devotion to the person of the prince. Thus there was born within him a new sentiment, which made him a man as twofold as his own interests, monarchial by reason of his position, revolutionary by reason of the roots of his power, and unable to found his monarchy except by keeping contact with the Revolution.

It was well said by Stendhal: 'Men say that Napoleon was deceitful. He was merely changeable.' And he changed, he had no fixed plan, he hardly even seemed to have sequence in his ideas — because he was always aware of how precarious, shifting, and contradictory was the ground he stood upon. That disappointing move by the Senate had taught him a lesson which served him in the establishment of the Empire. An Assembly's complaisance was of no avail. So he made a sudden resolve. He went over the head of the Senate, as over the other bodies, and appealed direct to the people, from whom he declared he held his authority, to have a delegation of the Consular power, no longer for a period, but for life. And he was sure in advance that the people would almost unanimously grant what was asked of them.

A Consulate *for life* — the very phrase was an incitement to murder, as the regime still depended on the existence of Bonaparte. But in the minds of the three-and-a-half million Frenchmen who approved this reign for a life-term was the idea that the results already gained would be maintained, that the new order would stand, that there would be no going back upon the distribution of property or upon the frontiers. The need for continuity still called for prolongations of the supreme magistracy entrusted to Bonaparte for the preservation of the Republic. And in this way the idea of heredity, which had no personal interest for him, and was even a burden to him, revived. Spontaneously it returned to men's minds, through that same concern about the future which had created a temporary authority and then transformed it into a lifelong tenure. As soon as the Consulate was extended to the last day of the First Consul's existence, the question of his death arose in the most pressing form. This was instantly realized by the men who most strongly adhered to the new order in politics and society and felt most closely bound up with it. It seemed to them that the opportunity was favourable to ask the people whether Napoleon Bonaparte, having been made immovable himself, should not be granted the right to name his successor.

It no longer seems strange to us that the First Consul struck out with his own hand the second question. We know now that he was not afraid of moving too fast or of asking too much at once; nor did he shrink before the Republican opposition, even that of the army. Heredity, no doubt, was monarchy undisguised. He could then be reproached with the dead bodies of all the men who had died to destroy the very thing he was restoring. But what successor could he name? He constantly brushed the question aside, but it was for ever being presented to him to the pitch of an obsession. The clan spirit, the Corsican spirit, had been exaggerated in the explanations and keys offered. For if there was one thing that Napoleon detested it was the idea of bequeathing his power to his brothers. Why should he? What claim had they? His brutal common sense mocked at their pretensions. Did they imagine, he said to his sisters, that it was a question of dividing the inheritance of 'our late father the king'? At this moment the hereditary idea had no more resolute foe than he. Napoleon had no child, nor had he the hope of having one by Josephine. When the idea was quietly broached to Bonaparte of adoption, he was no less opposed. Whom could he adopt? He was still so young — we must remember that he was now only thirty-three — that there was no great difference of age between himself and, say, his stepson Eugène. He was resolute in refusing to have beside him a substitute, a double, an heir-expectant who, even were he chosen as an adolescent, would grow up to be a vexatious mediocrity, or feel a grudge against his adoptive father if he were a man of parts, and at the same time, as heir-presumptive, be a rallying-point for opponents and malcontents. Bonaparte was a monarchist only for himself, and in that lay his only point of difference from the mass of those who put their trust in him. For him, the point of anxiety for the future lay in the remnants of elective principles in his power; for others, it lay in the gap which would confront them should he be taken from the scene. He was pressed to found a dynasty just when he believed that an hereditary dynasty could bring him nothing but difficulties. And those who incited him to seek it, desired it in other interests than his own, whether public or private. A strange conflict, but it helps in understanding what happened. That craving for duration and continuity felt by the new world sprung from the Revolution, had already given Bonaparte the life Consulate. It was to give him the Imperial throne. Men who had acclaimed the end of a long line of kings had at first hailed a master, and in their anxiety for the future, with importunate generosity, they sought to impose on their master the major right of self-survival and control of succession. Bonaparte, having no thoughts of his own death, would be content for the moment with a dictatorship moulded in the Republican form. Having gauged the difficulties, the vexations even, attaching to what could only be the founding of a fourth dynasty, he postponed the ultimate consequences of the rise until later. He would await events, having no measure of certainty as to what he should do.

The wait proved profitable. In the civil and pacific glory of the Consulate, the great captain stood out as the rival of Washington, the head of a resplendent and free Republic, who had attained the aims of the nation, sheathed his sword, and scorned a crown. He liked to stand as the legislator, the great administrator. The First Consul visited the manufactories of Lyons, the workshops of Rouen, the docks of Havre, the Ourcq and Saint-Quentin canals; and the visits offered fresh themes for popular prints, themes that were the bourgeois pendants to those of the bridge of Arcola and the crossing of the Saint Bernard. What with the Bank of France, the *Grand Livre* of the public debt, and the establishment of the Chambers of Commerce, this represented the sound, solid, prosperous aspect of his renown.

Meanwhile, anxiety dogged Bonaparte amid these civic occupations. He made perpetual calculations and estimates. He felt that to preserve his authority as it now stood, he must increase it, and to remain where he was, he must rise higher. The feat of strength did not consist in attaining power, but in maintaining himself there, and he could do so only if he had the instruments of governance. But he would still require the 'circumstances', to be taken on the wing, to be usefully exploited, to be stimulated if need be; and above all, he would have to lay solid foundations, to prepare institutions which would form the bases of the regime. That was the direction aimed at in all Bonaparte's innovations, and they still met with the shrewd opposition of the last of the Republicans sheltering in Corps Législatif and the Tribunat.

He knew his Montesquieu well enough to know that a system of honours, which by its nature calls for preference and distinction, is the principle of monarchies. He knew also that honours represent a noble sentiment through which almost everything can be obtained from Frenchmen. Stendhal has ably described the 'extreme spirit of emulation which the Emperor inspired in all ranks of society'. He has shown the chemist's apprentice in his master's back-shop, 'thrilled by the idea that if he made a great discovery he would be awarded the Cross and made a Count'. When Bonaparte wished glory to be 'the true legislation of Frenchmen', it was not merely to satisfy one of their cravings. The Legion of Honour, contemporaneous with the Concordat, was one of his master ideas, and he defended it, as he did the Concordat, with arguments as varied as his intentions. At Leoben he had scoffed at the ribbons and orders which the Austrian delegates would receive when they returned to Vienna.

But now he was saying that 'heroes were made with these much-despised baubles', that by suppressing them the Republic had gone counter to one of man's most legitimate and generous leanings, a need as potent as that for religious pomp. To restore a system of knighthood, he chose Roederer, a man who during the Revolution had declared that 'honours must be dishonoured'. The choice was perhaps a sign of his scorn for the human breed. The Legion of Honour found impassioned foes, almost as many as did the Concordat. The Tribunat especially was hostile to the creation of an order which recalled the orders of the old regime and would rekindle 'a sentiment of feudalism'. The First Consul thereupon expounded the view that society is not composed of 'grains of sand', and then that, to balance the visible organization of the Church, and the more secret one of the royalists and the old Chouans, it was important to form into cohorts the men who had distinguished themselves by services rendered to the Revolution and the new regime. Finally, he pointed out that, being civilian as much as it was military, his Legion of Honour derived naturally from the 'lists of notability' as conceived by Sieyès, and that it formed, with the Council of State at the summit, a pyramid, like the system of Sieyès itself. In all of which there was truth. The Legion of Honour had not really sprung fully armed from the brain of Bonaparte. It was a reversion to ancient usage, ingeniously adapted to modern France. It was many things in one. On the breast of the fighting-man, of the scholar, of the manufacturer, it was one more means of 'fusing' the French, as it was also a means of gliding over the suppression of the 'lists of notability', the last vestige of election in the institutions of the Year VIII.

And to harmonize these institutions with the life Consulate: he transformed them. They were already becoming the institutions of the Empire, and from the constitution of the Year X, it would need few changes to extract the Imperial constitution. All this was accomplished without violence, without a *coup d'état*. In spite of his annoyance with the obstinate opposition of the assemblies to everything, to his Civil Code, his Concordat, his Legion of Honour, and, less obviously, to his person, Bonaparte listened to the advice of Cambacérès to take no sudden action, but to eliminate the recalcitrant adversaries noiselessly. A renewal of one-fifth of the Corps Législatif and the Tribunat fell due in 1802. Sixty members of the former, and twenty of the latter, chosen from the most troublesome, were marked down to leave their seats: or rather, to make the exclusion less obvious, the remainder were marked down to remain. To replace them, the docile Senate appointed members of a docility equal to its own. And so the machinery of Sieyès continued to anticipate everything. To know how to use it sufficed to abolish the last vestige of the Republic. Before long nothing would be left but the Corps Législatif and the Senate, the new member of which would be appointed by the First Consul.

But what the constitution of the Year X gave him (or, at least avoiding the semblance of constitutional changes, the *senatus consultum* of the Year X), what he accepted in the end, what completed with neither crown nor title his monarchical power, was exactly the thing he had been refusing, the thing which for months men had sought to impose on him: namely, the right, like that of the Roman Emperors, to choose his successor. He had no son, and he resorted to adoption, 'an imitation of nature', as he termed it. Why did he now accept what had been, a few weeks earlier, so repugnant to him? It was not a caprice. But a nephew had been born, the child of Louis and Hortense. And this child of his breed, bearing the name of Napoleon, brought the solution. Between the adoption of an infant and that of a man, even a young man, there was a great difference. A difference of thirty-three years left no grounds for the fear of rearing a rival beside himself. And this child had the further merit of setting aside the ambitious and turbulent brothers, the princes of the blood, from the future throne. Bonaparte's dominant hope was to subordinate his kinsmen. But the baby Napoleon-Charles, marked out by the First Consul as his heir, and by Josephine as a safeguard against divorce, did not live. The idea of adoption died with him. And then the desire came to Bonaparte, who had so far hardly thought of it, to perpetuate himself, to follow nature instead of imitating her, to have a son who should inherit his succession. If the Empire had still to be born from the organic *senatus consultum*, the frail life of Napoleon-Charles held within it the Austrian marriage.

These thoughts and perplexities dogged Bonaparte from his park at Malmaison to the cities which he visited on these tours. Empire could hardly be far from his mind when he held the main attributes of monarchy, and especially when an Empire of the West seemed to be seeking him out. He was now, in the year 1802, the head of two States, First Consul in France, and, with more extensive powers, President of the Italian Republic, at the request of the body which had come to Lyons to offer him, as to another Charlemagne, something which already looked more like a civil magistracy than the Iron Crown of the Lombard kings. Was it ambition, an atavistic dream, that impelled Bonaparte to reign over that Italy in which, not so long ago, he had arrived unknown? But the transformation of the Cisalpine Republic into the Italian Republic under French tutelage, necessary to protect the young nationality against Austria, was an idea and an outcome of the Revolution. Similarly, the annexation of Piedmont, covering Lombardy, and the occupation of Holland, covering Belgium. Similarly, in Germany, the secularization and refashioning of territories, made the First Consul the arbiter of the Germanic Confederation. This, ere long, would succeed to the Holy Roman Empire to prepare the awakening of the German nation. Causes and effects were endlessly intermingling and multiplying in the great European hotch-potch called for by the conquest of the natural frontiers. For the moment, France rose up above the debris, and Bonaparte rose with her. Similarly, too, he became mediator of the Helvetic Confederation, arbiter of its parties, protector of Switzerland.

We may pause at this moment, when, from all sides, by the natural play of forces, the First Consul was brought to heights of greatness which lacked nothing now but the supreme consecration. An apotheosis was beginning from which he reaped the good grain of his sowing before he reaped the bad. And with that a doubt, an enigma, rises to the mind. Had Bonaparte shared the illusion of other Frenchmen? Did he believe that the Revolution was completed, abroad as at home? Did he believe in a definitive peace? Did he wish for a resumption because his authority and renown were linked up with war?

It would be vain to try to fathom his intentions and his conscience. But his actions imply unmistakably that during several months the First Consul behaved as if, the status of continental France being proof against any questioning claims and peace with England being assured, he wished to restore to his country what had been lost during the Revolution in the shape of a navy and colonies. The expedition designed to retake San Domingo, the pearl of the Antilles, from the liberated blacks, and the acquisition of Louisiana, bear witness to a plan that was all the less in doubt as Louisiana was hurriedly sold to the United States for eighty million francs as soon as the resumption of war with England became a certainty. The San Domingo campaign was to end in disaster. General Leclerc, the First Consul's own brother-in-law died there. The retaking of fertile Haiti was abandoned.

The restoration of France's maritime position was likewise abandoned. Already the first tokens of a maritime and colonial revival had kindled anew the jealous anxiety of England. The English could not but feel that France, beginning at Antwerp and stretching thence right to the finest Italian harbours, was a danger, and would not be long in supplanting their own navy and trade, choking them as if through their very lungs. It was not so very long since the rivalry of the eighteenth century had set England and France at grips with each other; and now, if England allowed to the Republic an expansion which she had always disputed with the monarchy, she would lose the fruits of a long warfare and sign her capitulation and defeat. England had hardly signed the Peace of Amiens before she was regretting it. The weight of mercantile and financial opinion decided Parliament and the British government to resume the struggle.

The carrying out of a treaty is no less important than the treaty itself. The responsibilities for the rupture are seen to be unequal, much heavier on England's side; she was not slow to raise difficulties, while the First Consul simply took up an attitude of distrust. The quarrel was born, and grew, round the island of Malta. The English refused to carry out the Amiens clause by which the island was to be restored to the Grand Master of the Order. Obviously they did not intend to relax their hold of that strategic key. For that matter, they hold it to this day. On the other hand, they refused to believe that Bonaparte had renounced Egypt. Suspicion was reciprocal, and the more determined England showed herself to retain Malta, the more did Bonaparte feel that a solid footing in the Mediterranean was necessary to France. Ill feeling centred round this rock.

But never did Bonaparte show more vacillation. His reason seemed to tell him that war was inevitable. He acted as if the peace was certain to last. In March 1803 he was still believing this, as he ventured a whole squadron at sea, bearing General Decaen, entrusted with the recovery of the Indian trading ports. And on the 13th of the same month, in front of the diplomatic corps, he violently attacked the English ambassador Whitworth, accusing England of bad faith and disregard for the sanctity of treaties; he threatened her and flung verbal thunderbolts at her, and then softened, as if he were still anxious to preserve peace, and then broke out afresh when he perceived that soft words were useless.

Malta, indeed, was only a symbol. The essential and insoluble point of dispute was still Antwerp. It hinged, as it did to the last, on the annexation of 1795. Bonaparte had been able to forget, to blind himself, for several months. But he now realized better than anyone in France. 'England will wage war on us,' he was to tell Molé in 1805, 'so long as we retain Belgium.' Even at the end of 1800 he had told Roederer and Devaisnes that England could not wish for peace. Why? Because, he said, France possessed too much. Because France held Belgium and the left bank of the Rhine and was bound to keep them, 'something irrevocably settled, and for which Prussia, Russia and the Emperor had been told that France would, if need be, make war single-handed against them all'. It was admirably clear-sighted — almost prophetic. The future was there, the deduction from a binding past, drawn line for line.

The emblem of the Consulate was a sleeping lion. How short was its rest! In July 1803, when the break with England had occurred, and six weeks after that rupture, the First Consul made an impressive journey through Belgium, as if to remind Frenchmen that, if they were going to fight, it was still for this land, for the annexations which he had received as trustee from the Republic, and which he was no less resolute than the Republic had been to hold in a lasting grip. In 1801 he had already told the Belgian deputation after the peace of Lunéville: 'Since the treaty of Campo Formio, the Belgians have been Frenchmen, like Normans, Alsatians, and men of Languedoc or Burgundy.' In the war which followed that treaty, the armies suffered certain reverses; 'but even if the enemy had placed their headquarters in the Faubourg Saint-Antoine, the French people would never have ceded their rights, nor renounced the union of Belgium.'

It was an oath. It was to be the oath of coronation. Napoleon kept it, even with the enemy at the gates of Paris. The history of the Empire is that of the struggle for the preservation of Belgium, and France could not preserve Belgium without subjugating Europe in order to bring England to her knees. But with the rupture of the Peace of Amiens, the great illusion of peace melted into thin air. The 'sleeping lion' awoke from his dream once more. The chase after impossibilities began.

CHAPTER XIII

THE MOAT OF VINCENNES

AT a distance, simply because it happened and because all things that happen seem easy, nothing looks more natural or straightforward than the establishment of the Empire. A ripe fruit seemed ready to drop into the First Consul's hand. But, just as with the 18th of Brumaire, the event had to be stimulated and it also had to be brought about by steel and by the spilling of blood.

One of Bonaparte's most trusted principles in war was that 'every operation must be carried out on a system, because nothing succeeds by chance'. In politics he worked likewise. Hitherto, we have seen, he committed no major fault, and he seized opportunities without hurrying. This accounts for his success and explains his steady rise. At the time of the succession question he exclaimed before a few trusted friends: 'Power is my mistress. I have worked too hard to conquer her to let her be taken from me, or even allow others to covet her. You may tell me that power came to me as it were by itself, but I know what pains and vigils and arranging it has cost me.' The rupture of the Treaty of Amiens was going to create circumstances which would enable him to rise still higher. But the crown would have been beyond his reach had he not formed fresh schemes and calculations. They were to prove deep and secret. Already, like Corneille's Augustus, his hero, he was speaking of 'this rank and fame that cost me once such travail. . . ' Ere long he was to complete the poet's line. He would add 'and such blood'.

The opportunity was provided by his enemies. Empire and Emperor were made by the English, and by the royalist and Republican conspirators. The life Consulate, enhanced by Bonaparte's power to name his successor, was a hybrid regime. But how was France to escape from it? The Jacobins, chastened and less rigid, had returned in large numbers to the assemblies and administrations of the Consulate, and were firm against any monarchy, if only to save their own faces. And the crowd too, though ready to want what Bonaparte wanted, felt humiliated by the picture of a throne when they remembered all the oaths of hatred against royalty, all the curses called down upon tyrants and tyranny. No doubt men were not yet far from the old regime. A crowned head was the aspect under which, for centuries, Frenchmen had seen and conceived power. But were not the memories of the Revolution still more recent, were they not still throbbing? The reports of many of the Prefects struck that chord. Only new sets of facts would prevail over sentiment and prejudice.

The rupture of the Treaty of Amiens dated from May 16th, 1803. The *senatus consultum* conferring the Imperial crown on the First Consul dated from May 18th, 1804. What happened between these two dates? How were these twelve months filled? With victories? Not at all. There had as yet been no fighting. The establishment of an hereditary monarchy in favour of Napoleon Bonaparte was not a reward for services. The intention behind that monarchy was that it should be 'a shield'.

Bonaparte had gathered no fresh laurels of war. England had not yet succeeded in reforming a coalition on the Continent. Contact between the two enemies, across the Channel, was difficult. From time to time a French port was bombarded. The First Consul replied with the usual reprisals of commercial prohibitions, and the arrest of all English residents in France. These somewhat theoretical hostilities, exhausting as well as desultory, might drag on indefinitely. And Bonaparte then turned back to the old idea of invasion — crossing the Straits, landing, and dictating a peace in London whilst William Pitt, restored to power, still toiled to make a European coalition. During those twelve months the future was taking shape whilst the past began again. The situation of 1798 was returning, and glimpses of 1814 were already visible.

France took up arms again without enthusiasm, with resignation, fatalistically. Bonaparte himself, with that mobility of mind which showed him affairs in their most varied aspects, would gladly have held on to this peace, the benefits of which had won him such popularity and gratitude; but reason told him that war was inevitable. And he was too intelligent not to see that it would be a duel to the death. He accepted it as a law of destiny, with which it was vain to parry. France accepted it likewise. Men saw that it was still the same war which had been going on since 1792. And to end it, on whom could they count if not on the First Consul?

The enemy themselves pointed him out as the indispensable man, and their threats made his life still more precious. Bonaparte had given France a government. He had restored order and strength by a single-handed control. So long as he was there, it would be difficult to wrest Belgium from France and push her back within her old boundaries. And so everything that made the French wish to preserve him also made the enemy wish to strike him down. Bonaparte had to be vanquished, or he had to be killed — which was quicker. Coldly the London Cabinet made that calculation, for the disappearance of this one man, to shorten an irreparable war — to spare, it might be, millions of lives.

England did not have to seek hired assassins. Agents and tools came forward, all prepared, the men of 'the essential stroke', fanatically disinterested royalists discouraged by the apotheosis of the Consulate, but with their hopes of finishing with the usurper revived by the return of war. With rare boldness, and an energy seasoned in the struggles of the Vendée, it was the Chouan element which they brought forward, right to the camp of Boulogne, to Malmaison, to the very doors of the Tuileries, without suspecting that if the 'stroke' failed, it would be the Corsican himself whom they would make 'essential'.

The state of war really prevailed in the interior. On August 23rd, 1803, Georges Cadoudal, brought by an English ship, clambered up the cliffs of Viville, and came to Paris for the man-hunt. He prepared assassination, or, preferably, an abduction. Once again these were days when the government was at the mercy of a pistol-shot. Fouché, in disgrace since his opposition to the life Consulate, still held the threads of the Ministry of Police, and gave warning from his retreat: 'There are daggers in the air everywhere.' It was more than a plot. It was a conspiracy in the strongest and fullest sense, for it gathered together widely different men animated by the same hatred, the hatred for Bonaparte, all wishing together for one thing — his disappearance. There were royalists, some recalcitrant Jacobins, and also those who were styled 'the friends of England', vexed by the rupture of the peace because it upset their interests and tastes. But principally there were soldiers. The army counted more Republicans than the Tribunat, more irreconcilables than the Faubourg Saint-Germain. Napoleon did not mince words, and he repeated to his last days — the army had 'traitors'. Who knew it better than the First Consul? He had had his reasons for sending Lannes and Brune as ambassadors to Lisbon and Constantinople, whilst Macdonald was despatched to Denmark. He was kept informed about Masséna, Saint-Cyr, Lacuée and others, not to mention Bernadotte, or those who had not yet shown their hand, the very closest to his person, who were to betray him at the decisive hour. The old army of the Revolution, the officer of Fructidor, the general who thought himself as good a man as Bonaparte — these were the worst enemies of the First Consul. To such a point, that Pichegru, a deserter like Dumouriez to the camp of Louis XVIII, was in friendly touch with the staffs. On January 16th, 1804, Pichegru returned to France by the same way as

Cadoudal, accompanied by the two Polignacs, Rivière, and some thirty determined men. It was he who interviewed Moreau. Pichegru acted as a link between Cadoudal the Chouan and the victor of Hohenlinden, the idol of the Republican army, who was more affected by the flattering incitements of the old Revolutionary officers than by his jealousy of his rival in renown. Such different conspirators were in agreement, no doubt, only on the suppression of their man. But it was enough to bring them together.

From the gentle handling of Moreau by the First Consul, from the exile which he inflicted, almost mercifully, after the trial, not daring to keep him in prison, one feels that this conspiracy had been quite as much a source of embarrassment as of alarm. People were afraid of discovering all of its associates, almost as much as of letting it expand, afraid of revealing its participants and even of admitting their stamp and number. Amongst Moreau's accomplices and 'sympathizers' there were found two highly placed generals, Lecourbe and, probably, Macdonald. Amongst the soldiers also would have been found Suchet, Dessoles, Souham, Liébert, Delmas and Lahorie; amongst civilians, it was said, twenty-three Senators, and Sieyès himself, who, a little later, was regretting having given the Republic a master. It was even whispered that Réal, the chief of the police, was suspect.

Probably Bonaparte was saved by the extent, the multiplicity, and the diverse composition of the conspiracy. One may wonder why so resolute a plotter as Georges, after planning the abduction of the First Consul in every detail, wasted four or five months and allowed devotion to cool off and secrets to get abroad, without taking steps to put it into practice. But royalists and Republicans were united only to overthrow the usurper, and Georges, the only man capable of making the enterprise successful, had no mind to be really working for another general of the Republic. He waited for one of the princes to arrive secretly in Paris, so that when the blow had been dealt the Bourbon restoration should be

forthwith proclaimed, Moreau being the dupe of the operation. The plan was really too complicated and too simple.
Weeks went by and no prince appeared. Time was wasted by
the conspirators, and Bonaparte turned it to advantage for
defence, whilst his adversaries, having neither the same
convictions nor the same goal, were not slow to betray each
other.

Threatened, hunted, aimed at by implacable and invisible
foes, Bonaparte certainly went through days of nervous
distress. He meditated vengeance, a counter-stroke. But
the idea of a vendetta quickly gave place to less summary
conceptions. He saw further ahead, beyond mere retaliation.
In all the rich unfolding of consequences, one act, both
terrible and bold, appeared to him as if brought by the con-
vergence of events to drive forward the action of the drama,
according to the rules of the school of tragedy which had
shaped his taste and in which he did not tire of witnessing
Talma.

Why seek to clear Bonaparte from the guilt in the death of
the Duc d'Enghien? He took it on his own shoulders. Before
God and men, before his son, at Longwood, he maintained
his final declaration of responsibility. Impenetrable at the
actual moment, and insensitive to tears and to blame, he
did not conceal, in later years, what he could not say on the
day following this deed, carried out as he had willed it to be
carried out. 'It was a sacrifice necessary to my safety and
my greatness.' Everything lies in that last word.

Few political crimes have been more coldly calculated.
Yet the idea of fixing on the Duc d'Enghien did not come
unaided to Bonaparte's mind. It was inspired by circumstances, and if, as there is ground for believing, Talleyrand
the Iago of the drama, suggested it to him, the very suggestion
emerged from the facts. That is no excuse for Bonaparte.
But at least we must see how the temptation was born and
grew within him.

We know why Georges delayed the abduction of the First

Consul. He was waiting for one of the princes to be in Paris, and this detail was known to the police. The plan, therefore of laying hold of this prince, whoever he might be, condemning and shooting him, rose to the mind, with the widespread consequences of so startling an example. Words of annoyance escaped Bonaparte, as from a mind beyond containing itself: 'My blood is worth just as much as theirs', he said of the Bourbons. He burned to have his hands on one. But which? None arrived. Would it be the Comte d'Artois, the Duc de Berry, or the Duc d'Enghien? The last-named lived at Ettenheim, in Baden, quite close to the frontier, within reach. He had the blood of Condé in his veins, a gallant, active, handsome man. He was typical of the active and militant *émigrés*, and had often been spoken of as a possible king. So, as Georges was expecting a prince to arrive, might it not be the Duc d'Enghien? Of all his family, he was the most capable of this bold stroke. He was watched. And the suspicions resting on him began to take shape when the name of a member of his entourage, badly pronounced in German fashion, suggested that Dumouriez was concerned.

It is now easy to reconstruct what followed. In one bodeful flash Bonaparte saw the possibilities of the summary execution of a prince of the blood royal. A Bourbon corpse would be the first step of the throne. He needed a Bourbon, at any price. There was a presumptive case against the Duc d'Enghien. That was enough. It did not matter that proof was lacking, that no participation in the plot could be brought home to the young prince, who was busy with other things and was deep in a romantic affair with Charlotte de Rohan. Nor did it matter that, being a soldier and unable to conceive of underground warfare, Enghien disapproved of the trap being laid by Cadoudal. The First Consul's plan was laid. Perhaps it was Talleyrand who whispered in his ear. It was also the 'genius of the Revolution'. The man who had formerly disapproved of the execution of Louis XVI, and suppressed the festival of January 21st as a sanguinary and repellant ceremony, now understood the meaning, the range, the symbolic utility of regicide.

Looking into the intricacies of this affair, it is beyond doubt that everything was carried out according to the First Consul's wishes. On March 10th a council was held, with Cambacérès, Lebrun, Régnier, Fouché and Talleyrand. The arrest on foreign soil was decided upon, with no heed for international law, or rather in the certainty that the Margrave of Baden would bow. Cambacérès ventured a word of protest. Bonaparte silenced the former president of the Committee of Public Safety with his retort: 'You have become very miserly of Bourbon blood.' When the decision was taken, Berthier, the War Minister, was entrusted with its execution, along with M. de Caulaincourt.

Mme de Rémusat must be believed in this part of her story, which has all the marks of authenticity. As a lady-in-waiting, informed by Josephine of what was in hand, she observed the First Consul. She saw him, on the evening before the night of Vincennes, resolute and impenetrable, brushing aside every allusion, then affecting gaiety and a joking mood, humming airs, and suddenly, as his habit was, repeating verses under his breath. Was it to put people off the scent, or was he actually giving spoken expression to an inward struggle? They were lines of his favourite poet, in which he spoke of clemency. He might also have repeated, from that same Corneille, tragedy the line:

'Those crimes of State, for conquering a throne. . . .'

During the night of March 14th-15th French gendarmes crossed into Baden and took possession, at Ettenheim, of the person and papers of the prince. Bonaparte's orders were given before even the possible charges obtainable from these papers were known. Vincennes was to be the place of detention. General Hulin, a staunch Revolutionary, was named president of the tribunal. Late on the 17th, Bonaparte received the dossier from Strasbourg; there was no proof of complicity with Cadoudal, and there had been a mistake about Dumouriez. Nevertheless, Harel, in command at Vincennes, received orders next day to prepare quarters for the prisoner and to have a trench dug. That same day, on two occasions, Josephine vainly appealed to her husband. Women, he retorted, should not mix themselves up with such matters: his policy demanded this *coup d'état*; the royalists had compromised him, and 'this action' would free him. On the 19th the dossier was sent to Réal, with instructions not to give any hint of what charges it might or might not contain, whilst Hulin, Murat, governor of Paris, and Savary, colonel of gendarmerie, were summoned to Malmaison, and received direct orders from the First Consul. Next day Bonaparte came to the Tuileries. He personally dictated the terms of authority for the judicial commission, which set out the heads of the accusation, involving the capital penalty. Réal was ordered to Vincennes to 'conduct' the preliminaries and to 'expedite' the procedure. Returning to Malmaison, Bonaparte again refused to listen to Josephine and his brother Joseph, who, it is said, asked for mercy. A courier from Strasbourg brought him the last papers from Ettenheim and the prisoner's denial of any part in Cadoudal's plots. The arrival of this courier meant that the prince also would soon be there. Immediately the First Consul sent again for Savary, repeated his instructions to him, and dictated to him a letter to Murat containing the formal order to 'finish the matter during the night'. At Murat's door Savary met Talleyrand, and learned that the Duc d'Enghien was nearly at Vincennes. He reached there soon after five in the afternoon. Since half-past three the grave had been dug in the moat of the fortress. Réal had not to intervene. Everything was well arranged.

At nine in the evening the commissioners appointed by Murat met at Vincennes. Savary consulted with them. At eleven o'clock the gendarmerie commandant Dautancourt interrogated the prince, strictly on the lines of the questions prepared in advance. The Duc still protested, and requested an audience of the First Consul. Dautancourt communicated the statements to the commission, who were already in session and had the accused brought before them, according to instructions, 'forthwith'. Savary stood behind the chair of Hulin, the president, who began his examination. The prince protested that he had not dabbled in any plot, that he had only opposed the Revolution, a Condé being able to return to France only if 'under arms'. The tribunal seized upon these words, and made them the crime. Instantly they passed sentence of death. And the warrant contained a blank space, left unfilled, for the text of a law of which the judges were ignorant — the only point which had not been provided for beforehand — and on which they based their decision.

This strange, unwonted lacuna seems to have inspired them with some scruples. They inclined to grant the prisoner his request for an interview with the First Consul. Here, however, obscurity falls again. Each man tries to shift the blame. But Savary took control. He had no further need of the commissioners: 'Gentlemen, your business is concluded; the rest is mine.' It was half-past two in the morning. Before daybreak the Duc was led out to the edge of the trench and shot by the firing-squad brought by Savary during the afternoon. To save time, the condemned man was refused a priest.

Such was the sequence controlled by the formal order to take speedy action. The crowning touch of art was to leave a measure of doubt, so that it came to be said that the Duc d'Enghien had been shot against Bonaparte's wishes. It was said that Réal had gone to bed and left orders not to be disturbed, and so had not received a message from the First Consul ordering him to question the Duc himself and to postpone the execution. Sometimes Bonaparte sheltered behind this fable put forward by his defenders and partisans. But did the Emperor Napoleon show displeasure with Réal, who could sleep so soundly when necessary? No more than with Savary, who was terribly awake. Savary became Duke of Rovigo, and Réal a Count. Quite enough for men who were supposed to have misunderstood their master's idea, to have been guilty of negligence or excessive zeal, to have forced his hand. The idea of postponement and pardon may have crossed Bonaparte's mind at the last moment; but that sleep of Réal's, and the speed of his agent, had served him better than all hopes. Chateaubriand, amongst others, has described the sorrow and reproach which Bonaparte read on the faces around him on the day after that night of blood: 'this death, at first, froze every heart with fear. Men were apprehensive of the return of Robespierre, and Paris felt that it was once again living through one of those days which come but once, the day of the execution of Louis XVI. Consternation seized Bonaparte's servants, his friends and his kinsfolk'. Chateaubriand himself resigned his office as French minister in the Valais. The protest would perhaps have impressed Bonaparte if it had been isolated. But he was watching, directly and indirectly, for every sign, and the one which he seized upon came from elsewhere.

Amongst the members of the Tribunat was a hitherto inconspicuous man named Curée, who was afraid that Bonaparte might be working for a Bourbon restoration. He had voted Louis XVI guilty of conspiring against the liberty of the people, but for his imprisonment rather than the death penalty. He was, in fact, a moderate regicide. When Curée reached the Tribunat the day after the Vincennes drama, he found his colleagues for the most part 'groaning over this tragic event'. He approached them, rubbing his hands, and exclaimed: 'I am delighted, Bonaparte has sided with the Convention.' And Miot de Melito, who tells this story, adds: 'The remark reached the ears of the First Consul, who had his spies in the Tribunat. He astutely realized that a man who had spoken so energetically against the Bourbons was the best man to raise him to the Empire. An Emperor sprung from the Convention would certainly, in the eyes of Curée, be a complete safeguard against the return of the old dynasty.'

Marked out by his simple saying, Curée was one in a thousand. He was the voice of the people who had made the Revolution, of the regicides who held it in trust. Having spilt the same blood, Bonaparte was one of themselves. Since 1793 it had been essential for a ruler to have voted for the death of Louis XVI. That was the unwritten law of the Republican constitutions. Sieyès had thus been a guarantee for the 18th of Brumaire. And to go further, to emerge from the Republic, but still through the gate of Revolution, was it not essential that this law of blood should be obeyed? Bonaparte could no longer seek refuge behind anyone to take that last step. He must himself trace the line of demarcation between the old royalty and the new monarchy.

Was it necessary? Did Bonaparte really need that blood-stained moat in order to be Emperor? The question is not answered by supposing the crime to have been the work of his two evil geniuses. To Talleyrand and Fouché, the First Consul did not seem, in Balzac's powerful phrase, 'so wedded as they were themselves to the Revolution', and they would have 'buckled him to it, for their own safety, by means of the affair of the Duc d'Enghien'. In that case, Bonaparte had understood their idea. He had grasped its wide bearings, and the hypothesis tending to exonerate him bears witness to the political design which controlled the drama at Vincennes. The desired effect was produced. Hortense observed very well the outcome, just as it would be desired by the chiefly interested party: 'From that moment all who had co-operated in the Revolution sided openly with the Consul. They were certain he would prove no Monk; here is his pledge and he can be counted upon.' A few long faces, some words of blame, some sulky looks, would matter little. What mattered a stain on the name of Bonaparte, if it was the ransom of a higher fortune, the price to be paid for inscribing the name of Napoleon on history?

There was an echo from Malmaison, when Josephine naively wrote the full truth: 'All these circumstances brought about a great event.' The execution of the Duc d'Enghien, the salvo of Vincennes, was the stroke which brought about the Empire, which settled the objections of Republicans, which determined and — mark the word — excused everything in the eyes of the France of the Revolution. Everything — even the coronation. Anointing would come before long, from a blessing and forgiving hand. That was the other aspect of the drama, which rounded it off — absolution in the apotheosis.

Shortly after the night of Vincennes the First Consul remarked in conversation, as if thinking aloud: 'I have imposed silence for ever on royalists and Jacobins alike.' And to Joseph, who had interceded for the Duc: 'We must console ourselves for everything.' That was easy. The stroke had succeeded, frightening some, delighting others. And those whom it had alarmed were quickly reassured; confidence was restored when it was seen that not only were there no further victims, but that Bonaparte, with a clemency as fruitful as the ferocity preceding it, spared the lives of the aristocrats compromised in the Cadoudal plot, Armand de Polignac and M. de Rivière.

And when we consult the calendar, can we deny that the affair of Vincennes was a success? The Duc fell dead at daybreak on March 21st. On the 27th, came the first official demonstration for a restoration of monarchy in the person of Napoleon Bonaparte. The Senate, that same Senate which so lately had allowed the First Consul no more than a ten years' extension, now took the initiative in offering him the crown.

How can this eagerness be explained if not by the fact that the Senate realized that the way was clear? On what main motive did it base its deliberation? It denounced the plots, and pointed horror-struck at the threats to Bonaparte's life. The government of France depended on one man. If he disappeared, everything disappeared. To prevent the conspirators being tempted to draw their daggers, the man must be replaced by an institution. The Senate's address to the First Consul was a request, a supplication. They besought him to take the crown, and thus closed the circle which had begun in 1789. Monarchy, as Thiers so well remarked, was the port in which the Revolution sought refuge.

The weeks during which the Empire was determined were those of the great trial of Georges, Pichegru and Moreau. An intransigent Chouan, a Revolutionary general, deserter to Louis XVIII, and another general, idolized by Republican officers — the strangeness of these bedfellows was also of service to Bonaparte, in that once again he seemed to be set above parties by being the target of hatred for so many adversaries. A man can be killed, but a dynasty cannot. Therefore one had to be made. Fauchet had said as much to the Convention, referring to Louis XVI: 'Will his family die under the same blow that strikes him? Does not one king immediately succeed another?' The death of a dictator ends everything. That of a king, nothing. And this was now to be the protecting shield which Bonaparte would assume.

But that word 'king' grated on the ear. The name of Emperor was the fitting progression from a Consulate. To a generation nurtured upon Roman history, the Empire, which is not royalty, was the normal succession to the Republic. Was it not even something greater than royalty? The title of Emperor had eluded the French ever since Charlemagne, and it suited a Gaul which had expanded beyond even his boundaries. Men's imaginations, and Bonaparte's was the most powerful, took wing upon time. The old enemy, the Germanic Cæsar, was vanquished. The Imperial dignity, usurped for centuries, would be torn from him. And Bonaparte, intellectual, almost bookish, conceived grandiose notions quite naturally. The crown of Charlemagne lay easy on his brow. There was no gap to be bridged between the utilitarian idea of a protective hereditary succession and the great idea of Empire.

Those were days which brought to pass one of the most extraordinary destinies that any man has known. And they showed all the reflective and impetuous strains in Bonaparte's mind, his continuity and his spasmodic quality, his consequent ability to adapt himself to the dramatic moments of his life, to calculate the exact sequence of events, to keep ahead of them, to overleap the stages — in fact, an exalted coolness of mind which would all be developed and accentuated in him as time went on. He was not feverish, any more than on the battlefield. Every element in the operation was present to his thoughts. He showed majesty, as if already identifying himself with sovereignty; he showed brutality, because man can thus be led; he showed affability and a coaxing spirit, because he knew that there were still things to be handled with care — such as the self-respect of Cambacérès, who would drop from his Consular rank (Lebrun, for his part, accepted everything); and, what is most pleasing as it shows the gleam of intelligence, he could contemplate the gentleman-cadet, the Corsican Tom Thumb in this prodigious incarnation, with cynicism, sometimes with a laugh at himself. One day he would scornfully remark that he had found the crown of France on the ground and picked it up; another day he was saying, magnificently, that, from Clovis to the Committee of Public Safety, he stood undivided from his predecessors and solidly at one with all. Another day there came those words at the Council of State: 'Before the Revolution, authority had fallen into the female line; we had a half-wit king; he was hanged and his family expelled. We pick up the throne and found the Empire. I have a strength and advantages which my successors will not be able to preserve. I must profit by them to set up a good government, a good system of administration.' The founder of the fourth dynasty had few illusions regarding the days to come and the end. He had, and kept to the last, a sense of living amid perils and on shifting soil. There must be no delay: he must profit by his omnipotence to attempt the work of construction.

But the greatest need felt by Frenchmen at that moment was for stability, and this continued to act in Bonaparte's favour and to push the throne towards him. The demand was for guarantees of the future. Napoleon's strength of character was well known, and alarmed infinitely fewer people than it encouraged. For those weeks when creation of the Empire was determined were the weeks during which the war with England took on a more serious form, when the conspiracy against the Consul and the Republic was brought into full daylight, when there was a renewed feeling that the Revolution was imperilled. The sequence is clear. On April 6th, three days after Curée, the Vincennes convert, proposed the creation of an Emperor to his colleagues in the Tribunat, Pichegru was found strangled in his prison-cell. If it was a suicide, it was a confession, and few people believed in the deliberate removal of the accused man, a political crime which would not be in the interests of the existing power. On April 18th, came the *senatus consultum*, conferring the Imperial status on Bonaparte, three days after the act of accusation against Georges, Moreau and their accomplices had been made public. All these things came together, explaining and precipitating one another. And meanwhile the English were becoming more enterprising; on May 5th, there was a serious naval engagement off Lorient. If England prevailed, the Revolution would be vanquished.

There was now an Emperor, his status ratified by plebiscite; there were dignitaries, marshals, a court and chamberlains, and a new dynasty, established by the nation 'to remove all hopes from the contemptible remains of the dynasty which it had overturned', as was said, in terms more or less imitated from these, by the countless addresses received by Bonaparte. And the Napoleonic monarchy had secured the approval of the masses, the safeguard of the hereditary principle, and legal status, when, on June 25th, Georges Cadoudal was executed on the Place de Grève, affirming under the shadow of the knife his lonely fidelity, and uttering a full-throated cry of 'Long live the King!'

Ten years later, less than ten years later, Louis XVIII would be there; and Napoleon, at Fontainebleau, would be almost as lonely as Georges on the Place de Grève. He could see what the *senatus consultum*, addresses, plebiscites, oaths were worth. 'Napoleon,' said Balzac, 'never entirely impressed the conviction of his sovereignty on those who had been his superiors or his equals, nor on those who stood for rights: nobody felt really bound by the oath taken to him.' He felt this. It was his anxiety at the peak of his glory. He regretted not having been able to rally a Cadoudal. He had heard the cheers of the Republican officers for Moreau. He was to hear them and think of them always, for his memory held on to everything.

Ten years; when it was hardly ten years since he began to emerge from obscurity; and a mere ten years before everything was ended. The headlong rhythm of his fortune willed it. A minor officer at twenty-five, he was Emperor at thirty-five. Time took him by the shoulder and pushed him. His days were counted out for him. They would flow past with dreamlike speed, so prodigiously crowded, broken by so few truces and breathing-spaces, in a sort of impatient frenzy to reach the catastrophe quickly, laden in the end with such a burthen of grandiose happenings that his reign, really so brief, seemed to have lasted a century.

On the throne, Napoleon was more at ease than if he had been born to it, because the very traditions which he revived were considered and intentional. In the first place, his monarchy was not, and could not be a military monarchy. In his palace he alone wore soldier's dress, as a reminder that he commanded all others, but he adopted a sober, half-civilian uniform, the green coat of the chasseurs of the guard. In the field, he wore the grey overcoat, its unique simplicity a clearer sign of the leader than plumes or gold braid. Swords, stripes and insignia were forbidden at court. The system of etiquette was not only designed to enhance the majesty of the sovereign. It subordinated his former commanders-in-arms, and made them courtiers, rather as Louis XIV had done with the last feudal lords; it effaced the dangerous memories of the old equalities and familiarities of camp and bivouac. It was against this, not against civil equality, that Napoleon set his face. He created marshals and appointed generals, and as the fountain-head of rank and rewards he controlled the military class by these, by hope and by fear, being sure of holding them only if they all depended on him, chamberlains in the palace, executants on the battlefield. The Legion of Honour had already been merging soldiers with civilians, and Napoleon pondered the foundation of a new Imperial nobility, starting from the same conception. Human vanity would be exploited. 'Men will let themselves be killed to become princes.' His old friends, Augereau and Masséna, were now to be the Duke of Castiglione and the Prince of Essling, as Fouché would be Duke of Otranto; Talleyrand the Prince of Benevente, and Maret, the clerk and secretary, Duke of Bassano. This noble status helped to demilitarize the great leaders, the men whom Napoleon had most reason to fear, merging them with diplomats and jurists in the ranks of the dignitaries. The conferring of titles was a reward and a stimulus; they were at once distinguishing marks and levellers.

All this took form in Bonaparte's mind through his dominant idea of laying a solid basis beneath his extra-ordinary adventure, of taking his stand upon the realities of society, upon the nature of mankind, upon the actual conditions of France as he found her emerging from the Revolution. He had risen abruptly from the common crowd, and he said at St. Helena: 'I felt my isolation. So I cast anchors of safety all round into deep water.' That remark is illuminating: it accounts for many things that seem to be mere vainglory. Thus, Bonaparte explained to Las Cases, that the thrones which he distributed amongst his brothers were likewise anchors cast to stabilize his immature dynasty. His brothers did not realize it, and at once conceived of themselves as 'kings by the grace of God'. And how many other calculations of the Emperor turned against him!

There is even something tragic in that unavowed anxiety of spirit. If the mind of a sovereign came to birth in him, it was not only by that capability of man to shape himself to the part he must play. He thought of the condition and the duties of a monarch, and of the flaws which a monarchy must not develop. He had seen the Bourbons fall, how unpopularity reached them, how their foes had made scandal their stalking-horse. He kept in his mind the affair of the Queen's diamond necklace. Josephine might still squander money with impunity, and the jewel-cabinet of Marie Antoinette might be too small for the wife of Napoleon. But might not the people murmur some day? The Imperial family must be honest, honourable, above suspicion — whence his stern attitude towards the ill-judged marriages of Lucien and Jerome. There must be no backsliding, only upward advance. And public malice must be given no fingerhold; the whole family must realize, like its head, that it will be harshly called back to its origins if it forgets them.

Nor was coronation the idea of a romantic megalomaniac. In reviving Charlemagne, Bonaparte doubtless sought to impress the imagination of the nations. But his real aim was the dropping of one more anchor in deep water. Perhaps he cherished the illusion that anointing would guarantee his power by giving it a sacred and legitimate character. Perhaps, too, he deliberately used that tool as he used all the others. If the moat of Vincennes had placed him beyond the suspicion of the purest of Revolutionaries, and carried them over the coronation, the coronation in its turn procured him absolution, washed his hands of d'Enghien's blood, and attached the Church and the Catholics to the Empire.

Not for always, nor even for long. In the confusions of his reign Bonaparte would undo what he had done, and would alienate Catholicism by maltreatment of the Supreme Pontiff. But at this moment he was conciliating everything, and everything succeeded. 'French Republic: Napoleon Emperor' — the words on the coinage were no hypocrisy. The Pope gave his blessing to the chosen man of the Revolution. The plebiscite had been a coronation under a different guise. Napoleon had on his side the voice of the people and the voice of God. And so who would listen to the voice of Louis XVIII protesting in Warsaw?

But the coronation was linked up in the wide sweep of his mind with another plan. The Holy Roman Empire would cease to exist, as willed by the Revolution, a desire which was covered by the old hatreds of France. That was not all. It was necessary that, by the hand of the Pope, Napoleon should become the real Emperor in the eyes of the world. All that then remained would be to drive back the old Empire, that of Germany, into its own Austria. And to Frenchmen that was 'well worth a Mass'. In September, when Pius VII had promised to come to Paris, the new Charlemagne proceeded to Aix-la-Chapelle, showed himself on the Rhine, and received the homage of the German princes, the electors and dukes and margraves, who all turned towards this star of the West.

And it was the new Charlemagne who summoned the Head of the Church to Paris, with an invitation so imperious, with such disguised threats, that it was like a command. 'The Holy Father was brought galloping from Rome,' said Cardinal Consalvi, 'like a chaplain summoned by his master to say Mass.'

It was no mean success for the founder of a fourth dynasty

to obtain the consecration which had been that of Pepin, founder of the second, and to hurl the Bourbon into the shade as the Merovingians had been hurled. Bonaparte's Childeric was not only Louis XVIII, but the Duc d'Enghien. In Catholic eyes, Pius VII came to whiten and pardon him. In the eyes of the others, the Pope absolved the murderer and condemned the third dynasty, bowing to the all-powerful, chosen head of the French.

But the Emperor was careful in handling the sentiments of Revolutionary France, those which we should call to day laic and anti-clerical. On Pius VII he inflicted petty humiliations. The Emperor met him out in the Forest of Fontainebleau, dressed and booted as if he had only come out on a hunting expedition, surrounded by a pack of dogs. The aide-de-camp who opened the carriage door, the first face seen by Pius VII, was Savary; and the man of Vincennes enjoyed making the white-haired old man walk in the mud, and arranging that he should sit on the left side of the carriage with the Emperor on the right. In the first escort given to the Pontiff pranced mameluke horsemen in turbans, with the intention of associating Mecca and Mahomet with Rome, in a sort of masquerade of religions calculated to please the philosophical group, the military would-be wits and the Institute.

There was more to come. The gentle kindliness of the Pope, and his paternal benediction in the Paris streets, silenced mockery. But there was one detail of which Napoleon omitted to inform Pius VII, although he can hardly have failed to recognize its importance. At Rome he was believed to have been married with religious rites. How should they suppose that he had himself dispensed with the rule he imposed on his sisters and his generals, and been content with a civil ceremony and Barras as witness? It is probable that he harboured the secret idea that he could be free to divorce, although the religious blessing was to concern him little enough when he wished his union to be dissolved.

More simply, he was perhaps annoyed at the idea of multiplying genuflections before altars, and, as he had obtained exemption from making solemn Communion before the coronation ceremony, he wished to avoid the ridicule of a blessing arriving for his marriage nine years late.

The idea of repudiating Josephine had crossed his mind before. His brothers had long urged him to get rid of her, using the strangest arguments, Joseph even saying to him: 'If she dies, you will be accused of poisoning her.' But it was not very long since they had ceased conjugal life, and he retained an affection for his wife. She remained his confidante and refuge. And when he saw the ambassadors pressing round her, and the authorities during his journeys at her feet as before a queen, he felt that there was no reason why he should not make her an Empress. He knew that she could not give him a child. But was he himself sure of begetting one? If he married another wife, worthy of his new rank, and still had no child, he would be laughed at.

These thoughts he hid from Josephine, though she guessed them in part. She herself was afraid of the Empire, of all this perilous grandeur. She was only partly reassured by her association with the coronation, as her husband willed. In the eyes of the Church she was merely a concubine: suppose that the coronation were not valid in her case? She then discovered scruples of religion and conscience. And to Pope Pius in person, under seal of the confessional, she revealed what was lacking in her marriage: it would turn the ceremony at Notre-Dame into a sacrilege. The trick was cleverly played; it was the last but the best of the stratagems she had employed with her little Bonaparte. The Pope let it be understood that he would refuse to crown Josephine at the same time as her husband if they did not regularize their position beforehand. Napoleon was furious, but could only yield. During the night preceding the coronation the belated pair were united, in great secrecy, at the Tuileries chapel, by Uncle Fesch, in the presence of Talleyrand and Berthier.

And now, duly married, crowned as well, enriched by two sacraments, she felt sure of the future.

On the eve of this fabulous event, they should not be pictured, either of them, as leaning over their past in meditation upon a destiny so far removed from the common lot of mortals. Great or small, the man who is suddenly successful does not linger over those backward glances. During the days preceding the ceremony Napoleon and Josephine were busy with their own affairs and interests, with the ceremonial and dresses, the rehearsal of the procession, the entry, the movements to be gone through, with all the spectacular side of the scene in Notre-Dame — studied on a plan with the aid of dolls dressed by Isabey — whilst up to the last moment, not counting the quarter of an hour reserved for the secret nocturnal marriage, the details of the great day had to be negotiated with the Legate.

There was one condition on which the Holy See insisted, but which Napoleon refused to accept at any price — that the crown should be placed upon his head by the hands of the Pope. Pius VII had come to Paris only after receiving the assurance that there would be no innovations in the traditional rite contrary to the honour and dignity of the Supreme Pontiff. Napoleon had promised everything, postponing a resolution of the difficulty on the spot. And he was an astonishing actor, moved as always by an artist's sense of glory. His gesture was 'at once imperious and calm', and so studied that it appeared spontaneous, inspired by a sort of inner genius — the genius of the Republic, perhaps. Forestalling the Pontiff, he grasped the crown to place it himself upon his head, with a gesture of such nobility and greatness that every eye-witness felt that it belonged to history.

It belonged positively to Napoleonic policy. Here again was seen the system of reconciliation of contraries on which the Consulate had rested, on which the new monarchy stood. The elect of the popular will became the elect of God, and summoned to himself the spiritual forces of Catholicism without denying those of the Revolution. Napoleon had the holy oil of anointment. It was a consecration whose importance he over-estimated, when one considers how the Catholic and apostolic Majesties, the faithful, the Church herself treated it less than ten years later; but for the moment it silenced those who declared that the usurper had not the benediction of heaven upon him. The Pope could only swallow the affront. On leaving Notre-Dame he let it be known that he would be obliged to protest, and to cite the promises he had been given, if the picking up of the crown were mentioned in the official account of the ceremony. A way out was found by publishing no account in the *Moniteur*. What did it matter to Napoleon? He had secured all the effects he had hoped from the coronation without compromising the other aspect of his sovereignty.

For the coronation oath was but one more oath of fidelity to the French Revolution. The Emperor swore on the Gospels to uphold equality, and even liberty, as also the property of those who had acquired the *biens nationaux*, and, above all else, 'the integrity of the territory of the Republic'. For that, to protect all these conquests, the Republic had delivered itself to one man, and entrusted him with the supreme power. And Napoleon would keep that oath because it was the essential reason of his monarchy.

On that day at Notre-Dame, December 2nd, 1804, in his state robes, sceptre in hand, already prepared for immortality, Napoleon made his human remark: 'Joseph! If our father saw us!' And what events had been required, during the twenty years since the death of their poor father, the tireless beggar of bursaries and pensions, for his sons to stand where they did! What chains of causes and effects, of well-matured scheming, of opportunities aptly seized! But the causes, like the ever-spinning Fates, were not to rest in their workings; with a movement no less rapid than imperious, they were to sweep away Napoleon, his crown, and his family.

CHAPTER XIV

AUSTERLITZ, BUT TRAFALGAR

Louis xviii had made his strong protest against the coronation of the usurper. And, from St. Petersburg, Joseph de Maistre had spoken of the 'hideous apostasy' of Pius VII. But the Pontiff was soon to recover himself. He had deceived himself about the benefits which the Church could expect from alliance with this new Charlemagne; and Napoleon had been no less deluded when he believed that he had become inviolable in his 'sacred person'. But at the moment, of what avail were protests, solemn or vehement? They were useless against Napoleon, no less so than, in time, he was to find his anointing, his entrance into the Olympus of kings. The essentials remained unaltered. For nothing would be gained so long as England did not accept the Empire, or all that the Empire represented and all that it was the Emperor's mission to preserve for France.

Ideas came to Napoleon one after another; he adapted and abandoned them with disconcerting rapidity. At one moment he was regarded as a knave, the next as a man drunk with power, as he struggled in an inextricable entanglement of which he was not the author. On the contrary, his task was to extricate France from it, by means of the unbounded credit allowed to him, and that endless, even absurd, supply of credit left him powerless to extricate even himself.

Why should he not be sincere, why should he not be deceived in the virtue of words and of the coronation a month since, when he adjured the sovereigns of Europe, his equals, and the King of England foremost, 'not to withhold from themselves the happiness of giving peace to the world'? He had already made that appeal to the Archduke Charles before Leoben. To George III he declared that his own conscience was touched by the vain spilling of so much blood. The fact was that then, as in 1797, peace was his most certain interest. War might make him indispensable to France, but he knew its risks. Peace would strengthen his throne even better than a coronation, and he was seeking every means of consolidation. If, after the failure of his move, he called France and Europe as witnesses of his self-denying moderation, that was the part he had to play. Nor did he invent that. Before him the Republic had believed itself moderate and the friend of peace, when she conquered Holland, annexed Belgium, invaded Switzerland, pushed to the left bank of the Rhine, and retained Lombardy as credit for bargaining with.

And was it less natural now that Napoleon should become King of Italy? The First Consul had received the crown of Charlemagne; the President of the Cisalpine Republic should therefore take the iron crown of the Lombard kings. The royal status was an act of homage to Italy freed from Austria, and a promise of Italian unity. Besides, Napoleon let it be known that it was not his fault that the two crowns were on two heads. That of Lombardy he had offered to his eldest brother. But Joseph, quick as usual to take offence, refused it because he thought it was a device to exclude him for ever from the Imperial succession. Louis also refused, and there were more family squabbles. It was comical — Napoleon was forced to a display of anger to make his brothers deign to seat themselves on thrones, that of France being the only one which they deemed worthy of themselves.

Eugène de Beauharnais, the model stepson, docile and filled with goodwill, was to be viceroy of this kingdom of Italy, a card-castle which would collapse with the rest when England had won the day. For England left unanswered the message of peace from the Emperor. The dice had been cast since the rupture of the Treaty of Amiens. Pitt was just then achieving a third coalition of powers, and for three months past had been negotiating a treaty with Russia, which was not only one of alliance. And here we must change our viewpoint and regard the Empire from outside. We leave Napoleon in Paris, on an unexampled pinnacle of triumph. But in London everything was being calculated and arranged against the moment of his downfall. Nine years ahead his defeat was being foreseen, the terms to be imposed on France were being established, and even the process of gradual adverse pressure whereby Napoleon would be forced to abdication was being mapped out beforehand, to such a point that in 1813 and 1814 it would only be a question of filling in the canvas.

The English plans for getting rid of Napoleon by murder had failed and were dropped. They were now turned to means of crushing him through warfare, directly and indirectly, and of forcing France herself to eliminate him.

To this end England was to work by first stating one principle, one quite small phrase which bore many fruits — that the Allies were waging war on Napoleon, not on France. Why? Through hatred of 'his Corsican Majesty'? To avenge the Duc d'Enghien? No more than the kings proposed to avenge Louis XVI in 1793. But it was manifest, if only by the coronation oath, that Napoleon could never sign a peace which abandoned the territorial conquests of the Republic. The Allies' aim was always to reduce France to her old boundaries, although this was no longer their ostensible programme. Revolutionary patriotism had been kindled by the Brunswick manifesto, threatening Paris with total overthrow. And that flame would be fanned by open threats against the maintenance of the Revolution's frontiers. The publicly-stated charge was against the 'excess' of the Republic's conquests, a vague and elastic term which seemed to be concerned only with the 'ambition' of the Emperor. It might be understood that the charge concerned Holland, Switzerland, and Piedmont and the later annexations, and not the Rhine or Belgium. But it was with these last that England was really concerned. The secret articles of April 11th, 1805, gave exact definition of the old frontiers ; but they were not mentioned immediately. Those requirements were to be kept for the end, after a series of loudly proclaimed offers, withdrawn, and always narrowed down when renewed, in proportion as France grew weaker and the fortunes of war inclined to her adversaries. And then, by proposing to Napoleon the very things which he could not accept, he would be made to appear as an enemy of the human race, he would be divorced from France, and the Allies would declare themselves ready to treat with France without him.

There lay the seeds of 1813 and 1814. Pitt's sagacity had foreseen and embraced these general lines of the future. But he was far from despising his opponent, and foresaw that it would be a long and exacting task, and that Napoleon, before he fell, would win many victories, knock out more than one of the Allies, and sign treaties of peace, perhaps of alliance, with them. That contingency must be nullified in advance. England was not sure of the others, but she was sure of herself. So she stipulated that a peace would be recognized only if it were unanimous, approved by all the members of the League — that is, with her own approval — when a congress had settled the prescriptions of international law, and set up in Europe a federal system to prevent the recurrence of war. A congress — that was Vienna in the distance. A feudal system — that would be the Holy Alliance to exile Napoleon and keep watch over him on St. Helena. Napoleon had to seize England by the throat and overcome her; anything else could only postpone the day of reckoning. He was lost.

If he had not realized that, he would not deserve his fame as an extraordinary man, and there would be a vast lacuna in his genius. And it is a poor tribute to his intelligence to suppose that the camp at Boulogne, the scheme for an invasion of England, the building of a whole fleet for transporting his army across Channel, were mere feints. Actually, it was Napoleon himself who, by prolonging his sojourn in Italy after the coronation in Milan, strove to delude the

English into a belief that his projects against them were a blind.

He might more justly be blamed for having, at that moment, conjured up enemies and having himself provoked the coalition by adding the Republic of Genoa to his Empire. But Genoa really mattered little to Russia, or even to Austria, to whom the question of Italy appeared as part of a different and wider whole. That, however, was the motive first advanced by Russia for her *volte-face*, when she accepted the English hold on Malta, and the reason put forward by Austria for joining the Anglo-Russian treaty and entering upon a war from which she hoped for her revenge and for the annulment of the Treaty of Lunéville. These two powers sheltered behind a pretext, and if Genoa had not offered it, they would certainly have found another. Diplomacy and Pitt's subsidies did the rest. For twelve years coalitions had followed each other to make France renounce her conquests. They were to go on and on.

Thus, far from Napoleon feigning an attack on England in order to surprise the Austrians and Russians, it was England who organized a diversion, through her extreme fear of invasion. If a crossing of the Channel at last succeeded and a French army landed, that would be the end of England as surely as on the day when William the Conqueror set foot on the island. It was a decisive game that was in play.

Decisive both to England and to Napoleon. His active correspondence, his elaborate schemings and conjectures, all bear witness to his being fully aware that his destiny was at stake. Far away in Italy he thought of it. Even in the festivities he thought of it, neglecting no information, preparing in detail the success of his maritime operation even as he prepared his wars on land. Every night before going to sleep he read his latest reports, to keep them constantly clear in his mind, just as in the field he always knew his exact position. All his intelligence and his care were now turned upon his sea squadrons, although he had here to reckon with the capricious element that upsets too many reckonings. He made his plan commensurate with the naval resources at his disposal, and if that was its weak point, it was at least not an unreasoned weakness.

He is sometimes blamed for here neglecting his essential principle of warfare — to destroy the principal strength of his enemy. One great naval victory would secure him a free passage over the Channel. The idea was too natural not to have occurred to him. But if his squadrons had been capable of beating the English, the problem was solved, and invasion of England would not be necessary to force her to yield. Napoleon was so conscious of the inferiority of his fleet that the dominating principle of his admirals was to sacrifice everything, provided that enough vessels remained to master the Channel, were it only for the space of one day. Everything rested on the schemes planned to allow passage for the splendid army of 132,000 men which was impatiently awaiting the moment for cutting the knotted coalitions in the heart of London, and 'avenging six centuries of insult and shame'.

Because the plan failed, it has been believed to be impossible, and therefore that Napoleon never seriously intended it. But there is ample proof that he applied his mind to it with passion. The book of fate was closed to him as to other men. He did not see himself in history as a shattered Titan, a Prometheus punished by the gods, a martyr hero. The glory that he desired was that of succeeding where his predecessors had failed. He was to be the man who, greater than Louis XIV, should dictate to the English the law of France, who should complete the national task, and be the first to win, over the ruins of Albion, the great hereditary contest. For he had no doubt but that, once having set foot on the oppposite shore, he would be another Julius Cæsar, another William the Conqueror. And indeed that was very probable. England had no soldiers to set up against invaders; and deprived of its bases, the English fleet would soon be disabled. Not even Nelson himself would have saved her.

After calling upon his admirals to assure him free passage for four days, then three, then two, Napoleon asked them for no more than twenty-four hours. Everything was calculated for the transportation of the army to Dover in two tides. In August 1805 the Emperor waited on the sands of Boulogne for his squadrons to carry out the diversion he had arranged. But men and elements combined to disappoint him. Never had Napoleon such complaints of being wrongly understood and badly served. Villeneuve had emerged from Toulon and slipped through Nelson's guard over the Mediterranean; he had rallied the Spanish vessels, which joined the French, for Spain and Holland at this moment were allied with France against England. The plan in brief was for the squadrons to meet in the West Indies and entice the English thither, and then to return at high speed to the Channel. But at Martinique Villeneuve did not find Admiral Missiessy, who had sailed again prematurely; and Ganteaume's squadron was becalmed and blockaded in Brest. Finding himself alone, Villeneuve sailed for Europe. None of the admirals had fulfilled his orders, and the original plan had to be abandoned. Thus remained the chance of giving battle, at any price, to enable Ganteaume to escape from Brest and penetrate the Channel with all available vessels. But despite imperious orders Villeneuve did not decide to head north and risk an engagement, and his timidity was to lose everything.

The clash between Napoleon and his lieutenants was to become habitual. He wanted them all to be like himself: the necessary effort should be made with the existing means. That was the meaning of his famous aphorism, that 'the word *impossible* is not French'. But his servants were like most men: they first considered their resources and measured possibilities accordingly. Villeneuve and the minister Decrès were skilled seamen, and saw every obstacle. It was with faulty vessels, ill-trained crews, and Spanish auxiliaries who had not even biscuits for their seamen, that Napoleon insisted on these vast operations. The contrast of the French navy disorganized by the Revolution and the fleet which had been that of Louis XVI overwhelmed Villeneuve, and the idea of measuring his strength with Nelson filled him with apprehensions that could not be set aside even by the fear of his master. In the end he let himself be encircled by Nelson, hurled himself against the English in despair, gave battle uselessly, and by losing it ruined the remnant of French naval strength.

We reach here the central point in the history of Napoleon. He had received the inheritance of the Revolution with all its burdens and hidden flaws. The task entrusted to this universal legatee was to bring about the capitulation of the world's greatest maritime power, and amongst the resources of France he found no navy. The sea had been, and always would be, fatal to Napoleon. Maddalena had been a foreshadowing of the Nile. The same causes worked to make invasion, as a means of disposing of England, a merely abortive project.

A new plan, a fresh combination of squadrons, allowed Napoleon some further hope before he resigned himself to striking camp at Boulogne. Nor did he do so altogether voluntarily. Grave news had been drawing his attention elsewhere. Soon he would no longer be at liberty to choose between land and sea. During a few crucial days, when he was master neither of events nor of the future, his fortune altered in aspect. He turned his eyes from London towards Vienna, Berlin, and St. Petersburg.

For the season was creeping on. For ten days Bonaparte had been chafing at Boulogne, where all was ready for the embarkation. Villeneuve, that Grouchy of the seas, did not appear. And meanwhile Austria, having entered the coalition, was threatening the frontier of the Empire. Russia made movements to join her. Over explanations, Austria quibbled. Napoleon began to see the need for facing up to this dangerous diversion, for meditating the plan which culminated at Ulm. If he did not reach London in a fortnight, he must be in Vienna 'before November'. His hope of reaching England had dwindled. But he had not quite abandoned it when, after days of waiting more cruel than bad news itself, word came that Villeneuve had entered the harbour of Ferrol, in Spain, and had not left it. The news brought on one of his most violent outbursts of passion. He was seen with 'a ferocious look', his hat rammed down on his eyes, his eyes like lightning: 'What a navy! What an admiral!' he cried. Then immediately the scene was shifted, and he became the man of realities and action, with the gift of driving away one thought at will, and putting another in its place. He dictated to Daru, as if spontaneously, the plan of campaign against Austria which he had been pondering. But he was still so uncertain of what decision to take that he held on to the supreme chance that Villeneuve might have only touched at Ferrol and might be heading north towards Brest. Napoleon did not know that 'the scoundrel Villeneuve', finding Ferrol unsafe, was already off Cadiz when, ten days later, having waited to the last possible moment, he began to turn his army towards the heart of Germany. His orders were given 'with that unmatched discernment of the relative urgency in the steps to be taken', and with a serene lucidity. He seemed to have had no hesitancy, to have foreseen and willed the very things he resolved upon. This is what still makes men doubt whether he seriously thought of crossing the Straits. It calls up the eagle glance, the swift inspiration of genius. Never was Napoleon so gladly followed by the rank and file, never was he so much their idol, as at that moment when he struck his sea camps, leaving England with a moral victory, the presage of another victory, and left her also freed thenceforth from a mortal anxiety. But Bonaparte's reason still told him that there would be no end so long as England was beyond striking reach. He did not abandon his great Channel project. He postponed it. He promised himself its renewal when Austrians and Russians were beaten. The root of the matter, he knew, did not lie in Vienna. 'When the Continent is pacified,' he said, 'I shall go back to the seas to work for maritime peace.' But he never went back.

We must now make a mental picture of both sides of this drama of shadow and light. The gleaming sun of Austerlitz still dazzles our eyes as it did contemporary eyes. And triumph on the plains of Europe overshadows the irremediable disaster on the Western seas. On September 30th, when Nelson was already cruising off Cadiz, the Grand Army received its title and achieved the crossing of the Rhine. From Strasbourg the Emperor proclaimed his promise to dissolve 'the new league woven by the hatred and gold of England', to bring 'unjust aggressors' to confusion, and to make no 'peace without safeguards'. Numbered in the series of wars that opened in 1792, this, the war of the coalition, was the third. Such was the circle in which men had revolved for twelve years past.

Once again Napoleon turned back towards the Revolution, as towards his mother, to gather strength. In that proclamation to the soldiers of the Grand Army, 'the vanguard of a great people', he stepped forward as the people's Emperor. Coronation, throne, etiquette, evocation of monarchy, would not stand unaided in times of storm. Bonaparte knew it, as he always knew it. He never left France without staking his power, as at Marengo. In 1805 as in 1800, he could feel the doubts and war-weariness of the public, and could hear that recurring question: 'What would happen if he were killed?' For his political fortune was born of the meeting within his person of two ideas — peace with order for the conservative feelings and interests and national greatness and conquests for the France of the Revolution. In reconciling these opposites he exhausted his strength.

When he set out for Germany there was a state of financial

embarrassment in the country. It was caused by the preparation of the naval expedition and of the new war, and was aggravated by the misdeeds of munition-makers and speculators. And it developed almost into a panic. Paris greeted him coldly. The strength which the principle of his own monarchy lacked, he could draw upon only at its source, and when he had now to ask a military effort from France and obtain a levy of 80,000 conscripts, Napoleon revived revolutionary passions, and spoke the revolutionary tongue. Before going to Strasbourg he promised 'to shatter the hateful House of Austria'. And even for his throne he paid homage to the nation: 'I sit upon it only by the nation's will. I am of the nation's making. It is for the nation to uphold it.' Nor was this rehash of the Republican style a mere matter of verbiage. A perceptible renewal of opposition had arisen. It was not only amongst the last friends of Moreau, nor in the Faubourg Saint-Germain; there were also nests of Chouan insurrection reported in the West and the South. Fortunately Fouché was there, restored to favour and once more Minister of Police, to smell out budding plots and shoot a few royalist agents; and at the same time he held such complicated threads that he contrived to pass for a man who might be useful to Louis XVIII, as if he were already preparing the ground with an eye to 1815, at once suspect and indispensable to the Emperor. Napoleon's dependence upon Fouché, at the very peak of his power and glory, was the confession of a secret frailty. And if the men who were reckoning with the risks of war and his possible downfall had seen, and known and understood everything!

The military annals of all the ages can show no more dazzling page than the campaign which resulted in the surrender of the foe in a fortnight. Napoleon's genius, as if inflamed by the failure of the English project, gave the impression of a strength more irresistible than that of arms — that of the spirit. There was little fighting, only what was needed for the safe execution of the plan, and also to repair the errors of the impetuous Murat. It was thus that Ney gained his title of Duke at Elchingen. By combinations of manœuvre, well-timed marches, the disposition of main forces, a complete mastery of the map on which hourly movements were precisely marked, Germany became a mere chess-board, and the French soldier was amazed at conquering 'with his legs'. General Mack had already disposed of Bavaria and was heading for the Rhine, alarming the German princes by this Austrian return offensive, when, at Ulm, he suddenly discovered that he was outflanked and surrounded, and could do nothing but yield.

Just when Mack was handing his sword to Napoleon, when the garrison of Ulm was casting down arms and flags before him, when the Emperor was proclaiming to his troops that without risking a great battle, and at small cost, he had ruined an Austrian army of 100,000 men — at that moment Nelson had blockaded the French and Spanish fleets in Cadiz, and Villeneuve, making up his mind too late, came out to give battle.

Villeneuve, perhaps, was the man who altered the history of Bonaparte, which is itself the standing proof of the personal action of individual men on the course of events. The failure of the Emperor's great project, and the consequent deviation of a war in which England was the chief enemy, were the fault of a sailor with a contradictory heart. Exact instructions, repeated orders, encouragement and congratulations had failed to achieve what reproaches and insults now did. But only disaster resulted. When the Emperor learned that Villeneuve had made for Cadiz instead of the Channel, he hurled cruel and furious insults at him. 'Villeneuve is a wretched creature,' he wrote to Decrès, 'to be expelled with ignominy . . . He would sacrifice everything to save his own skin.' His 'infamous conduct' had ruined everything. Villeneuve was not lacking in bravery, but in confidence, and refused to rest under the charge of cowardice. The order sent on September 14th from Saint-Cloud instructed him to use his squadron to make a 'powerful diversion' in the Mediterranean. He was to appear off Naples, which was an enemy ally, but, above all else, he was to keep the landlocked ocean from falling into English dominance. Villeneuve wasted a few days longer in hesitations. Was he now, under the worst conditions, to face the battle he had always dreaded? But his honour had to be cleansed. The luckless man rounded off his career by staking the fate of the French navy, in one day, in one despairing fling, against the English fleet under the command of its greatest captain.

Here then was the twofold picture: Napoleon at Ulm, in an almost bloodless triumph, with his Grand Army imbued with its sense of its invincibility; and, off Cape Trafalgar, a furious and disastrous battle in which foundered France's last hope of disputing England's mastery of the seas. Nelson was killed before he saw the completion of his victory. Villeneuve survived, was made prisoner, and soon afterwards was driven to suicide by despair. The French navy, with its Spanish auxiliaries, was annihilated, and did not rise again. Napoleon himself, after these costly and abortive trials of strength, lost interest in it; and indeed he had no time to reconstruct a fleet and the crews to man it. But he counted on the name of Austerlitz throwing that of Trafalgar into oblivion. He was even anxious to forget what he had known at Boulogne, that if it was impossible to impose the recognition of the natural frontiers upon England by invasion, it would be even more so to impose it when she remained undisputed queen of the seas. The French public turned its attention impatiently from projects of naval power, and did not really grasp the meaning of this disaster of Trafalgar; its mournful syllables took on meaning only after the knell of Waterloo. As for the Emperor, who wasted no time over regrets, he persuaded himself that wherever he did not command in person, the worst should be expected. And as he could not command at sea, his attention turned elsewhere, the more so as there was no visible change and he even seemed, as a conqueror on the Continent, to be more powerful than before Trafalgar. England, for her part, realized neither the extent nor the consequences of the maritime victory, which only became apparent as time went on. She was overjoyed at first at having escaped the dangers of invasion, but the blows dealt to her Continental allies left her in consternation. How hard it is for the greatest men to see a little way ahead! How veiled is the future to those who are in the centre of action! Why was Napoleon not mistaken here? Pitt was sick with grief when he learned of Ulm and Austerlitz; for him, they obliterated Trafalgar, whereas in actual fact Trafalgar was a decisive stroke which obliterated Ulm and Austerlitz, victories which had always to be started again.

Napoleon was advancing on Vienna when the news reached him. He seemed to show displeasure rather than anger or grief, and only asked that silence should fall over what had happened. Villeneuve himself was, as it were, dropped into oblivion, and that unspoken blame struck him so hard that there was nothing for him to do but vanish. But it is beyond question that the Emperor's calculations were modified by this turn of events. The failure of Boulogne and Trafalgar made him still more desirous of Continental alliances.

The swift campaign culminating in Ulm opened his way to Vienna; he had the satisfaction, which Frederick the Great never had, of entering the Austrian capital as a conqueror; and he lodged in the Imperial palace of Schönbrunn. But this war was not yet over. Austria still had troops, and Russia's were intact. Prussia, whose king was under the Tsar's influence, might join the coalition at any moment. Napoleon was too much a man of the eighteenth century not to admire Frederick the Great's Prussia, and not to follow the Revolution's quest for Prussian friendship. At Austria's expense he had heaped favours upon Prussia to bring her to recognize France's aggrandizements, and hoped to have attached her. But he hoped for more. If he could add the friendship of the Tsar Alexander to that of Frederick

William he could see his goal almost attained; England's naval victories would remain fruitless, and the bounds of the French empire would be left undisputed. Perhaps it was not fanciful to suppose that Trafalgar itself, by making Continental alliances still more essential to France, could even help to form them, and that Russia would come to dread an English mastery of the seas secured by Nelson's victory. That is why, before giving battle, Napoleon sought to negotiate with Alexander.

The time had not yet come when the two Emperors would embrace, and share the world between them. On the eve of Austerlitz Russia was asking the things which, in accord with her Allies, she would be imposing in 1814. The terms of peace brought by Dolgorouki were those of the Anglo-Russian pact, evacuation of Italy, restoration of the left bank of the Rhine, the relinquishing of Belgium and its union with Holland. 'What! Brussels too?' replied the Emperor. 'But we are in Moravia, and if you were on the heights of Montmartre you would not obtain Brussels!' The heights of Montmartre! A singular remark, not only because it foreshadowed a still distant event of the future, but because it revealed in Bonaparte what he concealed so well, and betrayed only in flashes and for very acute observers — his exact sense of a precarious situation, of walking on a tight-rope.

That sense accounts for many things otherwise obscure. The Emperor waited and hoped always for peace, and fought only to win peace. Every one of his great blows he believed would be the last. We now see Austerlitz in the crude colouring of a popular print, with the soldiers acclaiming 'the little corporal' as he passed among the bivouacs, improvising illuminations for the anniversary of the coronation on December 2nd, and then, in the morning, the great captain ringed by the rays of a winter sun which heralded one of his most splendid victories. In actual fact, Napoleon would have preferred that the Russians, seeing Austria beaten, should stop there. As they wished to fight, it had better be immediately;

AUTOGRAPHS OF NAPOLEON, 1785-1814

for time was against him, and he was still forty leagues from Vienna, a city which it would be difficult to hold if any check intervened, whilst the archdukes could still bring in reinforcements from Hungary, and Prussia was arming. By attacking too soon, the Russians rescued Napoleon from an awkward position. Furthermore, they were attacking him on a ground which he had carefully studied, so much so that, with the enemy's first moves, he was able to say: 'That army is mine.'

It was his fortieth battle, a battle of three Emperors, Alexander, Francis, and himself; and it was a dazzling triumph. The Russian Guard was annihilated, a hundred thousand men broken or dispersed within four hours. 'Those who escaped your steel were drowned in the lakes,' said the proclamation after the victory, with the famous phrase: 'Soldiers! I am well pleased with you!' And it ended with the apostrophe: 'It will be enough for you to say "I was at the battle of Austerlitz!" for the answer to come, "There is a hero!"'

The style was emphatic, calculated to appeal to middle-class and popular romanticism, to make a theme for the kind of pictures that hang over the mantelpiece; Napoleon had the secret of all that. Inwardly he applauded not so much his own sagacity and decision which had given him the victory, as the happy circumstance which had saved him from a grave peril. The third coalition was beaten. It must be dissolved. Immediate peace with Austria was essential, as with Prussia also. But peace with Russia even more. For Napoleon was continuing to seek the friendship of Alexander, and tried to charm him by the same chivalrous attentions which he had used with the Tsar Paul. He sent back the prisoners of the Russian Guard. To achieve influence over Alexander became one of his ambitions. If only Alexander would listen to his warnings against England and her snares! What great things they would do together! Two well-matched heroes could already unite, though far apart, in common mourning over the vain horrors of the battle-field. Napoleon must have known of the anguish with which Alexander, unable to bear the sight of the dead or the death-rattles of the dying, fled from the charnel-house where his army was rotting. So he resumed the humanitarian appeal, which he could handle as skilfully as he could the heroic: 'The heart bleeds! May all this spilled blood, all these woes, fall back at last upon the treacherous islanders who are their cause!' Since Trafalgar there was no longer any question of going to London to chastise 'the cowardly oligarchs'. It remained to unite Europe against them, if not voluntarily, then by force. Henceforward, Napoleon's fixed idea was the idea underlying Tilsit; peace, and the union of the Continent, through the Russian alliance, to make an end of England.

Talleyrand advised him to start with Austria. But he objected that an Austrian alliance did not accord with French sentiment, not yet dreaming of becoming the son-in-law of the Cæsar of the Germanies. But to some extent he showed mercy to Austria. He did not linger over the satisfaction of having received at his bivouc, two days after Austerlitz, a Hapsburg reduced to craving peace from the Corsican up-start. That peace, to be signed at Presburg, he granted, without destroying the old monarchy. To annihilate Austria would mean the continuance of a war whose main goal lay elsewhere. But to take nothing from her would be to leave her too powerful; and there were some things which Napoleon had to take from her. She must totally renounce Italy, through which she had so long dominated Europe and threatened France. She must also abandon the other shore of the Adriatic: he must hold the coasts of Europe to close them against England. The crossing of the Channel was now but a memory, and the other system, that of the Continental blockade, was being sketched. Austria had also to accept a wide reshaping of Germany, with the abolition of the Holy Roman Empire, from which she derived her prestige. She had also to promise — and the demand had an ingenuous air about it — not to form alliances with enemies of France.

To pledge herself to these terms, Austria could be no more sincere than after Campo Formio and Lunéville: too much was taken from her to be tolerable, and too little to leave her powerless. Austerlitz was a victory which settled nothing, any more than the others had done.

But now the new system of warfare against England took shape and substance. It was not only armies that Napoleon set marching 'with the swiftness of thought', but diplomats, chancellories, dynasties. In seven weeks he altered the face of Europe with an abundance of negotiations, orders, agreements, writings which it would take pages to summarize, a volume to recount in detail. The happy days of the Consulate, those almost restful days, were over. The reign was now to rush forward like a torrent, in unceasing turmoil.

But everything was linked to one central idea. Napoleon found that although the Russian alliance was not yet ripe, it was not an impossibility. He counted on it developing in two or three years; and, to avoid offending the pride of the Tsar, he allowed the remnants of the vanquished army to leave Austria unmolested. The generals could not understand why the victory was not more fully exploited. 'It's asking them to be in Paris in six years' time,' grumbled Vandamme. But really it was Paris on which Napoleon was keeping an eye; things were none too cheerful there, and he was eager to return. And besides, he had to make sure of Prussia too. If Austerlitz had turned out wrongly, the Prussians would have stepped in and cut off the French retreat. And, with that danger in mind, Napoleon strove to obtain the alliance of Prussia by threats and promises. Prussia would be given Hanover, the domain of the English king, provided that she closed her ports to the English. That was the essential condition, for already the Continental blockade, though as yet unnamed, was taking shape. Prussia yielded, but through fear. The Hohenzollern was no more sure than the Hapsburg, and hastened to annul his treaty with Napoleon by a counter-letter to Alexander.

Napoleon was suspicious and distrustful. No matter. Things must move quickly, and a Germany must be built up which would not threaten the Empire of the West, but protect and extend it. He improvised a rearrangement of the Germanic states, a Confederation of the Rhine corresponding to the old monarchy's League of the Rhine, kingdoms and principalities that matched the Revolution's improvised subsidiary republics. He made the Elector of Bavaria a king, and obliged him to give his daughter's hand to Eugène de Beauharnais, while the Prince of Baden, betrothed to that princess, was ordered to marry Eugène's cousin, Stephanie. It was matrimonial and dynastic politics. Murat, his brother-in-law, was to be Grand Duke of Berg and Cleves; Jerome, forcibly parted from his American wife, was allotted Catherine of Württemburg, and her father also was made king. The Napoleonic Empire was swarming as the Republic had swarmed. The Republic, in the train of its generals, had exported representatives of the people and of its principles. The Emperor, head of the dynasty sprung from the Revolution, and the consecration of the Revolution, sent forth his brothers and brothers-in-law, his stepson and step-daughter, together with his Code and administrations. But this was not in order to find food and lodging for his tribe. Far from it. The family was there to serve. The Emperor brooked no opposition, and did not consult their feelings. Joseph was set up to reign in Naples, and Louis in Holland — both by order.

And on January 26th, 1806, he was back at the Tuileries, four months after his departure. One hundred and twenty days, during which he had kneaded Europe without bringing the hour of final peace one minute nearer.

He had been in a hurry to undo the coalition. And now he was in a hurry to be back in Paris and pick up the reins of government, suspicious always of the intrigues of some, the incapacities of others, knowing that in his forced absences things went to pieces, and that his death was constantly reckoned upon. He returned victorious once more. But he would have no triumphal entry, for he knew that even Austerlitz had availed nothing. He turned immediately to serious affairs, to the threatened financial disaster and bankruptcy of the Bank of France. Barbé-Marbois, the Minister of the Treasury responsible for these shortcomings, came humbly to 'offer his head' to the lord and master. 'What on earth could I do with it, you great fool?' answered the Emperor.

There was a strange mixture of the heroic and the everyday in this, of calculated solemnity and the natural, which so greatly enhanced his legend and his popularity. Here, the Minister trembled before him as before an Asiatic despot, and the victor of Austerlitz replied with a retort fit for a farce; and here, on the day when the Batavian deputation came to offer Louis the throne of Holland, he followed the ceremonial of the Spanish Succession, that of Louis XIV for the Duc d'Anjou. The new sovereign was proclaimed at court, with all the doors of the palace open. But the serious aspect was elsewhere. Holland was not a conquest of Bonaparte's. It had come to him from the Republic, and had to be a 'customs post' against England, just as Joseph's new Kingdom of Naples was to be an 'advanced' Mediterranean post against England. The distribution of crowns to the family came from a system and from urgencies which were continually multiplying themselves. But on the day after the ceremony, in front of the new queen, Napoleon had the fable of 'the Frogs who Would Have a King' recited to the little son of Hortense and Louis. 'What do you say to that, Hortense?'

It was as if there were within him two men, one of whom occasionally, in rare moments of relaxation, found amusement in watching the other.

CHAPTER XV

THE SWORD OF FREDERICK

SEEING that Napoleon had struck camp at Boulogne to reply to the Austro-Russian diversion, it would have been natural that he should return to Boulogne when Austria and Russia had been knocked out. But Trafalgar was more than a passing reverse. The destruction of France's main naval force made the Channel an insurmountable obstacle. On February 6th, 1806, came a vague announcement: 'The Emperor is about to turn his attention to his navy and flotilla, and take all steps for the compulsion of England if she does not make peace.' But nothing followed. Napoleon had never time to resuscitate his navy after the blow of Trafalgar. France still awaited that peace which she thought had been obtained by Austerlitz, as she had thought also by Marengo; but how could England's hand be forced? Her island was more inaccessible than ever now that she ruled the seas undisputed. But there was one hope on the horizon.

On Napoleon's return to Paris he learned the glad news of the death of Pitt. The greatest enemy of France had vanished. William Pitt and Frederick of Saxe-Coburg — how long had the patriots of the Republic linked those two names in one hatred, the personification of opposition to the whole course of the Revolution! The second was beaten, laid low with the House of Austria. With Pitt in his grave, the voice of Liberal England, the good England of Fox, could be raised. Frenchmen had sworn never again to submit to 'tyranny', but had handed themselves over to one man to find a victorious release from war; they did not doubt that English policy likewise depended on one man.

It is strange that Napoleon shared this vulgar delusion. He always believed in peace with the English; he wished to make a new Treaty of Amiens with Fox. But Charles James Fox, whom Frenchmen misinterpreted because he had been the opponent of Pitt, was, for all his different stock of phrases, an aristocrat, an Englishman attached to the permanent interests of his country. In these negotiations there would be talk about everything, except the essential.

And Napoleon was not slow to realize that the essential had not changed. The long and pompous statement of March 5th rightly said that the aim of the third coalition was still to deprive France of the Scheldt estuary and the strongholds of the Meuse. 'England has scant interest in Italy: Belgium is the true source of the hatred she bears us.' Not once was the question of Belgium raised between Lord Yarmouth and Talleyrand. But while Napoleon still tried to soothe his anxieties with hope of a new Peace of Amiens, Fox strove only to prove that with Napoleon there could be no possibility of a real peace, and so to cast on him the odium of a war whose end would either be the annihilation of British power, or the withdrawal of France from her conquered territories. Pitt, the indomitable, had died heartbroken by Austerlitz, bewailing the plight in which he left his country. Fox, the humanitarian, took up the torch.

But the Emperor was for resuming where the rupture of the Treaty of Amiens had left matters. As Malta had been the cause of the break, he would abandon Malta to England. As if it were a question of that island! And whilst negotiating with Lord Yarmouth, Talleyrand also treated with the envoy of Alexander. Agreement with England would force Russia to negotiate, and this would be reciprocal. True, Hanover had been promised to Prussia to keep her out of the third coalition, and must be restored to the British crown. No matter. Prussia could be otherwise indemnified. There was plenty of room in Germany. On the other hand, Prussia was insistent on holding Hanover. She had nibbled the bait. Why, then, if peace with England and Russia failed, the Hanoverian spoils would ensure the fidelity of Prussia to the French alliance. Besides, Prussia remained the prime favourite of the Napoleonic Empire, as she had been of the Revolution; and was not the Minister of Foreign Affairs the same man who had held the portfolio under the Directory? Was not Talleyrand a pledge of tradition and continuity in this? With the sincerity of a systematic policy, the Brandenburg family were promised the succession of the House of Austria, as well as pre-eminence in a confederation of Northern Germany, and the transference of the Imperial crown from the Hapsburgs to the Hohenzollerns.

These threefold negotiations, so pitiful in their outcome, occupied only two or three months of the year 1806. After the stunning and unexpected successes of Ulm and Austerlitz, which left Central Europe at his discretion, Napoleon regarded his proffered terms of peace as very moderate. He had widened the girdles of France, which included now 110 Departments, to protect the conquests he had inherited from the Revolution and was sworn to defend. It seemed to him natural to treat on this basis of the war-map, the more so as the English and Russians affected to be bargaining over Dalmatia and Sicily just as if nothing else between Amsterdam and Naples were now in question. Napoleon did not see the trap set for him, which consisted in casting the wrong upon his side, in emphasizing his pretentions, in denouncing his ambition as a world-wide danger. Whilst England pretended to be talking and examining every hypothesis, she was secretly preparing a fourth coalition. And then the event which nobody had reckoned upon happened: Prussia went to war, alone. And her act of aggression disguised the mortifying failure of Talleyrand and his master and their joint diplomacy; and it brought back Napoleon to activity as a war leader, opening before him new illusions with new victories.

In all these dealings he had been mystified, from first to last, and he had reason to be disgusted with the finesse of Talleyrand and the subtleties of the diplomatic craft. Agreement with Russia had been reached, but not ratified. But the publication of the terms was far from bringing the English to negotiate in their turn. They were outraged, and the Russian ambassador in London was intimidated into inducing Alexander to withhold his signature. At the same time, Fox sent another plenipotentiary to Paris, and Lauderdale made the responsibility for a rupture fall upon the demands of Napoleon. Yarmouth had already revealed to the Prussian minister in Paris that the restoration of Hanover would be the price of peace with England. And this was the pretext seized by the anti-French party in Berlin to force Frederick William out of his hesitations and his policy of timorous wavering between Russia and France.

By the autumn of 1806, then, the peace with England and Russia had failed. Ere long the fourth coalition would be rising up, possibly even with Austria herself. If the three Continental powers marched in unison and concerted their action, France would be placed in a painful position, and would at the very least be forced to remain on the defensive until the tide ebbed again. Doubtless Napoleon was a great captain. Doubtless he had dictatorial control over the resources of a nation which had held Europe at bay whilst still convulsed by anarchy. But it was also true that Bonaparte had never had to fight all his foes at once. At Austerlitz the Austrian addition to Russia's weight was a small matter after Mack's disaster at Ulm. And here once more, through the premature aggression of Prussia, it was Napoleon's fortune to find the enemy dispersing themselves to receive his blows.

And when? Just when he himself was beginning to feel that the burden was heavy. The Empire's situation after Presburg was no easy one. To maintain itself on a line running from Holland to the Straits of Messina and the Gulf of Cattaro, passing through the German Confederation, called for mighty efforts which, even prolonged, would have been fruitless. Stretching from Friesland to Calabria, the French

Empire formed one vast sea-wall against England. That was the reason for its existence. But with all its outposts and extensions, its protectorates and feudatories, the great French Empire was not yet vast enough, and Europe was not closed enough, to make England surrender. She could still trade. And every moment brought fresh problems in the links that held the Empire together.

The cold violence with which Napoleon undertook to solve them was revelatory. It showed fury against obstacles which he failed to surmount. His mind, for all its lucidity, grew vexed as it strove to find a way out, where none existed, from a situation which, by its very nature, must be of increasing complexity. And forthwith, at the moment of Prussia's attack, came an instance.

The kingdom of Naples, a supply base for English vessels, had been transferred from the Bourbon rulers to Napoleon's brother Joseph. And now Joseph was claiming money and assistance. The burdens of empire were endlessly piling up. But between that kingdom and the kingdom of Italy, where Eugène was viceroy, lay the Papal States, which not only made communication between north and south uncertain, but also left a breach open to English commerce. Napoleon insisted that the Holy See should break with all the enemies of France, recognize Joseph as King of Naples, and pay no heed to the Neapolitan cardinals who had remained loyal to the Bourbons. Pius VII replied that the interests of Catholicism forbade this. The dispute grew embittered. Napoleon, already in occupation of Ancona, threatened the occupation of Rome; and there came into being a conflict with the Roman Church, which clashed with his policy within France, where he fostered the revival of religious feeling, made use of the clergy, and showed increasing favour towards the bishops of the old regime. It was the year of the abolition of the Republican calendar, when the feast of Saint Napoleon was instituted on August 15th (a certain Neapolis or Neapolas was ultimately discovered, a martyr under Diocletian, to be the new saint). It was also the year in which Jerome Lalande, the atheist astronomer, was forbidden to publish his works, and when, on the other hand, there appeared the Imperial catechism, which emphasized the duties of the Christian towards 'Napoleon I, our Emperor', to whom both taxes and military service were due in the name of the Deity. And these details go to show how the very things that had made Bonaparte's success, as the conciliator of the old with the new France, were now showing signs of becoming spoilt. Concessions to the Church at home, conflict with her abroad, would mean in the long run an untenable position. The entirely political intelligence of Napoleon was surprised when confronted by this unforeseen obstacle, the conscience of Pius VII, which soon was to serve as an encouragement, an example, a war-cry, for the Catholic peoples raised against him by the force of events that were to prove beyond his strength.

And the declaration of war by Prussia, supervening on these happenings, was already a rebound beyond the control of his will. He strove to the last moment to prevent the rupture of the Prussian alliance, which he clearly regarded as essential to his system. On September 12th he was writing of war with Prussia as a 'sacrilege' and 'a disaster'. Prussia addressed an ultimatum to him calling for the evacuation of Germany by October 8th, which amounted to the cancellation of Austerlitz and the terms of Presburg. His reply was the only possible one — a thunderbolt attack: for behind Prussia there stood Russia. Before the tomb of Frederick the Great at Potsdam, the Tsar had sworn fidelity to the Hohenzollern and to the fair Queen Louisa, whose *cavaliere servente* he was. The Prussians must be beaten before the Tsar could come into line. And the reply to the Prussian aggression was also that bulletin of the Grand Army, one of the most astonishing copies of that literature for soldiers' use, with dramatic effects, a dialogue setting Napoleon on the stage. 'Marshal,' says the Emperor to Marshal Berthier, 'We are given a rendezvous of honour for the 8th. A Frenchman has never failed in one. But as they say there is a beautiful queen who would witness the combat, let us be courteous, and march without resting by night for Saxony.' Then the romantic apostrophe to the Queen of Prussia: 'One seems to be viewing Armida in her frenzy setting fire to her own palace.'

But Napoleon was anxious and thoughtful. How could he replace the alliances with Prussia and the Tsar which were escaping him? From Wurzburg he informed La Rochefoucauld, his ambassador in Vienna, that he still hoped that war could be avoided. But in Prussia, the 'versatile and contemptible', he no longer believed. Yet 'the necessity of turning my efforts from naval directions makes an alliance on the Continent essential'. Why not seek that in Vienna? 'The navy flourished in France in past times by reason of the benefits of the Austrian alliance.' The ambassador should try. The scheme had no outcome for the moment. But here was a symptom of the uncertainty in Napoleon's mind. He no longer thought of the Austrian alliance as not according with the wishes of his people. He was plunging into Germany, farther perhaps, to put his shoulder to that eternal rock of Sisyphus — with a backward glance at Trafalgar, the navy, the Boulogne camp, all the failures! But action called him, necessity mastered him. Regrets were finished with. And there must be no wavering. The operations of war are precise and clearly bounded, as political schemings are not. Napoleon was not in the flower of his years and of his military genius. The campaign imposed on him by Prussia was, as it were, a relief to his spirit.

But great news came. Since Trafalgar, Spain had been turning away from the French alliance. Her all-powerful minister Godoy was doubtful whether an ally without a navy could help Spain to retain her vast colonies. He lent an ear to the English and prepared for betrayal. Thus, if he lost one battle in this renewal of the war, Napoleon might well have the whole of Europe against him. He had no more security in Madrid than elsewhere. And the dangerous seeds of the Spanish affair began to take root.

But neither Spain nor Austria moved, because his victories were even more overwhelming than in the previous year. Prussia collapsed under his blows within a fortnight. In the first clash, at Saalfeld, Prince Louis Ferdinand, one of the instigators of war, was killed. On October 14th the Prussians were annihilated at Jena, and simultaneously another of their armies was shattered by Davout at Auerstadt, a victory not without its uses for the Emperor. The Queen, 'Armida' herself, was very nearly captured, and the Duke of Brunswick gravely wounded.

Brunswick was the man of the famous manifesto of 1792, who threatened to leave no stone of Paris standing. Memories of Valmy were aroused, and a duchy was given to the aged Kellermann. A duchy and Valmy — once again Napoleon was successfully wedding memories of the Revolution and of the old regime. 'The battle of Jena has wiped out the affront of Rosbach,' said the army bulletin; and the Emperor, as he passed, razed the monument erected on the site of the Prussian victory over Soubise. The effect was calculated to impress Paris, where every new war brought the same murmurings, and where confidence and national spirit had always to be kept alive. We tend to look back upon the Emperor as a hero whom no man questioned. But there were still men, and soldiers too, in whose eyes Napoleon had done nothing until he vanquished the Prussian army and its lingering reputation. There were still opponents who came forward when his back was turned and when the empire was staked on the battle-fields. Fresh Chouan risings occurred in the west, even in Normandy, and caused apprehensions to Fouché and his police, the real 'regent of the Empire'. To blend the names of Valmy triumphant and Rosbach avenged with the new name of Jena was in no way superfluous. France needed such tonics. Fouché's reports again insisted, as after Austerlitz, on the growing desire for peace in the country. 'It is clear,' he wrote, 'that the Emperor is approved by every class in proportion as his sword is the further thrust within its sheath.' Vain counsels. Napoleon was justified in his impatience of them. Peace? He was still pursuing peace, further and further. After Jena it slipped away again.

Rarely had a more dazzling victory been so much at the mercy of uncertainties. Five days after Jena the French were on the Elbe, and the routed enemy were chased to the gates of Magdeburg. If Napoleon refused a premature armistice, which would only give the Russians time to advance, he still did not despair of splitting the alliance of Berlin and St. Petersburg; and from his camp at Halle he wrote to Frederick William emphasizing that he would view with satisfaction 'means of re-establishing, if it be possible, the former confidence that existed between us'. But when Napoleon was sure that the Prussian army 'had existed', and that his own military position was fairly safe, and so granted an armistice, Frederick William showed by his refusal to ratify it that he still counted on the arrival of the Russians.

Ten days after Jena, the Emperor was at Potsdam, in Frederick the Great's palace of Sans-Souci. It was one of Bonaparte's most glorious hours: to a man of the eighteenth century the King of Prussia, soldier, legislator, philosopher, had seemed the perfect hero. But in the imagination of the peoples, it was he who should take the place of that Frederick whose sword was his most glorious trophy, whose alarum clock he would take to St. Helena. He sent that famed and symbolic sword to the Invalides. At Potsdam he was at home as he had been at Schönbrunn, and he made his entry into Berlin, the second capital in which he appeared as conqueror. He took possession of all the Prussian states lying between the Rhine and Elbe. He 'had only to whistle', as Heine remarked, and Prussia, like her army, would have ceased to exist. The King and Queen Louisa had retired to Königsberg. And what next?

Here there is a special significance in the chronology and

itinerary. Having left Saint-Cloud on September 25th, 1806, Napoleon returned there only on July 27th, 1807. Out of his ten-year reign, ten months had been spent in Berlin, Poland, East Prussia, often in cottages and barns, snow and mud. What was he doing there? He was seeking and waiting for what he would go to seek in Moscow, what he would await there with an obstinacy that at last proved fatal, but an obstinacy that is explained by the memory of the success of Tilsit. These ten months were used up on the realization of the great task where Talleyrand's diplomacy had failed: the task of bringing about the capitulation of England, the union of the Continent against England, through peace and reconciliation with Russia.

Fox died in the middle of September. The leaders of English politics were men of smaller fame. Power descended to the followers of Canning and Castlereagh, who were to go through with the contest with bureaucratic method and obstinacy, phlegmatically accepting reverses, unwearying in their repetition of the same moves, those of a great business firm the more determined to smash its rival as the more capital was staked, men from which it would be as vain to expect a sign of sensibility as from a syndicate or a trust. During the ephemeral agreement between Napoleon and Frederick William, England had declared war, not because of Hanover, but the treaty of alliance closed the Prussian ports to English ships. That was the sensitive spot. As master of Prussia, Napoleon was able to close one more door into Europe against England. To strike 'Carthage' in the vital spot of her commerce had been the preoccupation of Revolutionary France, as we have seen, for years past. With all his power, Napoleon had found no better weapon against the rulers of the sea than the Convention or the Directory had found. And now, with the war-map favouring him, he enlarged the conception of economic reprisals to that of the Continental blockade.

Reprisals is the exact term, because England, on her side,

had already declared a blockade against France and her vassal states. A paper blockade – which raises an immemorial controversy that rises to the pitch of exasperation. The English claimed to blockade, by decree, the ports and coasts which were not patrolled by their naval forces, and thereby arrogated the right of forbidding even neutrals to trade with their enemies. Napoleon turned the tables. By a decree dated from Berlin he forbade any commerce with England to France, to countries dependent on or allied with France, and to the occupied territories, and proclaimed rigorous penalties against all who might defy the prohibition.

This formidable counter-stroke was dictated not only by Napoleon's logical imagination, but by sheer necessity. The Berlin decree of November 21st, 1806, was the act of a man confined to the land and struggling to force the encirclement of the waves. On reflection, it is not clear what else he could have attempted. No doubt, as events showed, the pressure of the Continental blockade was not irresistible. But it was the only thing to be done, short of immediate surrender to what came in 1814, a restoration of the old frontiers and, to that end, the return of the Bourbons. He explained to his brother Louis that the problem was 'to hold the seas by land power'. But it was an impossible, a chimerical, quest. An experiment, however. Certainly Napoleon was under no illusions as to the condition of success being a Europe united and dominated by his alliances. Possibly he did not see clearly enough that success would call for an unbounded effort. At any rate, he did not disguise from anyone the fact that it would be a gigantic task to conquer the rulers of the sea on land. Immediately after the Berlin decree he called up the 1807 class conscripts, and expounded the motive of his levy. 'I have not lost men,' he said, and said truly: 'but the project to which I have put my hand is the most far-reaching I have conceived, and I must henceforth be in a position to answer every turn of events.'

And it is likewise true that all his thoughts now hinged on

the Continental blockade, that is to say the blockade of England, which would become the proclaimed and fundamental principle of the Empire. The day would soon come when the Emperor no longer controlled the system, when he became its prisoner, as of a machine which he could no longer steer and which steered him instead. But at the moment, the task, as Napoleon saw it from Berlin in November 1806, was straightforward, if not easy. Prussia was in his hands. But the king was obstinate. Threatened in Königsberg, he fled to Memel, still nearer to Alexander, on whose victory he wished to count. Nor was Alexander in a mood of surrender; he burned to avenge Austerlitz. Then Napoleon's thoughts took another turn. When the Tsar had lost this fresh prospective war, which he had declared, he would realize at last the uselessness of the struggle. He would fall in with the desires of an adversary who only wanted him as an ally. The Russian alliance would bring the Prussian alliance, and the Continental blockade would cease to be a paper one. Europe would be entirely federated against the 'tyrants of the sea' and really barred to them; the final surrender of England would only be a question of time. Even naval operations could be resumed. This plan was well set forth by Napoleon to his brother Louis. At the moment it would be 'folly to try to persevere with the maritime struggle'. But not so in four or five years, because the combined powers could then unite numerous squadrons, if, as there was reason to think, an interval of peace could be enjoyed.

The question then was how to combine the powers, how to league Europe against England. It was a European federation that he sought when he took up arms against Russia, who was attacking again, forgetful of the generosity of the victor of Austerlitz. The twenty-ninth bulletin announced to the Grand Army that Russia was marching against them, and added: 'This war must be the last.' That is what the peoples and soldiers are always told, what

Napoleon had so often announced. This time he prided himself that he was speaking the truth. For alongside of a scrupulous preparation for more distant battlefields, he was elaborating a whole political system with equal solicitude.

Prussia was under his heel, but he handled her with care. He was at pains not to exasperate the people, and to keep in touch with the dynasty. After his spectacular pardoning of the Prince von Hatzfeld, about to be shot, he hastened to write to the Princess Ferdinand of Prussia a letter whose thinly veiled meaning was: 'You see that I am not an ogre. So please let your relatives know that I am ready to reach an understanding with them!' But there were moments of sternness, certainly, for this was war, and war has its necessities. The Prussian aggression had its accomplices, and some were not to be pardoned. The Elector of Hesse-Cassel, 'English rather than Prussian', was dispossessed on the humanitarian ground that he was selling his subjects abroad to be made into soldiers. His states went to the kingdom of Westphalia, which was to round off the Germanic system of the Emperor, and was destined for Jerome, his youngest brother. The Elector of Saxony also had followed Prussia. But Napoleon pardoned him, and even made him a king, like his colleagues in Bavaria and Württemberg, adding him to the clientele of the Empire, in which this Saxon, if not his subjects, was to be distinguished by his loyalty.

Thus Napoleon applied himself to leaving a few bridges both behind and in front of himself. Forced to fight against Russia, he wished to foster the means of a reconciliation with the Tsar. Herein Napoleon was more of a politician than a soldier. To discern in him the Italian, the Machiavelli, it is here we must look. He pushed subtlety, skill and calculation to the point of duplicity.

Marching forward to meet the Russians before they came near, he moved from the Elbe to the Vistula, and soon to the Niemen. He reached Posen, then Warsaw. He was in Poland. But now he was neither invader nor conqueror, but liberator. To revive the independence of Poland would be easy, as much within Napoleon's power as the annihilation of Prussia. When the Poles saw him in their midst, surrounding him, admiring him, touching him with their fingers, they beheld France — France, of whom in their days of distress they said it was too far off, as God was too high up — and imagined that the hour of reparation had come, that the iniquity of which they had been the victims would be only a brief, but sombre, chapter in their history. And Napoleon was alive to their patriotism, their chivalry, their enthusiasm. Alive also to the beauty of their women: for Madame Walewska was to be, if not the great love (he was too busy), at least the inclination of his maturity. And the loving and faithful Walewska was to give him more than fondness. He had doubted his capacity for fatherhood. A few months earlier a chance fancy for a reader employed by his sister Caroline had reassured him. And the fair Pole was also to give him a son. There awoke within him the sense of paternity, of natural heredity, the desire to be continued in his own flesh. And when? Just when the child of Louis and Hortense, in which he liked to see his successor, was carried off by croup. The death of that child, and the births of these others, meant the condemnation of Josephine. His mind welcomed what it had formerly rejected— the idea of divorce. The anticipated and glorious peace would be completed by a marriage uniting him with one of the Imperial Houses; and it was of the Russian that he thought, just when he was engaging the Russian armies, because his ruling idea was to secure the indispensable alliance with Alexander. If he in his turn married a princess, he would tighten the bonds of Europe, and make federation stronger by mingling himself with its monarchies and kingly families.

But what counted Poland, or Maria Walewska herself, beside these schemings? He needed the Poles. But not even for love of Maria would he create anything that would compromise his policy. He has been blamed for not having undone the work of partition in Poland, for having been content with a shadow of reparation and national independence, for having failed to prepare for himself the support of a great Poland, against the day when the peoples would rise against him. But his view was less distant and more immediately practical. To uphold the Polish cause would make peace impossible with the partitioning powers, Russia, Prussia, and Austria. It would even make them hostile. In Napoleon's mind Poland was already sacrificed to his great Continental scheme, and he allowed them to indulge in hopes of independence without making any firm promises, wrapping his words round with a prudent 'perhaps'. Murat, anxious to exchange his grand-duchy of Berg for the crown of Poland, openly offered his candidature. The Emperor rebuffed him. But the serious thing was that, at the same time, Napoleon informed Austria, on whose neutrality he pinned high hopes, that whatever happened he would guarantee Vienna her share of the Polish spoils — Galicia.

Napoleon made use of Poland. He had no mind to help her. His duplicity was dictated by vital interests. He saw clearly that his position was much less brilliant than it seemed. His inborn genius as a leader of men is to be seen not only in that energy by which, four hundred leagues from his capital, he kept everyone holding his breath; busied with everything, supervising everything, foreseeing everything, dictating ten or twenty letters a day — and what letters! — on the most diverse subjects. Nor is it only in his clear vision of things as a whole and things in detail, the operations proceeding for the total occupation of Prussia, the administration of occupied territories, organization of army supplies — biscuits and boots — not to mention diplomatic instructions and the governance of the Empire. There he would perhaps do too much, and the day was coming near when he would be submerged, for already it was plain that his impulsion was essential, that without him everything weakened. But the great leader is also seen in his self-possession. He never betrayed his anxiety, or only furtively, to acute observers. But anxious he certainly was. For he knew that a failure with the Russian alliance would mean the collapse of everything; that the Continental blockade was useless unless the whole Continent adhered to it. It only remained, no doubt, to force Russia to sign peace, but she had first to be conquered. And Napoleon's thoughts turned round and round in that circle.

But conquer he must: if not, the world which he upheld would fall and crush him. Prussia, he saw, was held down, but not truly subjected. The Prussian spirit, that of the October aggression, had been punished at Jena, but it was not dead. Magdeburg, Stettin and Danzig fell in turn, but Fichte was to issue his *Address to the German People*, and Major Schill and his irregulars were to take the field. At the other end of Europe, it would be necessary to impose respect for the Berlin decree upon Portugal, held on a tight rein by the English. There were fresh uncertainties in Spain. Louis in Holland, Joseph in Naples, were handling their profession as kings poorly; the Dutch were reluctant to break off their lucrative trade with England. To hold Europe in the blockade system would be a stiff task.

Everything pointed back to the need for a swift success with Russia. And here Bonaparte's great imaginative diplomacy was brought into play. He was not the inventor of that classic diversion against Russia through the Sultan of Constantinople; his demand for Dalmatia at Presburg was to be closer to the Turks and to be in communication with them. And to the Sultan he added the Shah of Persia. To strike the imagination of the troops he received the Turkish and Persian ambassadors, almost at the advance outposts, with the mud of East Prussia spattering their glittering robes.

The clash came on February 8th, 1807, at Eylau, after difficult marching and skirmishing amidst rivers and marshes, in a cruel climate and with cold, hunger and sickness in his train. It was a hard and murderous day. Victories now were not emerging straight and simple from a skilful manœuvre and the Emperor's brain; they were not giving the troops the impression of certain success at small cost. Even to Bonaparte fortune was sometimes fickle. And the Russians halted at Eylau and covered their retreat. In the cemetery, under the storms of lead and snow, a new picture of war appeared to Napoleon. He looked graver than usual. It was a new picture also to the Grand Army, which did not yet know these butcheries. The Grand Army remained masters on the field, but it was a field of corpses. The Russians and Prussians had been able to undergo losses twice or three times as heavy. But the losses of the Grand Army were cruel for an undecisive victory. In all there were 3000 Frenchmen killed, more than twice as many wounded. Such unaccustomed figures were startling. Both in France and outside France they were exploited, and Napoleon had to give orders that the word was to pass in newspapers and in foreign courts that his losses had not been important; the bulletin had acknowledged only 1900 dead. Talleyrand contented himself with an epigram: 'Eylau,' he said, 'was a slightly won battle'. And it was also said that it was a battle which the Russians claimed to have won and which the French did not wish to have lost.

Napoleon was certainly disappointed and tormented. Peace was escaping him with the undestroyed armies of Prussia and the Tsar. What would Austria do? And in the bivouac one evening he murmured what Jomini, the man who best read his thoughts, said aloud — 'If I were the Archduke Charles!' He had to stand firm against his entourage, Murat and even Berthier, who wanted to recross the Vistula. On February 13th, General Bertrand was sent to convey to Frederick William at Memel the Emperor's proposals, which offered to restore the King of Prussia in Berlin and to restore also his states as far as the Elbe. Poland was openly abandoned, as the occupation of Warsaw had produced not the slightest effect on Alexander.

The very explicitness of Bertrand's mission betrayed the hidden thoughts of Napoleon. Frederick William and Alexander, still in league, resolved to make sure. A Prussian colonel was sent on a pretext of exchanging prisoners to the Imperial camp, which was the wretched hovel of Osterode. He saw Bonaparte, and found him talkative, excited, distracted, like a man who was a prey to desperate anxiety. He chatted with Ney and others, and heard criticism and bitter complaints; some, like Bernadotte, seemed ready for instant defection. Frederick William decided that Napoleon's overtures should not be followed up. Driven back though he was to the extreme fringe of his kingdom, the King of Prussia, together with the Tsar, could feel the day coming when the French would be driven back beyond the Rhine.

The story runs that, during the council at this time, Queen Louisa, mistrustful of her hesitant husband, whispered in Hardenberg's ear the word: 'Constancy'. After the failure of his peace offer, that was Napoleon's motto. He always bowed to forces outside himself and was self-possessed when confronted by the inevitable. He had told the Prussian colonel, who interpreted it as mere boasting, that if he did not obtain peace he would smash the Russian army once and for all, that he could quite well force Alexander to accept his terms, and that then the King of Prussia would count for nought. He kept his word. Four months longer he stayed in East Prussia, working at frenzied pitch, preparing for the summer campaign, for the terrible thaw after which it would be possible for the troops to march again. His goal was unaltered — peace, and friendship with Alexander. He would beat his generals and win over the sovereign. And then the Continental federation would be more than a mere word. The greatest of his projects would be accomplished.

One of the most striking parts of his history is that, actually, he did obtain what he sought; that he secured Alexander's alliance after conquering him, as he had said; and that all that success still proved unavailing. But one circumstance gave pause already. In November 1806, after the Berlin decree, the 1807 class was called up to carry out the great project. In March 1807, to conclude it, to 'ensure the tranquillity of our children', the concripts for 1808 had to be summoned to the colours. From year to year the effort was magnified, the bow was drawn more and more taut. It would break unless Napoleon found peace and repose through the alliance with Russia.

CHAPTER XVI

TILSIT

IF ever a man could flatter himself on having forced the hand of destiny, it was Bonaparte in the month of June 1807. That summer solstice was his zenith. He blended with equal success his military and his political schemes, an armed force in the service of a reasoned diplomacy, a Mazarin who was his own Condé and a Condé who was his own Mazarin, a great captain who could say of his adversary not only, 'I shall beat him there', but also 'I shall embrace him there', and did in fact beat and then embrace him. At thirty-eight, he was giving a sense of mature fullness of power. 'The honest man,' he wrote then, 'always fights to remain master of himself.' His favourite tragedy added: 'as of the universe'. The world, and outward events, are dominated only if one first dominates one's self, and Bonaparte recalled his prudent beginnings, the toils that were the price of power, the fickleness of victory. 'If grave reverses took place and the country were imperilled . . .' — that phrase, recalling the anxieties of Eylau, came just two months before the double success of Friedland and Tilsit. It is evidence of his lucid vision, his exact sense of the position.

He was aiming all this time at reconciliation with Russia. Between Eylau and Friedland he took every possible means of appearing to be the victim of the coalitions fostered by England and of avoiding a provocative role. He kept the idea of an Austrian alliance in reserve against a possible failure of the Russian, just as, if the Russian marriage fell through, he would have an Austrian marriage to fall back on.

True, he had constantly to be on his guard; the Prussian

aggression had been a lesson to him. But was it any fault of his if Frederick William suffered for his obstinate alliance with the Tsar? The Emperor wanted only to come to terms with the Tsar. Then Sweden, who had joined the coalition, proposed an armistice. And Napoleon seized this opportunity for resuming the theme which had already proved useful with the Prussians. Why this warfare? Why this mutual butchery when French and Swedes had so many reasons for being friends?

And thus Napoleon was in a good position to stretch out a hand to Alexander, but with recommendations to Paris 'not to speak of Polish independence', and 'to suppress everything tending to show the Emperor as liberator'. Only one thing was needed for the crowning spectacular event which would bring the dénouement. And that was, that the Russians themselves should attack, when summer made a resumption of hostilities possible. If they retired, if they left Napoleon with a void before him, if they forced him to pursue (how far?) or to wait (how long?) — then that would be 1812 already. For the year 1807 was an 1812 which succeeded, bringing peace and alliance with Russia because the Russians, instead of breaking off contact, took the offensive and gave battle, enabling Napoleon to boast that they had again been aggressors, with that excuse of having been pushed on by England, the eternal 'enemy of peace'.

On June 14th, the anniversary of Marengo, the Russian army was totally defeated at Friedland. Alexander was even more totally defeated. He seemed to be filled with admiration for his conqueror, and perhaps really admired him. In any case, he yielded to the idea of coming to an understanding with him. And this shows why, within five years from now Napoleon would be going right to Moscow and wasting precious time there. It was because, after Friedland, he had seen Alexander fall into his arms. He would pursue, and, at the price of ruin, he would wait for another accolade of Tilsit.

He drove back the remnants of the Russian army to the Niemen. And what would he have done if, at that moment, the fascinated Alexander had not requested an armistice, if the Tsar had listened to his counsellors who advised him to let Napoleon enter the Muscovite empire, as Peter the Great, after his defeat at Narva, had allowed Charles XII to enter? Alexander did not see how great was Napoleon's hunger and thirst for the peace he had promised his soldiers on June 22nd, that peace 'which carried its own guarantee of permanency', because 'it was time to make an end and for our country to live in repose, safe from the malign influence of England'. To make an end — that was the need behind Friedland, and the illusion of Tilsit. For, eager through Napoleon was for Alexander's alliance, he did not see that the Tsar was only half sincere, because he had pressing reasons of his own for concluding peace. It was being loudly called for all around him; discipline had broken down into discouragement and disintegration, in which the Tsar himself was none too safe, and might even fear, as happened a hundred and ten years later to Nicolas II, a forced abdication in the middle of a war at the hands of a revolting army.

Alexander was sentimental and mystical, and subject to sudden changes of front. He made many calculations, but, like Napoleon and like most men, he let circumstances decide for him. Novossilov suggested to the Tsar that an alliance with France might, on his return to St. Petersburg, bring him the fate of Paul I. But just then, with his army powerless, Alexander received offers of peace beyond all his hopes. Napoleon's long efforts to make reconciliation possible were bearing fruit; he was going to dazzle the Tsar with the generosity and magnificence of his terms.

The two Emperors met at Tilsit on June 25th; and the theatrical character of the meeting produced in Napoleon's favour a strong moral success. That raft moored in the middle of a Northern river, on which, under the gaze of the two armies ranged on either bank, the two sovereigns who had but yesterday been at war and to-day were embracing, was staged with all the characteristic skill of Bonaparte, with that 'understanding of the imagination of the peoples' which was one of his master faculties, one of the chief reasons for his power over the minds of mankind.

Napoleon had vowed to win over Alexander, and was confident that he would not be won over himself. He came away from the first interview enchanted by this 'very handsome, fine, youthful Emperor'. Before long he was to find in him 'a Greek of the Late Empire'. But he was then naturally ready to enjoy his conquest of the Tsar, and he had the gift of charming men. Alexander saw the great man of the century, the formidable captain, amiable, soothing, magnanimous, and persuasive in this sincerity, and sincere because he had at last reached the goal of his policy. At one stroke the Tsar was conquered. He was to utter that feminine, but not really untruthful remark: 'I have never loved anything more than that man.'

And now Napoleon and Alexander were hand in glove, sharing their meals, their walks, their thoughts. The Tsar had but one vague remorse — for his abandoned allies, the King and Queen of Prussia, who had lost all because they had believed in him. Napoleon held in store for him that surprise, that sentimental delicacy, of divining the scruples of his friend and sparing him the bitter silences of the sad Frederick William, the scornful looks of the fair Louisa. Immediately Napoleon sent for the victims from their lagoon at Memel. In honour of Alexander, he had already resolved to restore part of their states to them. They also would be guests of the Imperial table, and receive the consideration due to misfortune. The picture to be formed of Napoleon at Tilsit is the opposite of that of a brutal conqueror. If he were intoxicated with anything, it was not with his victories but with his diplomatic, and as it were fashionable, successes. And what a temptation to believe that nothing was impossible for himself, when, under the tent of Tilsit, the Emperor of the French and the autocrat of all the Russias sat godlike together, modelling Europe in friendly conversation?

The treaty of peace and friendship with Alexander brought him to the peak of his desires. No doubt he was the dupe of Tilsit — but how many others were with him! 'This is the end of wars now,' the word went round the camps of the Grand Army; and the great days of Tilsit would leave behind them as many regrets as those of Amiens, and efface the memory of miseries and bloodshed, and enhance the magic of the reign. But nothing was ended, and Napoleon knew it. He ordered Fouché to see to it that the newspapers ceased to talk foolishly about the beaten side at Friedland and the Tsar, and added: 'Everything leads us to think that our system will be linked with this power in a stable fashion.' The 'system' was the Continental blockade. And three days later he was drawing up for Alexander's use a summary of joint policy directed to forcing England into peace. Henceforward Napoleon viewed the war as finished on the Continent; it only remained to conclude the maritime struggle. If England held out, Russian naval forces could unite with French to resume hostilities at sea. And what was necessary to decide Alexander? Napoleon knew that to renounce the resuscitation of Poland was not enough. And so, before the Tsar's dazzled eyes, he unrolled on the table the map of a scheme of partition more grandiose than the partitions of the eighteenth century, a settlement of the Eastern Question for the profit of Russia. The Turks as well as the Poles would have to be sacrificed, though they had provided a useful diversion in this last campaign. And it would have been painful to betray them openly, but just then a palace revolution overthrew the Sultan Selim and freed Napoleon from that alliance. And so the Danubian provinces, spoils of Selim, and Finland, spoils of Sweden, were the share received by Russia a few days after a bloody defeat, as if, in Thiers's phrase, 'the honour of being beaten by Napoleon were equivalent to a victory'.

The treaty of peace was signed at Tilsit on July 8th, three weeks after Friedland. Napoleon would have been the first to criticize its various contradictions and weaknesses, if he had not been subordinating details — and the partition of provinces, the creation of states were nowadays merely details — to the central idea of a Continental federation against England.

It is easy to say that Prussia should have been completely destroyed or completely restored, but she could not be obliterated, or her king dethroned, without dishonour to Alexander. It is likewise easy to say that the Duchy of Warsaw, the simulacrum of Polish independence, was also too much and not enough. Napoleon congratulated himself on the creation of that state as a moderate and prudent solution which took everything into account. He was doing something useful for the Poles, acting kindly towards these sincere friends of France in Eastern Europe, making them into a buffer state, adequate to put some distance between Russia and Germany, but too weak to be a source of affront to the Tsar. So at least Napoleon supposed, but wrongly. The Tsar could not but resign himself to this resurrection of a fragment of Poland. But it was to prove a lasting grievance in St. Petersburg against the French alliance, and even the choice of the King of Saxony, a kind of neutral, to rule over the Duchy of Warsaw did not suffice to calm the fears of the Russians.

But Napoleon had not intended that his brother Jerome should reign in Warsaw. The latter was still without employment, and must make himself useful like the rest, or disappear. The Emperor created for him the new feudatory kingdom of Westphalia. It had its place in the development of the 'system', continuing the kingdom of Holland, completing the Confederation of the Rhine, using the remains of Prussia, always with a view to withdrawing more coastline, more estuaries, from English commerce. And then, Jerome, by marrying Catherine of Württemberg, became a kinsman of the Tsar, who feigned not to understand — this was the disappointment of Tilsit to Napoleon — the allusions to the other marriage project, and seemed to be in no hurry to make his cherished hero into a brother-in-law. With Finland and the Danubian provinces, Russia was surely being given enough to ensure her fidelity to the alliance? But to offer her Constantinople straight off would mean making her so powerful that history would never have forgiven Napoleon for going so far. And there would also have been the natural temptation to Russia of securing the guarantee of her Tilsit acquisitions by England after receiving them from France.

These hasty constructions, these political huts raised by Napoleon after each of his victorious marches across Europe, continually extending the annexes with which the Revolution had buttressed its own conquests, were cloud castles. But there is no absurdity unless we forget the fundamental absurdity of a situation which had lasted for fifteen years, the law of an enterprise which consisted of making war on England without a navy, of conquering the sea on land. And now the English were less ready than ever to admit France's right to Belgium, when France, to keep Belgium, had been led on to dominating the whole Continent. War with England had begun again in May 1803, a year before the Empire was proclaimed, and it was to last until Napoleon's downfall; nobody has ever said how he could have escaped it. To condemn the means he employed amounts to a recognition that they were as useless as the struggle itself, for nobody has ever suggested better means. Only one would have been really efficacious — the immediate evacuation of Belgium. But that could enter less into Napoleon's calculations than anything, for the supreme power had been entrusted to him so that he might preserve for France that fundamental conquest of the Revolution.

At Tilsit Napoleon and Alexander agreed to leave Malta to England, but she would hardly pay any heed to that, as the island had never been out of her hands. As with small things, so with great. Nothing would be done so long as England remained undefeated, and the whole Napoleonic policy was directed to produce the capitulation of England, just as the whole of the British Cabinet's policy was turned to bringing about the renunciation by France of the conquests which they had banned since 1793. The Continental blockade, therefore, as Napoleon's unique weapon against England, must be made complete and hermetically sealed. To that end Tilsit had to serve, as the Russian alliance had to serve, to force the closing of ports in recalcitrant states. That treaty emphasized the 'he that is not with me is against me' rule which was in force on both sides of the Channel, and ceaselessly provoked coalitions and counter-coalitions.

Not for a moment did Napoleon lose sight of his objective. On his way back to France, at Dresden, he gave Talleyrand his instructions, based on the treaty signed eleven days before on the banks of the Niemen.

Wherever the blockade leaked, it must be stopped up. The Prince of Benevente was to busy himself instantly with closing the Portuguese ports against England. If Portugal held out, war would be declared against her in unison with Spain, who, as an ally of France, must appreciate the urgency of this measure. Note, this was the decoy that led him on into a tragic business; but logic and necessity willed it. Again, on August 28th, Napoleon wrote to his other great ally at St. Petersburg, to intervene at Vienna, backed by France, and secure the closing of Austrian ports to English ships. True, Alexander had not completely sealed his own; a fact from which the quarrel and rupture were to come. There remained the Papal States and the Scandinavian countries. And when they were brought in, the seamless coat of the blockade would cover the whole Continent.

'The work of Tilsit will rule the destinies of the world.' There was the work of Tilsit, the friendship of Tilsit, and even the style of Tilsit — that in which the two sovereigns had laid bare their hearts to each other. There was also, in

Napoleon alone, the intoxication of Tilsit. In spite of his knowledge and his scorn of men, he was not sufficiently versed in diplomacy to gauge exactly the weight he could lay upon the Russian alliance. He exaggerated its worth, its reach, its solidity, because it was becoming the basis of his policy; whilst Alexander was whispering into a Prussian's ear: 'The policy may well change with circumstances.' But Napoleon felt that only a few years of alliance with the greatest power on the Continent would suffice to make him irresistible. The underlying principle of his gravest errors lay there. He was a victim of the Russian mirage. He was not the first, and would not be the last.

After Tilsit Napoleon's touch became rougher. He forgot his caution, and his most blameworthy mistakes, the affairs of Rome and Spain, both date from the period following the theatrical effusions on the raft of the Niemen.

But if violence grew greater, Napoleon was not alone in the guilt. England's retort to the Franco-Russian alliance was harsh. On September 2nd, after a warning to Denmark, she bombarded and almost destroyed Copenhagen, in order to terrorize the neutrals and make the Russian coastal towns fear the same fate. On November 11th, a cabinet decree obliged the vessels of non-belligerent flags to pass through English ports and pay a tax there, or take up merchandise, under penalty of being declared lawful prizes. This was clearly arbitrary on the part of the 'tyrants of the sea', and it is only fair to say that 'Napoleon thought he could do as he liked because England did as she liked'. The reply to the London decree was the decree of Milan, on December 17th, which tightened the rules of the Continental blockade, and permitted the seizure of any vessel whatsoever which had touched at an English port.

We must see here the connection and sequence of events in the Anglo-French duel, with the inequality resulting from the fact that England had been since Trafalgar the undisputed ruler of the seas, whilst Napoleon was never to hold complete mastery over the Continent. He was to exhaust himself in the impossible task of rallying all the European nations, and joining them in a war of which the unvarying stake was Belgium and the left bank of the Rhine. To federate the peoples he counted on England's maritime tyranny, her exactions, her assaults on international law. Only one country, at the last, was to rebel and declare war on England in the name of freedom of trade, but she did so quite on her own account, and without adequate means, to make her indirect assistance of any value. That was the United States of America, not then a great power. But the European nations, summoned to battle for their independence, already felt the land blockade weighing more heavily on them than the maritime blockade. England seized ships at a distance. France installed customs everywhere, and her constraint was much more visible and actual than the English 'tyranny', which was exercised between sky and water. In vain did the Emperor plead that the 'unjust, illegal measures (of Berlin and Milan), which attacked the sovereignty of the peoples', were forced upon him by circumstance. In vain did he console the allied governments with fresh territories, their populations with progress, abolition of old serfdoms, good administrations. He was no less strongly obliged to see to the strict maintenance of his blockade, to set soldiers behind customs officials, to expand the customs by conquest and annexation, until the struggle against England for independence became the domination of France, and until Europe, quite soon, came to hail the English as liberators.

It was after Tilsit that the Emperor really applied the system, and the incredibly tangled skein became instantly visible. One has the impression of a kind of vertigo, a delirium of power, of an insensate demi-urge endlessly stirring the old world round and round; removing kings here to place them elsewhere, giving to some what he takes from others, reshaping, agglomerating, dividing, annexing; and it is impossible to follow it in detail without giving the narrative a fluttering disjointedness painful to the mind. But, to venture on a lowly but quite exact comparison, the most demented acts of Napoleon were as reasonable as the hither-and-thither scurrying of a rat caught in a trap. His trap, we must not forget, snapped down at Trafalgar, and he had had to rush from 'Gibraltar to Texel', to every gap open to English trade, as it was only through her trade that the new Carthage could be struck at.

But what a task, perpetually calling for fresh starts, now in Russia, now in Holland, now in Italy! Then there were plans for Portugal. Lisbon and Oporto were simply 'English counters'. One third of Portuguese territory should be given to the Bourbon Queen of Etruria, who had best be moved thither; one third to Godoy, the Spanish minister; and from the remaining third Napoleon himself would supervise the rest. This was the Treaty of Fontainebleau, the treaty of Franco-Spanish conquest and partition, to make an end of the Braganzas as an end had been made of the Bourbons of Naples, 'sold' likewise to England.

From the original Berlin decree to the Treaty of Fontainebleau the sequence of reasoning and action is clear. It was natural. But this development entailed others of equal necessity and fatefulness. Junot led an army across the Pyrenees to march on Lisbon. And this was the beginning of the Spanish affairs, alliance and military co-operation with the Madrid Bourbons, pending their coming dethronement, which developed into the occupation of the whole Peninsula. And in Spain, incalculable circumstances were to bring Napoleon face to face with a baleful temptation.

During that triumphant autumn of 1807 Napoleon was reluctant to content himself with this immobile war of prohibition, this battle of usury which was wearing down everybody, which consisted of ruining the English, which spread the news of their being at bay when they were always finding fresh resources. He thought again of an attack on

India through Persia. He urged the idea on Russia, who was sceptical. He reverted to a possible invasion of England, or at any rate to naval operations, and for a maritime renaissance he required the active assistance of his ally Spain. But was Spain a trusty ally? And what was her condition? She was deep, and sinking deeper, in decrepitude, threatened even by anarchy. 'He could not,' said Thiers, 'avoid a feeling of pity, anger, indignation, at the thought that Spain was not even in a state to equip a naval squadron.' And 'he assured himself that in the end he would have to ask her, for her own sake and for that of his allies, to alter her administration.' He had vague thoughts of rejuvenating Spain, of modernizing and regenerating her. She was asleep under Charles IV, that crowned Sganarelle who, like the Queen, had eyes only for Godoy, the 'Prince of Peace', a former member of the guard, the scandal of the court and nation. 'An imbecile king, a shameless queen,' an heir-apparent conspiring against his parents and their 'abject favourite' — such was the spectacle of Spanish government. How could he depend on it? Had it not been for Jena, Spain would have given herself over to England. For joint enterprises to be successful, this ally must not only be loyal; her strength must also be as well developed as that of France. Already certain flattering tongues, amongst them that of Talleyrand, more dangerous as he was in partial disgrace, were whispering in the master's ear that Napoleon should set up in Madrid a king of his own family, as Louis XIV had done with the Duc d'Anjou. But the Emperor was not yet ready to decide that the Bourbons of Spain had ceased to reign. It was not part of his policy to multiply revolutions. Nor was it in his interests needlessly to dethrone ruling families.

It was to take him some time to be convinced that this royal family of Spain was rotten, that its dissensions were throwing the Spanish state into chaos, and would end by ruining it, nullifying the alliance, and perhaps delivering it into the hands of England. To imitate Louis XIV could not be done at will. Before the Duc d'Anjou reigned in Spain, the throne had to be without an heir, and a will had to designate the great king's grandson. If Napoleon had wanted the Spanish crown for one of his brothers, pretext and opportunity would have been lacking. But chance willed it that a family quarrel at the Escorial brought him both. Admittedly, Spain was the grave of the Napoleonic Empire, but it must also be recognized that a malign destiny drove him to the brink. He believed in his star; here was his baleful star. Melodramatic circumstances, an imbroglio with an unpredictable outcome, brought him irrevocably into the mesh of Spanish affairs.

In October 1807, just when the Franco-Spanish force of Junot began its march on Lisbon to enforce the Treaty of Fontainebleau, scandal broke out at the court of Madrid. As Charles IV seemed in danger of dying, Godoy tried to secure his powerful position, aided by the Queen, by obtaining the disinheritance of the Prince of Asturias, who was to be Ferdinand VII. The Prince craved the protection of the Emperor of the French, and also asked in marriage the hand of a princess of the house of Bonaparte. Godoy and the Queen convinced the old King that his son was conspiring against him, and Napoleon was made arbiter by both father and son in their abominable quarrel. From that day, with the disgust inspired in him by this family, dates the temptation.

And worse was to come, as if the Evil One himself had taken charge of the work. In their hatred of Godoy, the Spaniards sided with Ferdinand, and called aloud for the French army, their ally against Portugal, to deliver them from the favourite. They themselves called for the troops which Napoleon had massed on the frontier as reinforcements for the Portugese expedition, and to be ready to intervene in Madrid if the deliquescent Bourbon government and dynasty collapsed. It was a legitimate precaution, as the object for driving the English from Lisbon and Oporto had led Junot's corps into a hazardous position, and he would be caught between two fires if the suspect Godoy betrayed the alliance.

At that moment Napoleon faced Spanish affairs with distrustful uncertainty. He had not followed up Ferdinand's request when a fresh turn came in the drama. Charles IV pardoned the Prince, who as fearful of Godoy as Godoy was of revolution, had denounced his own counsellors. And it was now the King, the Bourbon, who craved the hand of a Bonaparte for the son whom he had cursed a few days before. The Emperor thought of Charlotte, a daughter of Lucien's first marriage, still a child. But the project collapsed. The idea of marrying the granddaughter of a Provençal innkeeper to a descendant of Louis XIV, which would have avoided the dethronement of the Spanish Bourbons, came to nought. In Spain all the fates were to turn against him, to render vain the supreme checks of prudence.

In these origins of Bonaparte's most ruinous enterprise it is plain how, like other men, he was the toy of chance, and, more than other men, the victim of his calculating spirit that inexorably deduced the consequences of principles posited. But he knew well enough what he had weighed for and against never to have regrets. Within a few months from now his foot would have slipped in Spain. He was no longer able to avoid the slope.

And yet, during those brilliant days that followed Tilsit he seemed to be perfectly self-controlled. He reappeared after his long absence, a little stouter already, and fuller in the face. He was no longer the dark, rapacious Corsican, who looked so swarthy because he plastered down his hair with pomade. Men saw now his white skin, the beautiful teeth, the blue eyes, an imperial Roman mask, on which gravity mingled with good-nature and the slight plumpness that goes with success. His tension was relaxed. He had not yet grown irritable. His thought, always so swift in action, had a sort of Olympian serenity when he spoke of the government of peoples. It was at this time that he proffered counsel to his brothers on the art of ruling, and taught them, out of his experience, the uses of patience and reflection. 'Between pondering a thing and carrying it into execution,' he said, 'one should wait for three years — and you don't wait three hours.' That was how he had reached power. That was how he had attained what was perhaps the hardest objective, that Russian alliance, of which he was proud as of the finest fruit of his skilful preparations, and the Continental peace of which he was the author and protector. He kept an eye on the military men, who did not always understand him and often compromised him, and frequently scolded them for their rash speech: as for instance, Davout, the victor of Auerstadt: 'The rumours of war with Austria are absurd. You must constantly maintain the most pacific language: the word *war* should never be on your lips.' Who would think that so wise an Emperor must commit follies? Was he not 'master or friend of every king on the Continent', and allied to several by marriage of his kindred, sure of Europe through universal garrisons, through the Grand Army, through the territories he had partitioned, the treaties he had signed? What peril could threaten him? After his return from Tilsit he had taken up residence at Fontainebleau. There he spent two months of a brilliant court life, with foreign princes crowding his halls, a thing which had not been seen since Louis XIV and the great days of Versailles.

But he went to Fontainebleau rather as Louis XIV had gone to Versailles. In the stifling, malicious currents of Paris he felt uneasy. He even had thoughts of residing in the palace of the great monarch, and had the Château of Versailles put under repair, because, as he sometimes said, the Parisians had never forgiven him for the 13th of Vendémiaire. Behind that impressive mask, that Jove-like brow, reigned the secret idea that the Empire was brittle, that it had still to be continually stiffened, the same idea that his mother, the good Ajaccio housewife, with her wealth of canny Corsican proverbs, her patient savings against a rainy day, had translated with the exclamation — 'Provided it all lasts!'

The chief impression which the Emperor wished to obliterate was the widespread one that he was only a lucky gambler who, at the first sign of a change in his luck, would be ready to call in his stakes. He knew that Friedland and the subsequent peace had not completely effaced all the traces of anxiety that followed Eylau. Things had gone on fairly well whilst he was directing and supervising France from his Polish bivouacs. But would they continue to do so if he had again to stay away so long? 'The mere opinion that I was faced with any set-back in France would bring several powers against us,' he told Cambacérès. But where could opposition declare itself! In the Tribunat, where, however, the tribune was all but silent. Napoleon had returned from Tilsit resolved to close that establishment, to eliminate from the Constitution he had received from Sieyès this last vestige of an assembly endowed with the right of discussion, that is to say, of criticism and remonstrance. It meant, as he said, 'breaking his last links with the Republic'. He had already eliminated some troublesome figures — Benjamin Constant, Marie-Joseph Chénier, and Daunou. The members were still showing too much opposition, and Bonaparte had publicly exclaimed: 'They are a dozen metaphysicians — they should be thrown into the river. They are vermin on my clothes . . . Don't imagine I shall let myself be attacked like Louis XVI. I will not stand it.' Like Louis XVI — no. But in a different way — yes.

The suppression of the Tribunat passed off with no stir: the *senatus consultum* was used. It was hardly noticed. Against the despotism there were a few scattered voices, but there was not yet any opinion. The men whom Bonaparte had most to fear were those who speculated on the fall of his stock, ready to cover themselves whilst he himself was obliged to maintain and push up values to dizzy heights. There was Talleyrand, whose place at the Foreign Ministry was transferred to the docile, tepid Champagny, chiefly because he knew that the Prince of Benevente now had little faith in the Empire, or in his own principality, and displayed a premature pessimism in council. And Napoleon had also to fear the Corps Législatif, which refused him no levies, and the Senate, where obedience was exemplary in prosperity, where the former tribunes, most of whom he lodged in these silent strongholds, would not be the first to give the signal for desertion in the hour of collapse.

Bonaparte's real foe was doubt; and except in a small number of heads, doubt was dormant in France. But it buzzed in the ears of Alexander of Russia. In St. Petersburg many voices were asking whether it would be possible to end matters with England, whether Napoleon was not day-dreaming when he proposed a diversion in India by way of Persia. And whilst Napoleon was warming the zeal of France for the Russian alliance, letting it be known that he had worn all day his cordon of the Order of St. Andrew, whilst he informed Alexander that Vienna had decided on war against England and that the King of Sweden would follow suit 'when Your Majesty has spoken rather seriously to him', there was an Austrian ambassador in Paris of whom more would be seen. His name was Metternich. There was an embassy secretary named Nesselrode who would also be seen again. And Metternich whispered remarks to the young Russian diplomat which were meant to be repeated to his chief, and by them to their master, remarks which were all in one sense: 'Napoleon is powerful, but it is a precarious power. We should not be his dupes, you and we, but let us avoid coming into collision with him. And let us prepare for the great day of judgment on this astounding adventure.'

CHAPTER XVII

FIRST CLOUD FROM SPAIN

To understand the Spanish affair, it should suffice to recall that of Greece during the European War. In 1917 the Allies, for the Salonika expedition, required the ports, the roads, and the resources of Greece. It was essential that that country should not be continually on the verge of siding with the enemy and striking the Allies from the rear. To be sure of Greece, they had to be sure of her government, and for that reason, in the end, King Constantine was called upon to abdicate. Similarly, in this war against England, Napoleon required Spain to be in friendly, loyal and firm hands. Still, Charles IV was his ally, and to depose him forcibly was difficult. Napoleon was forced to temporize and to dissemble. He thought he had dealt a master-stroke when, with the course of events helping him only too well, he brought Charles IV to cede his rights to the throne and the Prince of Asturias to do likewise. His satisfaction inspired him with a confidence that proved an ill-omened successor to his long-drawn measures of precaution.

During the first two months of 1808, as if filled with a presentiment of danger, he remained hesitant and perplexed, torn between several plans. He was far from having formulated a decision. On February 25th he was again writing to Charles IV asking about the projected marriage of Ferdinand with 'a French princess'. He reverted to that because this marriage would settle everything, if only there were a princess capable of holding this great position. Through her Spain would be placed under the direct influence of France. But how much simpler it would be to have done with these Bourbons, to find instead a French prince of the Bonaparte blood! Would that be so difficult? Were not the Spaniards weary of the shameful mastery of Godoy? The passage of Junot's army through Spain to conquer Portugal had been a festival, and on its approach, the Prince Regent, with the Braganza royal family, had embarked for Brazil. It would suffice if Charles IV, the Queen, and their inseparable Godoy followed their example and proceeded to Mexico: the dynastic question would be instantly solved, and the Spanish throne would stand empty without France having interfered and without the Emperor having soiled his fingers. Perhaps even an attempted departure would have the same result as the flight to Varennes, and suffice to disqualify the Bourbons. In that case, someone must be at hand to replace them. Napoleon thought of Joseph or Louis, although he was discontented with the one in Naples, the other at The Hague. But his mind wavered between several schemes, settling on none.

But henceforth, whatever action he resolved upon, Napoleon could no longer dispense with intervention in the affairs of that Peninsula. With Junot in Lisbon, Napoleon saw that it would be absurd to share out Portugal with Spain, who had barely collaborated in the expedition and whose government was so unreliable. His hesitations, and the careful way in which he still handled these Bourbons of Madrid, then resulted in his resorting to oblique manœuvres which made him suspect to the Spaniards and laid him open to charges of double-dealing. Gradually he increased the numbers of his troops in Spain, doing so as an ally, no doubt, but also as a warder, and this pacific invasion raised the murmurs of the Spanish people. And further, in order to keep a closer eye on Charles IV and Godoy, he appointed Murat to be with them, with orders to observe, to wait, to be prudent, without unmasking his projects, for the reason that he had resolved upon none. But Murat's mission was to be the root of another mistaken judgment which would open up a whole string of sorry mistakes.

Meanwhile the Emperor's brother-in-law and his sister

Caroline were neither of them satisfied with their grand-duchy of Berg. Like the others, they wanted advancement, and more advancement. As Lieutenant-General in Spain, Murat began to toy with the idea of reigning there. He fancied he understood the Spanish people; his wishes became father to his thoughts. His letters began to persuade Napoleon that it would be quite easy to place one of his kinsmen on the throne of these decrepit Bourbons, that the masses hoped for it and would greet with enthusiasm the new sovereign provided for them by their powerful protector. Murat's interested ambition blinded him. But his illusions, coinciding with those of Napoleon, flattered and fostered them. Why should not the Emperor be 'admired and worshipped throughout all Spain!' He wished to benefit Spain according to the recipe which he had given to his king-brothers, to bring Spain light, liberty, equality, the Civil Code. He was convinced that he could rally Spain by proclaiming to the people that he had abolished feudalism and the Inquisition. If a few fanatics resisted, they would be quelled by swift and dire punishment. 'The Spaniards', he wrote to Marshal Bessières, 'are like other peoples, and do not form a class apart.' That was his mistake. He did not know the Spaniards. In all Bonaparte's vast knowledge which served him so well, in the libraries he had devoured, there was this accidental lacuna. When there was something he had not learned, he was on the level of other men, with no firm footing, and what was worse, he lacked positive knowledge and fell back on prejudice. And so, with his judgment devoid of information, fatalities became linked up with the errors.

Napoleon proposed shortly to cross the Pyrenees himself and investigate these present complexities. Pending his arrival on the scene, his advice to Murat remained the same. He was to be prudent and circumspect, to avoid clashes or hostilities, to be reassuring. He was to say that Napoleon was coming only to settle the succession, as a conciliator; he would not remain in Madrid — it was Gibraltar and Northern Africa that interested him. It would be dangerous to startle these people overmuch.

This wise counsel dates from March 16th. Napoleon still did not know what he would do. He hoped that things would settle themselves at the sight of his troops and with the news of his arrival, that the dynastic problem would resolve itself, one way or another, without violence. He had sided neither with Charles IV nor with Ferdinand, and was really rather embarrassed because the Spanish government had given him no grounds for offence, and Godoy himself had affected loyalty to the alliance and obedience to the will of the Emperor. For the idea was gathering strength in Napoleon's mind that it was time to be rid of this family divided against itself, corrupting and paralysing Spain, to have done with this servile and suspect favourite. He aimed at frightening Godoy by his impenetrable intentions into a flight to America, with the whole court, with Ferdinand himself, and so having the path left clear. The more imminent this flight seemed to become, the more powerfully was the Emperor tempted. Reigning over there on the other continent, like the Braganzas in Brazil, the Bourbons would still be a vexation. Deprived of her colonies, Spain would lose half her value in the association against England. What an advent for a new king, to present himself before his subjects without their overseas dominions! From these reflections sprang another scheme — a first ruse. The remnants of the French fleet beaten at Trafalgar were still lying in Cadiz. The admiral commanding them received secret orders to detain Charles IV if he came to embark at that port.

Only one element did Napoleon omit in these complicated schemings — the Spanish people themselves. And by a sudden spontaneous movement they upset his calculations. An outbreak flared up at Aranjuez. Godoy, as Napoleon hoped, had actually prepared for flight together with the court. But when these preparations became evident, the crowd rose to prevent the departure of the Prince, whom they preferred to the favourite. Rioting broke out and Charles IV was terrified into abdication in order to avoid a revolution.

Napoleon's next error, fostered by Murat, lay in his belief that this unforeseen event would settle everything by aggravating and confusing everything. Murat was overjoyed to see the throne of Spain empty. He refrained from recognizing the Prince of Asturias, whom the Spaniards accepted as their legitimate King Ferdinand VII. But then Charles IV, perhaps surreptitiously incited to it, retracted his abdication, claiming that it had been forced upon him. Murat subtly advised the quarrelling father and son to refer their dispute to the arbitration of Napoleon, and to go and plead their causes before him. The trap of Bayonne was already prepared when the news of what had happened at Aranjuez decided Napoleon to put an end to all this. He adopted Murat's stratagem, and, strangely enough, the factotum used for this snaring of other Bourbons was once again Savary. The trusted agent of Vincennes was entrusted with escorting Charles IV and Ferdinand over the Pyrennes and into the lion's den, just as he had been charged not to let the Duc d'Enghien go before bringing him to the moat at Vincennes.

He had embarked upon an adventure. He would regret it bitterly. Men and events were conspiring to deceive Napoleon into a belief that these Bourbons were an extinct race. Ferdinand had of his own accord taken the road for Bayonne, hastening to be recognized as King by the Emperor of the French. But Charles IV and his Queen hurried on his heels to plead their own cause, to conciliate the powerful ally and place themselves under his protection. Ferdinand hurried all the faster. But on the frontier he hesitated, perturbed by the appeals of a few clear-sighted Spaniards. He was no less perturbed when the astute Savary gave him to understand that he would compromise everything by not coming on to Bayonne, bringing him a captious, subtly perfidious

letter from the Emperor. Napoleon's course of action was
not resolved upon. He spread out his net, and Ferdinand,
afraid of his father, fell into it, abruptly deciding to continue
his journey. Orders were given to Bessières, commanding
the French Army of Spain, to arrest the Prince of Asturias
if he retraced his steps, for if he refused to come to Bayonne
he would certainly place himself under English protection.
The die was cast.

At last Ferdinand crossed the Bidassoa. He abandoned his
kingdom and his idolizing subjects, only to learn that he would
not have the throne and to perceive that he was a prisoner.

After long weighings of pros and cons, after admitted 'perplexities', the opportunity had at long last offered itself. As
usual, the Emperor seized it. He acted quickly and decisively.
He now felt that these dynastic affairs had taken too much
of his time, that these Bourbons would have to disappear:
otherwise everything would be spoilt. Junot was in danger
in Lisbon. Everything now appeared to Napoleon as a
succession of necessary events, their necessity compelling
swift, and therefore brutal and extreme, solutions, to be
handled at any risk, because delay itself would be a risk.

One pleasure remained in store for Bonaparte — to see the
descendants of Louis XIV held at his disposal and humbling
themselves before him. When he arrived, Charles IV threw
himself into the arms of his dear friend, hailing him as his
saviour; and when he realized that his prayers were vain,
that the Emperor's course could not be shifted, he played out
the last act of a palace tragedy before that reader of Corneille.
At the price of his own crown, the father avenged himself
on his son. He ceded his rights to Napoleon, and Ferdinand,
who had stupidly put himself within the power of the arbiter,
abdicated and renounced the throne in his turn. After
which the two kings humiliated themselves further by
accepting the lands and pensions which Napoleon hospitably
offered them, Talleyrand being entrusted to house and amuse
Ferdinand and his younger brother at Valençay. 'You

might bring Madame de Talleyrand and four or five ladies there. If the Prince of Asturias became attached to some pretty woman, there would be no objection.' Impassively the Prince of Benevente accepted this role. He was biding his time, feeling the end approaching. Talleyrand was disdainful, and Napoleon scornful. To what heights did his scorn rise when, at his orders, the former Bishop of Autun made himself the entertainer of these princes of the noblest blood, who had just humbled and degraded themselves before the upstart usurper! But he found an excuse to himself and to history. He had done wrong. But did not policy compel it? Did not the interest of France and of Europe, the conduct of the war against England, outweigh all else? Would not that silence any scruples?

A report of Champagny, a justificatory memorandum corrected by Napoleon's own hand, set out the Spanish affair in the form of closely reasoned arguments. After detailing the treacheries and the administrative debility of Spain, and after a reminder of the unvarying principles of French policy regarding security along the Pyrenees, the memorandum emphasized the supreme importance of the war against England, and of a sound and judicious government within Spain. The peace for which humanity called out depended on action against the common enemy, and 'anything conducing to that end is legitimate'. These were the circumstances which had obliged the Emperor to take his great decision. 'Policy counsels it, justice authorizes it, and the troubles of Spain compel its necessity. Your Majesty must provide for the security of the Empire, and save Spain from the influence of England.'

And that these were Napoleon's determining reasons is proved by the fact that, from Bayonne itself, as soon as the double abdication had been secured, he proceeded to profit by Spain's resources and to reconstruct her navy in order to revive the naval war against England as also by his instructions to Decrès, as numerous and urgent as in the days of

Boulogne. Ships were to be built in the yards of France, Spain, Italy and Holland. Things must move fast. He reckoned that within a year, including the Russian fleet, he would have at his disposal 130 vessels of the line, a force capable of dealing successfully with the English.

Nothing remained but the consent of the Spanish nation, which the Emperor had no doubts of obtaining. 'When my banner bears the words *Liberty, Emancipation from Superstition, Destruction of the Nobility,* I shall be received as I was in Italy, and all the truly national classes will be with me. You will see that I shall be regarded as the liberator of Spain.' Such were his words — the doctrine of the Convention in the time of the propagandist wars. But its style had never failed more completely in effect. The Emperor's proclamations, the solemn assurance that the crowns of France and Spain would always remain distinct and that the Catholic faith would remain the sole religion, were unavailing promises. Never yet had Napoleon so gravely deceived himself; and he did so as an ideologue. He knew that he was subject to error. 'I have so often made mistakes that I do not blush for them,' he had once said to Talleyrand, with the feeling that his superiority allowed him such an avowal. But here the error was all-embracing, and was thereby bound to make everything conspire to his hurt, to make the smallest circumstances turn against him.

It is possible that, after all, in the first moment of surprise before the vacant throne, Spain would have accepted a king from the hand of Napoleon. Murat was fairly popular. But Napoleon put him aside, thinking Joseph or Louis more worthy of the Spanish nation. But Louis, who was first sounded, refused; and Joseph raised difficulties. Time was wasted, during which the Spaniards began to tell each other that Napoleon wished to rule over them himself, to conquer and annex their country. His brothers' ill will was a fresh complication; his family, by doing a disservice to the member to whom it owed everything, did itself a disservice.

FIRST CLOUD FROM SPAIN

The Emperor's illusion was made complete by the popular rising which he had foreseen, and would rather have avoided, but which formed part of his calculations as an opportunity of showing Spain the folly of resistance. On May 2nd, the people of Madrid rose in opposition to the departure of the Infantas, who were going to join the royal family at Bayonne. A few French soldiers were killed, and in a few hours Murat's grape-shot had restored order. That commotion in Madrid deceived the Emperor completely. The respectable classes in the capital had been afraid of violent demonstrations from the mob, and wanted an authority under French auspices to prevent their recurrence. They prevailed upon the Junta to send a delegation to Bayonne offering the throne to Joseph. Murat's grape-shot, the heads slashed off by the terrible mamelukes as they galloped, seemed to have had a favourable effect; but the news, propagated throughout Spain, kindled insurrection and the spirit of vengeance. Suppose that after the Zappeion trap and the counter-stroke of King Constantine's deposition, the whole of Greece had taken up arms, and had had to be conquered, village by village to the end of the Peloponnesus: the Allies in 1917 would have been less surprised than the Emperor was when he saw the whole of Spain rising against him.

It was a principle of his that 'men will put up with evils when insults are not added'. He was concerned with the welfare and progress of the Spanish nation, and was bringing it order and enlightenment; and he thought he had paid enough attention to Castilian pride by his skilful solicitation of the double renunciation from the King and his son, by paying them royal honours and assuring them of a gilded retirement, manifesting particular consideration to 'the unfortunate Charles IV', as he called him. It would, in his eyes, have been insulting to overturn the dynasty brutally, and he was proud to have avoided that. He never imagined that Spain would challenge him in the name of legitimacy, when he was dealing with a family that had not reigned for more than one century, and nobody seemed less worthy of affection than Ferdinand VII. When he thought how the French had guillotined the worthy Louis XVI, it never occurred to him that the Spaniards would sacrifice themselves for that bad son, 'so stupid that I could not get a word out of him . . . indifferent to everything, very dull, eating his four meals a day and with ideas about nothing'. Like many intelligent men, the Emperor, always quick to find other men fools, counted too much on the human race's dependence on reason. Fanaticism disconcerted him.

While the Spanish people, from their hatred of foreigners and their determination to be independent, were taking Ferdinand VII as their banner and idol, Joseph was regretfully leaving Naples to Murat. He made a melancholy and ill-augured entry to his new kingdom. He was clear-headed in the letter he wrote to his brother the day after his arrival in the Escorial: 'You must be persuaded that the feelings of the nation are unanimous against all that has been done at Bayonne.' Napoleon had already arranged to 'flood' Spain with his troops, judging it impossible that bands of fanatics could possibly stand firm against soldiers who had beaten all the armies of Europe. One accident, one first betrayal of fortune, sufficed to decide otherwise. Spain, which was to be an auxiliary under her French king, was to become a bullet. Everything had been done to keep England out of the Peninsula, but it all led to the English entering there and so getting a footing on the Continent. And what was worse, though . invisible, was that the Grand Army, the instrument of his power, the invincible phalanx, was henceforth cut in two.

Bonaparte had already encountered fanaticism in Egypt, where he displayed all his virtuosity as a manipulator of men. In Spain, national and religious enthusiasm were preparing for him an exhausting war and unknown difficulties. And this happened just when the Emperor, for the same reasons that had determined his intervention in Lisbon and Madrid, had come into conflict with the Papacy.

Why did Napoleon, who had so well understood the importance of the Catholic Church, allow himself to be drawn into violences against the Pontiff which would destroy the moral effect of his coronation at the Pope's hand? The cause was the same. As a temporal sovereign, Pius VII refused to break with England, invoking the spiritual interests which he held in trust. The Emperor called upon the head of the Pontifical States to take the necessary measures for enforcing the blockade. Pius VII replied that, as Father of all the faithful, he viewed all nations as equal in his sight, and that to protect Catholic interests, wherever they might be, his duty was to remain in communication with all governments. The policy of the Emperor clashed with the duty of the Pope. The quarrel had lasted for a long time, and had no issue. But, as with Spain, it was not till after Tilsit that Napoleon felt he could take up this Roman question with the will and ability to bring it to an end and close up this crack in the blockade. Called upon to enter the Italian confederation and make common cause therewith, Pius VII again refused to take up an attitude that would make him a belligerent. One part of his States was already occupied by French troops. On February 2nd, 1808, the Emperor carried out his threat. General Miollis took possession of Rome.

Actually the scandal of the profanation was perhaps even less grave than that caused by the action of the new kingdom of Italy, sixty-two years later, in taking possession of the Pontifical city. Napoleon recalled complacently that St. Louis had ceded none of his rights; nor, he added ironically, 'did that prevent him from being beatified'. Europe was silent, and let things take their course, whilst the Emperor reckoned that the presence of a few regiments in Rome would be enough to force the Pope's hand into surrender. As with Spain, his mistake was in believing in a rapid settlement, through combinations of skill and force, and in his belief that he had anticipated every development. Thenceforward he doubtless envisaged the absorption, pure and simple, of the Papal States into the Empire, if the Vatican did not happen to yield, but he flattered himself that everything would pass off imperceptibly and unnoticed. And he believed himself to be well-informed. At Rome itself, the Papal entourage, the majority of the Sacred College, thought that a rupture should be avoided at any cost. From Paris, the terrified Legate, Caprara, sent word that it would be mad to . resist the Emperor and to refuse him this essential element in his policy, the entry of the Holy See 'into a federative system with France against the English'.

Napoleon was gravely disappointed and vexed when he learned that, far from yielding, Pius VII was protesting against the occupation, recalling the Legate from Paris, and showing no fear of a rupture. Moreover this news reached him at Bayonne, in the midst of his uncertainties about the Spanish settlement. He saw clearly that to dethrone both the Pope and the King of Spain would multiply his difficulties, and that it was inopportune to 'burden his arm at once with a religious war beyond the Alps and a political war beyond the Pyrenees'. And he realized that, just when he was trying to reassure Catholic Spain with promises that her faith would be respected, a clash with the Church would be disastrous. He was inclined therefore to temporize. But just then, after obeying his conscience, Pius VII himself let himself be carried away by the contest. The Pontiff who had been happy to sign the Concordat and had anointed Napoleon at his coronation, now denounced the religious indifference of the Emperor, the protector of every sect and every cult. He exposed to the eyes of the faithful 'that system which supposes no religion', with which Catholicism could never join hands 'any more than Christ could ally Himself with Belial'. And in the end the subjects of the Sovereign Pontiff, lay and ecclesiastic alike, were forbidden to take oaths to the French authority, to serve, help or support that 'interloping government'.

FIRST CLOUD FROM SPAIN

This was just the time when Joseph, newly mounting his throne, was also styled an 'interloping King', when the Spanish clergy were rousing the people, when Spain was insurgent, when every day made Napoleon see more and more that this was no question of a handful of fanatics to be overcome, a few bands of brigands to be scattered, but that a difficult task of conquest was beginning. The Roman affair increased his ill-temper. He did not discuss them, and affected to be uninterested, to be letting things take their course, as he could no longer make his retreat. When Miollis took stern repressive measures, Napoleon neither approved nor blamed, but was content to advise silence. When he heard of Miollis having arrested Cardinal Gabrielli in the Papal palace itself, the Emperor hastened to write to the viceroy, Eugène: 'Take care that this is not mentioned in any gazette and is not talked about in any way.' That was on July 17th. Two days later came another event, which could not be concealed from Europe — the disaster of Baylen, in Southern Spain, the first military check of the Empire, the first crack in the edifice.

One moment of weakness in General Dupont led him to capitulate to the Spanish insurgents, wiping out the results of the day of Medina de Rio Seco, when Bessières had won a victory that seemed to assure the throne for Joseph. Baylen was a Trafalgar on land, but a shameful Trafalgar, as Dupont had surrendered without making a final effort against an enemy, who, as it turned out, were short of munitions, and also because instead of an unequal contest against the finest navy in the world, there had been 20,000 picked French soldiers pitted against inferior Spanish troops aided by peasant bands. And it is no arbitrary comparison to mention Trafalgar here. One disaster was to summon forth another. Dupont had doubtless ventured too daringly into Andalusia, and from afar Napoleon had been following his march with some anxiety. But it was necessary to reach Cadiz speedily, for there the remnants of the French fleet were in peril.

As help did not arrive, Admiral Rosily and his sailors had to give themselves up to the Junta of Cadiz. This meant an end of the hopes of Napoleon, who six weeks earlier, thanks to a regenerated Spain, had seen himself at the head of a fleet equal to that of England.

The Emperor instantly saw the dire consequences that would come from Baylen. They exceeded his fears. The loss of 20,000 men was nothing. These were still the days when he had 'an income of 100,000 men', and, as Thiébault said, his loss in Andalusia was not even two months' revenue. But such a prodigy of success over the finest army in the world had roused enthusiasm amongst the Spaniards. The moral effect was immense, and it unleashed the strength of the insurrection, to the humiliation and disheartening of the French.

In a few days things crashed. Joseph, hardly having made his entry to Madrid, decided to leave his throne there and come nearer to France. Bessières himself, the victor of Medina de Rio Seco, moved back towards the Pyrenees. And the English set foot on the Peninsula under a leader named Sir Arthur Wellesley, who was later to be Wellington. Communications with Portugal were cut, and there too came a rising and an English landing. Junot, thus isolated, lost his head and let himself be beaten at Vimeiro. One month after Baylen, the newly created Duc d'Abrantès capitulated in his turn, although the honourable convention of Cintra ensured the return of his troops to France, which Dupont's soldiers did not obtain. But the Russian fleet, on which Napoleon had counted for the naval war, was captured at Lisbon and conveyed to England. Thus foundered the political enterprise which, emerging from the Berlin decree and the Peace of Tilsit, began with the Treaty of Fontainebleau.

What was Napoleon's attitude towards this reverse? It was no longer to Madrid that his eyes were turned from Bayonne, but first to Paris, and then to Berlin, Vienna, Rome and St. Petersburg. He wrote to Joseph on the day that news

271

came of Baylen: 'Events of such a kind compel my presence in Paris. Germany, Poland, Italy, etc., are all linked. It is truly painful to me that I cannot be with you at this moment, and amid my soldiers.' This was his first check. He was anxious, and in a hurry to gauge the state of opinion. He might now be glad that the Tribunat had been suppressed, as it might perhaps have criticized, blamed, asked for explanations. But he must be assured that his still new authority was not shattered, that his prestige remained intact, that the great Empire was not tottering. Despite his haste to be back in his capital, he made a detour into the Departments of the West, determined not to omit his promised visit, to see for himself 'the spirit of the people of the Vendée', and several times declared his satisfaction. Doubtless he had feared that the rising in Spain, that large-scale Vendée, and the clash with Rome, might have had repercussions there.

It was a very small matter, a minute satisfaction. His anxieties reached further. If the Bayonne affair had succeeded, the forced abdication of the Spanish Bourbons would have been passed over as the execution of the Duc d'Enghien had been. But the French army was in retreat, Joseph had left Madrid, and Ferdinand VII had there been proclaimed sole and true King of the Spanish nation. In the eyes of Europe, Bayonne was a mere trap, an outrage which men, with belated indignation, compared with the abduction at Ettenheim and the drama of Vincennes. Such was the world's justice. His first failure brought about a display of virtue. Europe had seen, committed and accepted many acts of violence — beginning with the partitions of Poland — but she now began to talk with a sense of outrage of Napoleon's violence. After Vincennes, the court of Vienna had declared that it understood the necessities of policy. After the entry of Miollis into Rome, she had replied to the Pope's protest that his circular letter would only bring fresh troubles on his head. Now that affairs were going badly in Spain, Austria was arming, well supplied with

English money, and claimed that no throne could be secure after the provoked abdication of Charles IV. On Napoleon's birthday, August 15th, he had a striking scene with Metternich in Paris, at the reception of the diplomatic corps. There was no storm, but a firm courteous argument, 'a pacific move, an effort to tie the cords again'. He seemed to be trying to convince rather than to intimidate, whilst showing that he himself had no qualms: 'Well, is Austria wanting to wage war on us, or is she wanting to frighten us?' And then: 'You have raised 400,000 men. I shall be raising 200,000. Soon even the women will have to be armed.' It was true that, to be ready for anything, he would be raising a further 80,000 conscripts. Austria must realize the risks of provoking him. Napoleon thought he was sure of Alexander. 'The Emperor of Russia will be against you,' he said, looking at the Russian ambassador Tolstoy to get a sign of assent. Tolstoy's face remained frozen. But he went on, seeking to attract Austria by bringing her into a partition of Turkey and his vast, always misty, Oriental projects. And he ended on a good-natured key, seeking reconciliation and trust: 'Justify your peaceable dispositions by your acts as well as your words. For my part, I shall give you all the security you can desire.' A fresh war with Austria would be a most undesirable complication, and Napoleon was using every argument to avert it.

For if it broke out, what would become of his supposed work of Tilsit? Would not the great task of his policy be again in the melting-pot? Nevertheless, it was still on the Russian alliance that he fell back, and in this hour of doubt and alarm it was that alliance which he used to hearten the French people. 'My alliance with the Emperor of Russia leaves England no hope for her schemes,' he said in a message to the Senate. If he returned to Paris instead of going in person to help Joseph in insurgent Spain, it was because he needed tranquillity in Europe if he was to withdraw troops, from as far off as the banks of the Elbe, and use them to inundate Spain. The security which he had just promised to Austria was something which he needed for himself. Thinking aloud before Savary, he said: 'If I leave my army in Germany I shall not have war; but as I am obliged to withdraw it almost in its entirety, will that bring war on my head?' And he added: 'This is the moment to gauge the solidity of my work at Tilsit.'

The idea behind the meeting of crowned heads at Erfurt, in the last days of September, was to make plain to Europe the unalterable friendship of the two Emperors, to declare it with compelling brilliancy. The Emperor Francis of Austria was the only monarch absent. He had not been invited, because Napoleon proposed to ask Alexander's word that he would not leave the threats of Austria unpunished; but the court of Vienna did not fail to send to the congress its best diplomats. There were eighteen days of glamour and show and gala, staged as sumptuously as the setting of Tilsit had been natural and less sincere. The minor actors in the play were the vassals of the Germanic confederation, three of whom owed their crowns to Napoleon. To one of them, in his desire to astound the table at which he entertained all these illustrious ones of the world, he uttered the famous remark: 'Be quiet, King of Bavaria! Look at the living man before concerning yourself with his ancestors!' — drama again, but of Victor Hugo, not Corneille. And similarly, he enjoyed talking to these princes, like a Ruy Blas, of the days 'when I was an artillery lieutenant . . .' He used everything and everybody, French actors and actresses from the Comédie, French cooks, great names of the French nobility, but choosing the old – 'excellent for court purposes!' – rather than the new. He showed the virtuosity of an impresario, forgetting neither Goethe nor Wieland, whom he summoned in homage to literature, to that 'culture' of which the Germans were proud — and it was important to please Germany. He laid himself out to be charming, and used every resource of strength, wealth and intelligence. Erfurt was to be a greater Field of the Cloth of Gold, to cover up those far-away reverses of Baylen and Cintra, the raising of the first siege of Saragossa, the insurgent Spaniards with their monks and crucifixes.

But the spirit of Erfurt was not what that of Tilsit had been. Alexander had recovered himself, and the spell was less binding because the Tsar no longer had the same interest in letting it bind him. He confided in his sister Catherine: 'Bonaparte takes me for a fool. He laughs best who laughs last.' In another letter, to his mother, he explained that after Friedland he had 'for a time to adopt French views', in order 'to be able to have a breathing space and to augment our forces during that precious interval'.

But Napoleon, in spite of Spain, was still too powerful to break with. The Tsar calculated that it would be best to keep him deluded, and, by obtaining the right to occupy Finland and the Rumanian principalities, to compensate himself through this alliance which, to one Emperor, was the keystone of his system, to the other a means of gaining provinces and time. Napoleon had also to consider the question of divorcing Josephine and marrying one of the Grand Duchesses, and so creating a family link with Alexander. Which of his sisters would he ask for? Catherine, or little Anne? But Napoleon was afraid of being refused, and this fact made for many reticences which caused the Tsar to be 'very different from what he had been at Tilsit'. Above all, Alexander refused to threaten Austria, and to please him, Napoleon evacuated part of Prussia and reduced her war tribute. He was still pursuing his idea of federating the Continent. With the Prussian joined to the Russian alliance, France would truly have nothing to fear.

Napoleon was to be the dupe of Erfurt. After setting Talleyrand aside from the conduct of affairs, he had brought him back. Why? Because the Emperor, always inclined to be variable when he felt insecure in the saddle, required for this task of diplomatic consolidation a subtle and tactful man, a diplomat of the old school and of wide renown. Talleyrand was accused of treachery at Erfurt, of conducting a policy different from his master's, and of revealing his instructions to foreign powers. Actually he was playing a very complex game. Talleyrand fancied that, being more perspicacious and reasoning than Napoleon, he was really serving him. Alarmed by the extent of the conquests, he wanted to apply his 'law of possibilities' to a state of affairs which had become a search for impossibilities. He felt that all this lack of proportion was bound to lead to trouble, and tried to bring Napoleon back to a sense of proportion. Unable to convince him, Talleyrand adopted the perilous plan of constraining him. He would calm his fever by driving Austria and Russia to resistance. Talleyrand's penetrating eye saw that the Emperor was blinding himself with regard to the Russian alliance, and he feared that he might go even farther astray and let a partition of Turkey lead him into Oriental adventures. If the Tsar kept his head against Napoleon, the Emperor would be stopped, halted for his own good. But Talleyrand was the blinder of the two men in imagining that the conquests could be preserved by limiting their extent. He misunderstood the requirements of an unequal struggle against England, and also the secretly or openly avowed resolve of the great powers to push back France within her old boundaries and to leave her not one of her annexations. The game which Talleyrand thought subtle then became naive. When he advised Alexander to stand out against Napoleon, it was in order that the shock to the alliance should stop the latter from thinking that he could do just what he liked. When he informed Metternich of the Emperor's Eastern projects, and suggested that the court of Vienna should act as arbitrator between the Emperor and the Tsar, he thought he was continuing that policy of equilibrium which had been France's before the Revolution. He failed to see that, in the eyes of the other powers, circumstances had altered, and that the equilibrium had been destroyed by the annexation of Belgium and the left bank of the Rhine. Alexander and Metternich thereupon encouraged Talleyrand's confidences. They used them for their own ends, concluding that confidence in Bonaparte had lowered, since one of his entourage, invested with high powers, did not hesitate to have communications with them which ensured for that prophet of days-to-come a place at the congress of the future peace.

Napoleon left Erfurt deceived and betrayed, not admitting to himself that the spirit of Tilsit was no more, but melancholy, as after an unsuccessful party. After a stroll with Alexander on the day of departure, he was seen returning silent and pensive. The two Emperors were never to meet again. But he had gained objects of immediate importance. He had renewed the Russian alliance at a reasonable cost, for, less rash than Talleyrand supposed, he had dropped the partition of Turkey and reserved Constantinople. He was suspicious of Austria, but felt assured that she would not attack at once. He would have three months to straighten out affairs in Spain.

He did not hope for a reply from England to the offer of peace which he addressed to her in concert with the Tsar. It was a formality, designed to convince public opinion that England was still the cause of the continued hostilities. And Canning's negative response expressed English sentiments, which blamed the generals for not having kept Junot's army prisoner at Cintra as Dupont's had been at Baylen. The British government insisted that in any peace discussions the Spanish insurgents must take part. It recognized only Ferdinand VII as King of Spain, and still affected not to know that there was an Emperor in France. Thus there was at least one place left undazzled by Erfurt and unimpressed by the Russian alliance. That was London.

There was no question now of crossing the Channel and taking his grenadiers of the Guard to pitch their bivouacs in St. James's Park. It was a sad falling-off from the high hopes of Boulogne. He must now turn back to Madrid and drive the English army into the sea.

Returning to Saint-Cloud on October 18th, Napoleon set off reluctantly and listlessly for the Pyrenees on the 29th. Spain wearied him. To fight against peasant bands in the country of fanatics, with enemies ambushed behind every rock, where there was neither government nor state, and consequently no possibility of ending matters with a few thunderbolt marches, was a wearisome toil. 'Will you never stop making war?' Josephine asked him. And he retorted in ill-humour: 'Do you think I enjoy it? You know I can do other things than waging war, but I am the bondslave of necessity; I don't control events, I obey them.' And he was even more discontented with men than with things. He could still see that his absence only brought mistakes, that his orders were badly executed, that his instructions were not followed or not understood, and that he must be everywhere now that the course of events multiplied the difficulties confronting him.

A month after he left France, on December 2nd, he arrived before Madrid. He entered only for a moment, to show himself, but without his brother Joseph, whom he kept at a distance during this campaign. While the Emperor of the French came as a chastiser, an officer of police, Joseph must not be compromised in his subjects' eyes, and he was even given opportunities to obtain pardons and exercise his clemency. It was no good reckoning now on the Spaniards taking gladly to the new monarchy; the only thing to be done was to make them desire Joseph so as to escape conquest and domination by Napoleon himself. He left to Joseph the role of intercessor and protector, even forbidding him to take up residence in Madrid before he was asked to do so, as he had likewise forbidden him to be at his side when the bands of Palafox and Castanos were mercilessly cut down. And as it turned out, the solid classes of Madrid accepted Joseph, alarmed at first at the prospect of bombardment, then by the atrocities of the mob opposed to the handing over of the town, and completely resigned when news came of the defeat of the English rescuing force.

To beat the English, and beat them quickly, was the second task that Napoleon had given himself. With his fortieth year he had perhaps grown stouter and heavier. He was still the man of action, the trainer who spared himself neither fatigue nor pains, who crossed the passes of the Guadarrama on foot, through snowy days that seemed to anticipate the retreat from Moscow. Spending a night in a wretched posting-house, he chatted with the officers in comradely fashion, talking of the extraordinary adventures which had brought him from the school of Brienne to this Spanish hovel. 'And to-morrow, who know where?'

Napoleon pursued General Sir John Moore, who was retreating. He counted on inflicting a severe defeat on the English, as he would ere long be able to confront them on land, his own element. During the night of January 12th, 1809, a courier from France reached him. He read the despatches by the light of a camp fire, and Savary noted that 'although his face hardly ever changed, he yet seemed to have been reading something that made him thoughtful'. He had learned that Austria was arming and preparing to attack whilst he was in the recesses of Spain. They also confirmed news that had already come from Paris, contributing to the moodiness that he could no longer dissemble. Fresh plans were on foot in Paris against his possible death. Talleyrand and Fouché had become friendly again, and were showing themselves arm-in-arm in public, as if they were already the provisional government. The Emperor had, in fact, been warned that to replace him they had their eyes on Murat, with the assent of Caroline, who was even more embittered than her husband at losing their chance of the Spanish throne. This information, reminding Napoleon of the frailty of his monarchy, made him the more anxious because, six months earlier, a plot had been revealed to him regarding which he had not been able to discover precise details. It was a Republican conspiracy, in which were mentioned the names of General Malet, an adherent of Moreau, La Fayette, Lanjuinais, the liberals of the Senate, the former Girondin minister Servan. In all, something rather obscure: Fouché had minimised the affair to nothing, although the rumour ran that he himself was compromised. This vagueness made the Emperor anxious. And this vexation pursued him. The despatches he had received renewed his suspicions and alarm. Instantly he decided to return. Leaving to Soult the task of driving Moore into the sea, he paused for a few days at Valladolid, whence communication with both France and Madrid was easier, and he drew up his instructions before leaving Spain.

There he showed his irritability and short temper. On one occasion he suddenly revealed his innermost thoughts. During a review at Valladolid he happened to be near General Legendre, who had been one of those who surrendered with Dupont at Baylen, and there was a terrible scene in front of the troops when Napoleon, in a voice of thunder, hurled reproaches at one of those responsible for the catastrophe. Baylen, like Trafalgar, was a red-hot brand that seared him; and without thinking that every soldier of his guard could hear, he relieved his feelings and his nerves on the man before him, detailing the consequences of the disaster — Madrid evacuated, the insurrection raised to fever-pitch, the English in the Peninsula, the course of events altered, and the 'destiny of the world' perhaps altered too!

A few days later Napoleon was riding back to Paris. To Joseph's New Year greetings he replied with dryness that was like a shrugging of the shoulders: 'I have no hopes of Europe being pacified during this year. I have so little hope that I have just issued a decree for raising one hundred thousand men.' And he truthfully added: 'The hour of repose and tranquillity has not yet struck.'

CHAPTER XVIII

RETRIEVAL AT WAGRAM

NAPOLEON had gone to Spain grudgingly. He left Spain under pressure, discontented with himself, with others, and with events over which he had less control with every year that dawned. He had restored Joseph to Madrid by a fresh *tour de force;* but he knew that he was leaving guerillas everywhere, the English ready to land again, the troops weary of their tasks, the marshals in a bad frame of mind, and Joseph perpetually complaining. And he also knew that nobody was any more deluded about affairs than himself, in London or Vienna, Berlin or St. Petersburg, or even in Paris. 'A man who was not born to a throne and who has tramped the streets', as he defined himself, does not deceive himself with words or illusions. He knew that he would have to bear on his own shoulders the weight and the blame of the mishap of which he had been able to repair only the most obvious part. He would know that during his absence Austria must be preparing to attack him, whilst within France itself men were preparing to betray him, and those who had counselled him to dethrone the Spanish Bourbons would be quick to blame his ambition, his folly, his pride.

He left Spain in exasperation, having promised to return there in a month — he never returned — and came back to Paris like a thunderbolt. What reflections were his during that galloping journey! He had two instruments of rule — at home, success; abroad, fear. If he ceased to be fortunate, if he ceased to impose fear, his monarchy would crumble, and there could be merely an abyss in front of himself. Spain was the touchstone of all loyalties, those of servants, of allies, of fortune.

But that first, single check, though half-effaced by Joseph's return to Madrid, was enough to raise an opposition in France. It was no longer a question of intrigues and conspirators. Here was the Corps Législatif itself turning restive, and quibbling about — about what? About the code of criminal procedure! There were forty black balls, forty malcontents, a symptom unmistakable to a trained eye. And the boldness of Austria was another sign. Not only did Vienna believe that the hour had come to draw in Europe against France, but she did not fear Russian intervention. This was a straight blow at the policy of Tilsit. Napoleon did not know just how far Talleyrand had betrayed him at Erfurt, but he now understood better the coldness and reticence of Alexander. He could gauge the insufficiency of his anchors, the weakness of his power, so vast and yet so transitory — so transitory that now men were reckoning not merely on his death but on his downfall. He saw how the Empire might well founder within a few weeks. He must consolidate, consolidate, consolidate, and he had not even a child to avert the perilous problem of the succession. To have a child he must have a wife. A marriage with a princess, a family bond with a great dynasty, would give him the stability he lacked. But the Tsar — another disquieting symptom — did not follow up the Erfurt projects or the allusions to the grand-duchess, his sister.

And Napoleon was soon to leave Paris, where intrigue was rife and the Bourse was showing its own symptoms of unrest in the falling public funds, setting off again although he declared that there was 'no presumption of war'. During his absence everything would start again if he did not alarm the conspirators, at the risk of himself furthering the plot. Before Cambacérès, Lebrun and Admiral Decrès, there took place the great scene, the rumour of which sped instantly beyond his study, with Talleyrand and Fouché, the two accomplices. They were thunderstruck by words and looks, especially Talleyrand, whom Napoleon treated with the greater cruelty, as if he could not pardon the great seigneur, the married bishop, the minister who had held the conduct and secrets of his policy. The reproaches and insults left nothing veiled of what the Emperor knew. Sternly he reminded Talleyrand of his treacherous counsels, and the way in which he flattered him to his face in order to criticize him behind his back. He added graver insults — accusations of corruption, of wealth accumulated in ways of which he had been told by the confederated princes. As yet Napoleon did not know all. He was unaware of the double-dealings of Erfurt, of Talleyrand's advice to Russia and Austria. And the Emperor's apostrophe to these two witnesses of his life did not shrink from a reminder of the frailty of his throne: 'Remember that if a fresh revolution should come, it would break both of you the first, whatever part you took in it.'

The great scene of January 28th, 1809, calculated for public notice, was chiefly remarkable for the absence of any subsequent punishment. Fouché this time retained his ministry. Talleyrand lost his post as High Chamberlain, but his title and rank of great dignitary were not taken from him. These two 'forestallers of the future' would be only the more careful not to be overwhelmed by the collapse of the Empire, and would take up the challenge by helping the Restoration. What inconsequence or weakness made Napoleon threaten without punishing, as if he found comfort enough in just giving vent to his wrath? He himself wrote to his brother Louis; 'A king who is spoken of as a good fellow is a lost king.' But he showed singular indulgence, both now and later. No one was more often betrayed, or had fewer illusions about it, and yet was more sparing with punishment. And when men spoke of his despotism, he shrugged his shoulders. Within his Empire Napoleon was not so fully the master as is thought. Astonishing as the word may be, he had in him a certain timidity. Carnot, the Republican, spoke of his 'inconceivable weakness'; and said that 'he was for ever repeating his fault of threatening without striking, and of leaving the power to do harm in the hands of those whom he had injured, great and small'. Was it a fault, or was it, in Savary's phrase, the 'misfortune of his position'?

Carnot speaks also of his successive moods of soft-heartedness towards Austria, Prussia and Russia. But the Emperor needed allies abroad, just as at home he needed to gain the attachment of men through their interests. After the outburst of January 28th, he was afraid of disturbing too many people by taking sanctions which, says Mollien, would have left everybody without a sense of security. The feebleness was not in Bonaparte, but in his position, the instability of which was brought home to him daily, sometimes preventing him from being firm enough, sometimes making him brutal to the point of temerity.

This new war was of all things the most likely to increase that fatigue, the symptoms of which Napoleon could discern better than anyone. Signs of nascent exhaustion did not escape him, nor that yearning for rest and peace which he had made use of in the past, at Leoben and Campo Formio, to win popularity. This Austrian aggression was a bludgeon-blow to public opinion. Everywhere men saw themselves pitched back into the current of war without end. Presburg had not brought peace, any more than Campo Formio and Lunéville. Metternich boasted of the 'disguised armistices'. Graver still, it was realized that Austria, pushed on by England, was resuming hostilities because Spain was robbing France of troops and good generals, while the Grand Army, cut in two, lost the strength of its unity. 'If only I had here the three corps of Soult, Ney and Mortier!' Napoleon was to sigh after the cruel days of Essling and Wagram. There was no need to be a skilled soldier to foresee that in this coming campaign Soult, Ney and Mortier would all be missed.

So well did Napoleon divine this public anxiety that his watchword after Valladolid was that war was not in sight. Then he had to make admissions, to bow to the evidence. This war could not be averted; Austria willed it, and had brought forward half a million men, one of her greatest efforts. Already Prussian volunteers were joining the Austrian forces, and Prussia herself might be carried away by her patriots. And then the Emperor began to reassure everybody, Frenchmen as well as the princes of the Rhine confederation, with talk of the Russian alliance. He still believed in it, or pretended to. He wrote to them all that Austria would disarm when she saw 'the French and Russian armies ready to invade her territories', the integrity of which both Emperors guaranteed. Throughout March he repeated that formula, informing Munich, Stuttgart, everywhere, that the Tsar was indignant at Austria's conduct, that he had reiterated his promise to join his forces to those of France, and that he would lead his own armies in person.

To encourage morale he infused others with a certainty which he lacked himself, listening patiently to comments, as always when things were going badly. And meanwhile Caulaincourt, ambassador at St. Petersburg, was told to remind the Russian government that notes to Vienna were not enough, that words should be supported by threatening forces, and to make it plain, in fine, that the peace would not have been disturbed if the pledges of Erfurt had been firmer and more definite, more in accordance with Napoleon's desires.

Tilsit was being tested. This was the moment to gauge its solidity. At Erfurt it was already suspect. A few days more, and the myth of the Russian alliance would collapse. Alexander alleged that he was busied with Sweden on account of Finland, as also with the Turks, new allies of England, on account of the Danubian provinces. It was becoming clear that Austria was attacking France with the assurance of Russian neutrality. It might not end with mere neutrality. Alexander was under fire from within: the partisans of England wanted him to march against France.

From that he refrained. The right moment for a break had not come. France was still too strong: Friedland too recent. The interest of Russia demanded, for the moment, that Napoleon should wear himself out with a new war. And by the same token Prussia would also stand clear. Since Jena it had been her rule to keep on good terms with France, 'not to be swallowed up'. The coalition that came in 1813 was not yet ripe, and this time Napoleon was to have one adversary only, Austria, in the field against him. But Russia's inactivity was in itself a political and moral defeat for him. 'That is no alliance — I am duped!' he cried when the last hope of Alexander keeping his promise vanished. And there was also that cry from his heart, that he had counted too much on Russia, ventured too much by leaning on her: 'If only I could have suspected this before the Spanish affair!' At Tilsit he seemed to have reached his goal: peace had only to be made with England. England alone was still standing out. Once all the parts of the Continent were united, federated, well in hand, the defeat of England would be a certainty. Eighteen months later Napoleon had to wage war with Spain and with Austria; and this, as one of his entourage accurately remarked, was for British policy equivalent to a continuation of his wars with Prussia and Russia.

The diplomatic task of Tilsit had to be resumed. And it had to be refashioned by the same means — by victories. But every year made it harder of attainment. Not only was he continuing to consume man-power one year in advance, but he raised the annual tribute on youth from 80,000 to 100,000 men, and enrolled those conscripts who had been exempted from earlier classes. The famous '100,000 men income' was beginning to prove inadequate. With gathering difficulties, the bow was being strained more and more every day, to breaking-point.

Then, by miracles of activity, clear-sightedness and decision, Napoleon for a second time opened the road to Vienna: but at high cost, after five days of bloody fighting at Abensberg and Eckmühl. Four years earlier, at Ulm, the same enemy yielded and surrendered their capital without putting up a fight. This time the French lost Ratisbon, which had to be retaken by assault, and under its walls Napoleon was struck on the foot by a cannon-ball, a bruise, not a wound, like a warning of fate, a token that the times were becoming unkind. It proved more costly to conquer Austria alone in 1809, than the Russians and Austrians together in 1805.

After another murderous engagement, at Ebersberg, Napoleon entered Vienna for the second time. Before the city itself surrendered he had still to quell the working-class districts with a few cannon-shots: for this easy-going, pleasure-loving city was itself now swept with a sort of national fervour, a proof in itself that everything had to be fashioned again, that the goal was unattainable. The Emperor was back at Schönbrunn, amid the furnishings of the Hapsburgs, but only to receive bad news. Eugène had been defeated in Italy. The Tyrol was in revolt. In Poland, Poniatowski had had to retire before the Austrians, abandoning Warsaw to them; and Alexander looked on without moving. And heaven knew what was happening away in Spain and Portugal! Macdonald was hurried off to bring help to Eugène in resuming operations on the Adige, whilst other complications arose. An English squadron threatened a landing on the Italian coast and kept Murat on the alert. Rome was restive, and the occupation of the city led to daily conflicts with Pius VII. General Miollis was irritated, and perturbed by the resistance offered by the Pope and Cardinals, by their desire to shun a contact which he had at first tried to keep courteous in character. The Pope complained aloud of the attack on his independence. His assertions of sovereignty might at any moment kindle the Romans into a rising against the French. To put an end to this, and to strike terror, the remainder of the Papal States were annexed to the French Empire, four days after the fall of Vienna. The Pope would remain in Rome as a spiritual sovereign, but was deprived of his temporal power. With haughtiness Napoleon said that he was taking back the gift of Charlemagne; but he was once again beginning what the Revolution had attempted with the

Roman Republic; as Emperor, crowned and anointed, he was doing what he had refused to do as a Republican general in 1796. Where was the Concordat, where the reconciliation with the Church? Confronted by opposition to the achievement of France's destiny and the logical necessities of preserving the natural frontiers, he was reverting to Jacobin ideas, using the same methods, the same resorts to force; and the result was that all the forces which had ranged themselves against the Revolution in 1798 would now rise against the Empire, but with a multiplying strength so great that now the flood could no longer be stemmed. In the affairs of Rome, as in those of Spain, as in those of Russia before very long, the immediate reasons of Napoleon are readily understood, always deduced from circumstances, dictated by the need for immediate solution. But that is just how he heaped up what eventually would fall and crush him.

The break with the Papacy was not an access of the vertigo of power. He had not gone to Vienna for the sake of a hollow triumph, but because strategy ordered him to march directly against the undestroyed forces of the enemy. These forces surpassed his own. He had still battles to fight, and he might lose them. Before the bad days of Essling he was in an exposed position, observed by all Europe, abandoned by Alexander, and, after the high festivals of Tilsit and Erfurt, rather ludicrously 'duped'. His greatness consisted in not letting his anxiety be seen, in keeping his pulse steady, like the pulse he once let someone feel after an outburst of rage to show that he only let himself be swept away deliberately. But he had to uphold his credit, which was based on his prestige; and his prestige was based on the fear he inspired. He challenged in order to intimidate, and to show that his hand was steady.

He was in a hurry to be finished with the Austrians because he still feared that Prussia might move, and because he was not sure of Russia. His haste was such that he was himself seen carrying planks — for the building of the bridge on

288

which he was to cross the Danube. 'Politics, as in all the Emperor's wars, had to be considered as much as strategy.' But in this respect his haste, though 'indispensable', became headlong, and headlong to the point of temerity. It might be thought that Napoleon was lost when he undertook the passage of the Danube in face of the Archduke Charles's army, and, after the stern battles of Aspern and Essling, where Lannes met his death, when he had to fall back upon the island of Lobau. There it was that he felt the effects of the defection of the Tsar, who kept on writing to his dear friend, but sent never a Cossack — compliments and flatteries in lieu of an army corps.

Eylau had been a disputed battle. Essling was a reverse. For the first time the Emperor, commanding in person, was forced to withdraw in face of the enemy. A disaster was averted only by dint of energy and sacrifices. Napoleon had not anticipated that the sudden swelling of the river would imperil him. He ought to have anticipated it, and it would not have served as an excuse for one of his lieutenants. The successful passage of the Danube would have been an operation of genius. Failing, it was merely a rash move. Napoleon saw the consequences, especially the moral effect of an event which was to make every German head seethe, and left him – far from France and with a populous capital in his rear – in a position of greater danger than the Archduke's army could threaten him with, worn out as it was by the terrible days of May 21st-22nd. What he had to fear was the disheartening of his generals and troops. He thereupon, as at Mantua, held a council of war to strengthen morale. He explained why it was necessary to remain entrenched on the island of Lobau, waiting for the meeting with the army of Italy, and not landing on the right bank at any price: otherwise the retreat would not halt until Strasbourg, passing through an insurgent Germany, with Prussia, and even perhaps Russia, in pursuit of the French— a vision of what was to come to pass in 1813. Safety lay in clinging to this island of Lobau, a well-chosen camp too, in order to have it as a jumping-off place for another and a victorious battle.

Such a victory was necessary for the salvation of the Empire, and Napoleon was not exaggerating. He saw how very near everything was to turning against him. The view-halloo was on the point of being heard. There were signs in plenty — those obscure insurgents, partisans, leaders of bands, patriots and apostles, the Prussian Major Schill, the Tyrolese innkeeper Andreas Hofer, and upward to the head of the Catholic Church, who did not fear to lay him under excommunication. Nor did the Romans, despite the presence of French troops, fear to paste the bull of excommunication on the walls of the three basilicas.

The excommunication was issued a few days after Essling, and Pius VII, who had made no secret of his intentions, would not have hesitated, even if the battle had turned in the Emperor's favour. In his actual situation Napoleon received the sentence as an insult, and, more serious still, as an act of hostility when he was in difficulties, confronting the enemy. The ban hurt him all the more because he could not leave it unanswered, and his answer aggravated everything: he arrested the Pontiff and conveyed him away from Rome by the hands of General Radet's gendarmes. As in the episodes of Vincennes and Bayonne, Napoleon was able to say that the deed was not done by his express orders. The agents, however, interpreted and understood his real thoughts. Far from blaming Radet, he made him a baron, and contented himself with repeating his maxim: 'A thing should be accomplished if you are to admit to having thought of it.' In any case, the removal of the Pontiff took place on the same day that Wagram was fought, and its effect was diminished by that victory. The assault on the person of the Holy Father, to the Catholic Courts, and to his Apostolic Majesty himself, would be one more 'necessity of policy'. Both inside and outside of France the faithful would be able to style Napoleon the Antichrist. This did not matter so long as fortune was loyal to him. But when the great reverses came it was to be one of the elements in the catastrophe.

His attention, however, was fixed first of all on the battle which was to restore his position. Six weeks were spent in vigilance and preparation so that, this time, all the chances should be on his side: he could no longer afford a failure. It then looked as if his military genius grew greater with his difficulties. Far from being made anxious by the gravity of the stake, as he had been at Marengo, as he would be on his last battle-field, he was marvellously in control of his wonderful faculties. After planning everything to the last detail with complete lucidity of mind, and physically alert on the day of decision, he carried out, under fire, one of his finest manœuvres which both saved and won the day. The Danube was crossed, the Archduke Charles's position was carried, the reverse of Essling wiped out, the enemy forced to retreat. 'From the standpoint of art, it was perfection, in reasoning and inspiration, in boldness and caution — the masterpiece of Bonaparte's maturity.'

'And yet the Emperor was only moderately pleased with the battle of Wagram.' It had been costly, both in officers and men, almost as costly as to the beaten side. Both from generals and from rank and file he had demanded an effort which could not be continually asked. Circumstances had favoured him, the Archduke John's army having failed to rally that of the Archduke Charles, whereas Prince Eugène, Macdonald and Marmont had fortunately arrived in time. Napoleon contrasted Wagram with Jena and Austerlitz. Here was no longer the winged victory: the Grand Army no longer existed. He felt his instrument to be less supple; and as Thiers said, there was the beginning of 'a confusion to be imputed, not to the mind of the commander, but to the quantity and diversity of the elements of which he was forced to make use if they were to suffice for the immensity of his task'. The beginning of fatigue, too, with everything strung taut, almost to excess, in the physical energy, the courage, and even the powerful brain of the leader. The beginning, in fact, of the struggle against the nature of things.

And Napoleon was 'only moderately pleased' because the days that followed Wagram were no longer those that succeeded Austerlitz. The essential result had been attained by a superb, and indeed necessary, retrieval. But no more. He was clear-sighted enough to see that this was not so much a victory as the illusion of victory. This time the Emperor of Austria did not come to his bivouac to ask for peace. What would Napoleon have done if Charles, whose army was sorely tried, but not destroyed, had taken refuge in Hungary, where he would have found fresh soldiers and resources? This grave embarrassment to the victor was avoided by a false move on the part of his adversary. The Archduke withdrew into Bohemia.

The pursuit was nerveless. Napoleon had too many reasons for desiring an end to this campaign. He was tired, and filled with doubts, and always regretting the 200,000 men away in Spain. If things turned against him, might not the Russians emerge from their cruel and insulting neutrality to overwhelm the French? 'No, enough blood has been spilt.' Wagram was fought on July 6th. On the 12th the armistice was signed at Znaïm. Davout's corps camped at Austerlitz. A few weeks later the Emperor held a review there, and at dinner he asked his generals, as if sounding them: 'This is the second time I have been here: shall I come a third time?' They answered: 'Sire, in the present circumstances nobody would dare to wager against it.' The idea of interminable warfare, with all its consequences, was entering men's minds, and already the weaker among them were thinking of withdrawing from the game. Bernadotte had to be rebuked for unjustly attributing to himself and the Saxons under his command the credit of Wagram. The man who was to draw the prize of the throne of Sweden would become an enemy. As a sort of compensation, the restive and long suspect Macdonald was made a marshal. The Emperor was feeling the necessity for manipulating his circle.

Back again at Schönbrunn, he experienced many other
cares and anxieties during the peace negotiations, which
continued until mid-October. Everything conspired to
thwart him. He felt himself beset by fools and traitors. Blow
followed blow. The trusted Soult had conceived the idea of
carving out a kingdom for himself away in Portugal, which he
was not even capable of holding in the face of the English.
For a second time Portugal was lost. Wellesley had entered
Spain after Soult's defeat, and fought a battle which he ought
to have lost, but from which he escaped; and the engagement
remained as a check to the French through disagreement
amongst the leaders and growing indiscipline in the army. The
story of that absurd affair of Talavera made Napoleon shrug
his shoulders in pity. 'I really ought to be everywhere!'
And then some donkey decided to bring the Pope into France,
as far as Grenoble, and everybody was kneeling as the persecuted Pontiff drove by. Orders were given to go back and
intern Pius VII at Savona. And then the English had landed
on the island of Walcheren; the 'cowardly' and 'incompetent'
General Monnet had surrendered Flushing, so that Antwerp
was threatened.

To crown matters, Fouché, Acting-Minister of the Interior,
spread alarm through the country. He raised the national
guard, as if invasion were imminent, and called up soldiers
who had been retired on account of Republican sentiments —
in fact, he armed the malcontents. He asked Bernadotte,
so recently disgraced, to take command of this national guard.
What did Fouché want? In the Emperor's absence he was
the ruler of France. At first glance Napoleon missed the full
meaning: he approved of Fouché's action, seeing only a
means of augmenting the Empire's forces. But France was
startled by this mass levy, this reversion to '93. Complaints
and protests against Fouché flowed into Schönbrunn. The
Emperor was disconcerted, and then furious. He saw a crisis
springing to birth, and no longer knew what he ought to do.
He had just made Fouché Duke of Otranto. He withdrew his

portfolio, but signed his letters patent. He deprived Bernadotte of his new command, which left him with a running
sore, and ordered the dissolution of the national guard, re-
proaching Fouché for having unreasonably alarmed the
Empire, discerning beneath this episode one of those plots
which always arose whenever he was far afield. The abduction of the Pope had provoked agitation amongst French and
Belgian Catholics, troubled the clergy, and revived the hopes
of the royalists. And the Emperor grumbled: 'I am weary
with intrigues.' Above all, they made him anxious, and
although he wrote stern letters to Fouché, he once again did
not dare to remove him from office. Where would things have
been without the recovery at Wagram! From every point of
view it had been time for a victory. It was time now to sign
peace. 'If peace is not made,' said Napoleon at Schönbrunn,
'we shall be surrounded by a thousand Vendées.'

Here there supervened one more of those abrupt reversals
of plan customary to Napoleon. He still found himself in
what he called 'forced situations', which were, as he knew, the
successive aspects of the insoluble problem. When Austria
attacked him, when the Emperor Francis violated the word
he had given after Austerlitz to wage no further war, Napoleon,
for his part, had vowed to make an end of Austria. But the
Austrian army had put up a better resistance than he had
expected. It was beaten, and its leaders were demoralized
because they had thought victory was theirs — but it was not
destroyed. If Napoleon then talked of deposing the Emperor
Francis and sundering his triple crown, he did so in order
to intimidate, to get what he wanted. And what he wanted
was always the same thing: it always came back to the strict
enforcement of the Continental blockade. In that, if not
elsewhere, there was a rigid sequence in Bonaparte's ideas,
because therein lay the sole solution, the essential tool, for
a problem that had not changed since Trafalgar. Trieste and
Fiume would complete the 'Illyrian provinces', which, annexed to the French Empire, would form an uninterrupted

coastline as far as Turkey. And this was no longer a road to the East for the 'great objective', the realization of which, always postponed, was emerging from Napoleon's thoughts since the languishing of the Russian alliance. It was a matter of customs barriers, one more bulwark against the admission of British goods into Europe, one more padlock added to the blockade.

During these negotiations, made difficult by Austria's expectancy of some accident supervening to spare her fresh sacrifices, the English evacuated Walcheren, and the insurgents received set-backs in Spain. Austria became more tractable again. And Napoleon, feeling himself master of the discussion, also changed his tone, and, as if by some sudden inspiration, he disclosed the thought which was crossing his mind. Let France and Austria join hands, let them unite for the preservation of peace. An Austrian Tilsit would make Wagram the means for obtaining the Austrian alliance. If Europe were not federated from one end, it would be from the other; the Austrian alliance would make amends for the Russian. It would be a buttress and a means of consolidation.

For everything counselled consolidation. On the eve of the signature of this new peace a new symptom showed itself, opening a view into strange depths. During a parade at Schönbrunn, a young German student approached the Emperor. He was found to be carrying a knife, and unconcernedly confessed that he had wanted to kill the tyrant of the country, and moreover, that if he were allowed to go free, he would again seek to kill him. It was impossible to show mercy to Friedrich Staaps. And it was still more impossible to carry out the Emperor's recommendation that the news of the facts should be kept quiet. It was soon known in France. The ever-possible accident, so often taken account of, returned to men's minds in a new light — that of the national fanaticism which was raising armed hands against the Emperor in Germany, as political fanaticism had formerly done against the First Consul.

And then Napoleon began to think of the future, of safeguards, of the stability he lacked. These European affairs grew more complex wherever they were touched. This Austrian war had revived the difficulty of Poland. For in this last campaign the Poles had been the only really militant allies of France. The contingents of the Germanic confederation had fought, but only in middling style. But the Polish legions had gone with spontaneity and zest; and in Spain also these valuable auxiliaries were not sparing with their blood. They could not be repaid with ingratitude; and after all, a strong Poland would be useful to France. But to set up once more a large Poland would completely alienate Russia, and the difficulty became the same as in 1807. How could everybody be satisfied without alarming anyone? Galicia, taken from Austria, had to be allotted to somebody, and Napoleon attempted a judgment of Solomon. One part of Galicia would go to enlarge the grand-duchy of Warsaw; another, 'more than their winnings', would go to the Russians; the chief part remaining in Austria. He reiterated to St. Petersburg, with clarity and insistence, that the idea of a renaissance of Poland was not present to his mind, declaring that he 'approved the disappearance of the words Poland and Poles not only from all political transactions, but even from history'. But, small though it was, the extension of the grand-duchy of Warsaw was disquieting to the Russians, and they made it a grievance against the French alliance. A 'phantom alliance' now: but Napoleon persisted in maintaining it. 'The very fact that the Emperor no longer believed in the Russian alliance made it all the more important that the belief which he himself had lost should be shared by the rest of Europe.'

To preserve that simulacrum was useful, not only to keep Europe respectful, but to secure another buttress, since experience had proved that Russia did not respond when she was required. Why should not Austria have her Tilsit? An attack on France had brought her nothing but invasion and losses of territory. It was rash to drape oneself in honour and in the pride of the Hapsburgs, whilst it was simple to feign friendship and gain time. That was the example given by Alexander, and he had just shown that such commitments cost little!

Thus Napoleon had admitted, a few weeks earlier, that in the case of Russia he had been duped, that he could no longer show Alexander 'a confidence which he no longer felt', and not only did he seek to preserve the illusion of the Russian alliance, but he was ready to start again with Austria. He still wanted one solid, and he hoped durable, European system. And he found only opportunists to ask his friendship, such as Prussia, who still affirmed her loyal subjection — opportunists whose only thought, like Prussia's, was to gain time and avoid being swallowed up. Wagram produced the same result as Jena and Friedland, but produced nothing more. If victories ceased, if Napoleon's strength was cut into, the 'phantom alliance' would vanish into thin air.

Speaking of Alexander, Francis, and Frederick William, the Emperor had remarked: 'They have all given each other a rendezvous on my tomb, but they dare not turn up.' The day was not so far off when they would dare. To forestall their league, Napoleon had one last chance to try — a family alliance, stability through marriage, entrance to the most exclusive of the world's clubs, to the inner circle of kings. When he was there, he would have a real buttress for his system, a guarantee for his Empire . . . It was a new illusion, greater even that that of Tilsit; but, shared by the peoples, it was to bring a renewal of splendour before the setting of his sun.

CHAPTER XIX

SON-IN-LAW OF THE CÆSARS

EXCEPT perhaps after Tilsit, all of Napoleon's returns to Paris were care-ridden. Even more than the others, the return from Wagram was laden with preoccupations. Everything went to confirm his feeling that he was not gaining strength, and this time he was made strongly aware that the first squall might carry him away, his crown and his Empire too. On men and their loyalty he had never had any illusions: 'Men rallied to me to enjoy security; they would leave me to-morrow if everything became dubious.' And it was at this time that he one day asked Ségur what people would think if he happened to die, and when the latter became confused in his courtier-like answer, he retorted: 'Not at all! They would say "Ouf!" ' He knew that by now he was not so much loved as put up with, that those whose fortune he had made would quickly cut their links with him if adversity befell, and that he would find few to share to the end the risks that he himself ran. Observers discerned in him a sort of 'hidden bitterness' against everyone; and whilst his aged mother still shook her head wondering whether things would last, his thoughts were turned to finding means of making them last, because he had felt the ground quiver beneath his feet, caught a glimpse of the beginning of the end.

Cambacérès was the first to be summoned to Fontainebleau, and to him he spoke more freely than to anyone else. He told him of his intentions, of part of his anxieties. The Austrian aggression, complicated by the Spanish insurrection, had been a dangerous blow. Disaster was averted at Essling by inches. The Russian alliance was cracked. The Germanies were in a ferment, and Staaps had produced effects undreamed of by that young fanatic. It was no longer the stray cannon-ball, the chance bullet, that threatened the Emperor's life. That was known, and there were many anxious to have foreseen all eventualities. Plans were being laid in Paris. After Murat, it was of Eugène that men were thinking as the possible heir. Eugène would certainly be the least bad. But who would accept him? Napoleon saw none of his own brothers capable of replacing him, and he knew that on his death they would dispute the throne with the heir he might have named. Would they even wait until Napoleon was actually dead? In Madrid, Joseph's entourage were already talking of the succession as if it were open. Joseph dreamed of the rare prospect, and saw himself as a liberal Emperor, favoured by the Senate. He would be sensible and cautious; he would give up superfluous conquests, satisfy England, conclude peace. It was already a commonplace, and history would repeat it interminably, that a little moderation would settle every-thing — as if moderation depended on Napoleon.

'Only a son of my own can bring things together.' He had the illusion that by ensuring his descent he would ensure his throne. He was now feeling the craving for an heir of his flesh and blood; and Josephine had understood as much when, some time before, to avoid repudiation as a sterile wife, she had whispered to him the absurd idea of a supposi-titious child.

He had long opposed the notion of divorce, to which he was pushed by all who were concerned about continuity. His own family were motivated, in their narrow outlook, only by their jealous hatred of the Beauharnais family, but there were also political forces favouring a dynasty to rob the Bourbons of every hope of return. The ideas of 1804 reappeared with the shocks, light though they were as yet, dealt to the Napoleonic system. What was a dynasty without a direct heir? The foundation of the Empire, the institution of the Imperial heredity, had been fathered by one great reason of state. No satisfaction had resulted. Men of weight regarded it as calamitous that the crown might possibly descend to any of the Emperor's 'revoltingly incompetent' brothers, And Fouché summed it all up when, in October 1807, referring after Tilsit to the Russian marriage, he wrote to the Emperor that 'the English were encouraged in their enterprises against him . . . by the single thought that, being childless and consequently without an heir, the Emperor, in the event of his always possible death, would bring down the entire government'. The death of Josephine was desired by the most coldly calculating. 'That would remove many difficulties. Sooner or later, he would have to take a wife who would bear children.' And for four years Fouché had renewed these themes. He even tried to persuade Josephine. What a noble page in her story a voluntary sacrifice for the common weal would be!

Would it really cost Bonaparte so much to repudiate Josephine? His attachment to her was habit, and it had been said, a superstition. He might lose in her a lucky charm. But really he felt the need for a surer talisman. Policy now demanded divorce, just as, on his return from Egypt, it had counselled forgiveness. Napoleon did not feel that fortune would desert him when he had repudiated Josephine. He repudiated her because he felt that fortune was going to desert him. He required an alliance close enough and strong enough to protect him from utter ruin in the event of reverse and danger. Only an impervious alliance with one of the great states of the Continent would enable him to close this series of wars from which he wished to emerge at any price, because he knew that in the end he was bound to succumb. But he was not exaggerating the value and the durability of family pacts. When Daru advised him to choose a Frenchwoman, as a choice that would meet with the approval of the nation, Bonaparte replied that the marriages of sovereigns are affairs of policy, not of sentiment. 'My own must not even be determined by motives of internal policy. It is a question of assuring my influence abroad, and of enlarging it by a close alliance with a powerful neighbour . . . It must rally to my crown, at home and abroad, those who have not yet rallied to it. My marriage offers me the means of doing so.' There was no element of pride, or of mystery. His marriage was to be an assurance, the child a 'shield', the wife a lightning-conductor. Such were the motives and thoughts with which he returned to Fontainebleau on October 27th, 1809.

A veil of melancholy is wrapped round the episode of the divorce, and over the figure of the deserted wife. When Bonaparte thought of forestalling the fall of what was bound to collapse, when he was on the brink of ruin, legend was already flowing into elegy. In fact, he himself was seeking a safeguard and a means of salvation. She herself played her last card, and her wiliness was seen once on the last page of their novelette. On the day when Napoleon, returning from Austria, decided to inform her of the rupture, Josephine swooned. To avoid any scandal, the Emperor summoned the chamberlain on duty, and together they carried the Empress into her apartment. But, after tripping on his way down the narrow staircase, M. de Bausset was surprised to hear Josephine whisper to him: 'Take care — you're holding me too tight!' How well she could play the woman's part! On December 15th, at the family meeting before which the pair announced their separation by mutual consent, she stopped with consummate art in the middle of her statement, choking with sobs. Not that her tears were forced: after all her struggles to keep her husband, she might well be nervously exhausted. Nor need one rule out her sensibility, her regrets and even the humiliation arising from a failure, nor yet the memories of her youth and her former love. Josephine no longer hoped to shake the resolve of her 'little Bonaparte'. But she could at least soften him. She had to assure the position of her own children, and her own status as a discarded royal consort. She excelled in winning the sympathy of the public, and of history. And it was Napoleon who was awkward, moved, constrained, and who cut a poor figure:

301

for in the politics of life the woman is always superior to the man, however extraordinary he may be. Malmaison remained her domain, and from there she continued to be dexterously useful. Her taste for the old regime inclined her towards Austria. She was on very friendly terms with Madame Metternich. And the discarded spouse took her part in helping on the Austrian marriage.

That was really only the second choice of Napoleon. The idea that he had pondered for two years past had been to tighten the Russian alliance by marrying a sister of the Tsar. But the weakening of the alliance left things very much in the air. Later Alexander began to shelter behind his mother, in whose hands family affairs were vested. The Grand Duchess Catherine was then of age, but she had been hurriedly married to the Duke of Oldenburg, as if to avert a request for her hand from the Emperor of the French. It was not a good sign of the feelings of the Russian court, and there remained only the Grand Duchess Anne, who was still a child. Everything had been delayed too long.

But now Napoleon could not wait. His separation from Josephine had been a clear indication of his intention. The Emperor's marriage was a universal topic in Europe, and, although little Anne was hardly fifteen, she was doubtless the bride whom Napoleon would have wished for. The 'invariable' union with the Tsar, despite all the blows to his trust, remained the fixed pole of his policy. There was need to confirm the alliance in the eyes of France and Europe, for the fickleness of Russia during the Austrian campaign had been plain for all to see. Napoleon's dream was that Alexander should come in person to Paris, bring his sister, for the 'marriage of Charlemagne and Irene'. Caulaincourt, the ambassador in St. Petersburg, was instructed to say that 'no importance was attached to the conditions, not even to religious ones'. The future Empress could remain in her own faith. Only one thing mattered: 'start from the principle that it is children that are wanted'. So long as the Grand

Duchess was deemed capable of bearing them, there were no objections or problems from Napoleon's side. The Russian court, and the ambassador Kurakin, were treated with every consideration. A loan was desired in St. Petersburg — as is the custom of the country — and the loan was granted in advance. The Polish question was raised, and on January 4th, 1810, the new treaty with Russia was signed, including an article declaring that 'the Kingdom of Poland will never be re-established'. In such terms did Alexander conceive and practise friendship. He got all he could out of it, giving as little as he could; and in any case he did not give his sister.

Caulaincourt, newly made Duke of Vicenza, was to carry on the negotiations with sufficient skill to save the Emperor of the French from being shown the door. But Alexander's lack of zeal, his everlasting plea that everything depended on his mother, the slowness and questionings of the old Empress, notoriously hostile to the Corsican usurper, kept things dragging on, and brought doubts of Russia's good faith. Refusal was in the air. Napoleon did not abandon his project, but he began to feel the necessity for arranging an alternative marriage. He had not repudiated Josephine for nothing. He certainly could not fall back on the daughter of the King of Saxony, marry nothing better than the German princesses given to Jerome and Eugène, or bring himself to a level with Berthier, become a nephew of the King of Bavaria, one of those Kings of the Emperor's own manufacture. Besides, the King of Saxony's status as Grand Duke of Warsaw would make Alexander take umbrage at such a union. In the end the Tsar did not grant the hand of his sister. The Emperor was almost offering his daughter. Whatever Bonaparte's reasons for preferring a family link with Alexander, this other match would fully compensate them. If Napoleon could not enter the family of the Tsar, he could enter that of Marie Antoinette and Louis XVI, both of whose names were borne by their grand-niece and goddaughter, the Archduchess Marie Louise of Austria.

Cambacérès, hostile to the Austrian marriage, like most men of the Revolution, had formerly declared his certainty that 'within two years France would have war with one of those two houses, the one whose daughter the Emperor did not marry'. He should have added, to make the prophecy complete, that within four years the Emperor would also be at war with the other. Through the traditional match-making diplomacy of Vienna, the Emperor Francis was anxious to forearm himself against fresh blows, to prepare a revenge without rousing suspicions. Metternich would admit as much; Marie Louise was handed over to the ogre so as to obtain 'a halt that enabled us to gather strength again'. For his own part, Napoleon reckoned that a father-in-law had as much weight as a brother-in-law, and that the Emperor of Austria would be more interested in maintaining his daughter on the throne of France than the Tsar would be in maintaining a sister there. Francis and Metternich allowed him to think so. Here was the political realist basing his investment on family principles, family sentiment, just as if he had not been enlightened by his own family history, and on reasons of the heart, as if he were incapable of resisting them. Did he not see how little the condemnation of the Pope must count with his Apostolic Majesty, if there was no hesitation about accepting as a son-in-law an excommunicate whose divorce was possibly not even regular?

For, in order to break the religious marriage of Napoleon and Josephine, it was impossible to apply to Rome, or rather to the exile of Savona. The annulment was pronounced, under orders, by the ecclesiastical court of Paris; and that body, after due consideration, could find no better motives than the absence of the appropriate priest, because Fesch had united them in secret, and the 'lack of consent' on the part of Napoleon.

In the Austrian marriage, Napoleon was the dupe of an aulic deceit. It was one more act of the 'august comedy' of the kings who were battling, not against regicide France, but against the France of the natural frontiers. They would put the amorous lion, the flattered hero, to sleep. But in his own view, this was one more anchor dropped, an addition of strength to his war map. He realized from experience that Austria was still formidable and could not be despised. At the great family and state council when Napoleon sought the advice of the dignitaries regarding the match, Lacuée remarked that 'Austria was no longer a great power'. And Napoleon answered him sharply: 'It is clear, sir, that you were not present at Wagram.' He also discerned the influence and prestige which close kinship with the Germanic Cæsars would bring him over the peoples of Germany. An intimate link with Austria, whilst the Russian alliance survived in form at least, would be the continuance, perhaps the con- clusion, of his Continental policy. Ever since the Spanish affair, enemy propaganda had represented him as a dema- gogic Cæsar, a Jacobin aspiring only to overturn all thrones. And this reputation did grave harm to his system of a general federation of the Continent, the only weapon by which he could overcome England. Entrance to one of the greatest sovereign houses of Europe — and the Hapsburgs were more historic than the Romanovs, and Catholics as well — would preclude anyone from representing him as the man of revolutions. The mingling of his blood with that of the most conservative of dynasties would legitimate him in the eyes of all; he would join up their preservation with his own; and this would be, as he thought, the definitive stabilization that he sought for himself.

These thoughts, which were so many illusions, filled his mind more and more as it became clear that the Russian court was slipping away. The Emperor of the French could not remain the patient suitor for ever. A Parisian bourgeois would not have suffered so many evasive replies and post- ponements. There were successive delays for the Tsar's mother to declare herself, and the month of January, 1810, was nearing an end without bringing the 'decisive news'

There could no longer be any hope of its being favourable. When Napoleon received it, he had already, and rightly, made up his own mind. It was a thinly veiled refusal, and Napoleon had obviously been 'led by the end of his nose'. He had taken a long time to discover it.

He was now in danger of ridicule if, after openly aspiring to this exalted marriage, he did not instantly make another, and one even more astounding and flattering. He did not engage in fresh matrimonial agency negotiations. He addressed himself to Prince Schwarzenberg as on a matter to be taken or left, giving him one day to say yes or no, an ultimatum which did not leave him time to consult Vienna. The Austrian ambassador consented, disposed of the hand of his imperial master's daughter, and was not disavowed. He must have had grounds for knowing that he would not be. And forthwith Napoleon drew up the marriage contract on the model of that which had served for Marie Antoinette and Louis XVI.

It was a bold stroke, this well-trumpeted marriage which would bring another 'Austrian woman' to Paris. Napoleon was later to say: 'When the Empress arrived here, she played her first game of whist with two regicides, M. Cambacérès and M. Fouché.' Certain highly placed supporters of the Empire represented to him that the Austrian marriage would be a challenge to the France of the Revolution. Murat was particularly indignant; revolutionary feelings had revived in the King of Naples through fear of the possible consequences in Italy of this union with the Hapsburgs, closely related to the Neapolitan Bourbons. Talleyrand voiced the Emperor's mind when he recalled the alliance of 1756, which had enabled the Bourbon monarchy to resist England. The argument was in the direct thread of the reign, both logically and practically, and all the better as it was a question not of reversing, but of completing, alliances. So high a price did Napoleon place on the alliance with the Tsar that he was above all things anxious not to break it. The meaning of the refusal had certainly been clear. If Alexander had wished, he would surely have given one of his sisters to his friend. Was it conceivable that this autocrat could be ruled by his mother? The move had been jointly staged by mother and son; and the proof was found in Kurakin's papers. But injured pride would hold fast, and in any case the hand of Marie Louise was an adequate satisfaction for Napoleon's self-respect. And he tended the self-respect of the Tsar with care, pretending to sympathize with the reasons of age and health and religion which had been put forward, and assuring him that the choice of another princess 'would mean no alteration of policy'. Far from damaging the friendship of Tilsit, this Austrian match should draw the three Emperors closer together, Vienna being their uniting, not their sundering, force. 'Gentleness, discretion, prudence. Avoid anything that might wound.' Those were Caulaincourt's instructions for the moment.

But it was difficult. After so many signs of middling good faith, who could say of what this too Byzantine Alexander might be capable? Possibly, as the Tsar's brother-in-law, Napoleon would have ratified the treaty already signed by Caulaincourt, which pledged France not to allow the tomb of Poland to be reopened, not even to suffer its name to be uttered. But if Cambacérès was right and the Emperor would be at war with Prussia in two years' time, he would still need the Poles, and by humiliating them he would have discouraged them, and dishonoured himself to no purpose. Thereupon, after reflection, Napoleon was willing to promise never to re-establish the Kingdom of Poland, but not to participate in the armed repression of a Polish revolt. He consented to recognize only a Grand Duchy of Warsaw, and not, as Alexander wished, to guarantee the limits of that state against all other powers. The Tsar could not help feeling, through these slight and adroitly formed restrictions, that Napoleon was on his guard. Mistrust increased on both sides. But something more serious than the matter of Poland would be necessary to alter alliance and friendship into war. The official relations between the two Emperors remained in the same harmony, and Kurakin was shown every honour on the day when the triumphal marriage was celebrated. And if only men could see Marie Louise with the same eyes as Napoleon! Beyond doubt he was proud to take to his couch the daughter of these haughty Hapsburgs. He had the satisfaction of being treated as a sovereign of ancient race, of attaching his dynasty once more to that which the Revolution had overturned, of amalgamating in his own person revolution and legitimacy, of fulfilling his great idea of fusion. His taste for women made him alive to the eighteen-year-old freshness of this German girl, this 'lovely filly', a rose most delicately tinted, an enticing flower, and docile — which, with her, was the same as facile, as she was to show with Neipperg. For Napoleon she had another attraction in her walk and bearing, the inimitable simplicity of a princess, well trained for her role of Empress by her Hofburg education, so perfect in every way that she would not fail to give a son to the husband chosen for her by policy, an heir to this Empire over which she was coming to reign.

Above all, Napoleon saw the wider aspects of this marriage, not only in its promise of a successor, but in the fulfilment of his constant thought, a unified Europe, a federated Continent. Already the wedding festivities were almost another Tilsit, heading for an alliance, in all but the word, with Austria. French and Austrians were fraternizing; soldiers who had fought one another at Wagram were clinking glasses. When Berthier came to Vienna to conclude the marriage by proxy, he was welcomed with particular eagerness by the military, and he brought to the Archduke Charles, the adversary in so many encounters, the cross of the Legion of Honour, that cross which the Emperor wore, the cross of the soldier, the same that Napoleon had with his own hands given to the bravest of Alexander's grenadiers on the banks of the Niemen. In Vienna, France was favourite; in Paris, it was Austria. The effusion and gestures and spectacles of Erfurt were repeated. Metternich handled that enthusiasm admirably. He represented the Emperor Charles at these ceremonies and fetes which repeated the rejoicings at the marriage of Louis XVI, and at the nuptial benediction with its surrounding pomp of crowned heads, although, to Napoleon's great annoyance, thirteen of the cardinals assembled in Paris were missing — their absence a reminder of the excommunication. During the wedding banquet, Metternich appeared at a window and called out a toast to the crowd, raising his glass: 'To the King of Rome!' Then every miracle had come to pass! The Emperor of Austria had already renounced the Holy Roman Empire, and was abandoning to France the ancient title of the future Germanic Cæsars — King of the Romans.

Paris thronged to see Napoleon and Marie Louise in their crystal coach — the same Paris that had applauded the beheading of Marie Antoinette. Opinions are but changes of clothing. Men will accept every idea in its turn, and every metamorphosis. How many characters had not Napoleon himself concocted already, without counting those still to come? The bitter philosopher within him knew the fickleness of crowds, a fickleness equal to that of kings. And this would seem the finest chapter in the reign, because France believed that, this time, wars were really over and done with — forgetting the war that still went on with Albion. The Austrian bride was popular because she was seemingly a pledge of peace. Seated on the throne of Louis XVI, Bonaparte seemed to have raised it higher. This was the moment when he looked, and felt, most kingly. But he did not forget whence he sprang, nor overlook his great idea of reconciling Frenchmen. 'Always heedful not to affront the memories of the Revolution,' he forbade Chateaubriand's discourse in the Academy, that 'diatribe' against the Revolution. There are words, and there are facts. Napoleon knew men well enough to discern that the new nobility felt that they were gaining something by the legitimizing of the Empire's status. A 'genuine aristocracy' was taking shape, whilst the Tuileries, the assemblies, the prefectures and staffs were being invaded by the former *émigrés* and royalists, freed from their last scruples and more warmly welcomed than ever. This was the 'reaction of 1810', which corresponded at home to the political and dynastic alliances abroad. Social and dynastic self-preservation followed his admission to the great club of sovereigns, which he mistook for a syndicate for mutual protection. Furthermore, the Europe which he sought to federate was a Europe of kings. In order to unite it more efficaciously he adopted its own modes of thought and proceeded to make himself in every way regal. In any case, was not everything tending in that direction? The dynasty of the Vasas in Sweden was dying, and during August 1810, that year of magnificence, Charles XIII named as his successor, and Sweden elected as heir-apparent, Bernadotte, the brother-in-law of Joseph. Napoleon approved. Almost everywhere on the Continent he had kings as allies, kings as kinsmen, and — or so at least he understood — kings to serve him.

He had become confident. He had anchored himself securely. He had no coalition to fear. And now that his hands were free, and he disposed of all his forces, Spain would be brought into subjection. It was only a matter of time. Once again he began to believe in peace through England's standing down. She might become convinced that a comprise would be as profitable as a continuation of the struggle was vain. The state of war still persisted with the English, but as far as he could he gave tokens of what, in his view, was a spirit of understanding, goodwill, and moderation. He withdrew troops from Germany, leaving only two divisions. The one had to occupy Bremen, Hamburg, Lübeck and Danzig, as indispensable to the maintenance of the Continental blockade, his essential weapon; the other, in Westphalia, was to keep an eye on Prussia, which remained suspect since that aggression of 1806. But Napoleon did not wish to give the absurd impression that he wanted to retain all his conquests. They were only 'instruments of negotiation'. He would discuss terms with his war map, as England would with hers, and cautiously, with nothing committed to writing — which might spoil everything — he renewed advances to the British government. The banker Labouchère, a go-between often used by Louis, was authorized to convey messages to London. 'There can be no doubt that no circumstances could be more favourable to peace if England had the slightest inclination to make peace on a footing of perfect equality and independence.'

And that is where there was not, and never would be, agreement. To Napoleon, equality and independence meant leaving out of discussion the very matters which, to the English, were the aim and object of the conflict. Whatever the Emperor might do for the 'restoration of an equilibrium', the root of the matter would still have been missing. And unhappily, for both parties, the root of the matter lay in the same places. Where did Napoleon take Marie Louise, three weeks after their wedding? To Antwerp. They spent nearly the whole of May in Belgium, as if to show the gallicized Belgians the daughter of their former sovereigns, to attest the consent of the house of Austria to Belgium becoming inalienably a part of France. From that moment Labouchère's mission could only come to grief.

And many people came to grief with it. Talk of peace brought forth a crop of intrigues, so weary was everybody, and so many were those who wished to have had a hand in bringing it about. Fouché joined in, and with him the famous Ouvrard, the business men, the intriguers who wanted to drag Napoleon into a perilous negotiation where he would be in a position of inferiority and compromise his alliances — for he would be brought to state what concessions he could not make, whilst he knew well those which England would demand. But here again the steadiest and most complete view was Napoleon's, not that of the partisans of the 'policy of possibilities'. He wanted to sound the English, no more. His weapon against the rulers of the sea was the Continental blockade, and he let it be known that he would strengthen it if England refused to yield. England remained unmoved by the threat. She was no longer alarmed by the indefinite expansion of the Empire. Napoleon might subjugate and annex the whole of Europe: England was only the more certain that in the end he would have to give up everything. Thus no peace was possible; there was no escape. Those who sought what the situation did not contain, a moderate solution, were the most chimerical of all. 'And so it's you who decide for war or peace?' Fouché was staggered by the question, although he had been once forgiven and had become almost unmovable. He had struck at the basis of the Empire. His crime was not so much a usurpation of his master's power as that he had compromised him and lessened his greatness in the eyes of England and Europe. The only peace to which Napoleon could put his name was that of Amiens, and he was striving to re-establish it with all the more perseverance because the English, being unwilling to have it, were set upon refusing it, and were resolved upon perpetual war, as they had said. This had not been realized by the Duke of Otranto any more than by the Prince of Benevente, and it was the turn of this other 'forestaller of the future' to meet with disgrace. The Emperor was thus freed from the men who have often been styled his evil geniuses, and it meant his final break with the Republic. He would commit neither more nor less faults by having no other men of the Revolution in his counsels. His new-fashioned legitimacy, his latest promotion, his new incarnation, all left untouched the difficulty which he had found on assuming power, the difficulty which had lifted him to power. The crowd was mistaken. With Marie Louise as Empress, with Napoleon admitted to the family of kings, 'it seemed to everyone that notions of war were going to be abandoned', whilst that war which kept rekindling the others still persisted.

Nothing had altered. So little, indeed, that Napoleon recovered that confidence which had already misled him after Tilsit. Once again the extreme measures dictated by his reasonings seemed to him practicable and devoid of dangers. That year 1810, which, after the supreme satisfaction of his marriage, was to bring him the hope of survival through paternity, found him laden with cares regarding his next decisions, and inclining to the most far-reaching because the idea of his family alliance with Austria enabled him to venture still more boldly. He was deluded rather than intoxicated. But he did not strain the taut bow through lightheartedness. Spain was still causing him anxiety. Joseph and his lamentations weighed on him. Sometimes he thought that the best way of liquidating the Spanish trouble would be to set up Ferdinand VII in Madrid with the safeguard of a French queen. This led to a fresh approach to Lucien, but to a fresh mortification. Lucien consented to send his daughter Charlotte to Paris, again the possible bride for Ferdinand. But when her letters were read by the secret service, her mocking of her uncle and the whole court showed that she could not be counted on for a marriage of political utility, and she was sent home. There was a break between the two brothers, and Lucien embarked for the United States. A ludicrous accident on the way left him in the hands of the English, who brought him to Plymouth, and received him with every consideration, as living evidence of Bonaparte's tyranny, a victim who could find asylum and liberty only on English soil.

Joseph would continue to reign in a kingdom which was unaware of him. And things went badly with the rest of the Imperial family. It was coming to pieces. Lucien was ruled out, and Louis ceased to be a king. Almost simultaneously with Lucien's departure from Civita Vecchia, Louis fled from Amsterdam, quitting wife and throne. It was the pitiable end to a long quarrel in which Napoleon had shown patience, and where the wrong was not all on his side. Louis, his favourite, was a hypochondriac, a sick man who made others, including Hortense, unhappy. And so Napoleon had found nobody at his side to understand him or serve him. By dint of energy and scheming he maintained himself and his circle on incredible, dizzy heights. His brothers trifled with everything as if their position was in all respects permanent. The bitter blow to the Emperor was not that he felt people to be ungrateful: it was to discover that they were fools.

The basic reason for the existence of Louis's kingdom in Holland was the intention that it should control the strict observance of the blockade in a commercial country which was one of the great doorways of Europe. That kingdom, like the rest, could survive only if England was vanquished through the blockade. Louis uncomprehendingly let his subjects circumvent him. He was blind to contraband, and even shielded it, and the Emperor, tired of remonstrance, had to place French *douaniers* and French soldiers in the ports. In the end he had even to decide on a military occupation of part of the states entrusted to his brother, and by Louis's orders the governor of Breda and Berg-op-Zoom closed their gates against the Imperial army. Painful and ludicrous incidents multiplied. For six months Napoleon, in vexed embarrassment, scolded and pardoned and adjured the 'prince of his own blood' whom he had set upon the throne of Holland to 'be a Frenchman first and foremost', and threatened to remove forcibly those ports and coastlines from the administration which made them the chief channels of trade with England.

In a burst of passion Napoleon had declared that he would 'eat up' Holland. More accurately, one of the comminatory notes which he had had to send to The Hague coldly stated that a return would be made to the state of affairs existing 'from the time of the conquest made by France in 1794 until the moment when his Imperial Majesty had hoped to make

a general conciliation by setting up the throne of Holland.'
The abdication of Louis, followed by his nocturnal escape,
on July 2nd, 1810, left the Emperor unexpectedly in a
difficult position. Louis had followed Lucien in openly
bringing against the tyrant of Europe the further charge
of being a family tyrant. That was Louis's offence. And
further, it left Napoleon with the embarrassing problem of
what should now be done with Holland. To restore her
freedom would mean delivering her to England and opening
a wide breach in the blockade. To hand her over to Hortense,
as queen or regent, meant female government, and matri-
archy is possible only in times of calm. Holland might be
put back to the status of a conquered country, reverting
to the days following the conquest by the Republic. But all in
all, union with the Empire seemed the least unsatisfactory
solution. It was the least oppressive and the most honourable
for the Dutch themselves, for, bound to observance of the
blockade, they would be under the same obligations as the
French and could not complain of being treated as a sub-
jugated people, being admitted to the Empire on the footing
of equals.

Napoleon's reasoning was always serious and powerful.
Having full regard to the circumstances and motives which
determined his decisions, it is clear that often it would have
been difficult for him to decide otherwise, because his
'forced situation' left him neither freedom nor choice. Good
or bad, his reasons mattered little; the result was the same,
and obvious to all. The great Empire was expanding further.
Here were more annexations. Where would they end? With
a reign over all of Europe, a universal monarchy? The effect
produced was deplorable, even in France. Where were
things tending? Would there be no longer any free corner?
Holland was a banking-house for every country, the haven
of money. The signal was given for a 'new crusade' against
the conqueror, that of the capitalists and financiers.

The mysterious part of Napoleon's thought, the only

part perhaps which cannot be deciphered, is to be found here. Did he really believe that he would keep this inordinate empire and be able to bequeath it to his successor? Was he even thinking of preparing a still more fabulous heritage for the child already promised him by Marie Louise, a child who, with the aid of his star, would be a son? If it were so, he must have become completely mad, with a reasoning madness that left him otherwise lucid. And even in his own days there were those who said that his mind was darkened and deranged. But he himself never explained, unless at St. Helena, as it were metaphysically, by what miracle and why he would have retained all his conquests, added to those of the Revolution. He never stated on what basis or terms he would have concluded peace with England, assuming that England were willing to negotiate. It was totally absurd to imagine Napoleon and his successors eternally masters of the land while the English for ever ruled the seas. If such an extravaganza filled his mind, Napoleon would have given other symptoms of mental derangement. Only one idea can be attributed to him, always the same one — that of England brought to her knees by the blockade, asking mercy, liberating the seas, restoring the colonies, accepting a just and honourable dealing.

And England was still thought to be on the eve of collapse, overwhelmed by her commercial losses and her rising debt. Men calculated the day on which she would drop, just as the Germans, over a century later, calculated that she would be forced down by the unrestricted submarine campaign. When all was over, there were those who claimed that England was on her last legs, that within a very short time she would have given in. That was Alexander's view in 1814, during the Paris conversations, when he declared that in his opinion the blockade was a terrible and admirable weapon. So terrible, indeed, that it turned back against the man who, having almost perfected it, was imposing it everywhere. Nobody knows whether it might not in the long run have laid England low. Russia was the first not to resist it.

The 'supremacy of economics' does not seem a thing of our own day when we observe how the Continental blockade, failing to make Napoleon victorious, provoked the collapse of his empire. 'A bold and gigantic project, but its success is impossible,' said the banker Lafitte. And he proved it. But if Napoleon had accepted the demonstration, he could only have abandoned everything. We must see him here applying his mind to matters which he absorbed and mastered as quickly as others, leaning over the customs statements as he did over his campaigning reports. How far removed from the hero of legend, the hero of the popular prints! He was deep in statistics and tariffs, arguing about net costs. Even at St. Helena he still thought of possibilities he might have tried. His misfortune was that, for a long time, his fecund brain had been working only against itself. The Continental blockade condemned him to annexations and absorptions, to a policy of invasion which sowed fear and hatred. For the moment, at least, that was beyond remedy. But the blockade had its other disadvantages. Though strictly applied in the French Departments, the toleration of contraband by the allies and neutrals opened a thousand clefts elsewhere. The result of this was that the cost of living was higher in France than in other countries. Impressed by this idea, Napoleon authorized the importation of certain raw materials necessary for industry, in consideration of a tax equivalent to the premium charged by the smugglers. He set up the system of licences, as fruitful to the French Treasury as it was favourable to French industry. The Emperor investigated every scheme, such as the replacement of sugar-cane by beetroot, whereby Europe could dispense with things sold and produced by England. But then, although the effects of the blockade became less exacting within the bounds of the Empire, they became more so for the rest of the Continent, for the friendly, allied and auxiliary powers, where the strictness of the prohibition had hitherto been mitigated by fraud. These licences, planned to restore equality, gave France a privileged position. Being a more highly developed manufacturing country than the other European nations, she assumed the place of England in their markets. And what did the English lose thereby? The licence system allowed them to continue the traffic in colonial products, whilst, as masters of the sea, the rest of the world was open to their trade, which took hold of a monopoly. The efficacy of the blockade was already being undermined by the fact that England was finding compensation for her exclusion from Europe in America, in Africa, in Asia.

Napoleon's commercial strategy was even more seriously at fault in another respect. The other Continental countries, it was well pointed out by Lafitte, were losing on their products which they could sell to nobody; they lost on those which they could buy only from Europe. But these foreigners were allies, members of the anti-British federation, and the blockade laid a double burden on them, for a cause which, after all, was not theirs. Impatience and discontent were bound to be aggravated. France would be ruffling too many interests, and a clash of interests means a clash of affections. 'Our allies will move towards our enemies, and fresh wars will possibly again make our future doubtful.'

The first of the allies to fulfil this prophecy was the ally of Tilsit. Wood, rye, and the falling rouble destroyed the alliance more surely than the refusal of the Grand Duchess or the Austrian marriage. Threatened with the fate of Paul I, Alexander yielded to the complaints of his boyards and his ruined merchants. On December 31st, 1810, he issued the ukase which carried the seeds of war within it. Freedom of trade for neutrals in Russian ports; and neutral flags, of course, the American especially, covered English goods; and how many notes passed between Paris and the United States in that connection! After this, through the whole of Central Europe as far as Mainz, sugar and coffee imported through Riga would be marketed. This inevitably meant conflict with Napoleon, as Alexander well knew: for six months he had been making military preparations . . . The alliance of Tilsit was foundering on the rocks of the Continental blockade. The two great ideas of Napoleon did not accord. He could not simultaneously federate and constrain the countries of Europe.

And yet, at the close of that year, he still seemed to be moving on in the assurance of his glory. Before long the succession would be assured; the heir was expected. An end to the Spanish trouble was surely not impossible. In Vienna, the father of Marie Louise answered for the friendship, or the submissiveness, of all the princes. If Alexander broke the pact, there would be another Friedland, but this time with the help of a European coalition, and a fresh Tilsit. The excessive confidence already inspired in Bonaparte by Tilsit was not given to him by his marriage. 'I have been blamed for having let myself be intoxicated by my alliance with the house of Austria,' he said. And he said so because he felt it to be true.

CHAPTER XX

THE KING OF ROME

THE life of Napoleon is a series of scenes ready-made for legend. Behold, in 1811, the triumphant hero beside the cradle of the king-child. And the next year would see that happy father tramping the snow, staff in hand. What artist ranged these pictures on the wall of history?

The man over whom hovered a great misfortune grew tender. Bonaparte, at the approach of the dark days, is represented as dulled by the satisfactions of his marriage, in love with his wife, 'in love with Austria'. He is represented as intoxicated by his paternity, dreaming of an empire for his son that will never be too wide. And he himself remembered those moments of paradise with a sigh: 'And was I, too, not to have my few moments of happiness?' Perhaps he had savoured those moments because his heart was heavy. During the months of looming catastrophe men tried to see the Emperor, to penetrate him, to lift his conventional mask. And few men observed him coolly at a time when every man was beginning to think of himself, when many felt a grudge against him for risking his own fortune and theirs. Always careful to show a serene front, not to spread abroad the trouble that he felt within himself, he still deludes posterity. His inmost reflections have left but faint traces. One must go deep to discover his hesitancies and anxieties, the battle waged within him before he followed his destiny, or rather rushed into it, as if he knew that disaster could not be avoided and he were eager to see the end.

No man had 'reflected more on the reasons that govern human actions'. He had never been able, added Mme de Rémusat, to conceive that other men act without plan or aim: he himself had always had a reason. In each of his

THE KING OF ROME
After Sir Thomas Lawrence

movements a motive can be found, and the unhappy Russian campaign was debated with himself as long as was the unhappy affair of Spain. The whole of 1811 was taken up with those deliberations.

Ever since Trafalgar Napoleon had sought the means of conquering the sea by power on land. His weapon was the blockade, which was based on the Russian alliance. What was he to do if that alliance failed? Wait? But wait for what? For things to arrange themselves? And how many days, months, years? Méneval heard him, 'in the silence of his study', giving utterance to his preoccupation: 'The bow has been strained too long'. And another time he murmured: 'Time? Always time? I have lost too much already'. If England joined hands again with Russia, the European federation would go to pieces, and France would be brought back to the same position as before Austerlitz. What then did reason say? That Friedland had been needed to found the alliance. To start again on a Friedland, or even threaten to do so in order to obtain a new Tilsit, to profit by the submission of Prussia to intimidate Alexander, to profit likewise by the honeymoon with Austria — such was the idea germinating in Napoleon's mind. He weighed it long, because he appreciated its risks. It had come to him early. On July 1st, 1810, he had told Caulaincourt: 'Does Russia wish me to prepare for her defection? I shall be at war with her on the day she makes peace with England.'

Once Napoleon agreed that in Spain he had committed 'a stupidity'. He never admitted that of Russia. He did not feel that he was doing anything against his system by going to Moscow, even less than in going to Madrid. To those who wanted him to 'rein in his horse', he replied: 'I have no bridle to pull up the English ships — and that is where the whole trouble lies. Why have not people the wit to feel it?' But the system continually drew him on. There was nothing to take its place, and it had to be applied to the very end, whatever the price. Otherwise the blockade, an 'epic conception', consecrated by decree as the fundamental law of the Empire's being, and carried out unfalteringly for five years, would be merely a hollow idea, and England would have won the match by endurance and doggedness.

These events were not controlled by the two friends of Tilsit. One had genius; the other was not without subtlety in politics. But they were both pushed forward along their separate paths by a will outside of themselves. We must look where their eyes were for ever turning. After all, the impassivity of the London Cabinet was in a way fascinating. The King was mad, the Regent without authority. The government, made up of men with small prestige, was a mere executive council, a calculating-machine, and all the more obstinate for its lack of sensibility. Nothing affected it. At one moment the financial crisis was so serious that England seemed to be cornered. She held firm. And none of Napoleon's successes troubled her. He might marry the daughter of the Cæsars, threaten to absorb Holland and then fulfil his threat, redress for a time his position in Spain and Portugal. The automaton did not change one of its movements. Napoleon kept on making annexations. Albion seemed only to be saying: 'Annex as much as you please.' But meanwhile Alexander was fortified in his plan of breaking away from the tentacles which the Napoleonic Empire was now pushing out towards the Baltic coasts. He was further impressed by the prodigious calm with which England faced these aggrandizements. How sure she must be of herself, and of her final triumph! That confidence in the ultimate outcome was like a magnet to the Tsar, who was tired of the blockade laws, and disturbed by the discontent which they caused amongst his subjects. What interest had he in prolonging this fight against England? To Russia, the freedom of the seas and naval tyranny were mere words. Much more vexatious was the rule imposed on Russia by Napoleon. After Friedland Alexander had concluded an alliance only to escape from his awkward plight. At Erfurt he had enveloped it in reticence. The hour for which he was keeping himself seemed to have struck. 'He laughs best who laughs last.'

It is hard for us to imagine a time, near though it is to our own, when news came only by courier, when communications were hardly speedier than they were in the century of Julius Cæsar. It took quite a fortnight for Paris to know what was happening in St. Petersburg. The age of the telegraphic ultimatum, of instantaneous mobilizations, of the irreparable brought to pass within a few hours, had not yet dawned. Each of the Emperors pursued his 'evolution' far from the other, and before the final impact came nearly two years went by.

'The Continental system will be efficacious only if it be established everywhere.' This self-evident proposition had already burdened Napoleon with the affairs of Spain, Portugal, Rome and Holland. It was not imagination, it was not the demon of conquest or of glory that led him on: it was the spirit of deduction. The absorption of the Hanseatic towns was announced to the Senate on December 13th, 1810. Bremen, Hamburg, and Lubeck were to extend the coast-line of Holland. Wesphalia was bereft of its coasts, and Oldenburg ceased to exist. The estuaries of the Scheldt, Meuse, Rhine, Ems, Weser and Elbe rivers were 'new safeguards which had become essential'. 'It is not my territory that I have wished to enlarge, but my maritime instruments,' Napoleon explained, after his action had been taken. He was shutting other doors, with irrefutable logic. But in the south he had also to close the Turkish gap, through which English goods entered Central Europe; and in the north, the gap of Sweden, which led to Bernadotte, as the heir to the Swedish throne, crossing into the enemy camp. And there was still Russia, who was now not only failing to observe the blockade, but was protesting against the deposing of the Grand Duke of Oldenburg, the Tsar's brother-in-law. The Continental system was cutting into the living flesh. And there were cries.

Meanwhile, what of Alexander? For his contemplated attack the Tsar needed the help of both the Poles and the Prussians. He made dazzling promises to the former, who did not trust his word and allowed Napoleon to get wind of the move. He sounded Prussia as to her intentions, but she sheered off, afraid of a fresh Jena and of being the first to be chastised. Alexander then thought that Bonaparte was not yet so greatly weakened after all. He postponed his plans of attack till better times. But he had made considerable preparations, and he pushed them on. He had certainly meditated an attack on his friend of Tilsit, who had gradually discovered the truth. And Napoleon, put on his guard, and always afraid of the revival of a coalition, took certain precautionary measures, against which Alexander protested the more loudly because of his bad conscience. He declared that he was being threatened, attacked, victimized; and Europe in her weariness believed him. From that time onwards, as Albert Sorel has pointed out, the long-accepted idea took shape that Napoleon hurled himself upon Russia in a delirium of domination and pride.

On the contrary, everything goes to show that he viewed with the utmost annoyance the approach of a conflict which would bring a check to his policy and throw everything into the melting-pot. During January and February, 1811, Russia was already his preoccupation, and he kept turning over the same thoughts: if the Northern powers stood out of the blockade, the Continental system would cease to exist. If Russia made peace with the London Cabinet, Napoleon might be attacked by her just as he had been by Prussia in 1806 and by Austria in 1809. In any case, it was clear that she was making her escape, that she no longer accepted the harsh rule of the blockade, even as other peoples subjected to its iron grip were dreaming of breaking free. Their impatience was rising, and already they had a tacit understanding of one another. Napoleon was respected because he was regarded as an irresistible force. If he gave any impression of weakness, he would be treated 'like a little boy'. Once Russia was rid of her war with Turkey, Alexander's hands would be free and he would become more aggressive. Perhaps it would suffice to show him the point of the sword, to startle him into a return to a complete and sincere acceptance of the alliance, to make Russia as docile and submissive as Prussia and Austria. Was it impossible? By appearing on the banks of the Vistula with strong forces, the results of Friedland might be obtained without having to risk an engagement . . . The Russian expedition had some of the same elements as the affair of Spain. The idea can be seen coming to birth, growing, and taking hold of the Emperor's mind, until, in accordance with a growing inclination of his temperament, he regarded as accomplished something which could be and should be accomplished, simply because his reason had conceived it.

But, as with Spain, there were long perplexities. 'I was not sure of my balance,' he was to tell Gourgaud later, referring to that year 1811. His uncertainties and secret anxieties remained hidden. And perhaps he was trying to deceive himself as he imposed upon the peoples, when the day came for him to present to them the new-born heir to the Empire.

How fallacious were the omens! That birth seemed to bring Napoleon the only thing still lacking in his immense power. His succession was assured. He wanted a child. Here it was. And on March 20th, one hundred and one cannon announced that it was a son. How could one question the star of Bonaparte? Whatever he desired, whatever he calculated, came to pass. And Savary expressed the relief of all who looked to the future: 'Fortune had been constantly loyal to us; and she seemed now to crown her efforts with the gift of an heir to that power which had been so laboriously erected, and which, had it not been for that child, seemed to be opening up great gulfs on every side of us. In all good faith men hoped for a deep-seated peace, and reasonable ideas completely excluded any war or occupations of that kind.' The Revolution, which had taken refuge in the hereditary principle, rejoiced to behold the posterity of the man to whom the right of hereditary succession had been given as a shield and buckler.

Napoleon excelled always in the art of striking the imagination. He surrounded the cradle of the King of Rome with magnificence, but destiny vied with him. To perfect the story, no detail was to prove lacking — the father expiring on his rock, the son, in his princely prison, dying like another Marcellus. The child was from the first made the idol of the monarchy. At his nurse's breast he was Majesty. Towards this King in long clothes signs of respect — an almost Asiatic cult — were ordained, to an extent that had never been thought of with the Dauphins of the old regime. The solemnity of health bulletins of this suckling matched the emphasis of the father announcing to the Senate the birth of an heir to the throne: 'The great destinies of my son will be fulfilled.' What dreams did the Emperor weave round the child who should have been Napoleon II?

The same enigma recurs. Did he believe that he would bequeath to his son the Western Empire as it stood in the spring of 1811 — a monster, a shapeless state with one hundred and thirty departments, from that of the Tiber to that of the Elbe Estuary, and the great mass of vassal states over and above these? That Empire had no future. It had been brought into being by a governing idea which itself was governed by circumstances. It was a war map, a kingdom of coastlines and ports and river-mouths, a configuration ordained by the requirements of the Continental blockade. He further annexed the Swiss republic of Valais, a connecting link with Italy, and announced the project of a canal which, within five years, would join the Baltic with the Seine. And after declaring that the English, for their part, had 'torn up the public law of Europe', he added this strange sentence: 'Nature has altered.' Did he really believe that one could govern and rule against Nature, changing and constraining her permanently? Did he believe that after his own day that challenge would be maintained? He himself recognized that the Empire was too large, too distended, when he wrote to his war minister: 'Orders are not carried out because they are given indistinctly to men in the recesses of Italy and others in the recesses of Germany . . .' What likelihood was there that, when the new Charlemagne had disappeared, his heir would be successful?

One hesitates to attribute plans for a remote future to the man of whom his aides-de-camp asked: 'Does the Emperor know what he will do to-morrow? It will depend on circumstances.' Nothing was stable; a crack might be stopped in the north, but another would appear in the south. Not a month after the birth of the King of Rome came the defection of Murat in Naples. With him, and with Caroline, Napoleon was to be even less fortunate than with his brothers. Murat also wanted to consolidate his throne, having fears of the former Queen of Naples, an Austrian, on account of Marie Louise. He even intrigued with England, because his subjects too were weary of the stringencies of the blockade. He even sent away Frenchmen in his service who refused to become naturalized Italians. The Emperor was annoyed. He muttered that he had not spared his brothers for drifting away from the blockade, and he would spare Murat even less. The King of Rome was a fortnight old, and the boundless Empire of his heritage was showing its tares. Nevertheless Napoleon would overlook and pardon, here again, because he was afraid that Murat, pushed to extremes, might go over to the English side.

Napoleon's mind was obsessed with England, Russia, and Spain. On April 2nd he was explaining to the King of Württemberg his attitude towards Alexander: 'My war in Spain and Portugal, spread over a country larger than France, is taking up sufficient of my men and resources; I cannot be anxious for another war . . . But although I do not wish for war, and am far from wishing to be the Don Quixote of Poland, I have at least the right to insist on Russia remaining loyal to the alliance.' A few days later, his instructions to Lauriston, the new ambassador to St. Petersburg, were 'to use every means of proving that French policy is not directed towards Poland, but solely towards England . . . It is probable that the smallest sign of a peace between Russia and England would be the signal for war'. And again, in a letter to the Tsar himself, after reminders of the spirit of the alliance and of the precautionary measures to which Alexander had forced him: 'My troops will take up arms only when your Majesty has torn up the Treaty of Tilsit.'

But if only, to face these perils of the East, he could have an easy mind regarding the other end! There was still Spain — and how vexatious that was! He would have to go there in person, as he had promised. His horses were awaiting him at Bayonne, and now it seemed as if he dared not leave France, hardly even Paris, as if he dreaded being again brought back by bad news. And things were going badly again in the Peninsula. He had tried his best generals there. He had placed his trust in Masséna; and the Prince of Essling, the defender of Genoa, after reopening the road to Portugal, had been checked by the English on the lines of Torres Vedras. He would need more troops than Napoleon could give him. He refused the 60,000 men lately asked for by General Foy. He even took back some to reconstitute the unity of the Grand Army, with thought of the Russian danger. Spain had never been so burdensome or so importunate. Reason told him he ought to hurl all the forces still at his disposal beyond the Pyrenees against Wellington, sacrificing the rest. But policy forbade sacrifices. It must not be said in Europe that he was not master of Spain, which would make men suspect that he could not long remain master elsewhere. The outcome of this dispersal of efforts was that Soult stood checked before Cadiz, Suchet in Aragon, and that Masséna himself fought a bloody and indecisive battle with Wellington at Fuentes d'Onoro. That was how things stood in May, 1811. Napoleon was annoyed. He was aggrieved with men and things, and Masséna was disgraced. He did not know either how to cope with Spain or how to get rid of Spain. Complete evacuation? The restoration of Ferdinand? Withdrawal to the Ebro and the incorporation of the northern provinces into the Empire? Any of these steps would imply impotence. And Spain then became to him 'intolerable'. He refused to think about it. Sometimes he left despatches unread for three days, asked for résumés, and finding even these too long, would leave them unread on his table. Did he think of leaving the Spanish millstone to Napoleon II, along with the huge and shapeless empire?

But the birth of his son must be celebrated, a pretext for fetes and rejoicings and ceremonies. Napoleon stressed the dynastic note. As a guarantee of duration, continuity and security at home, for the interests attached to the empire, that spirit corresponded to the external utility of the Austrian marriage. The empire became legitimist and conservative. A lady of the Montesquiou family was appointed governess of the 'Children of France'. The Duchesse d'Orléans, the Duchesse de Bourbon, the Prince de Conti, fugitives in Catalonia, received pensions. Napoleon was moving beyond his original conception of a reconciliation of Frenchmen, of the 'fusion'. He would like to be closer to legitimacy even than Louis XVI. The father of Marie Louise was styled 'His Sacred Imperial Majesty', and the title made him think: 'power comes from God, and only by reason of that can it be placed beyond the attack of men.' There could never be too many consecrations. The King of Rome was borne to Notre-Dame to have the coronation confirmed by a solemn baptism.

That day saw a silent, chill, unenthusiastic Paris. There were even hisses in the Carrousel. Men were saddened or vexed by the sense of approaching war. Trade was poor, public stocks were low. And things would have been worse if everything had been known, if the Emperor's anxiety had been divined, if his thoughts could have been read! The phrase escaped him: 'if the English held on much longer he did not know what would happen, nor what he would do'. The blockade forced him to scatter his efforts, the threat from Russia to concentrate them. 'For peace to be possible and durable, England must be convinced that she would find no further allies on the Continent.' It followed that Alexander must be brought to heel if he did not once more show loyalty. To do that, threats were the only weapon, and threats are efficacious only if the conviction is given that war is the sanction. Napoleon could not decide upon a war against Russia without 'cruel tortures of mind'. The work of Tilsit would have to be restarted. It always came back to that. Sometimes the prospect 'discouraged' him — a few observers used the word.

And we should look here at the reverse side of a power and renown to which nothing seemed outwardly lacking, although they lacked the confidence of the man who trod these dizzy heights. 'I have heard M. Monnier tell of the anxieties and care-ridden meditations which possessed the Emperor without his confiding them in anyone,' said Barante. Napoleon did not fail to understand the risks of a war in an unknown country, seven hundred leagues from France, leaving behind him, in Spain, an English army and an insurgent people, and with Germany also 'ready to break him at the first reverse of fortune'. In France herself he discerned 'a tired obedience', a craving for repose, weakening devotions, a sated soldiery. 'To anyone living in close touch with him and observing him attentively, it was plain that he was beset by these thoughts; long insomnia troubled his nights; he spent whole hours on a sofa, brooding. In the end his reflections overcame him and he would fall into an uneasy sleep.' Here we are reaching the truth. The Emperor was often strange, distraught, and curiously dreamy. Thiébault describes the scene during a great reception at Compiègne, when, to the astonishment of the court and of ten princely guests, he was seen suddenly standing motionless, his eyes fixed on the floor, as if completely absent. Masséna came up to him, imagining he must be feeling unwell; and Napoleon replied to him in a furious voice, as if he had been dragged from sleep: 'What are you meddling with?' His health was said to be affected; perhaps he was epileptic. He was uncertain, uneasy, tormented.

He reverted to the idea of grappling with the chief enemy, and had thoughts of a Boulogne camp in the summer of 1811. Decrès was asked to prepare a report on whether Brest or Cherbourg would be the better place to assemble an expedition aimed as a threat to England. The threat would perhaps hasten peace. He became interested in the navy again, and on a visit to Holland stopped at Flushing and spent two days on board the *Charlemagne*. But no serious expedition could be ready before two years. Less remote results were needed. The Emperor thought of a landing in Ireland, or, more modestly, in Jersey, and then dropped the subject. He knew the vanity of these diversions, these old schemes. If he revived them for a moment, as also the idea of a new Egyptian campaign, it was because his mind was toiling to find a means of escape.

Napoleon did not find one, because he had already exhausted all the combinations within his reach. For lack of maritime power, he had to return to the idea of Tilsit, the union of Europe against England, the common foe, the foe of the Continent. If Russia stood out and became allied with the English, her example would corrupt the other European countries. The Tsar had already sought to beguile Prussia into renewing the pact of 1806. The Prussian government resisted the temptation, through fear. The 'regeneration' for which Stein was working was not yet ripe, and Frederick William, remembering the lesson of Jena, would take no risks. But an active alliance between Russia and Prussia was a probability, it was now even a matter of time, no more.

And Napoleon became convinced of the need of forestalling this coalition.

In the Russian alliance he had sacrificed Sweden, Turkey, and Poland, former friends of France; and from that alliance Alexander had gained Finland, the Moldavian and Wallachian provinces, and the assurance that Poland would not recover her independence. And now, with his hands filled, Alexander was threatening. Still Napoleon kept on negotiating throughout the summer of 1811. Over and over again he told St. Petersburg that Russia's preparations for war in themselves forced France to place herself on a war-footing. Russia had armed secretly; France had armed publicly and when Russia was ready. Who was violating the alliance? Russia. One hundred and fifty vessels flying the American flag, really English, had just entered Russian ports. 'Make Lauriston understand that I desire peace, and that it is high time that these things came to a prompt end.' Armed conflict would be the last resource. The Emperor did not conceal his extreme vexation: anyone who averted this war would do him a great service. But his thoughts were becoming inured to it as to something inevitable; and the knowledge of the imposing forces still at his disposal, the preparation of the vast army he was organizing, the measures he took in all parts of his Empire, fortified him in his idea that Alexander would yield in alarm at the approach of these legions, and that, at the worst, one battle would suffice to renew the friendship of the two greatest sovereigns of the century.

Meanwhile, in May, Alexander had written confidentially to the King of Prussia: 'The system which had made Wellington victorious by exhausting the French armies is that which I am resolved to follow.' His plan was laid. He would let Napoleon attack, and prepare a new Spain for him in Russia. In June Caulaincourt warned the Emperor. It was the sole topic in St. Petersburg: they were resolved to draw him on as far as possible into Russia, not opposing his entry, and refusing him battle, after which the climate would overcome the Grand Army. But Napoleon remained incredulous and even impatient. A battle? He would be able to force the Russian generals to stand and fight. The rigours of winter? But 'the whole of Europe has the same climate'. He had already said so at Warsaw in 1806, and when the Poles replied: 'Sire, we wish it were so,' he reaffirmed it because he needed to affirm it. Things must be as he wished them, because there was no alternative to this extreme measure and he had to make the most of it, and because he could not wait for his European federation, which was coming to pieces where it had been begun, to flow back in arms on to the Rhine.

But he did not take the risk without weighing it, without putting on his own side all the chances he could lay hold of, without an attempt to foresee every eventuality. And there was no gap in his plan except the hypothesis that he would be caught by the Russian winter; for his plan definitely precluded that hypothesis, and would be absurd if it were admitted. He foresaw everything, except furs for the soldiers and ice-shoes for the horses. His anticipations were political, those of the head of a government. It was important that everything should be calm within the Empire while he was far from the scene. His ministers were urged to see to provisions, to food-prices, to avoid making malcontents and to refrain from arbitrary arrests. He was preoccupied also with the religious consequences of his rupture with Pius VII: dioceses were left without bishops, as the Pope refused to approve those named by the Emperor, and there were murmurs amongst the faithful, especially in Belgium. The council of July 1811 was viewed by Napoleon as an attempt at conciliation with Catholic opinion. It was none too happy. 'Everything was becoming difficult, so complex had he made his position', or rather, so complex had it become of itself. The assembled bishops resisted him. To force their obedience he simulated anger, and sent the most recalcitrant to Vincennes: it happened that two of them held Belgian sees.

The project of transferring the Holy See from Rome to Avignon was repulsed. But having decided to place the Pope in France, and not to leave him at Savona, where the English, whose vessels were cruising off the port, might be able to liberate him, the Emperor had him brought as a kind of hostage to Fontainebleau shortly after leaving for Russia. He was plunging into a great adventure, as he well knew, and he remained distrustful. He certainly did not embark upon it lightly. From his librarian he asked for 'everything most detailed in French regarding the campaign of Charles XII in Poland and Russia.'

The same day, December 19th, 1811, brought forth the decree that paid Napoleon his dividend of men, the levy of conscripts for the coming year. It was an unmistakable and too well-known sign, and that New Year's Day of 1812 was pregnant with dark forebodings. Anxiety lay over Paris. The rumours of vast preparations foretold a war greater than had gone before, and if men had been 'tired out with miracles' at the time of Jena, they were now more wearied with waiting for still greater happenings. Then 'the Emperor decreed that men should amuse themselves'. Festivities and balls were the order of the day everywhere. He himself maintained his own crushing toil, and kept his secrets; and despite himself he was seen in complete absorption, and occasionally humming to himself, like a man reluctant to be thought worried.

But he had reasons for worry. He wanted now, as he had wanted at thirty, to see everything, know everything at first hand, control everything himself. But the machine of an empire was heavy to handle. He could not do everything himself, though he knew every branch of activity, and he entrusted executive duties to men who 'thought they had fulfilled their task by writing a letter to someone, who wrote another to somebody else, and so on'. It was a vast military and civil bureaucracy, which did not help him with any ideas, which did not even give warning of oversights, obedient enough, but beginning to have excessive zeal for detail and passion for control; and as he could not go everywhere, it sometimes misled him with false reports.

The organization of this Grand Army which set off from all quarters of the Empire to concentrate on the Vistula was a new conception of Napoleon's, more extraordinary than the others. Europe in movement, an idea of which the medley of its effectives was the expression. The foreign auxiliaries served not only to augment the French forces, raising them to a figure of over 600,000, a crowd with its train of convoys like one of the great migrations of the early ages. Those legions, comprising Northerners and Southerners, Latins, Teutons and Slavs, represented the Continental federation on the march to force Russia to return to the duties of the alliance. At the same time it was a calculated precaution. The Emperor had long felt that Prussia was very near to siding with the Tsar. He had frightened Frederick William, obtained the dismissal of the most notable anti-French ministers, together with a treaty of offensive and defensive alliance, and 20,000 men in the event of war with Russia. Austria contributed 30,000 against certain exchanges of territory. General Yorck's Prussians and Schwarzenberg's Austrians would answer for the fidelity and tranquillity of Germany. The Emperor prided himself on having thought of everything in his deep-laid schemes. Nevertheless, Frederick William was writing to Alexander, excusing himself for having yielded to irresistible force and fatality. 'If war breaks out, we shall harm each other only as much as is strictly necessary, remembering constantly that we are at one, that we must one day be allies again.' Metternich, on his side, communicated to the Tsar the treaty just signed with France, which did not prevent Russia and Austria from 'continuing their secret understanding relative to their political views'. The coalition of 1813 would not be difficult to form. It already existed in the half-light. Neither Russia nor Austria nor Prussia had ever recognized the essential conquests of the Revolution, any more than England had. No general peace or congress had ratified them. The treaties, alliances, and military co-operations secured by Napoleon were still only opportunist measures, like the Austrian marriage itself. Fear gave him the upper hand. But the possibility of a great reverse to Bonaparte was always in the background.

And because Alexander still felt him formidable, he abandoned his project of aggression. He now said he would retreat 'right to Kamchatka' before he would sign another peace that was still only a truce. And although Napoleon was aware of the Tsar's new design, he remained persuaded that 'one good battle would prevail over his determination'. They both knew that the conflict was inevitable. But neither wished to be the aggressor.

So fully did Napoleon believe that 'one good battle' would restore the repentant Tsar to his side, that he made provision for the future reconciliation. He persisted even in his belief that the approach of the Grand Army would suffice. The war then would not be a struggle to the death; it must not be irreparable; there must be no action to make negotiation and friendly approaches impossible, nor any resurrection of Poland or promises of freedom to the peasants. The Emperor needed the Poles; it was necessary to encourage them, but not overmuch. His intention was to wage a political and diplomatic war against Russia. But he was to find it a war of nations.

And it is possible that the Tsar might have weakened in his costly resolve to let his adversary enter and lay waste his line of advance before him; possible too that he would have offered the battle which Napoleon desired, if he had not known that he could not count either on Prussia or on Austria. Meanwhile the Grand Army flooded Germany on its northward march. A simulacrum of peace still united France and Russia; and it was the Tsar who took the initiative of an ultimatum, calling upon Napoleon to halt at the Elbe so as to force him to declare his intentions. This was in April, and the Emperor had not counted on hostilities opening until June.

For a moment longer he avoided picking up the gauntlet. Without slowing up the charted advance of his huge army, he again appealed to the alliance, declared his wish to avoid war, his 'constancy in the sentiments of Tilsit and Erfurt'. This was the letter of April 25th, composed with a view to the coming peace, and concluding, in the style of Tilsit, in remembrance of the raft and the accolades, with these words: 'If fate should make war between us inevitable, it would still make no difference to the feelings which your Majesty has inspired in me, and which are surely protected against any vicissitude or any alteration.'

Equally convinced of the 'inevitable', both Emperors still wove schemes with fate. A fortuitous incident hastened the break. The Tsar's ambassador in Paris was already in an awkward position because an affair of espionage had involved the attaché Chernichev. Receiving no answer to the ultimatum, and no instructions from St. Petersburg, Kurakin lost his head and requested his passports. Maret only sent them after a month. But the Russian ambassador, on his account, had put an end to the temporizing of his own master as well as to Napoleon's.

It was May 7th. The Emperor left Saint-Cloud on the 9th. He was not free from anxieties or forebodings, and he cast a backward glance over the state of affairs he was leaving behind him. On April 17th, he had addressed a fourth offer of peace to the British government. If English and French troops evacuated Spain, Portugal, and Sicily, the integrity of Spain, with a national constitution, would be guaranteed, and the Braganzas would be recalled to Lisbon. Castlereagh again remained unmoved. If the Emperor had been anxious to prove the responsibility of the British cabinet for 'the blood that might still have to flow', he showed too clearly his desire to find relief on the side where the saddle chafed. Inwardly he had already renounced Spain, with all its dangers, and

that accursed Portugal. He spoke about them with bitter
irony, contrasting what he was about to do in Russia with
what his lieutenants were doing in the Peninsula. Marmont
applied for troops and money and foodstuffs for the Peninsula,
and the Emperor replied: 'And here am I, about to plunge
into the middle of a country that produces nothing!' And
then, as if emerging from deep meditation, as if speaking to
himself: 'But how is all this going to end?'

And the day before his departure he gave his last instructions to the prefect of police. Pasquier did not conceal
that he anticipated dangers, the consequences of an 'insurrectional movement of some extent', if one should arise as a
result of the high prices of food, or from some other cause.
The Emperor listened in silence, and walked over from the
window to the fireplace with his hands behind his back,
'like a man in very deep thought'. Then abruptly he spoke
his thoughts before Pasquier. 'It is one difficulty more added
to all those I have to face in the greatest and most difficult
enterprise I have yet attempted. But what is begun must be
finished. Good-bye.' And Pasquier adds: 'He was quite
aware of the dangers into which he was about to throw
himself.'

But he had so often before wondered how it would all end.
Never had he wielded so powerful an army. Never had he
counted so many auxiliaries. His matured strategic plans
were the finest he had ever conceived. He had scrupulously
avoided anything that would make him appear the aggressor.
He had taken good care of the means for negotiating with
Alexander. Why revert to the earlier perplexities? It was
no longer a question between the Alliance and war. The
indispensable Russian alliance had to be refashioned by
means of war, as it had already been established by means of
war. Bonaparte would have no regrets, because he knew that
by inactivity or idle waiting he would have lost everything.

338

CHAPTER XXI

THE TWENTY-NINTH BULLETIN

It is easy to say, after the event, that Napoleon was punished for his incredible rashness, that he could not escape disaster if he led the Grand Army as far as Moscow. But was it of set purpose that he really led it there? He may have said on occasion that he would go as far as Moscow if it proved necessary. But there was no sign of such an intention at the moment of his departure; and far from having had any feeling of rashness, his plans seemed to him perfectly prudent and reasonable. Furthermore, blamed for having undertaken this war, he was also accused of having lost it by an excess of circumspection, not to say timidity.

Again, it is easy enough to argue that, with a little patience, he would have got the upper hand of England, who was now faced with the hostility of the United States, rebelling against the embargo laid upon them. True, the English were none too happy in this fresh American war, but there were only small numbers of men involved. All in all, it was a mere episode, and could not alter the course of events in any way.

It would be fairer to urge that perhaps the Emperor increased his own embarrassments. He was always reverting to Alexander's armaments, and not only to provide himself with a grievance against the Tsar. He was afraid of them. And that is one of the reasons which make one doubt the authenticity of many presumptuous remarks attributed to Napoleon with regard to the coming campaign. Napoleon was resolved on this war, but it did not for a moment cross his mind that it would exceed the limits he had set down for it. Before leaving Paris he had reassured the wise Cambacérès, who put forward certain objections interpreting the public's alarm. Did they take him for a madman? And what he told

Cambacérès, he repeated to Metternich: 'My enterprise is one of those whose solution lies in patience. The triumph will fall to the more patient.' The campaign would reach its end at Smolensk and Minsk. In no eventuality would Napoleon go beyond these two points, on the limits of Poland and the old Russia. If he had not defeated the Russians before the fine weather ended, he would set up his headquarters at Vilna, and possibly even return thence to spend the harshest months of winter in Paris.

Such were his intentions as he still declared them in Dresden at the end of May, to an assembly of kings and princes more brilliant even than that of Erfurt. All Germany was there to do him homage, and he could have applied to politics what he said of war: 'The repute of arms is everything, and is equivalent to the real forces.' Those who had taken their precautions against the failure of his fortunes were no less cordial than the rest. The King of Prussia and the Emperor of Austria were both present. His august parents-in-law were there in token of the intimacy of the two houses and the two Empires. Fourteen months would pass, and in the city which had seen that family gathering, Bonaparte would receive a declaration of war from the court of Vienna. Provision had been made equally against his triumph and his reverse. And if the festivities of Dresden had their undercurrent of whisper and rumour, the chances of both adversaries were counted as equal. The Tsar, exposing himself to the blow of such a colossus, seemed sometimes the more insensate of the two.

Napoleon entertained no doubts: Alexander would have to sue for peace, 'because that outcome was at the basis of his scheme'. He did not believe the Tsar, subject as he was to emotions and sudden changes of mind, could persevere in the cruel plan of yielding his empire or laying it waste before the advancing invader. That seemed quite fanciful to Bonaparte, who would rather have ranged the Tsar amongst the lovers of drama, with changes of scene and shiftings of development. Napoleon did not discern that at this moment Alexander had entered on a new role, that of liberator of the peoples – nor that he would be bound to it – by the alliance he was about to renew with England, by the national fanaticism he would kindle in his subjects, and by vanity as well. His court was becoming the rallying-ground for Napoleon's enemies, and a salon of liberalism. In St. Petersburg Mme de Staël was welcomed and feted as the adversary of the tyrant of Europe, and she celebrated the virtue and conscience of the Russian autocrat. The style was not that of Tilsit, but it was still a style, and one which matched a new set of circumstances. It flattered and intoxicated Alexander.

The wish is often father to the thought; and that grave mistake was at the root of the mistakes which Napoleon was about to make. The essential reason for his failure, which lay in his mind, has been sought in a deterioration of his bodily health, a pastiness of physique which is thought to have left his intelligence clouded and his activity sluggish. This has been much exaggerated. A man is not worn-out at forty-three. Napoleon was to stand the Russian winter well, as also the physical rigours of retreat, hard for all, even for himself. His ideas were still lucid, his imagination lively, even too ardent. His only symptom of oncoming age was his refusal to admit the possibility of his errors, and the way in which, when he found himself in circumstances where his calculations had previously proved correct, he fell back on them again. He was imitating himself, like an author whose manner has been successful. He returned completely to 1807, by the self-same stages and scenes, almost the same resting-places; and the seeming resemblance was so strong that he thought aloud, and there came the proclamation of June 22nd: 'Soldiers, the second war of Poland has begun; the first closed at Friedland and Tilsit.' And ten days later, the message to the Tsar: 'If fortune must again favour my arms, your Majesty will find me, as at Tilsit and Erfurt, full of friendliness and esteem.' But one cannot bathe twice in the same stream, and the symbolic raft was not to float again upon the Niemen.

Just as he crossed its treacherous waters, himself reconnoitring the ford, a queer accident befell the Emperor. A hare ran between the legs of his horse, which reared and unseated his rider. His suite saw an evil omen in the fall, and half-serious, half-laughing, the headquarters staff declared that the Roman legions would have gone no further. Napoleon dreaded the superstition of others, the more because he was not superstitious himself, and was concerned with keeping the incident quiet. Then, shaking off this childish idea and endeavouring to persuade himself, he declared that within two months Russia would be suing for peace. Next day he had crossed the Niemen — to find, instead of Alexander's open arms, some Cossacks who took to flight, and to find that for three days the Russian army had been in retreat.

It was now June 24th. On the 28th, Napoleon entered Vilna. He spent eighteen days there waiting for Alexander to make a request for peace. With the Grand Army occupying Lithuania, threatening to raise the population against its Russian oppressors, and to join the Letts with the Poles, Alexander would surely become alarmed. He would give in. Napoleon did not doubt it, because he had so decided. 'When once the Emperor had an idea which he thought useful lodged in his head,' said Caulaincourt, 'he deluded himself. He adopted it, fondled it, and became imbued with it.' Vilna, in his plans, was a political and military headquarters, the place from which the intimidation would succeed, or from which the 'thunderbolt' would be discharged. Alexander, as his correspondence proved, was apprehensive of a restoration of Poland; and Napoleon was certain that he would be worked upon through this dread. From Dresden he had sent instructions to the ambassador in Warsaw, directing that Poland should be roused 'to a kind of intoxication', that a kind of Vendée or Spain should be

prepared there for the Russians — the Spanish bogy, repro-
duced at this extremity of Europe, being the one brandished
by both adversaries. The difficulty was still how to call
upon the Poles to rebel without annoying Austria, who had
to be carefully handled in order to avoid making Alexander
irreconcilable. Now, as in 1807, Napoleon used Poland,
but did not help her. On July 14th, still at Vilna, when the
deputies of the Polish confederation came to thank the
liberator and invite him to continue his work, he wrapped his
reply round with 'buts' and 'ifs', reservations and conditions.

The political menace, therefore, did not impress the Tsar
so long as a military decision was not secured. After all his
judicious planning, Bonaparte was being disappointed and
led on. He proposed spending a year at Vilna, two if need
be. From Vilna the peace with Russia would be arrived at,
because it would be from there that his operations were bound
to end by destroying the two main Russian armies. Obstinately and methodically the enemy generals avoided contact.
The Emperor pondered subtle and unavailing schemes.
Bagration's retreat must be cut, Barclay de Tolly overwhelmed by superior forces, according to the style of victories
which the French used to win 'with their legs'. But on a
difficult terrain, over vast tracts of forest and marshland,
exact time-tables could not be kept. Napoleon urged on his
brother Jerome and his generals. He rated them, and spurred
them with his orders and reproaches; he was amazed that
they were not at the prescribed place on the prescribed day,
refusing to admit the excuse of natural obstacles, lack
of supplies, fatigue of rank and file, bogged cavalry. He
repeated his bitter refrain: 'I am badly served . . .' He was
insulting and wounding, without ever punishing. And meanwhile Bagration escaped, while Barclay slipped away, and
both effected a junction further on, beyond the Dnieper.
Every engagement had been victorious, but they were only
engagements, none of them comparable to those shattering
decisive battles which Napoleon usually fought at the

opening of his campaigns and which he had prepared for this one. Thiers maintains that Napoleon was wrong to stop at Vilna, that he wasted valuable time in resting his troops after their long march and in a meticulous regrouping of troops and convoys. 'Once the madness of this war had been started,' true wisdom should have consisted in being 'still madder'. He should have advanced by forced marches, at the risk of leaving still more laggards behind, and struck swiftly and terribly with the best of his forces. Yet Thiers takes into account the declining quality of the Grand Army, the excessive youth of the French recruits, the dead weight of the foreign auxiliaries. The Emperor was well aware that his instrument was not what it had been; he had known that since Essling and Wagram. And Thiers notes that although the conception remained bold, the execution was wavering. Have we not already seen Napoleon's mind invaded by that uncertainty, tormenting and paralysing him to such a pitch that it is often tempting to regard this man with his brevity of speech and imperious commands as a man hiding his own indecision and whipping up his own hesitancy? Was he perhaps a gambler unwilling to play except for sure stakes, startled by the idea of losing his all, and raising his risks by excessive prudence? In Paris his mind had wavered over the question of making war. At Vilna it still wavered painfully. Should he spend the winter and organize in the conquered country, waiting for the Tsar to offer peace, or should he continue the pursuit to strike the great blow which would certainly bring the peace? He shifted abruptly from one idea to the other. He abandoned the idea of winter quarters at Vilna because he saw a chance of grappling with Barclay. The 22nd or 23rd of July was fixed for the 'great battle' that was to end everything. On the 28th he thought he had it within his grasp on the Lutchega. It was there that he anticipated his new Friedland, and he cried to Murat: 'Till to-morrow, at five — the sun of Austerlitz!' No sun, no enemy. Once again the Russians had retreated.

The French entered Vitebsk behind them. Perplexity was renewed. At first Napoleon announced that this town would be his winter quarters, and even asked for a troupe of actors from Paris 'to pass the winter evenings'. The campaign of 1812, he declared, was over; that of 1813 would do the rest. And still the only news of Alexander was rumour, all confirming that he was neither intimidated nor inclined to turn back in Napoleon's direction. The Tsar had formed an alliance with England, another with Sweden, through the treachery of Bernadotte. Envoys from the Cortes of Cadiz had been received at St. Petersburg. Peace was imminent between Russia and Turkey. And so the occupation of Vitebsk was no nearer to forcing the Tsar's hand than Vilna had been. 'We shall not repeat the folly of Charles XII,' said the Emperor on his arrival. And then he reflected that he was losing time, that events would go on whilst he stood still. From Vitebsk he projected a move forward to Smolensk. (And Charles XII?) Whereupon he was again seized by cruel anxieties, and Ségur describes him from Barante's dry account, 'unable to settle, continually taking up his work, setting it aside, resuming it again, walking aimlessly about, asking the time, looking at the weather, humming in a preoccupied way, and walking about again'.

His ceaseless reflections showed him that he could no longer cling to his original plan, because his reckonings had proved untrue. He had formed several hypotheses. None had materialized. Alexander had not sued for peace, and the military decision had not been obtained. To stop before entering Russia proper, with the idea that the Tsar would submit rather than risk the restoration of Poland, was a third conjecture, and like the others it excluded the danger of plunging into the heart of the country. Once on the spot, Napoleon saw for himself that, for all sorts of reasons, his apparently judicious project of wintering there was not practicable, that the billeting of the men would be too widely scattered, and that they would be poorly supplied. As the cold weather came on, they would be exposed to surprise attacks; the frozen streams would offer passage to the enemy instead of being lines of defence. Besides, to enter on a campaign in June and to rest in August, meant demoralizing the army by inactivity and admitting a check — a grave admission, because in the rear there was Germany, and Spain farther away, and even France, concerning which Napoleon had still some anxiety. Prestige must be saved at any cost. In any case, granted that the winter passed off successfully, everything would have to be restarted in the following summer, and in what respect would things have changed? The Emperor handled troops reduced in numbers by fatigue, sickness and desertion. What remained was the hardiest and bravest, the men of whom anything could be asked, who would push right on to India, and sometimes thought they were bound for there, who preferred risk and adventure to the boredom of winter quarters in a land of desolation. It was fallacious wisdom to cling to the original plan. On the contrary, the Emperor should march on the enemy, force battle, compel the still-lingering peace, and have done with 'this fever of doubt', as he said to Duroc. Napoleon then held a council, as he always did when he had a great decision to take, to secure approval, to be told that he was right. He lost his temper with Berthier, who counselled caution, and reproached him with being the greediest for rest amongst those whose only aspiration now was to enjoy their high rank and high incomes. He ill-treated this 'cousin' of his, Prince of Neuchâtel and Wagram, and bullied the faithful Duroc himself; and with those who agreed with his views he was kind and ingratiating. After all, he was the master, the war leader. The idea of spending a long winter in this gloomy Lithuania weighed heavy on men of action. The new manœuvre, that of advancing on Smolensk, would be carried out. And once more the Emperor was persuaded that this could not fail to bring the thunderbolt which would end everything. He ought to have stayed

patiently in Vitebsk until the next summer. He stayed there
a fortnight.

For eight years now Bonaparte had been chasing an impossibility. Everything was now creating fresh impossibilities.
At Vilna he had let Barclay and Bagration escape because he
would not leave anything to chance. The superiority he had
gained in the first encounters decided the Russian generals
to refuse battle with him, and this helped to draw him farther
into the interior. The more science and genius Napoleon
put into his schemes, the more he forced the Russians
to withdraw. They retreated by plan and by necessity, in
obedience to the general order, and because they 'could not
do otherwise'. Napoleon complained of their lack of resolve
when they slipped away. Whenever they were within his
reach they felt disaster so near that, despite themselves, they
fell back on the plan of methodical and deliberate retreat.

On August 18th Napoleon entered Smolensk, with no
further result than he had found in Vitebsk. This had been
the very farthest point which he had assigned to himself
before leaving Paris. He was to have gone there only if
peace had not been concluded before then, presuming
that the Tsar would seek friendly overtures when the Grand
Army had reached the intersection of the two roads, one of
which led straight to Moscow, the other to St. Petersburg.
Napoleon found a bare and deserted town. He understood.
The Russians were leaving a hollow void in front of him.
All the more reason to hurry on faster, not to waste time as at
Vilna, or hesitate as at Vitebsk. The question of wintering
at Smolensk hardly arose, for the town had been stripped of
resources. Nor was there any question as to whether peace
would be imposed at Moscow or at St. Petersburg, for it was
the Moscow road which the Russian army had taken, and
he would have gone to Kiev if they had taken the Kiev road.
The retreating army was within his grasp. A rapid march,
and the main enemy force, once overtaken, would be annihilated. And so, chasing 'the phantom of victory', Napoleon

found himself continually drawn farther and farther, led on where he had forbidden himself to go. Circumstances were ruling him. He was not the master of events; he was commanded by the need of obtaining the solution. He was now finding reasons for heading towards Moscow as he would have found others for turning to St. Petersburg.

And why did nothing succeed? The manœuvres conceived by his alert and fruitful imagination were of the kind in which he usually triumphed. To outflank the enemy, encircle him and cut off his line of retreat — it was all skilfully planned, and it all failed. Contact had been made with the Russians before Smolensk, at Valutina. Again they escaped. The great battle always melted away between his fingers. At Valutina he had not been present, being detained by state business which beset him even here. When he heard of the engagement, furious at not having directed it himself, he again stormed against his lieutenants who had not exacted from that day of slaughter the cost of its sacrifices. 'I cannot do everything,' was his constant complaint. His wrath was violent against Junot. It subsided, like other outbursts, without any penalties being taken. Everything evaporated in words.

By words he also reassured himself, convinced himself and convinced others. At Smolensk he declared: 'Within a month we shall be in Moscow: in six weeks we shall have peace.' His obsession was now binding him to the fatal path. As peace had to be wrenched from Russia, Alexander would yield when the French had seized the holy city. During that march on the Kremlin, whence he counted on bringing back a triumphal treaty, Napoleon lost no opportunity of repeating that this was a political war, with neither personal nor national animosity, that he had no ill-will against either Russia or the Tsar. St. Petersburg must realize that he did not plan to resuscitate Poland, and that actually, since seeing Poland again, he disliked it even more than in 1807. Let the Tsar break with England and declare himself against her.

He asked no more, because that was the only thing which had brought the Grand Army into Russia. Napoleon still aspired to a second Tilsit. There too he was imitating himself, and was behind the times. He pursued the ghost of the past as vainly as he pursued Bagration and Barclay.

And if, during that twenty-day march on Moscow, he was perpetually in a state of irritation painful to his entourage, it was because he would not confess the truth, would not recognize that he had done what he was unwilling to do, that he had changed his plan while the Tsar had remained faithful to his, and that he had repeated the action of Charles XII after pouring scorn on those who warned him of the marshes of Poltava. It was agony to be plunging unwillingly into the heart of Russia in search of the military or the political decision — he knew not which — and without the certainty of either. 'He was,' says one witness, 'like a man in need of consolation.' He affected to mock at these Russians 'who burn their homes to prevent us from spending a night in them', and could not shut out forebodings as he saw the deserts left in his rear. He tried endlessly to work out the motives and intentions of Alexander, trying to persuade himself now, that the Tsar would become conciliatory, now, that the Russians would give battle. And when battle showed itself, when old Kutusoff, his new adversary, gave signs of saving honour by at least trying to defend the holy city, Napoleon was strangely troubled.

It has been thought that some mystery lay behind the battle of Borodino, on the Moskowa river. Bonaparte is supposed to have been no longer himself. Ill, weakened in will and intelligence, the almost immobile spectator of this murderous day, he is thought to have compromised its success by his phlegmatic heaviness. It has also been said that he was affected by news from Spain, the defeat of Marmont at Salamanca and Joseph's second flight from Madrid: Spain was probably lost. The refusal to give the 18,000 men of his Guard to exploit the victory seemed inexplicable. Murat's indignation has been described, and the scornful words of Ney quoted: 'Let him go back to the Tuileries!' Actually it seems that Napoleon was afflicted that day by a violent fever, which did not however prevent him from following the battle. As for the despatches from Spain, they had as usual only excited his pity for what was happening away there. Meanwhile his desire was to measure himself against Kutusoff, for he still clung to the idea of the great battle, which would be certain to bring peace and, as he promised his soldiers, a 'prompt return to their homes'. But at the height of the action, which was fierce, he remained obsessed with the idea that the Guard was his supreme resource, that it would be rash to let it be shattered. To the supplication of Ney and Murat, his reply, approved by Bessières and Berthier, was that 'last reserves are not risked eight hundred leagues from France'. At bottom his anxieties did not leave him. He flattered himself on his prudence and foresight, on leaving nothing to chance, answering that he wanted 'to see things clear on his chess-board'. Perhaps also he had some unconscious idea, as at Austerlitz, of moderation with Alexander, and not making this a war without quarter. His prolonged uncertainties weighed on him more heavily than his fever. Hesitating between the different methods of securing an elusive peace, he no longer knew whether he would obtain it by terrifying the Russians through the destruction of their army, or by giving a sign of his humanity and desire for coming to terms. But the combats had been bloody. This was butchery, a battlefield even more sinister than Eylau. Over forty French generals had been killed or wounded. The Russian losses were enormous. Napoleon was at pains to diminish the enemy's losses in despatches and bulletins, as if reluctant to humiliate or to exasperate the Russians. Kutusoff, for his part, having retreated and saved the remnant of his forces, declared his readiness to fight fresh battles, so that Napoleon, though victorious, was not completely so. 'Well! We have not had the fifth act', he said to Narbonne with that detachment which he attained at moments of supreme crisis. He had not produced the effect he expected, either by a defeat of the Russians or by a show of clemency in victory to facilitate the renewal of the alliance for which he constantly hoped. He had had the great battle upon which he had reckoned before leaving Paris. His victory was insufficiently complete, and it remained sterile.

It even became fatal, as sinister as all the circumstances which had gradually brought him nearer and nearer to Moscow, because it brought him right into the city, and Moscow was to be his tomb.

Napoleon headed for Moscow instead of St. Petersburg because the enemy themselves pointed out the road to him. Russia had two capitals, and Napoleon was persuaded that it was at Moscow that this war would reach its end. This too he believed because he needed to believe it, and he needed to believe it because beyond Moscow there was nothing. It would simply have to be at Moscow that he would receive Alexander's messenger. He refused to believe otherwise, because in that case he would find himself confronted by a void, by the thing that could not be conceived because it was the dead-end of action and of thought. At that moment Bonaparte reached the limit of his efforts, of his military and political schemings, of all that he had tried in vain for ten years past. If this supreme feat of strength failed, there remained only a fall into emptiness. Moscow was the last stage. Was it possible that he had come so far to set off again as he had come? That was the idea which would prove fatal to him. He was now a slave to the illusion that he would find another Tilsit at the Kremlin.

He comforted himself again with the thought that he was not Charles XII. Had he not thought out and organized everything throughout this march, with his care for exactness and details? Right back to Paris stretched unbroken lines of communication; the seat of Empire was borne east to Moscow, and in the Kremlin the Emperor would be installed as in the

Élysée. If it must be, it would be better to winter in the great city of Russia, where more weight could be exerted on the Tsar's will than at Vilna or Vitebsk. Surely the surrender of this city of gilded cupolas and three hundred churches would shake that resolve, which Napoleon had never taken seriously, to retreat 'right to Kamchatka'?

The day — September 14th — on which Moscow came into view of the Emperor and the army was probably the day of their greatest mistake. These men who had accomplished so many wonders had the sense of having accomplished one which surpassed all the rest, and the fact caused them to feel that they had reached the limit of their efforts. It was a strange moment, when the soldiers seemed to be awaiting the reward of their efforts, and their leader the solution of a painfully pondered problem. 'It was high time,' he murmured; and Ségur shows him with his eyes fixed on these walls which 'enclosed all his hope'. An Oriental imagery rose to men's brains. From these gates would come forth the boyards, bearing the ritual offering of bread and salt; and they would proffer the gates of the city, kneeling before the Tsar of the French, imploring him to show mercy to Russia. The hours passed, with neither keys nor boyards. At dusk he had to yield to the truth. Like Smolensk, the city was evacuated, deserted. Napoleon grew impatient, and demanded the deputation of notables. Only five or six poor wretches could be brought to him. He shrugged his shoulders, according to Ségur, and 'with that air of contempt with which he overwhelmed whatever thwarted his desire', he exclaimed that the Russians did not yet know the effect which would be produced by the taking of their capital. That same night they set fire to the city.

Thereupon Napoleon was the man who is obliged to deny the evidence, who obstinately wishes things to be other than they are, who elaborately proves that what is held to be baneful is beneficent, that whatever destroys his reckoning really confirms it and helps it. Around him men were saying that his conquest was going up in smoke. He himself, before the reddened Moscow, could not check his cry: 'This foretells great ills for us!' He had hardly entered the Kremlin before the flames drove him out. Hardly had he returned when he recovered confidence. The savagery of Rostopchin, the governor, would provoke the Russians and open the eyes of Alexander. Had not the French extinguished that barbarous conflagration, unsparing of their own lives to save those of others, to save churches, palaces, treasures? The Tsar would surely respond to such humanity. He would see that this was not a war to the death, that renewed friendship and alliance were possible, that only one thing — always the same — was wanted: a break with England, measures against English commerce, observance of the blockade — the questions, in fact, at the root of this unhappy conflict. All this Napoleon kept repeating, as if he were talking to his friend Alexander, the 'handsome and fine young man' of Tilsit, just as he kept repeating that Moscow was a 'political position', excellent for awaiting offers of peace. He came near to adding that it is only right and proper that a sovereign whose capital is conquered should ask terms of the victor lodging in his palaces. However, with memories of the past, it was Napoleon who took the first step. On September 20th, he wrote to the Tsar: 'I have waged war upon your Majesty without animosity. One note from your Majesty, before or after the last battle, would have halted my march, and I should have been willing even to sacrifice the advantage of setting foot in Moscow.' And he ended cordially: 'If your Majesty retains any of your former sentiments towards me, you will take this letter in good part.' And his wish that Alexander should do so was too clearly manifested.

It was clear now that he had come as far as Moscow in pursuit of the phantom of Tilsit, and that he would not leave without grasping it. But October came, and there was still no sign from Alexander, no news from St. Petersburg. But at the outposts (for Kutusoff still prowled about the neighbourhood) Murat was becoming friendly with the Cossacks, and even enjoyed some popularity amongst them; and just as he had dreamed of becoming King of Spain and King of Poland, he was tempted by the idea of becoming a hetman. Why not? After so many prodigies nothing seemed impossible. The Russian officers then confided in him — he was quite ready to exchange his crown of Naples for another, or to don a second one — that things were in a bad way in Russia, that the nobility, the merchants and the people were all war-weary, and that they themselves were anxious for peace. And, just as formerly in the Spanish affair, Murat's illusions fed those of the Emperor. He amazed everybody by his assurance, spending three evenings in drawing up the regulations of the Comédie Française, as calmly as if he were dating the decree from Saint-Cloud, and, watching the days pass, he answered the anxieties which he could feel growing round him by saying that the climate was not so rigorous as the pessimists had declared. 'Look,' he said with an easy-going air, 'the autumn is finer, and even warmer, than at Fontainebleau!' And although 'everything cried aloud to him that the Tsar would not negotiate', and whereas his own need for peace was crying, he obstinately and unceasingly declared that the Russians would be worn out before he was, and that the capitulation of Alexander was only a matter of days.

This fine confidence concealed secret alarms. On October 4th, he sent Lauriston to Kutusoff's headquarters with another letter to the Tsar. And he was beginning to tell himself that Moscow was not a good position, that between France and the Grand Army lay the Prussians and Austrians, allies for the moment, but quite capable of being foes again. In fact, there had reached him an enigmatic note from Schwarzenberg which made him fearful of an Austrian defection; and after reading it he murmured some bad tragic verses about the supreme law of destiny. Winter in Moscow? The burnt and deserted town offered no resources, and, what is more, there was ground for believing that the road would soon be cut. Cossacks had appeared in outlying quarters. Some of the couriers bringing mails and ensuring communications had been chased. These were symptoms. There would still be time to get the army back to Vilna before the bad winter weather came on. Napoleon delayed because he still hoped that the Tsar would decide to negotiate. And why should he leave without the results for which he had come so far? How was the departure to be explained? Caulaincourt cogently remarks that 'the embarrassment of his difficult position kept him as it were chained to the Kremlin'.

Faced by danger, he had to decide on departure. The Russians were beginning to cut the Smolensk road. Communications with France were becoming irregular. Napoleon had no news of his empire, could no longer correspond daily with his ministers. The army, receiving no letters from home, felt its isolation, and its morale was affected. Inwardly, the Emperor had already realized that he could not remain longer in Moscow. He would not as yet admit it openly, because an announcement of retreat would ruin the last chances of peace. With time vainly lost, an improvised departure and inadequate measures against the cold were to bring disaster on the Grand Army. Napoleon let himself fall asleep at Moscow, and in order to give him a fallacious sense of serenity and buoy him up with fatal hopes, the wily Kutusoff even simulated a suspension of hostilities.

These last days in the Kremlin were those of the gambler denying to himself that he has lost, and trying fortune once again. On October 16th, he addressed Kutusoff direct, resigning himself to a request for peace. The reply was a refusal. Napoleon then thought of the weapon he had been reluctant to use. He had an act drawn up to emancipate the serfs. And then the proclamation was withdrawn, 'avenging bolts of which he showed only the flashes and always held back the thunder'. As the founder of a dynasty, the kinsman of crowned heads, could he once again become the

Emperor of the Revolution, compromise alliances now more necessary than ever, ruin a whole policy? And to no end: for it was brought home to him that it was too late, that the peasants, with their fanaticism kindled, would pay no more heed to him than had the Spaniards when he proclaimed the death of feudalism and the Inquisition. Instantly — but it was not for long — he reverted to the style of the legitimate and conservative sovereign, and he called Rostopchin 'the Russian Marat'.

His mental excitement was betrayed by other symptoms. The departure had to be explained. Whereupon Moscow become merely 'an impure and unhealthy sewer . . . of no military importance and now of no further political importance'. Which was only too true. A move was made towards Vilna, supposedly to threaten St. Petersburg, for in his innermost heart Napoleon had not yet completely resolved upon retreat. One more manœuvre, then, which might set everything right, or at least a punishment that would make Kutusoff harmless. And so Napoleon was giving himself pretexts for not abandoning, and he left Mortier in the Kremlin whilst he himself was to try to engage the enemy. But Kutusoff still kept out of reach. 'This is becoming serious', said the Emperor. He had delayed; he had let winter gain on him, and compromised the retreat, because the road he was going to take was that of decline. Did he have presentiments of the coming catastrophe? Yet he refused to believe, just as lately he had wanted to believe. The Tsar was bound to be going to make a peace offer. He made no more mention of it. Now he was reluctant to admit that the army was already melting, falling to pieces, and that winter in these parts comes with no transition, as abruptly as the summer. He shook off warnings by saying: 'It freezes for the Russians as hard as for us.' Caulaincourt reminded him of what Alexander had replied to the armistice proposals brought by Lauriston: 'My campaign is beginning.' The Emperor shrugged his shoulders: 'Your prophet Alexander has been wrong more than once.' But he admitted to Caulaincourt his deep, gripping anxiety. What were men thinking and doing in France? At the end of October he told him his great secret, his settled intention to leave the army as soon as he could and get back to Paris.

That retreat from Russia, which adds another picture to his history, might have had an even worse ending. Just when it seemed that his star was abandoning him, it served him in a different fashion. Twice he nearly fell into the hands of the Cossacks. He may be imagined being made prisoner, being killed in a skirmish, or avoiding captivity by taking poison, with which he had supplied himself as a precaution. His destiny would have been then cut off short, he would have left behind the reputation of an adventurer, and his history would have lacked a conclusion made worthy of what had gone before by a catastrophe on the grand scale. Or let us suppose an adversary less cautious, less temporizing, less apathetic than old Kutusoff — the retreat cut off — the remnants of the Grand Army destroyed or compelled to surrender. That would have been the end which befell Charles XII, whose marshes Napoleon almost found again at the crossing of the Beresina. He was shielded by his reputation and prestige, by the fear inspired by his name, a capital which only fifteen months were now to exhaust. For cruelly long though the days of that retreat seemed, everything after them was to advance towards the final downfall with gathering speed. In any case, Napoleon still remained like himself during that tragic return, when every stage brought a disappointment, a misfortune, the threat of annihilation. His health? Excellent. He was no longer the depressed and sick man who had apparently been seen at Borodino. He remained hopeful, counting on the orders he gave, and on the provisions which should be found on the line of march, not doubting his fortune, always in expectation of a lucky turn of events which would right everything — possibly a diversion by Schwarzenberg. For these very reasons, says Caulaincourt, he was 'as undecided, as uncertain on the last day as the first'. And then, when it became impossible to blind himself to the ruin of the Grand Army, his attitude became 'grave, silent and resigned, and though physically he suffered less than the others, he suffered more in mind, and accepted his misfortune'.

After the army had been seventeen days on the march, pushing off the harrying and pursuing Russians, the snow began to fall. And with it began the direst miseries. On that same day came a courier, bearing news from Paris. And what news! A sort of political Baylen — the worst that could happen, with the Emperor absent and enduring his first great reverses. A Republican soldier, General Malet, involved in the plots of the past few years, had escaped from the asylum in which he was confined, announced the death of the Emperor and the proclamation of the Republic. For a few hours he was the master of Paris, and arrested Savary, the minister of police, and Pasquier, the prefect of police. The affair was unmasked and checked, and its only outcome was the ridicule cast on the Imperial authorities, and the odium of twelve death sentences. At first Napoleon consoled himself by declaring the whole affair to be the work of imbeciles — on both sides — but at bottom he was gravely affected. 'It cannot be the work of one man,' he repeated. He pictured a vast plot, almost a revolution. He was chiefly struck by the fact that nobody remembered that, if the Emperor were dead, he had an heir and successor. 'And did nobody think of Napoleon II?' The monarchy, the hereditary empire, its institutions, his marriage, his son — did all these count for nothing? The forgetfulness showed the measure of his weakness. He realized that his power remained as brittle as in the time of the Consulate, that he himself was at the mercy of a great reverse. And these thoughts filled his mind just when everything was bringing home to him that, at any moment, the Russians might inflict that great reverse upon him. Powerless to dissemble his alarm, he tried to find out what others thought of the events in Paris, and, instead of keeping silence, he announced the astonishing news himself, so as to observe its effect on his generals.

He ceased talking of it, but without ceasing to think of it, still hurrying to get nearer to France, still separated from home by a host of dangers. Every day made the retreat more hideous. On arrival at Smolensk, the food supplies were found pillaged, and high hopes were turned into distress. Napoleon remained in his own quarters, shunning the spectacle of these scenes, these battles between comrades-in-arms for a few remnants of victuals. Then the march had to be resumed in disorder and vanished discipline, only a few handfuls of men showing how far endurance and heroism can reach, Ney in the rearguard putting up a fight twice daily to shield the sorry convoy. The Emperor was now trudging on foot himself, surrounded by the 'sacred squadron', burning his papers and clothes with his own hands on the day when he was nearly caught. Once the remark escaped him that 'great reverses were often prepared by too consistent a habit of great successes, but there was no question of recriminations'. Sometimes, on hearing disastrous news, he struck the ground with his stick, and 'cast a glance of fury at the heavens' with the words: 'And so it is written up there that whatever we do now shall be wrong.'

In this way the Beresina, of baleful memory, was reached, and he was apprehensive of some still more fearful disaster. When he saw that stream of drifting ice, the bridge destroyed, the Russians resolved on crushing the shattered remnants of the Grand Army, and when for a moment he had to think of turning down towards the Dnieper, he remembered with a pang how assured he had been when he declared that he knew what he was doing and would not repeat the history of Charles XII. And it was perhaps this idea of not letting history so gloomily repeat itself, which gave him the energy he needed for these tragic days, and the determined clear-sightedness of a war leader. Nor was his trusted star to abandon him. The very point which he had chosen to cross the fatal river deceived the enemy. Further on he had still to cross the marshes — too much like those of Poltava — which would have swallowed up all who escaped the horrible rush over the river, if the Russians had not forgotten to destroy the bridges in the marshland.

'I have played the Emperor long enough: it is time I played the general,' said Napoleon in that extremity of danger. On the other bank, saved from great perils, the Emperor reappeared. He thought of the morrow, of his throne. He was in Poland; he could communicate with France; he was greedy to know what had been happening whilst he had been on the point of vanishing. For a fortnight he had heard not a word of news. He was anxious to know what Europe was thinking. And men must know, first and foremost that the Emperor was alive and well, and would soon be back, because there must be no doubts, in Germany, in France, anywhere, of his still formidable presence, which, during forty terrible days, had held back Kutusoff in fear and respect, and had helped Ney to save the honour of what had once been the Grand Army.

He took the full measure of the disaster. To-morrow Europe would know that the Emperor had escaped from this gigantic adventure only with routed and ragged troops, and that of the finest military machine ever known there remained only famished, half-dying men, and leaders covered with glory but in ill-temper. Russia and England would redouble their efforts. Prussia, and even Austria, would no longer be safe. The ferment, perceptible in Germany since 1809, would have reached the countries of the Confederation, Holland, Belgium and Italy, not to mention Spain, already insurgent; and in France the discontents already revealed by the Malet affair would strike deeper roots. Neither tricks nor dissembling would be of any avail. And he must reach Paris simultaneously with the news of the disaster, so as to minimize its effect. The news must not run ahead of him. If it did, Prussia would rise, join hands with Russia, and all would be lost.

The Emperor reflected thus and took his decision during the days following the passage of the Beresina, days which were hardly less tragic than that when so many poor fellows were swallowed by the icy waters. The Russians had continued to pursue, and sometimes Ney and Maison could muster only a handful of men still capable of holding a gun. It was in this plight that Napoleon composed the most difficult and perhaps the most surprising piece of his military writings. This was the 29th Bulletin, which makes everything clear, and envelops everything in a noble gravity of language, wherein the words are skilfully graduated, moving from the 'painful situation' to the 'hideous calamity', whilst the two aspects of the retreat are set forth with the serenity of one who is well versed in men, a psychologist, touching here those 'whom nature has not sufficiently tempered', men shattered and dreaming only of catastrophe, and also those who preserve their cheerfulness and ordinary ways, and see 'only fresh glory in the difficulties to be surmounted'. Everything is there — the men falling by the way from hunger, cold, or despair, the horseless cavalry, the abandoned wagons, the generals acting as captains and the colonels as corporals, the Emperor himself impassive in the midst of his sacred squadron. The narrative is calculated to give an impression of calm and complete self-possession, and ends with the words: 'The health of his Majesty has never been better.' The Emperor was identifying himself with the Empire. He was thought to be dead, sick, worn-out. Let them take care. He was coming.

But the most difficult thing was not this stylistic rendering of an unprecedented disaster. He had to leave the men who had survived all these agonies and horrors, abandoning them, deprived of the presence of the chief and the magic of his name, to dangers not yet ended. Ségur describes how

361

he coaxed his marshals and won them over separately to his project of departure, 'now by arguments, now by bursts of confidence'. Then, having assembled them, he distributed praises and thanks, and sought to convince them that to save them, and with them their status and emoluments, he must first of all save the Empire, that their safety rested only with himself, and that all of them had from the start entered jointly with himself upon an adventure. 'If I had been born on the throne, if I had been a Bourbon, it would have been easy for me to make no mistakes!' It was still the generals that Bonaparte feared; he was less sure of them than the soldiers. And he found the words that kept them to their duty. Only Berthier stood out, and wanted to depart also. The mameluke Roustan has described the scene with barbaric simplicity. 'I am old. Take me with you.' 'You shall stay with Eugène and Murat.' And then, as Berthier insisted: 'You're ungrateful, you're a coward! I shall have you shot in front of the army!' It was a foreshadowing of the revolt of the high command, the scenes of Fontainebleau.

On December 5th Napoleon set off, 'on a simple sledge, surviving his army, his own glory, and, so to speak, his own power. On his way he offered to his governors, his allies and tributaries, the spectacle of a kind of phantom, which a breath of wind might carry away, but whose very name still imposed terror and compelled respect'. Here was one more chapter of his adventurous life — this Emperor, under a secretary's name, traversing Poland and Prussia with three companions, exposed to all the hazards of the road if he were recognized. Bonaparte had already left Egypt in the same kind of way, trusting to fortune. Nothing astonished him. He had always expected anything. During the journey he spoke of himself as of a stranger with that readiness to watch himself living which is the mark of the artist. He took Caulaincourt with him, as if curious to be *tête-à-tête* with the man whose advice he had refused to listen to. With him he discussed his case as if it had been someone else's: 'I was wrong, not about

362

the aim of political opportuneness of this war, but about the manner of waging it. We should have stayed at Vitebsk. Alexander would be at my feet to-day.' Of Malet's conspiracy: 'I still think that everything I've done is very fragile.'

On December 18th, almost unrecognizable, he arrived at the Tuileries without warning. The 29th Bulletin had been published in the *Moniteur* forty-eight hours before. Napoleon knew that he would find Paris stricken. The consternation exceeded his expectations. Men spoke of the expedition of Cambyses, of the end of Charlemagne's empire. The Emperor would have to take everything in hand, and work, as soon as he returned, with Cambacérès, Clarke, and Savary. He called for information about the Malet affair, to which he attached prime importance. He spoke of it with 'a worried brow', and cast harsh remarks at everybody concerned. 'You thought I was dead . . . But what about the King of Rome — your oaths — your principles and doctrines? You make me tremble for the future.' Punishments were expected. Savary and Pasquier seemed to be doomed. They underwent a burst of temper like the rest, and remained at their posts. Only the simple Frochot, prefect of the Seine, was dismissed. He had gone too far, and had 'kept open house for the conspirators in the Hôtel de Ville'.

Then no more was said about the Malet affair. All presentiments were thrust away, and silence was imposed on everything connected with the Russian expedition. The Emperor explained matters to his ministers in a few words: 'Fortune dazzled me. I was at Moscow. I thought I should sign the peace there. I stayed too long.' That was the whole story, told with sincerity and disdain. The Senate was given even less: 'My army has suffered losses, but they were due to the premature severity of the climate.' To the men whom he felt to be ready to betray him, and who were again playing the sycophant before him, he replied in the customary formula, through which his scorn showed itself: 'I accept the expression of your sentiments towards me. . .' To some, a shrug of the shoulders; to others, a turned back. The bitter philosopher had reappeared, unmistakably. And since Moscow his whole policy had failed. Who knew it better than himself?

CHAPTER XXII

EBB-TIDE AND DOWNFALL

How was it that Bonaparte, who always realized the frailty of his power, did not feel the danger of his position on his return from Russia? None of his 'anchors' held. The Russian alliance was the basis of his policy, and the Tsar had become a resolute foe. The birth of his son was to abolish the vexing question of the succession, and 'Malet had revealed a fatal secret — the feebleness of the new dynasty'. It was astonishing that he gave so much thought to that surprise of one morning. 'Paris is talking only of the events in Russia; he seems to be struck only by events in Paris.' But the two things went hand in hand. He had long foreseen the eventuality of grave reverses. On a shaky throne he was at the mercy of a defeat, just as much as on the eve of Marengo. He repeated to himself that he was not a Bourbon, a king of ancient lineage; and later he was to remark: 'If I had been my own grandson, I could have retreated as far as the Pyrenees.' His thoughts turned to those whom he regarded as his predecessors. One evening in February, 1813, talking with Barante and Fontanes, he mentioned Louis XIV with admiring envy; 'so weighty a sovereign, with so strong a sense of his dignity, and of France's; after splendid victories he was able to resist the whole of Europe.' The whole of Europe — what would happen if Napoleon had that against him?

And things were much worse than they had been when he climbed into his sledge with Caulaincourt. When the Emperor left the Grand Army, its disintegration became complete, and it was 'devil take the hindmost'. Obedience was ended. Indiscipline spread even amongst the leaders. Everything was demoralized, and the spirit of defection was born. Murat, to whom the command had been entrusted, was not listened to, and he himself set a bad example. In the mud of Lithuania his only thoughts were for his kingdom, his endangered crown, and once he openly treated his brother-in-law as a madman. What arrived at Königsberg was merely the flotsam, the phantom of what had been the Great Army. The disaster was now there for Germany to see with her own eyes, and she drew her own deductions. Prussia was still the ally of Napoleon; in Berlin, Saint-Marsan, Narbonne and Augereau were with the King, dining with him, when, on December 30th, 1812, General Yorck, commanding the Prussian auxiliary corps signed an armistice with the Russians on his own initiative. Treason began with the Prussians; it spread to the Saxons at Leipzig, the Bavarians at Hanau. Frederick William was at first 'petrified' by the news of Yorck's headstrong disobedience; but he let himself he drawn on by the patriots, by his people, as in 1806, and within two months he had renewed the alliance with Alexander which they had, by common accord, suspended for their own preservation.

And so Napoleon was in the same position as before Jena, at grips with Prussia and with Russia. There remained Austria, the father of his consort, the grandfather of his child. Whatever happened, whatever the chance of arms and the accidents of the battlefield, whether the Emperor were killed, captured, or beaten, the Empire must remain, and nobody must be able to say that power was vacated. From every point of view, it was important to attach Francis II to the future of his daughter and grandson. And Bonaparte then sought a measure of protection in a new investiture.

It was the idea of an anxious man, whose ever-working brain had not reached the end of inventions to obtain an elusive security. This time he held before him the gown of Marie Louise and the swaddling-clothes of the King of Rome. Before rejoining the army, he was to set up a regency, and it was to the Empress that he entrusted it. Furthermore, the

King of Rome also was to receive the coronation anointing. A symbolic ceremony would affirm that Napoleon outlived himself. The coronation which had not sufficed for the father would be redoubled for the son. Henceforth the Emperor of Austria would be unnatural and sacrilegious if he did not protect his son-in-law's empire, along with the regent and the heir. And as Napoleon loved precedents, he caused investigations to be made concerning the regencies of queen-mothers, or wives of the kings of France, with special emphasis on Blanche of Castile. Researches were ordered regarding the crowning and the oaths of the eldest sons of kings during the lives of their fathers, since the days of Charlemagne. By the Emperor's orders, the dusty archives were searched, whilst he himself dictated daily notes for the organization of the army which 'he made to spring from the earth'. He also planned a spectacular reconciliation with Pius VII. One winter evening the recluse prisoner of Fontainebleau saw the Emperor entering unexpectedly. Everything would be forgotten, and the link would be reforged with the days of the Concordat. The Pope would extend the coronation to Marie and the Prince Imperial. Within the Empire, the disaffection of the faithful would be at an end. The Catholic courts would be satisfied. The manœuvre would have wide repercussions, and the Emperor hastened to inform his father-in-law, who had deplored the abduction of Savona, of the success of the interview at Fontainebleau. The solemnity of the second coronation would seal the reconciliation. And so Napoleon, who had already sought to legitimate his Empire by his marriage, was to take refuge in a kind of ultra-legitimacy. It had only needed the half-wit Malet, and a few panic-stricken officials, to bring the Emperor back to his obsession with conspiracies, to this desire for another application of the chrism of inviolability, for fresh anointing to confirm the guarantee he had sought through his marriage and his entry to the family of kings.

Before long, on the remonstrances of his cardinals, Pius VII repented of his continued weakness for Bonaparte. It was a weakness which he never quite lost. But in the end the Pope retracted, and rejected the new Concordat. The double coronation had to be abandoned; Notre-Dame and the throne erected beside the altar would have to be replaced by the oath being taken by the Regent in a room at the Élysée, before the ministers, the dignitaries, and the court. The times when everything succeeded were over. Napoleon would have to do without divine institutions. There remained human institutions. 'The Emperor calls upon his ever-victorious armies to confound his enemies, and to save civilized Europe and its sovereigns from the anarchy which threatens them.' Such was the peroration of the first speech recited by the Regent. It was not entirely false. Bearing the spirit of nationality, the ideas of the Revolution which so often startled Frederick William were fermenting amongst the Germans. In France Napoleon would need to revive the patriotism of the Revolution. And it was he who became the bulwark of the 'sovereigns', more dynastically-minded than the representatives of the old dynasties, without yet being at the end of his metamorphoses and incarnations.

The reconciliation with the Pope had failed; the 'affairs of Christendom' were not 'arranged'; the religious pacification, which was especially important in Belgium, was not obtained. But the one thing in which he refused to doubt was that he could count on Austria, on the bonds of blood that linked the two Imperial houses. Austria took the place of Russia as the basis of his policy. He believed, because he had to, in 'the religion, the piety and the honour' of his father-in-law. Putting aside every reminder of the dire check of Moscow, he affected an Olympian calm. Molé described him at this time 'governing, administrating, and concerning himself with the smallest details as if he had neither pre-occupations nor memories'. But one month after Yorck, Prince Schwarzenberg had signed an armistice with the

Russians. Austria was no longer the ally of France. She was neutral, and with a suspect neutrality.

Napoleon's illusions were in part wilful. If in 1813 he recommenced 1805 and 1806 and broke up the new coalition before it had united its forces, would he then be any further advanced than in 1807? Was not the stake still the same? He knew it, and said it: 'England insists on the disruption of this Empire as a condition of peace . . . If the enemy had their headquarters in the Faubourg Saint-Antoine, the French people would never renounce the union of Belgium.' And he repeated it to Schwarzenberg: 'The English believe that France is crushed; they will ask me for Belgium.' He knew well that France was worn out and sighing for peace. If he made peace at any price, he would first of all hear cries of gladness, and then, when the fatigues and anxieties of war were forgotten, he would be accused of having lost the conquests of the Revolution. He did not forget how he had reached power, nor what had carried him to power. He said so before, during, and after. It was of no avail to legitimize himself, to invest himself with regality; his power was only one 'of opinion', both abroad, where he had to maintain 'the appearance of an extreme confidence in his own strength', and at home, because he was chained to the mission he had taken over, to the duty of preserving for France the annexations of the Republic.

One party — and by now it included nearly everybody, even the marshals — declared that a sincere desire for peace would suffice, and that peace was still possible. For another, not for himself. He had bound himself to France, and France had bound herself to him, by this war for the natural frontiers. France and Napoleon could now be separated only by triumph or by defeat. In the former he still affected to believe. But if he beat the Continental powers, there would still remain the English, rulers of the sea; and then the blockade would have to be refashioned, and Spain reconquered, and everything would have to be started afresh to reach the same point as before. He could, if he chose, restore to Prussia and Austria what he had taken from them. But he had taken from them only to constrain them to peace, that they might become his auxiliaries. Would he hand back Italy to Austria? The Treaty of Lunéville had been signed by Austria only when she had been driven from Italy.

Frederick William had just deserted. Napoleon blamed himself for his gentle handling of Prussia, but that had been at Tilsit, to please Alexander. Prussia was calling upon Napoleon to choose between the line of the Elbe and war. Would he really have peace so cheaply? In 1806 the King of Prussia had summoned him to evacuate Germany. Since the Russian disaster he had fallen back from the Niemen to the Vistula, and thence to the Oder. Would the Prussians consent to stop at the Elbe? It was clear that the line of the Rhine would be imposed on him. And it was to protect that line that he had had to cross it and organize the Confederation. Annulment of the treaties of 1809, 1807 and 1805, would bring things back to 1800 and 1792. Napoleon knew that 'in defeat one had always to withdraw, just as in victory, it had always been necessary to advance'. The effect, says Sorel, would have been the same if the Emperor had consented to withdraw peaceably. By re-establishing Prussia and Austria in their former power, he would have given them the means of forcibly taking back from him what he might have kept. And at St. Helena he explained how, on his return from Moscow, he had resolved to make sacrifices. 'But the moment for announcing them was delicate. One false step, one word spoken inopportunely, might have destroyed all the prestige for ever.' And he lived on the prestige of his name. It was better, then, to make use of the reverential awe which he still commanded, to run the risks of battle, to consent to sacrifices only after success, and by using Austrian mediation, instead of negotiating under the cloud of the Russian disaster, a cloud of defeat.

With all this complexity, the ideas of the Emperor were

bound to become fluid again. He was no more clear in his mind about his possible concessions than the coalesced kings were about those which they might be able to ask: their demands were to go on increasing, just as his would have been augmented had he been victorious. He based everything on the mediation of his father-in-law. But his reason put him on his guard against Austria. He did not overlook the fact that the English were still at war with him, and that his reverses in Russia and Spain made them all the more resolute to pursue the struggle until Belgium was freed. Having no grip on England, he left her out of his reckoning. He admitted as much to Barante and Fontanes in talk at the Tuileries when he said: 'I am the creation of circumstances.' The creation at first, but now the slave, and he obeyed circumstances with a resignation that had more weariness than fatalism. Marmont, during the campaign of 1813, was to discover in him what others had so often discerned, 'a capricious confidence, an endless irresoluteness, a degree of mobility that resembled weakness'. In his last phase, this tendency to irresoluteness grew more pronounced with the greater scope of the decisions which had to be taken every hour of the day.

Prussia had declared war and invaded Saxony. The situation of 1806 was repeated. Two days before rejoining the army in Germany, Napoleon received Schwarzenberg, who was soon to be commander-in-chief of the coalition, and requested his assistance against the Russians, just as in 1809 he had expected Russian aid against Austria. From that moment Metternich and Francis II were resolved to cross over to the coalition, not openly, but by donning a mask. A skilful play of politics began, a tissue of illusion and deception, all the secrets of which Napoleon himself did not pierce and which misled him for a long time. After his first victory, at Lützen, he wrote to his father-in-law: 'Being well aware of the interest which your Majesty takes in every good fortune that befalls me . . .' Even if the Austrian alliance were now a mere counterfeit, he would prolong the fiction as he had prolonged that of the Russian alliance.

Leaving Saint-Cloud on April 15th, 1813, he was on the plains of Lützen on May 1st. His conception was unvarying, and still powerful. It was that of Jena, the thunderbolt to throw the enemy into disarray. But his resources were not the same — troops were too young, a hurried levy of tired veterans, few cavalry, an improvised army, the nation's last effort but one. Napoleon knew it. Throughout the battle he remained exposed to fire beside his raw troops, to hearten them with his presence. Was it not at Lützen that Gustavus Adolphus had perished? One has the impression that during this campaign Napoleon frequently courted death, or at least that he showed himself careless of death, as if it would have been a way out for him, and the means of handing on his succession to his son, through the regency of Marie Louise, without shock or convulsion. He knew all the dark side of events — the difficulties of conscription, the growing number of refractory recruits, especially in Belgium, the troubles in Holland, the final flight of Joseph from Madrid, the loss of Spain, the tide of hate in Germany, and lastly the 'shaken confidence' of France, as Maret, most complaisant of all the ministers, made bold to describe it.

None the less, on the evening of Lützen Napoleon was radiant. But Lützen was not Jena, and the Russians were not, as in 1806, on the other side of the Vistula. They were now doubling the strength of the Prussian regiments. Three weeks later, at Bautzen, these allies had to be beaten again, in one of those victories where the enemy escaped destruction, as at Smolensk and Borodino. At the end of the second day, that of Wurschen, he felt his conscripts to be collapsing. 'What! After all that butchery, no result, no prisoners?' At that moment one of his escort was killed. 'Duroc,' he said, 'fortune has a heavy grudge against us to-day.' A few hours later a ball struck Duroc, one of the very few beings whom he loved. He was seen all that evening, sitting silent in front of his tent, with clasped hands and bowed head, answering Drouot's requests for orders: 'It can all wait for to-morrow.' 'Poor fellow!' said his grenadiers, 'he's lost one of his children.' But a month later he was saying, 'A man like myself cares little for the lives of a million . . .' and Metternich dared not repeat the expression. But if the Emperor stiffened after a moment of tenderness, nothing checked the increasing discouragement. After Bautzen he heard the remark: 'What a war! We shall all spend the rest of our days at it.' He again became brutal with his generals. 'I know quite well, gentlemen, that you no longer wish to make war.' So-and-so would like to go hunting at Grosbois, and another to live in his mansion in Paris . . . And the ironic retort came: 'I agree, Sire: I have small familiarity with the pleasures of the capital.'

With this frame of mind he had to reckon. It now became important for the Emperor that nobody could 'any longer doubt his desire for peace'. And of that desire he gave proof, 'at the cost of his highest military interests'; for, having arrived again on the line of the Oder, he decided on a suspension of hostilities in the hope of arranging matters with Austria. On May 17th, between Lützen and Bautzen, he informed his father-in-law of his readiness to negotiate with Russia, Prussia, England, and even the Spanish insurgents. On June 4th he halted his forward march, and signed the armistice of Pleisswitz. Not without hesitations: he had felt that Austria would use this stoppage of hostilities to draw closer to Prussia and Russia after completing her armed preparations. But not to lose touch with the court of Vienna was his principle. Hitherto he had been confronted only by the Russians and Austrians in alliance, or by the Prussians and Russians in alliance. He had not had to fight a general coalition. And above all else, that was what he wished to avoid, because, at the moment when the strength of France was draining away, he felt that this would be the end.

And the end it was. As soon as he failed to obtain decisive

results from the first month of the campaign, the entry of Austria into the enemy ranks became certain, whether he signed an armistice or not, whether he accepted Austrian mediation or not. Metternich's decision was already taken, and Francis II was not to stop at the obstacle of a daughter or a grandchild. He had already sacrificed Marie Louise to policy when he gave her to her husband. He would sacrifice her a second time, when the hour had struck to wipe out defeats, abolish treaties, and compel France to return within the bounds which she had overstepped through the Revolution.

The last act had not come, but it was approaching. By rapid stages the former situation of 1792 was being reached, that which had determined the appeal to the soldier — Brumaire — the Consulate — the Empire. This reign had flowed past like a torrent. Bonaparte, together with France, was brought back to the point where he had been when he came back from Egypt. Europe had held him in awe. But she had never really believed that he would endure for ever, that he had opened anything more than a parenthesis, that his prodigious efforts would really assure for France the lasting ownership of the territories conquered by the Revolution. And now the kings grew bolder. They told one another that the hour had struck. 'The alliance of 1813 killed Napoleon, because he could never persuade himself that a coalition could maintain the spirit of union among its members and persevere towards the goal of its activity.' That remark of Metternich is true twice over: firstly because, when the coalition had taken form, Napoleon sought refuge in the hope of dissolving it; and also because the Emperor, and France with him, was lagging behind the course of events. The kings of Europe were driven to this resumed offensive against the Revolution and its crowned general, and driven by their own peoples. Now it was the old monarchies which received the force of the warlike zeal that animated the Republic twenty years before. And whilst the

374

peoples gave the impulse, these governments had acquired experience. In its long school they had formed their own generals and statesmen. If Napoleon's collapse came quickly after the formation of the general coalition, it came not only from the number of his foes, or of his faults, but from a policy perfectly calculated to provoke his fall. He had to fight forces greater than his own, and also against an idea which the fertility of his mind could no longer oppose.

It was a simple idea, based on an accurate knowledge of the French, and consisted of drawing a distinction between France and Napoleon, in order to separate her from Napoleon. This subtle and pernicious manœuvre began from the date of the armistice. In the middle of June, Prussia and Russia signed the Treaty of Reichenbach with England, stipulating that peace could be concluded only by common accord between the Allies. Here already was the convention of 1805, which Austerlitz had shattered, and now restored to vigour. Austria in her turn was secretly preparing to adhere to the Treaty of Reichenbach. The method, which would develop with the military successes of the Allies, was taking shape. Austria must first pass from the status of mediator to that of belligerent. In the course of the *pourparlers* entered upon after the armistice, either Napoleon would reject the peace terms to be put forward, and Austria would be given grounds for declaring against him, or else he would accept these terms, and others would be immediately announced in order to provoke a rupture. In maintaining the principle that her mediation was an armed mediation, Austria justified her military preparations, whilst giving Napoleon reasons for distrust which in themselves would lead no less surely to a break. Subsequently, at each stage, it would only be necessary to apply this diplomatic pattern. Honourable and moderate proposals would be made to Napoleon by the three coalesced sovereigns. If he rejected them, his obstinacy and pride and folly would be blamed. He would give the appearance of refusing the clauses of a definitive peace, whereas, if he accepted, these would be merely preliminaries, to be backed by additional articles held in reserve — not to mention that everything would still have to be submitted to the British government. It was a question of isolating Napoleon by gradually suggesting to the French that a solid, reasonable, honourable peace could be secured only by his abdication. The goal of the coalition was still, as always, the withdrawal of France into her old limits. But an open threat to deprive the French of the natural frontiers would risk a revival of national unity around their Emperor. Accordingly, there was talk in vague terms of lawful frontiers, or of the Rhine, the Alps, the Pyrenees, and so the French would assume that the Allies were leaving them all that was included on the left bank of the Rhine. This, in Metternich's phrase, was the 'bait'. Nobody saw that more clearly than Napoleon, and no bullet seemed to be aimed more directly at himself than the Allies' great proclamation of Frankfurt. When he read it he exclaimed upon the 'ruse'. That ruse was aimed at a tired people whom it was yet essential not to 'embitter'. It succeeded so well that history has been permanently mistaken about it.

The eight weeks of armistice were the last during which Napoleon, in the heart of Germany, still seemed powerful. The circle was already closing in about him. His long conversation with Metternich at Dresden, on June 28th, was that of a hunted man. He saw that he had been wrong to count on the Austrian alliance, that the policy of his marriage had been as unavailing as that of Tilsit, and he gave vent to sterile reproaches. Anger, threats, the legendary hat flung on the floor and left there by Metternich — such was his first response to the pressure now exerted on him by the Austrian mediator. Francis II was resolved on his course of action, and no family consideration would hold him back. He would listen only to 'the interest of his people'. Napoleon would have to yield to his father-in-law, or else he would have to fight one more enemy. 'Yes . . . everything confirms my opinion that I made an unforgivable mistake. By marrying an Austrian I wished to unite the present with the past, Gothic prejudices with the institutions of my century; I was mistaken, and to-day I can feel the extent of my error. It will perhaps cost me my throne, but I shall bury the world beneath its ruins.' And he reverted again to the idea which haunted him, that as an 'upstart soldier' he was not as these born sovereigns were, capable of twenty defeats and still of returning to their capitals. Metternich listened to this painful talk coldly. It was the inconsequent talk of a worried man seeking a way out and unable to find it. 'Do you suppose you can overthrow me by a coalition? The more numerous you are, the more easy I shall feel in my mind. I accept the challenge. In October next we shall meet in Vienna.' Then with a return to bonhomie in conclusion: 'Do you know what will happen? You will not make war.'

To this last remark Metternich flatters himself that he replied: 'Sire, you are lost.' He had discerned that Napoleon clearly recognized the inclination of Austria to join the enemy powers, but still refused to believe that she would really make the decision. At Dresden Metternich had seen the tense faces of Napoleon's general staff, and heard their anxious questionings. The Emperor himself, though denying that his army was weary, had admitted that his generals wanted peace. The news of the disaster at Vittoria, and of the evacuation and loss of Spain, was known at Dresden on June 30th, and gave renewed force to those murmurs and discontents and solicitations, without which the desertion at Fontainebleau eight months later would not be comprehensible. On his own showing, Napoleon had more interest than anyone in making peace: 'I knew it, and if I did not do so, it was because apparently I could not.' His manifest discouragement, coupled with the impression produced by Wellington's victory in Spain, was bound to have a bad effect on the negotiations.

But Napoleon engaged in them partly to satisfy the need for

repose which he felt growing around him, partly in a lingering hope of retaining the Austrian alliance. But the growing disarray was reflected in his mind. The Pyrenean frontier was threatened. Would it be wise to fall back on the Rhine, in case the armistice were broken? But that would mean granting the Allies their first group of conditions in advance. After looking for a moment towards Alexander again, he returned to the family alliance with Austria which, a few days before, he had described to Metternich as a piece of folly. Marie Louise was summoned to Mainz. Perhaps through her Francis II could be brought back to a different frame of mind. Within a few days, in this parlous extremity, Napoleon went through the whole series of his arrangements to insure against his downfall. They were already exhausted. When the dangers of his position at Dresden were pointed out to him, he exclaimed: 'Did I not take risks at Marengo, at Austerlitz, at Jena, at Wagram?' He was like a sick man, thinking in a crisis of the bouts he had already overcome and of the remedies that relieved him.

And how useless they all were! At Prague Caulaincourt was playing the part played by Talleyrand at Erfurt. In the interests of the Empire and the Emperor himself, he was suggesting to Metternich that Austria's demands should be exigent and stern. Just like Talleyrand, he imagined that this was the means of making Napoleon more moderate and ensuring his safety. Metternich stood in no need of this advice. Caulaincourt was still under the delusion that Europe would leave France with the fundamental conquests of the Revolution. The decision of the Allies had been taken, their plan settled. Whatever Napoleon's responses, Austria would declare war on him, and schemes were laid, not to make peace possible for him, but to bring him in any case to give the equivalent of a negative answer. After fixing the preliminaries on three points, he was presented with six, variable and elastic, and not to be open to argument. It was insisted that he should abandon every means of combating the English. He would want at least, in the last spasms of his policy, to save Trieste and Hamburg, the great ports without which he must perforce abandon the blockade and admit defeat by maritime supremacy. When he sent his acceptance of principle to Prague with a reservation regarding details, the Allies replied that they admitted no counter-proposals and that their conditions formed an ultimatum. On August 10th, at midnight, the Russians and Prussians announced that hostilities were resumed. Next day, to fresh offers of concessions, Austria replied that she was tied and could do nothing further. It was war. The armistice had been only one long intrigue. Austria had gained time to complete her armed preparations, the Russians and Prussians had received reinforcements, and Bernadotte brought in his Swedes.

The hunt was up. The kings had given one another a rendezvous on the tomb of Bonaparte. This time the coalition would not only be general, but it would be under a single command, that of Schwarzenberg; it would have a plan; instead of fighting separately, it would avoid a direct trial of strength with Napoleon, unless to crush him by superior strength; it would attack his lieutenants — 'Wherever he is not present, success is certain.' The coalition even had ideas — to call the peoples to battle for liberty, to turn against France the phrases, and even the men, of the Revolution. Moreau, the soldier of the Republic, had enlisted in the ranks of the liberators. By a bold transposition, the gods were changing camp.

In the 'great game of war' Napoleon once again rose to his own level. His virtuosity seemed to be exalted by the struggle against so many foes at one time. If he won, it would be one of the most difficult and astounding of his deeds. On August 23rd he had thrown back Blücher in Silesia, and the road to Berlin was opened for Davout and Oudinot. On the 26th he was at Dresden, to resist the 200,000 men who had come from Bohemia with Schwarzenberg. Two days of battle, when the Emperor, heedless of danger, remained in the

mud and rain, as formerly at Ulm, the rim of his hat running
with water and drooping on to his shoulders. It was a soldiering job, and he took it up as he had done in his early days,
because he had been brought back, and France along with
him, to the same situation as when invasion was threatened.
What memories of the past! During the fight a French
bullet struck down Moreau. The victor of Hohenlinden,
Bonaparte's rival, Georges, Pichegru, the plot, the trial — all
seemed so long ago, and was but yesterday! They had not all
vanished, the actors of this twenty-year drama, which,
dominated now by the figure of the Emperor, would have
ended far sooner without him and could now be concluded
only through him, and which he himself now looked upon
with strange serenity. When Napoleon was informed that the
enemy, who the evening before had reached the gates of
Dresden, was everywhere making a fighting retreat, he 'received this news' (wrote an eye-witness) 'with his features as
calm as if it were a question of winning a game of chess'.
Men told him that the days of Austerlitz and Wagram had
returned. But he was content to reply: 'Things are not
finished yet.'

On August 30th Vandamme's rashness led him into defeat
and capture at Kulm. The results of the effort at Dresden
were wiped out, and henceforward Napoleon knew success
no more. He learned of Vandamme's disaster as coldly
as he had received news of his own victory. He had 'seen at
a glance all the consequences of the event, envisaging them
calmly, and even with stoic resignation'. The only important
point seemed to be whether he himself had made any mistake
in military art. He verified his minutes, and those of Berthier.
Vandamme was alone to blame; he had not followed the
instructions he had received. Then, according to Fain, the
Emperor turned to Maret and said: 'Well, this is war — right
up in the morning, right down at night!' And gazing at the
map he recited some mediocre lines from a tragedy which
he used to declaim with Joseph, commonplaces about the

narrow edge between triumph and downfall, the accidents on which the fate of nations depends, and the destiny of men. He might have been at the play.

And now calamities and fatalities came fast on each other's heels. One after another the Emperor's lieutenants were defeated; Macdonald in Silesia, Oudinot at Gross Beeren, Ney at Dennewitz. A march on Berlin was out of the question. A bad symptom was that the German auxiliaries gave way in battle. From Dresden Napoleon marched to all the threatened points, and drove back now Blücher, now Wittgenstein, who, following the Allied tactics, broke when he faced them, and advanced when he was occupied elsewhere. Everything was going badly. The Austrians attacked in Italy. Defections were announced in the Confederation of the Rhine. At any moment Bavaria might cross to the coalition. The French were no longer safe in a Germany riddled with patriotic leagues and secret societies. Anxiety and discouragement increased around the Emperor, devotion grew less, and even respect was disappearing. What the malcontents used to say behind his back, they now dared to say to his face, and the bitterest of all were the marshals, those men whom he had 'crushed beneath loads of honour and wealth'. There were quarrels, scenes, insults. Murat was called a traitor by his Imperial brother-in-law, and Berthier greeted as an 'old imbecile', and told to hold his tongue. Emperor, king, and prince, were all reverting to the guardhouse. As the end drew near, the heroes of the epic found themselves as they had been at its opening.

Those things then befell Napoleon which he had so long anticipated. His authority did not survive defeat, and it was the military leaders who first threw off the yoke. Moreau, Bernadotte, even the obscure Malet — were not these names and examples which cried aloud? In Paris the far-sighted were taking their bearings in view of the catastrophe, although the political scaffolding of the Empire still held firm. The mass of the people and the soldiery remained loyal, and

Napoleon did not cease to represent for them what Bonaparte had represented. The leaders in the army, for their part, again saw Bonaparte behind Napoleon. They too were coming back to the Consulate, and they would be left as they would have been if the First Consul had been beaten at Marengo.

In fact, the Emperor was no longer master of his general staff. He had conceived another plan, of singular boldness and possibly capable of saving everything; it was to carry the war between the Elbe and the Oder, and to march on Berlin by holding out a hand to the French garrisons still in the strongholds of northern Germany. When this project was made known, the marshals raised their arms heavenward. Those who were already sulky made open resistance. They were tired of endless scheming, and quite incredulous. The Emperor no longer convinced; he met with argument and opposition. Ney and Berthier, impressed by the defection of Bavaria, were violent in opposition to this adventurous enterprise which would bring back the army towards Magdeburg just when, to-morrow, the whole of the Rhine Confederation might cross to the Allied camp. They insisted on getting nearer to France, to join up with arriving reinforcements. There were three days of argument, ending in Napoleon yielding, 'against his inner feelings', but resigned and impotent.

Thus he turned back towards the plain of Leipzig, where the enemy proposed to envelop him to shut him up in Dresden. He had wished to avoid this battle by a march on Prussia, because such a battle would decide the fate of Germany. Beaten, the French would only be able to fall back on the Rhine — if they got as far — and the loss of Germany, as the politicians saw in Paris, would be the beginning of the end. It was also necessary that Napoleon should preserve a line of retreat: if not, it would be the immediate and unmistakable end.

At Leipzig, from the 16th to the 18th October, took place

that 'battle of the nations', in which the French lacked everything — men, munitions, and confidence. It has been said over and over again that Napoleon there was unrecognizable: he was a sick man, according to some, and according to others, he was overburdened with business, the details of Imperial administration distracting and absorbing him at moments when he ought to have been thinking only of his 'chess-board'. And yet the first day had its gleam, perhaps an omen. A prisoner was brought to him, the Austrian general Merfeldt, who had come forward with the white flag at Leoben and had returned as a spokesman after Austerlitz. Again, everybody was meeting, and again, everything seemed at once so distant and so recent! And now, in this hour of danger, Napoleon still saw his supreme hope in Austria. He sent back Merfeldt to his Imperial father-in-law with words of reconciliation and the offer of a reasonable peace. Merfeldt did not return.

How quickly things were now to fall apart! This downfall of an army was the downfall of a system, the crumbling of what had been built up by twenty years of striving. In the midst of the battle the Saxons turned their guns upon the French; and Germany rose, overturned the Confederation of the Rhine, the barrier of those kings created by Napoleon to protect the frontiers conquered by the Republic. Jerome and his Westphalian Kingdom were to vanish in a few days. And after the guns of Saxony came those of Bernadotte, soldier of the Revolution and elected king. The Battle of Leipzig was a kind of Last Judgment, avenging the past, mingling the living and the dead, revealing what was hidden — the weakness of the Great Empire raised upon prestige and illusion. 'Cold, thoughtful and concentrated,' Bonaparte learned the sorry news with barely a trace of discouragement on his features. A hundred thousand French with their munitions exhausted were faced by an enemy three times as strong. He ordered a retreat, and, as with the return from Moscow, the end of his misfortunes was not yet come. The sappers blew up the bridge over the Elster before the whole army had crossed, and Poniatovski was drowned, the symbol of Poland's vain trust and vain loyalty. From that day, October 19th, the end of the Empire must be dated. The road back led them past places whose names recalled victories. They came by Erfurt, where, five years before, Napoleon and Alexander had exchanged the accolade. At Hanau, to open their road, they had to pass over the impeding Bavarians, allies of yesterday, who had turned their coats as the Saxons had done. The Emperor was prepared for anything. When Macdonald saw danger ahead and appealed for reinforcements, he answered with indifference: 'What do you want me to do? I give orders and am no longer listened to'. Macdonald insisted, and again Napoleon replied coldly: 'I can do no more.' Discipline too was only a memory. Marshals and generals had never been automata or mute worshippers of the idol. They continued to talk, to think, to maintain a critical mind. After the disaster they became insolent, and there were mutterings of mutiny. 'Does the damned fool know what he's doing?' cried Augereau, Duke of Castiglione, quite openly. 'Can't you see he's lost his head? The coward! He would leave us in the lurch!' Once in discussion with his staff, the Emperor turned to Drouot, and 'begging a vote at the price of a flattery', said that he would need a hundred such men. 'Sire, you are wrong,' said Drouot, 'you would need a hundred thousand!' And if Napoleon sometimes hit out and complained of the lack of zeal, if he occasionally admitted that his position was a painful one, he generally remained 'gloomy and silent', feigning not to hear what was said, not to understand what was going forward. On the day when Murat left him, called back by letters from Naples, Napoleon received him peevishly but said no more about his being a traitor. He even embraced him publicly several times. Was he a dupe? Was he wilfully blinding himself? So many words had become useless, and so many things had come to pass!

GERMANY EVACUATED

On November 2nd Napoleon was at Mainz. Germany was evacuated, except for the garrisons remaining in the north, destined to serve as counters if there were any negotiations now possible between equal parties. But would not the enemy wish to drive still further an army which, during that year, had been brought back from the Niemen to behind the Rhine? Napoleon's only hope now seemed to lie in delay, in the reluctance of the Allies to engage on a winter campaign. But he was not blind to the catastrophe, to all that the evacuation of Germany meant, to what the loss of Italy meant. Coldly he watched destiny declaring itself. 'I am annoyed not to be in Paris', he wrote to Cambacérès from Mainz. 'There I should be seen to be calmer and more tranquil than at any juncture in my life.'

With catastrophe the true stature of Napoleon appeared. He was the man who understood his own history, who dominated it and took it all in at one glance. He knew that he was returning to the origins of those wars which, ever since 1792, had been but one and the same war. He knew that after all these efforts of every kind he had arrived at the inevitable. Daru, remarking that he, more perhaps than anyone else, had been able to penetrate Napoleon's thoughts, added: 'I never perceived in him the least concern with the erection of an imperishable edifice.' Or rather, he knew that it was all ephemeral and fated to perish. He did not really cling to existence, even less to his throne, to the pleasure of power, and to his palaces and money not at all. Pitifully he watched his brothers grasping at hollow titles, and still, having lost their kingdoms, styling themselves 'King Joseph' or 'King Jerome' — and Eugène, his adopted son and favourite, troubled by the fear of losing the vice-royalty of Italy — and Murat, striving to purchase his crown by treason! To save his own at any price never entered Bonaparte's head, because it would be a useless thought, and one that he scorned. What interested him now, as a man of letters and an artist, was his own destiny, his name and his place in history. The comprehension of his own veritable glory was what now grew up within him. Having reigned over men by appealing always to their imaginations, he would still reign over the future by means of other images. One secret of his incredible rise had been that he always saw things largely. And for that reason his end could not be petty, and would help more than anything else towards his greatness.

CHAPTER XXIII

THE MUTINY OF MARSHALS

HENCEFORWARD the drama of Bonaparte's history grew more and more taut. Time, which had always been measured out for him, was throttling him. He returned to Saint-Cloud on November 9th, 1813, and he was to abdicate on April 7th, 1814. Only five months. And then a hundred days. Days of grace — but how crowded!

If the extraordinary man finished the 'romance of his life' and gave it an epic turn, it was because he was superior to the rest of mortals, and especially superior in the infallible sense of his destiny. In this crashing of worlds, what other man would not have weakened? It was not enough to have will and force of character. The Emperor had an historical view of his own situation. What was happening to-day was what might have happened ever since the first year of the Consulate, the risk of that single and identical war which it had been his mission to pursue to a victorious end, as the delegate of the Revolution for the preservation of the frontiers. He would not juggle with that mandate. Rather would he perish with the dream of the French nation in the last entrenchment, the dream of the inviolable territory, the reason for all that he had done.

Invasion loomed nearer. The Corps Législatif in a speech were reminded of the mass-levy and Valmy, of the year VII and Zurich, of the year VIII and Marengo. This chain must be forged again, strength must be drawn from these memories. The circle was closing, and Bonaparte himself had made the round of political ideas. A Jacobin soldier at twenty-five, he was now only forty-four. Since his marriage he had entered upon the role of a legitimate monarch, but he was not so far removed from the day when he shot down the royalists on the steps of Saint-Roch. Obedient to circumstances, he had changed with them. Why should not he change again, now that they were again becoming what they once had been? He had only to look round him. Everything had been so swift that his elders were still in the field and the characters in the drama nearly all on the stage. Barras was in exile, but an order would be given for the readmission of the former Director. Augereau, the Augereau of Castiglione and Fructidor, was still in the service, a marshal and a duke. Bonaparte wrote to him: 'it is essential to put on again the boots and the determination of '93 . . .' Augereau was to be among the first in the army to flaunt the white cockade; and in the Senate it would be Sieyès who voted for the recall of the Bourbons.

For the truth was, that it was not enough to put on the boots and the parlance of 1793. The vital spirit had to be found again, and the mainspring was broken. The efforts demanded of France by Napoleon had brought fatigue, and after fatigue, disgust. Thiers, recalling the talk overheard in his childhood, wrote that 'the horror formerly felt for the guillotine was at this time felt for war'. Eighteen-year-old recruits, refractory conscripts everywhere, the malcontent spirit in the towns — these were not the elements that made Valmy: if indeed Napoleon believed in a spontaneous victory, an irresistible enthusiasm, a military miracle, and in his own view Valmy had been only 'the ludicrous retreat of the Prussian army before our unorganized legions'. He would beat Blücher, and Blücher would not retreat as Brunswick had done.

The invader, at the end of 1813, was no longer only Brunswick, but 600,000 enemies crowding forward on the Rhine, at the gateways of the Pyrenees — Europe coalesced to bring back France within her ancient limits. Napoleon saw the problem with lucidity: 'A year ago the whole of Europe was marching alongside of us. To-day the whole of Europe is marching against us.' So he told the Senate. The choice now lay between the old frontiers and himself — between Louis XVIII and Napoleon. The Bourbons had been almost forgotten by the mass of men. The Allies hardly thought of them. But the Emperor foresaw their return with more certainty of mind than the most faithful royalist. Himself — or these others? Or what, when all had been tried? Would France wish to defend herself with the Emperor whose coronation oath had bound him to maintain the integrity of the territories of the Republic? Barante, a prefect and an observer of the internal state of the country, said that, with Bonaparte gone, 'the France of the Revolution had no point of resistance'. Would she offer a point of resistance to Napoleon?

He tried the experiment which he was to try again during the Hundred Days. He sought the support of public opinion. As public opinion accused his minister Maret of driving him to intransigence by servility, he replaced Maret by Caulaincourt, that is to say, by the school of Talleyrand, necessary sacrifices, and the sense of proportion. The Emperor was blamed for not having negotiated Prague. He informed the representative assemblies of the details of his negotiations. An attempt to give free voice to the Corps Législatif resulted in complaints against the absolute power, demands for immediate peace, and remonstrances which 'discredited him in the eyes of Europe and the nation'. The experiment had failed, and the Corps Législatif would be adjourned. As a measure of public safety, Napoleon would resume the role of dictator. And on January 1st, 1814, came his apostrophe to the deputies, marked by the return of the short, sharp sentences of Brumaire: 'What does France need at this moment? Not an assembly, not orators, but a general. Is there one amongst you?' And then: 'What is the throne? Four pieces of wood covered with a piece of velvet. But in the language of monarchy, the throne is myself.' And to conclude, he made accusations: 'You have been led away by men devoted to England, and M. Laîné, your chairman, is a mischief-maker in correspondence with the Bourbons.' The deputies were sent back to their departments, where more than one made haste to work on behalf of Louis XVIII. What Bonaparte always needed in politics was easy things, succeeding by the prestige of his name, by the authority that imposed itself unaided. And now all this was drifting away from him, just as there were already absentees from his court and the first signs of abandonment.

Success was passing to the subtle manœuvres of the Allies. To separate France from her leader, to let it be understood, though ambiguously, that the natural frontiers would be recognized, was the development and perfecting of the system of Prague. 'Napoleon would understand, and answer No; opinion would misunderstand and condemn the Emperor.' Frenchmen believed that the Allies could offer only a return to the treaties of Lunéville and Amiens. Nobody disturbed this illusion. Exact terms were likewise held back. In the overtures of Frankfurt in November 1813 there was a refusal to make clear the extent of territory which would be left to France; everything was to depend on the outcome of the war; the so-called bases of discussion were essentially mobile. Moreover, the consent of England was still kept in reserve, and the 'overtures' made to France by Russia, Austria and Prussia remained 'officially unknown' to England. Napoleon had wished for guarantees before discussing the bases which Metternich himself was careful to call 'general and summary'. Such as they were, they were welcomed in France with enthusiasm. The Emperor was pressed to agree to them instantly. Prague was repeated. When he had agreed, the Allies demanded something further. Metternich replied that the sovereigns must consult the Cabinet in London, whose opinion was contained in the note from Castlereagh to Lord Aberdeen, reminding him that to deprive France of Antwerp was, above all else, the most essential object for British interests.

The full meaning of the war and the invasion was now to be

seen. In January 1814 Holland, revolted and recalled the house of Orange. The Allies had crossed the Rhine, and violated the neutrality of Switzerland, under the pretext that they were striking only at the preponderance of Napoleon. This was another 'feint' which the Emperor saw through. Carnot, the staunch Republican who had deliberately held aloof from the Empire in its days of triumph, came forward from his retirement and offered his services to the hapless Emperor. He had been the chief worker in the annexation of Belgium, and was instantly appointed governor of Antwerp. Here was the spirit of 1793. It was about this time that Napoleon said to Caulaincourt: 'Do they want to reduce France to her old boundaries? That is degrading her. It is a mistake to think that the misfortunes of war can make the nation desirous of such a peace. There is not a French heart which would not feel the disgrace of it after six months and would not condemn the government cowardly enough to sign it.' Soon after his return from Russia he had told Molé that he would lose the confidence of 'this war-weary nation' if he obtained peace for it on terms which would personally make him blush. He added: 'You would see the French who have given me such admiration, and perhaps such fear, laughing at me more than at any of their governments.'

Driven to 'the stern alternative of submitting to everything or risking everything', he would risk everything. In any case, he was a man unchanged, free in mind, almost detached from these matters which he scrupulously prepared in view of the struggle, never ceasing to act as if success were certain, overlooking nothing to obtain success, and scrutinizing his own position as coolly as if he was gauging somebody else's. He proceeded to liquidate the most vexatious of his commitments, lightening his burdens like a harrassed speculator. He would hold on to the strongholds of the Elbe and Italy, as counterpoises against the day of negotiation. But the Pope was sent back to Rome, and Ferdinand VII to Spain. Napoleon shook off the Spanish millstone that had dragged him down for five years, without even consulting Joseph, who now tried his patience more than his other brothers. 'He? The eldest? For our father's vineyard, I dare say!' Austria still remained a hope, but his relatives by marriage were no better treated. During a family dinner, according to Hortense, he said with strange gaiety to Marie Louise: 'We haven't lost our skill. Don't worry — we shall go to Vienna again to beat Papa Francis!' At dessert the King of Rome was brought in, and the Emperor, laughing heartily, made the child repeat: 'Let's beat Papa Francis!' Mollien proposed placing the Treasury in safety beyond the Loire, and Napoleon, ironic and intimate, tapped him on the shoulder, with the words: 'My dear fellow, if the Cossacks reach Paris there will be neither Empire nor Emperor.'

On January 25th, in the morning, he left Paris. He had burnt his most private papers, and for the last time embraced his wife and son. He was never to see them again. He left things in proper order, and conscientiously carried out all the formalities, leaving Marie Louise as Regent and Joseph as lieutenant-general of the Empire. Only victory could bring reality to this setting of the stage, if indeed victory was still possible — and Bonaparte had so few illusions! 'My troops?' he exclaimed to Pasquier. 'My troops? Do people think I still have an army?' Nor was he under any illusion regarding the services or fidelity to be expected from his kinsmen. He knew of Murat's desertion to the coalition, hoping to save his throne, but falling into the nets of Metternich. 'It is part of my destiny to see my constant betrayal through the dire ingratitude of the men on whom I have conferred the most benefits.' The approaching end would be ugly. But there was one means of shortening it and freeing himself. Napoleon cared little for things, and for men not at all; and during those few weeks he cared little for life. He was hardly listened to on January 1st, when he concluded his lofty harangue to the deputies with the words: 'Before three months have passed, I shall have made peace, and the foe will be driven from our land, or I shall be dead.' A phrase — a trick of style. But deep within his heart lay a desire for the great escape, and the taste of ashes was in his mouth.

The campaign in France was splendid in the audacious genius of its conception — but how ugly was its underside! It was punctuated by Napoleon's refrain. He was ill-served, he was unhelped. Nobody had initiative or ideas. Even his orders were now being disputed, and were badly carried out, or not carried out at all. Absence of goodwill, aggravated by inferior numbers, was the undoing of his finest schemes; there were too many raw young soldiers, those eighteen-year-old 'Marie Louises', many of them unable to load their muskets; and after all these murderous campaigns, the subordinate officers who had been a main strength of the Grand Army had disappeared. His operations failed also through the dying of enthusiasm, the distaste for war, the quenching of confidence, and lastly by the sense that all was futile because the end was near. Napoleon himself, so often seen to be seeking death that would have none of him, was discouraging without knowing it. At Arcis-sur-Aube, Sebastiani held back Exelmans from warning the Emperor of danger: 'Leave him alone — don't you see that he's doing it on purpose. He wants to be finished with it all.'

He did want to. And then, ever shifting, ever uncertain, he clung to hope again. First, he found himself once more at Brienne, at his old college, where his first days in France had passed; and he found one of his old masters, Father Henriot, now the curé of Maizières, who acted as his guide and offered him a bed. This linking-up with his past seemed like a rediscovery of his star. He fell asleep with dreams of rebuilding the burnt town of Brienne, of founding there a great military school or an imperial residence. Next day, at La Rothière, he had to retreat and fall back upon Troyes. He was then prepared to accept the Allies' terms, and gave *carte blanche* to Caulaincourt for the Congress of Châtillon. When victory returned, he would forbid him to sign at any

393

price. He still expected miracles. He had seen so many, he had wrought so many! 'One more success,' he said on the evening of Champaubert, 'and the enemy will recross the Rhine faster than they crossed it, and I shall be on the Vistula again'. Such were the alternating swings produced in him by the results, now good, now bad, of an inventive strategy, which he renewed and pursued with — in the view of distant observers — 'an incredible vigour', reduced sometimes to a force of 10,000 men against the forces of the coalition and holding up before them the remnant of his old guard like 'the Medusa head'.

After Champaubert, Montmirail and Vauchamps, where he seemed to have recovered his youth, there was a revival of animation in soldiers and population, with the new hope of driving forth the invader. It was the military leaders who hoped no longer. And the Emperor complained of the delays and negligence which prevented his successes from being properly followed up. Victor, the Duke of Belluno, was deprived of his command after a violent scene, and two generals were threatened with court-martial. Then Napoleon's heart softened towards the old soldier, his old comrade of Italy — who was soon to cross over to Louis XVIII, like the rest. Less than ever was it the moment for venturing upon chastisement. Those who escaped him the first, those whom he had always feared, those who in two months' time were to overturn him, were the military leaders. After Montereau, where he aimed the cannon himself and made the gunners murmur at his rashness, he was gloomy and agitated in spite of a fortunate day; and during that night, in the château of Surville he said again what he had so often said before — 'I'm no longer obeyed! I'm no longer feared! I ought to be everywhere at once. . . .'

These superhuman efforts to repulse an invasion which, for over twenty years, had been merely postponed, were carried on in conjunction with negotiations of which he clearly discerned the character. He was always sceptical regarding the Allies' good faith, and especially dubious of England's desire for a peace such as he could accept. Castlereagh had arrived and was now conducting affairs. The terms of Châtillon were no longer those of Frankfurt. They were the frontiers of 1790, and when Berthier and Maret urged Napoleon to accept them, he appealed to the coronation oath. He had so often been reproached for not having signed peace in time, and he felt such a desire for haste in France, that he was several times on the point of yielding, despite his certainty that all this was 'a mask'. He was sure that further demands would be forthcoming. He would have to give safeguards, the first of which would doubtless be his renunciation of the throne. Did Francis II himself sincerely wish to save his son-in-law, his daughter, his grandson? Caulaincourt did not think so. He noted that Austria had always subordinated family considerations to 'other views which she did not then dare to avow, because she was not bold enough to anticipate their realization'. The disciple of Talleyrand further observed that, when Napoleon might have bowed to the principle of the old boundaries, it was not even certain that France would be admitted to the general settlement. Would the Allies proceed without her to dispose of her former conquests, in particular of Belgium and the left bank of the Rhine? If Napoleon went so far as to admit that, he was humbling himself so far that his government was becoming impossible. If he did not bow to it, his insistence would ruin the peace. Things still depended on the outcome of war. But if some incredible turn of fortune enabled Napoleon to inflict upon the Allies the great defeat for which he planned, would he have gained more than from so many other victories? Would he have secured anything better than all those magnificent treaties of peace which had proved to be no more than truces?

The first of his manœuvres, destined to destroy Blücher, collapsed on March 3rd with the capitulation of Soissons. Napoleon's fury was inexpressible. He called for the immediate shooting of the commandant of the surrendered stronghold. From that day, 'a profound sadness' was seen in the Emperor, forced smiles, tightened features, a seeking of death in the last engagements. One resource, and one only remained — the raising of France against the invader, not only in that spirit of resolve of 1793, but in the fiercer spirit of Spain and Russia. His thoughts ran upon the idea that 'when a peasant is ruined and his house burnt down, there is nothing better he can do than take up a gun'. Some such intentions, hardly recognized, hardly divined, increased the desire for peace in the uninvaded regions. And the Duc d'Angoulême was about to enter Bordeaux.

For a few days Napoleon had the illusion of grasping victory. Between the 16th and the 19th of March his offensive on the Aube threw back the Allies in disorder. Francis II, 'Papa Francis,' was within twenty-four hours of capture. But on March 20th, Augereau evacuated Lyons at the approach of an Austrian corps and fell back on Valence. The southern army, on which the Emperor counted for a flanking movement, became useless. There had been the defection of the Duke of Castiglione before that of the Duke of Ragusa.

But the climax lingered. And to precipitate it, there was needed the intervention of one man, clear-sighted in his thought and his hatred; and destiny willed that this hatred should be Corsican, that an island vendetta should be woven into this great history. Respectful fear of Napoleon still kept the Allies advancing only with care and circumspection. They were still afraid of Revolutionary Paris. But there was one man at their headquarters who proclaimed ceaselessly, and more boldly than any other, that a direct march on Paris would end everything and bring everything tumbling down. This man was named Pozzo di Borgo. He had an old score to pay off against this little Bonaparte, of whom he had been saying twenty years earlier what the Allies were now repeating in their proclamations — 'Napoleon is the cause of everything.' In the Ajaccio troubles Pozzo had sided with

Paoli. He had driven the Bonapartes from Corsica, before being driven out himself with the English, and with a price on his head. Entering the service of Russia, Pozzo had been filled with an enthusiasm for vengeance. The idea which he kept whispering in Alexander's ear, and through the Tsar to the other hesitating sovereigns, was a deadly one for his enemy. And here was Corsica, so far off, so forgotten, reappearing with its clannish quarrels and hatreds, in search of Napoleon just when he himself, between the Aisne and the Marne, was hardly more than a faction leader, holding the *maquis* in Champagne on behalf of the conquering and militant Revolution, and almost back to the status of an adventurer, as in the Ajaccio days.

The enemy's bold and decisive march on the capital left Napoleon in cruel perplexity. What was he to do? He 'spoilt himself by his thinking', conceiving of a still greater audacity in response. Leaving Paris to the Allies, he would cut off their retreat and make use of the resources offered by the patriotic East of France to wage a murderous war upon them, compelling them to the capitulation which he had twice thought he was obtaining. It would have been a war without quarter, like Gambetta's idea in 1870. Even if Paris were captured, might not the Allies find it their grave as he had found his at Moscow? It was an 'extremity', and he put forth 'every effort to familiarize himself with the resolves implied', for it would mean staking all for all; and he would be no more than an outlaw if it turned out that his dethronement was proclaimed while he was still in the field, as was threatened since the Allies concluded the Pact of Chaumont, in virtue of which they were to fall upon him a year later. Further, for this supreme throw, he needed a sense of devotion around him, and the generals, even less than the Emperor, were not minded to become mere Imperial Chouans. On March 23rd, after the break-up of the Congress of Châtillon, when Caulaincourt reached Saint-Dizier, the discontent oı the general staff broke loose. Napoleon pretended to pay no heed to their stormy explosion, but he paused, and pondered. To obtain peace he was ready to renounce even the left bank of the Rhine, when, on March 28th, chance brought into his hands a prisoner of note, the Austrian diplomat Weissenberg. He sent him to his father-in-law with a confidential mission, with as little result as had come through Merfeldt the year before. What bargaining could now save him? He was decided on his own lot. But meanwhile Ney and Berthier wearied him with the danger to Paris, with the impossible position into which he would place himself, and into which he had placed them. He had no following; he was no longer master. Ever prompt to change his mood, he now thought only of Paris and of what was happening there, of all that had so often obsessed his mind, of the crumbling of a power which he knew to be fragile — so fragile indeed that, with his brutal realism, he styled it a 'monarchy by the week'.

And whilst he hurried towards the capital, still hoping to save it, there came about what might have happened almost any time since Marengo. Napoleon had been right in saying that when the Cossacks appeared before Paris there would be neither Empire nor Emperor. On March 30th, he was at Juvisy, a few hours too late. Paris had surrendered. Marie Louise and the King of Rome had left two days earlier. Ten green coaches watched in silence by three or four score bystanders — such was the funeral of the Empire. And Joseph, the lieutenant-general of the Empire, had vanished, leaving Paris even more ingloriously than he left Madrid.

Here at last was the end so often foreseen by the Emperor. In a post-house beside the main road he learned that everything had gone, in a fading-away rather than a catastrophe. Like death, necessary and incredible things never come with the aspect lent to them. This one left Napoleon in sore bewilderment. Forgetting that he himself had given instructions for the departure of the Empress, the King of Rome, and the government if Paris were threatened, he burst into reproaches,

398

fury, trooper's curses against those who had surrendered, and especially against Joseph, 'that swine Joseph'. And then, unable to believe in the end, leaning over his maps from habit, he sought for his next move. 'Four days and I shall have them.' The road to Fontainebleau was open. He took it, still busy with projects for operations and manœuvres, reckoning up the forces still left to him, drawing up instructions for Berthier. On April 2nd, when the Senate was voting his dethronement, he was meditating an attack on Paris with Marmont's divisions. On the 3rd he harangued his guard, and was acclaimed. 'To Paris!' called the soldier. That evening he received the visit of his marshals.

The visitors whom Bonaparte saw entering Fontainebleau, headed by Ney, might well have presented themselves before! These were the men of whom he said that they had always been ready to rip him open. He had summoned them in order to find a prop in them. They brought him a summons. The Bonaparte venture had failed, and was done with. They were its liquidators. Napoleon was now only a troublesome individual. He had been chosen in order to avoid the Bourbons, and he had said himself that only the Bourbons could succeed him, unflattering though the idea was to himself. He had had his meed of greatness and power. So he must let other men live, and, as it was inevitable, put up with Louis XVIII.

What had Napoleon done by loading these men with honours and riches? He had made them conservatives. He complained to Las Cases that his generosity had been of no avail. 'There must have been fatality on my part, or essential vice in the persons chosen.' His wish had been 'to found great families, real rallying-points, flags in great national crises'. They stood before him, his Prince of Neuchâtel, his Prince of Moskowa, his Dukes of Danzig, of Reggio, of Tarento, of Conegliano, and they were there to dismiss him. What chiefly horrified these old soldiers of the Revolution now was the idea of disorder, civil war, anarchy. Augereau, Duke of

399

Castiglione, in his order of the day to the army he had taken from the Emperor, went so far as to rebuke 'Buonaparte' for not knowing how to die like a soldier.

The 4th of April at Fontainebleau was the 18th of Brumaire reversed. The marshals had come, as to the rendezvous in the Rue Chantereine, with escorts of staff and other officers 'to defend them if need be', and also to threaten. It was a picture of military rule, the government which Napoleon dreaded most, and also despised most. At all times he had been reserved and aloof with the generals, hardly addressing them 'and then only on indifferent subjects'. And here they were under his roof, raising loud their voices. Ney, Lefebvre and Moncey burst into his private study, and it was Ney who called for his abdication. There was nothing noisy or dramatic, only a cold determination. Napoleon spoke to them. It was like speaking 'to statues'. Macdonald entered in his turn with Oudinot, bringing a letter from Beurnonville, another veteran of the Revolution, a soldier of Valmy and Jemappes, and member of the provisional government of Paris, who had already inwardly rallied to the Bourbons and sent word that the Allies refused to treat with the Emperor. And Macdonald followed Ney in making it plain in the name of the army that everybody was weary, that everybody was resolved to end it all, that a march on Paris was impossible, and drawing the sword against Frenchmen even more so. 'I should have expected him to break out', wrote Macdonald. On the contrary, Napoleon replied calmly and quietly. He even complimented the spokesman of the delegates, who interrupted him with a brutal 'No compliments! It is a question of making a decision'. Beurnonville's letter was the argument — 'Well, gentlemen, in that case, I shall abdicate.' But he abdicated only in favour of the King of Rome, in the hands of his marshals, who had become the commissioners of the army with the provisional government.

In the suddenness of all this Napoleon was left as it were incredulous. His mobile wits saw one supreme chance to try. Throwing himself on a couch, slapping his thigh, he suddenly exclaimed in an easy-going way: 'Bah, gentlemen! Let's drop this and march to-morrow. We'll beat them!' Icily the marshals repeated that their decision was irrevocable, and he insisted no longer. But as a precaution they agreed that the command should be transferred to Berthier, who pledged himself to execute no further orders from Napoleon. 'The army will now obey nobody but its generals.' Ney had said so to the face of the fallen and now powerless Emperor. It was indeed the military power which had deposed him.

The whole fault, and even the shame, has been put upon Marmont, who at the same moment surrendered and signed a capitulation to Schwarzenberg. His defection robbed the Emperor of his last surviving force, his last weapon of resistance. But he was only applying at Essonnes the pass-word given at Fontainebleau.

Once again, confronted by this revolt of high officers, Napoleon was seen (as he had always been with those who betrayed him or served him ill) timid, and more afraid than ever of chastising. And in this abrupt fall from the heights he again passed through successions of ideas of such rapidity that his mind seemed uncertain and drifting to the point of incoherence. Within the space of one hour, on that 4th of April, he had abdicated and he had suggested a march on Paris. On the 5th, after again talking of a retreat on to the Loire, he renounced the Empire, disgusted. He was like the dying philosopher wrapping his head in his cloak. His proclamation to the army was the farewell of a misanthrope: 'If the Emperor had despised men as he is accused of doing, the world would recognize to-day that he had reasons to induce his scorn.' He desired nothing further; he was the stoic. The amateur of tragedy even recited lines of *Mithridate* and applied them to his position. And with Caulaincourt, the defender of his interests with the Tsar, he went into the question of what provision would be made for him. The throne was now no more than 'a piece of wood', to which he did not cling. A hundred louis a year were adequate. 'It needs no great space for a soldier to die.' And a moment later, he would not be content with less than Tuscany as a place to live worthily with the Empress. Next day he was proposing to the marshals to start the war afresh in Italy. 'Will anyone follow me once more? Let us march for the Alps!' Nobody replied, and in the silence another image rose before him. He saw himself leader of a faction, seeking adventures; and this incarnation went against the grain because it did not accord with his conception of greatness, the conception which had never left him, which had guided his destiny and would yet save him.

On April 7th everything was finished. No Emperor, no dynasty, no succession. The marshals had demanded abdication pure and simple. It was just as Napoleon had said: only the Bourbons could succeed him, because it was to prevent their return that the Republic had made him Consul, and then Emperor. It was all ending according to the rules. Even 'the great act' of January 21st, the act of regicide, had to be borne in mind. The major law of the Revolution, that which had sent the Duc d'Enghien to the moat of Vincennes, was observed by the victorious coalition of kings. They had not waged this war to bring back Louis XVIII. They only decided in favour of him when informed that the Senate, the very men who had voted for the regicide in 1793, had now adhered to the Bourbons.

It would have been too much to ask Napoleon to savour fully and serenely all this historic irony. Between his abdication and his landing on Elba, the island domain allotted to him, and accepted, he had his hours of human weakness. He could still make movements of disdain. On April 12th, on the day of the Comte d'Artois's entry, Berthier asked leave to go to Paris. 'He won't come back,' said the Emperor coldly. He thought of Berthier as he did of the others. After the chief of staff, a prince of two principalities, the mameluke Roustan would go, and Constant, his body-servant, too. The last desertions were the worst. During the night of the 12th-13th Napoleon uttered the Calvary cry of his agony. 'My life is unbearable,' he said to Caulaincourt. He wanted to die. He still had poison which he had aways carried on his person since the retreat from Moscow. But death refused to come, and again his star preserved him for a less vulgar epilogue. He had the feeling that he ought to live, that all was not over, that this was not the escape he should seek.

A few scenes remained to carry on the sequence of history. That of the farewell at Fontainebleau, ready-made for the engraver, would long be seen upon the walls of French homes. It was the beginning of the Napoleon of sentiment, a print with a sure appeal. The man who knew so well how to address the imagination was to surpass himself in this genre. The old soldiers in tears, the general, the flag kissed by the unhappy hero — it was perfect in its emotional appeal, the composition of an artist, of a man of letters who knew that one of his remaining tasks was to embellish his tragedy, to transpose the magic of his name into memory. 'If I have chosen to outlive myself, it is that I may serve your glory still further. I wish to write the great things that we have done together.' To write — that is the ruling word of those farewells to the Grand Army. Napoleon felt himself passing into legend.

But there were moments of pitiable collapse. From Fontainebleau to Fréjus the prisoner's journey, guided and guarded by the foreign commissioners, was his first martyrdom. Near Valence he met Augereau, who addressed him with vulgar familiarity, and reproached his ambition for having led him to this pass. The Emperor submitted to the insult of the deserter of Lyons without answering. He had said: 'It is not the people who lack energy; it is the men I have placed at their head who are betraying me.' He lost countenance, and courage, before the insults and threats of the people. He had not yet seen unpopularity at close quarters. In Provence he encountered hatred; knives were brandished.

At Orgon the mob broke the windows of his carriage. Before the inn when he halted, he saw himself hanged in effigy, a dummy figure in his likeness smeared with blood. He sat back in his carriage behind General Bertrand, refused wine and food for fear of poison, and was found, when alone, in tears. Believing that he was no longer safe without disguise, he put on a white cockade, mounted a post-horse, and galloped in front of the procession like a courier. Then, harassed and anxious still, he asked the commissioners to change clothes with him, and put on the uniform of the Austrian officer, and the cloak of the Russian. It was a humiliating journey, worse than the flight to Varennes, and Bonaparte showed, as in the 18th of Brumaire, that, with his intellectual's nervousness, he could not bear contact with the crowd. One of his escort, in a cruel narrative, says that he wearied them with his alarms, and — what struck this Prussian more forcibly — 'with his indecision'. On the way south Napoleon saw his sister, the beautiful Pauline, who made him ashamed by her refusal to embrace him unless he doffed the Austrian uniform. He was a sorry figure, a piece of wreckage.

On May 4th he landed from the English frigate which had brought him over to the island of Elba. He took possession of his new kingdom, with a grimace at first, for his new capital of Porto Ferrajo was like one of those small Corsican ports he knew so well. The mayor and vicar-general brought him the keys of the town, and led him under an arch of gilt paper to the church, for a solemn Te Deum. It was a parody of sovereignty, with the speech from the throne delivered in the town hall. Then the notables were presented; he spoke to each of them, and the usual miracle came to pass. He knew the whole country, better than any of its inhabitants, its history, customs, products, administrative peculiarities, and even its latest municipal incidents. At Fontainebleau, as soon as he knew of his place of exile, he asked for the files concerning the island of Elba to be sent from Paris, and for books dealing with it. And during the time covered by the abdication, the attempted poisoning, the farewell to the guard — amidst all the scenes of pathos — he was still absorbing information. He had read, learned, and remembered, driven by that longing to know and to be interested in things, that desire which lived on within him beyond catastrophe. Bonaparte remained what he had always been, a prodigy of activity. He could not possibly end up, at the age of forty-five, in the bourgeois tranquillity of an island which was a twin to that of Sancho Panza.

CHAPTER XXIV

EMPEROR AND ADVENTURER

NAPOLEON spent ten months of his life on Elba. Intending to stay there? Or to leave it? How could he tell? As always, he waited on circumstances to decide. He accepted philosophically this freak of fortune which made him sovereign of a kingdom barely twenty miles long. Confronting the island of his own birth, he once more found a little town that reminded him of Ajaccio and Bastia. He felt he was not so very far from home.

The Emperor had not been boastful or untruthful when he said that he cared nothing for grandeurs. Sated with everything, and with mankind especially, what did it matter to him where he lived? The only vexing thing was to be so young, so far from the age for retirement, with that insistent habit of busy activity which he had not yet lost. 'My island is very small,' he sighed, having explored it, and given orders for the building of residences and fortifications, cutting of roadways, improvement of mines, the reform of the finances and administration of his state. Even the style was unaltered. His letters remained imperious, as urgent as in the days when he ruled his great Empire. He was not a shattered man. With Bertrand, grand-marshal of the palace, Drouot, the faithful artilleryman, and Cambronne, commanding the four hundred men of the guard, and a naval lieutenant as admiral of the flotilla, he put himself into ceaseless activity. After those days of darkness and agony since his abdication, he relaxed and tasted of security.

But sadness and boredom came quickly enough, and anxiety afterwards. Josephine had died on May 29th, and he was seen shedding tears over bygone days. He was awaiting Marie Louise. It was the fond Mme Walewska who came with her son. He did not wish to keep them there, for fear of scandal in the island and in Europe, where the word would soon have gone round that he had renounced the Empress. Meanwhile Francis II advised his daughter to seek consolation, and gave her a consoler in Count Neipperg. He was bereft of his wife and of the King of Rome; he was deserted and lonely; and the void was only accentuated by the arrival of his mother and Pauline. These circumstances were among the reasons for Napoleon deciding once more to tempt fortune. At first he had mentally planned an existence like that of the archdukes, his kinsmen, whom he had seen installed at Florence or Würzburg. Marie Louise would have come to Porto Ferrajo, and he would have paid her visits at Parma. Shortly after taking possession of his new state, he went to the ball given by an English man-of-war for King George's birthday. It could not be said that this was already a cloak for his plans. He went rather as he might have gone to court in London.

His thoughts perhaps turned to the possibility of escape at the time of the opening of the Congress of Vienna in November. There was talk of putting Bonaparte in some safer place, further removed from Italy and France: the Azores, or one of the British West Indian Islands, or even on St. Helena. Word reached Napoleon, through his frequent visitors and messengers, that the projects for his removal were serious, that at any moment he might be carried off, or murdered. He had himself guarded, and ordered his forts to fire on any suspect vessels that might approach. At the same time, he was short of money. The pension of two million francs promised at Fontainebleau was not paid. Campbell, the English commissioner entrusted with his surveillance, observed his mental agitation and anxiety. When he was told that the French were regretting him, he answered: 'If they are so fond of me, let them come and fetch me.' He enjoyed repeating that he was finished, that he was a dead man. And throughout Europe the story was spread that he was used up, finished, harmless, a ball of fat incapable of mounting a horse. But meanwhile Fouché and Talleyrand, who knew him, remained mistrustful. Hyde de Neuville said: 'Even dead, he would still have to be feared.' The fear which he inspired gave him the measure of his prestige, of the magic that his name still held.

And the return itself hinged on trifles. His means of returning to France was very nearly removed from him. One day the brig *Inconstant*, which made up nearly the whole of his navy, was almost shattered by a storm. Hurriedly the Emperor had her refloated. In January, 1815, his decision was made. Boredom, disgust, and the difficulties of his daily life had made his sojourn on the island intolerable to him. Would he finish his existence here, in idleness and haggling? Was this an end worthy of his history? 'Could he,' as Chateaubriand asked, 'accept the sovereignty of a cabbage-patch, like Diocletian at Salona?' A thousand times No! Then he must not delay. With passing time, his memory would pass, his old soldiers vanish. And the partisans and emissaries from France told him of the discontents in the country, of the clumsiness of the Bourbons, and that many of the dignitaries and officers who had rallied to Louis XVIII, through necessity or in resignation, would turn again to the eagles if the Emperor came forward. He was also informed that military and republican plots were hatching, and that if he did not make haste, government might fall into the hands of Carnot, or Fouché, or of a general. In any case, there were all the signs of a movement stirring. It would seem that the information brought by one of his old officials, Fleury de Chaboulon, decided the Emperor on departure.

Once clear of indecision, he carried forward his idea, at all risks, to the very end. Forgetting his rancours, he concluded an agreement with Murat, whose treachery had not been in vain, as his desertion left him King of Naples. The departure from Elba was planned as carefully as a campaign of the Grand Army, and with as much dissembling as the drama of

Vincennes. The King of Elba feigned such concern with the affairs of his kingdom as if he never intended to leave the island. Three days before his escape he was still issuing orders for works to be carried out: 'three small bridges will be necessary near Capoliveri.' Since February 16th Campbell had been in Florence, to indicate what was going forward. He knew nothing, but felt anxious. Cook, the under-secretary of state, who came from the Congress of Vienna, would not listen to the commissioner, and laughed at his fears. When Campbell returned, the King of Elba had flown. From this can be understood St. Helena, Sir Hudson Lowe, and all the bickerings. Napoleon was to be the convict who had once before escaped, who had been brought back to jail, the bugbear of his warders.

On the evening of February 25th, he took his mother aside and confided his decision in her. If the account of their interview is true, Letizia approved, telling him that he could not end where he was, 'in an idleness unworthy of him'. He had not yet had his fifth act. At Fontainebleau the curtain had fallen prematurely.

The wise Drouot did all that was humanly possible to hold back the Emperor, but in vain. He pointed at the danger of civil war, and of invasion, all the incalculable consequences of the adventure. And who could be sure that Bonaparte did not see them, and was affected by them? When the die was cast, he was heard murmuring: 'Ah, France! France!' To return thither, to win acclamation, was not the hardest thing. He had been told, and truly told, that it would suffice if his hat were planted on the coast of Provence. The hat, and the tricolour flag. The proclamation which he drew up and had printed at Porto Ferrajo shows that he was informed about the morale of the army, and even suggested that he counted on intelligence and assistance. He prophesied: 'The eagle, with the national colours, will fly from spire to spire, right to the towers of Notre-Dame.' It was afterwards that the difficulties would begin. As usual, Napoleon persuaded himself of what he required to believe. When France had received him with open arms, Europe, disgusted with the Bourbons, would not hesitate to recognize him. England, satisfied with the restoration of the old frontiers of France, would no longer rebuff him. And so he was very anxious not to have to fire upon any English vessel when he raised anchor, or during his crossing. Francis II would be happy to see his son-in-law back, and to have his daughter once again on the finest throne of Europe. In fine, Napoleon would reassure the legitimate monarchs, and would be more constitutional than the Bourbons. Never had he compounded so chimerical a plan. Without his chimera, would he ever have set off?

On February 26th he set sail on the *Inconstant*, followed by six timorous feluccas. He had a thousand men, and a few cannon. His main armament consisted of his proclamations, images, reminders of glory, appeals to popular imagination, a style, a literature — and himself, to whom distance had already lent enchantment. As had happened with the journey to and from Egypt, the aid of circumstances, his star, did not fail him. The southerly wind drove the flotilla across to France whilst it held up the English frigate that was to bring back Campbell from Leghorn.

Landing in the Gulf of Jouan, the Emperor spoke with a village mayor, who said to him: 'We were just beginning to find happiness and tranquillity, and you are going to upset it all.' And he confided in Gourgaud: 'I cannot express how much these words disturbed me, nor the pain they gave me.' That irresistible march on Paris, that conquest of a country achieved simply by showing himself, the prodigy of an invasion carried out by one man — as Chateaubriand described it — left the Emperor full of qualms. The triumphal ascent, which would have intoxicated other men, filled Napoleon with a melancholy, a lack of confidence, a pessimism, which haunted him throughout the Hundred Days. Of the dangers he ran, he thought nothing. If one single regiment barred his way, he might easily be shot, as Murat was soon to be when

NAPOLEON'S RETURN TO THE TUILERIES, 1815

From a contemporary print

he followed Napoleon's example and landed in the kingdom of Naples. Bonaparte set his glory higher than his life. But he was intelligent enough to realize that, for him as well as for the Bourbons, times had changed. France would not be France that he had known before defeat and invasion, before the charter of Louis XVIII and the repudiation of absolute power. The language that must now be used, that of the Revolution, was imposed by the facts of the situation; and nothing could be easier for Napoleon. But it would be harder to make his actions harmonize with his words, to find new forms for the Imperial government. And what lay especially heavy upon him was the sense that the spell was broken, the memories of Fontainebleau and the desertions, the feeling that things were not as they had been, whatever the success of his boldness. Armed with the tricolour in his famous hat, he marched forth to conquer France with unflinching heart and troubled mind, sure of each step and without faith in the future. He was a virtuoso of popularity performing his last great air, an artist adding one new feat of strength to his list of triumphs. This unparalleled return, this unique perform-ance, with scenes ready-made for engravings and for pos-terity, was one more element to lend a touch of the fabulous to Bonaparte's story.

But he was true to his axiom that nothing can succeed by chance alone. His escort of a thousand men was needed for the first stages, to avoid an ignominious arrest by the police. His spoken words were as carefully chosen as his route. The detour by way of the Alps avoided the hostility of royalist Provence, and brought him into instant contact with a populace whose feelings were known to him, and garrisons where he had accomplices. He would certainly avoid a clash with the government's troops by taking the mountain road, and would no less certainly be welcomed in the Dauphiné: 'at Grenoble, he would be in Paris'. It was the peasantry and workpeople whom he called to his side. And he did not flatter the noblest of their passions. He spoke less of national honour and glory than of feudal rights and the tithe, of the oppressive nobility, of privileges, of the resumption of national property. He was putting on 'the boots of 1793', and for good. He was no longer the conservative and conciliating First Consul, the legitimate Emperor. He returned as a demagogue flattering the mob and menacing the aristocrats.

The only danger which Napoleon ran during that adventurous march, when he was at the mercy of one musket-shot from a disciplined body of troops, came in the defile of Laffrey. It was there that he stood forward with breast uncovered before the 5th battalion of the line, and cried out: 'Soldiers! If there is one among you who wishes to kill his Emperor, here I am!' Not one obeyed the order to fire; but Napoleon had been careful to spread his proclamation among the infantry barring his road, and to send two of his own officers to shake their steadfastness; and he had with him fifteen hundred villagers acclaiming him. At Grenoble and Lyons, with an increasing force, the same things happened. The crowd intimidated the officers and swung the army over. Above all, Napoleon had counselled his followers never to be the first to fire, certain of being shielded by popular feelings by the memory of victories, and by the horror of shedding the blood of old comrades-in-arms.

He had landed on March 1st; he was at Lyons on the 10th, still greeted by shouts of 'Down with the priests! Down with the nobles!' and by the Marseillaise. Macdonald, for all his determination not to let him pass, was reduced to the same impotence as the commander at Laffrey. The marshals, the conspirators of Fontainebleau, were bound to be the most ardent in preventing his return. But the cold Macdonald could only turn back.

Master of the second city of France, Napoleon had won the game. 'I have reascended my throne,' he wrote to Marie Louise. He had already formed a small army from the garrisons encountered on his journey, augmented by half-pay officers, the whole numbering 14,000, more than was necessary to reach

Paris without mishap. From Lyons he issued his first Imperial decrees, dissolving the royal chambers, being yet forced into too many promises which would be a vexation and a source of regret to him. He convoked for his arrival in Paris, and as an earnest for his conversion to liberalism, a great national assembly, styled that of the Champ de Mai, an outlandish, romantic idea. The rumour was skilfully circulated that the foreign powers were in favour of the re-establishment of the Empire, that the English favoured his return from Elba and intentionally left a free passage for his flotilla, that the Emperor of Austria was protecting his son-in-law. And the same moment, in Vienna, the powers were actually declaring that 'Napoleon Bonaparte had placed himself outside of civil and social relations, and that as an enemy and disturber of the peace of the world, he had delivered himself to public prosecution'.

One man had vowed to be the instrument of that prosecution, the leader of the conspirators of Fontainebleau — Ney. Having done more than anyone else to overturn the man whom he now called 'the wild beast', he pursued his end with passion and hatred. He had sworn to bring back Napoleon in an iron cage — which made Louis XVIII remark with calm prudence that he was not called upon to do so much as that. And he was accompanied by Lecourbe, the Republican general of the Moreau conspiracy. When the Emperor learned that Ney had assumed the task of hunting him down, he was divided between two sets of feelings. He knew that Ney was the most violent and immoderate of these soldiers who had always been prepared to rip him open, and he knew also that he was the most liable to abrupt changes. Ney is represented as having fallen into his Emperor's arms. As a matter of fact, several well-chosen emissaries depicted to him the triumphal march, the hourly increase of his strength, the certainty of his success, the futility of an ill-matched contest. Ney was perturbed, but recovered himself enough to declare that he would take a musket and fire the first shot. But would his soldiers obey him, or Lecourbe, any more than they had obeyed Macdonald? Napoleon put the crowning touch by writing to him that he would welcome him as 'on the morrow of Borodino'. Ney yielded to the current, 'to the storm', as he said during his trial. He was at Lons-le-Saunier, and Napoleon at Mâcon, when he abandoned the pledges he had given. Ney rejoined the Emperor at Auxerre, handing him a declaration in the Fontainebleau style: 'I am your prisoner rather than your partisan if you continue to govern tyrannically.' Napoleon tore up the paper, affecting gaiety as he remarked that 'the worthy Ney had gone mad'. This was not enthusiasm, no meeting of true friends: it was one more cloud over the joy of return.

The *Moniteur* of March 20th published the news: 'The King and the Princes left last night; His Majesty the Emperor arrived this evening.' It was a magical and miraculous return to the Tuileries, into which Napoleon was carried in triumph, a man no longer merely extraordinary but supernatural. 'It was like witnessing the Resurrection of Christ', said an eye-witness. Next day disenchantment set in.

Bonaparte now saw only the embarrassment of his position. He did not even conceal his pessimism. Back in Paris, he was powerfully reminded of the defections and the forced abdication; he counted up the missing, and they were so numerous that he immediately left the vastness of the Tuileries, devoid of courtiers, Empress and ambassadors, for the more modest palace of the Élysée. When Mollien congratulated him, he answered: 'The time for compliments is over. They have let me arrive, just as they let the others go.' Louis XVIII had been destroyed as much as he had been, in many cases by the same men; and his opinion of human nature was not heightened. His downfall in 1814 had struck deep, and now had come this further experience to incline him to a nihilism which he expounded at St. Helena, still full of bitter impressions. 'I no longer possessed the sense of definite success; my early confidence was no longer there

. . . I instinctively felt a disastrous outcome.' He was no longer capable of hiding his perplexities, of which his intimates had formerly been the sole witnesses. Carnot, his new minister of the interior, was taken aback: 'I can no longer recognize him; the audacity of the return from Elba seems to have drained him of the sap of his energy; he is vacillating and hesitant; instead of acting, he talks . . . he asks everybody's advice. . . .' He was seen to be gloomy, distracted, sleepy. He seemed to be a different man, whereas this was simply an aggravation of his tendency to indecision and contradiction. In his most glorious days he had been a prey to instability and insecurity; might they not now be overwhelming him? Thiébault was at the Élysée when news came of Berthier's death through falling from a window in Germany. That conspicuous deserter had left the country because he could not face Napoleon in his uniform as a royal officer. But when he heard of the end of his chief of staff, the Emperor sank into gloom. He was feeling his solitude. He could count on devotion no longer, and his eyes looked round for old servants.

And into what contradictions he fell! After Waterloo he exclaimed that he would have done better to perish in Russia. And when the answer was given that, in that case, he would not have had the triumph of his return from Elba, he answered: 'Yes, good and bad. Bad, because there was not resistance. If there had been bloodshed I should still be in the Tuileries.' He had not wanted bloodshed. He let the princes go unmolested. The terrorist threats of Lyons were followed by an amnesty for 'the crimes of 1814', only a dozen persons being excepted. He retained fully a quarter of the prefects of Louis XVIII — in many cases men appointed by himself, often chosen from amongst the men of the old regime. And what was he now himself? What sort of sovereignty did he represent? He did not know; he could not give a definition of himself. The Empire was a ghost from the past, in a land which a bare twelvemonth of parliamentary royalty had already altered. Bonaparte had returned as a liberal, almost a revolutionary. He felt the need for the support of republican opinion, and he feared it and coaxed it. He thumped his paunchy belly, and parodied a classic saying: 'Is a man as fat as myself ambitious?' Nevertheless the Republicans were rallying to him. He had with him Bigonnet, Duchesne, and Carnot. Along with Fouché, once more minister of police, Napoleon had two regicides in his council. His personnel consisted for the most part of marshals, generals, senators and functionaries who 'through egotism or the workings of fate, had stained themselves in one year with a double defection'. There were also men who acclaimed him because they hated all monarchy and demanded safeguards against despotism. It was difficult for Napoleon to do less than Louis XVIII and his charter. Thibaudeau was right in remarking that 'the Empire returned to life feebler than when it succumbed in 1814 . . . The Emperor assumed liberalism despite himself, under compulsion; no matter, he mutilated himself. Dragged one way by these exigencies, dragged the other by his nature and habits, he was enfeebled and no longer himself'. It is even doubtful what title to give him. The headings of his decrees hover between 'Napoleon, Emperor of the French', and 'Napoleon, by the Grace of God and the Constitutions, Emperor'. Sometimes there reappears 'King of Italy'.

Was this newborn Empire the old one, or a new one? Was Napoleon still the autocrat of other days, the legitimate sovereign blessed by the Church? Was he a constitutional monarch, or that lesser thing, 'the chief representative of the people', or a Jacobin dictator?

He hesitated. His proclamations, his promises in the Dauphiné and Lyons, his enforced demagogy, had committed him more deeply than he could have wished. His danger now was of being an Emperor of the mob, and of alarming the middle classes and conservatives, at a time when the royalist West and South were already rising. In Paris, the populace who cheered him and forced him to show himself at windows, was that of the red bonnets and the pikes. The review of the *Fédérés* was too much like the great 'days' of the Revolution. These were things that Napoleon did not like. They made him anxious and uneasy.

He had moved forward too far to be able to swallow his words and withhold a constitution from the French. The days of absolute power were over. Bonaparte found himself in the same position as Louis XVIII the year before. Like him, the Emperor claimed that his reign had been continuous, and like him, he granted a charter, under the name of the Additional Act to the Constitutions of the Empire. And as adversaries had to be disarmed and the opposition won over, he appealed for a plan of the liberal Empire to Benjamin Constant, the writer who had only lately been comparing him to Attila, and vowing that 'he would not trail, a wretched deserter, from one power to the next, stammering profaned words to redeem a shameful life'. Napoleon thought of Benjamin Constant as he thought of other men. He required a constitution; he asked for it to be supplied by the expert in political liberty.

These things were only expedients. The divergence between the Emperor and France was graver than that bearing on forms of government. The difficulty that Bonaparte had in being a crowned Washington did not lie altogether in the abandonment of his Cæsarean habits, his tastes and dislikes, his 'eleven years of rule', his whole past. It arose from the other promise he had had to make — in good faith, no doubt, and one which it was outside of his power to keep. He knew that the French were tired of war and conscription. When he seized power again he had announced peace, declared that he would respect the Treaty of Paris and accept without reservations the old frontiers, and that there was no further question of the great Empire. He wrote fraternally to the Allied monarchs, informing all the powers of his good intentions, and urged Marie Louise to return to Paris. The sovereigns did not reply. Since March 25th they had renewed the Pact of Chaumont, undertaking not to lay down arms until the foe of public tranquillity was overthrown. With the powers all assembled in Vienna, concerted action had been easy, and Napoleon regretted that he had not waited for the Congress to end before leaving Elba, forgetting that one of his reasons had been his fear that the Congress might incarcerate him elsewhere. As for Marie Louise, she informed him that she was no longer free. The daughter had abdicated to the hands of her father. The wife was in the power of her consoler.

Everything was a disappointment: the Empress not returning; the Prince Imperial (for Napoleon had dropped the child's kingly title in token of his moderation) still a prisoner; war a certainty; a constitution which was not sufficiently Republican for the men of the Revolution, whilst it lessened the authority of the Emperor in the face of danger; and there were 'cries of liberty when defence should have been the only thought'. Nobody believed in the duration of this miraculously restored reign, and Bonaparte believed in it less than anyone. 'Anxiety, fear, discontent, were the dominating sentiments, and there were no signs of attachment or affection for the government.' The Emperor himself felt the bad auguries, and took no pleasure in a situation which was more precarious than any he had known before in its sense of fragility. Lucien's arrival only awoke ideas of decadence and misfortune. The Emperor awaited Marie Louise, the daughter of the Cæsars, his pledge of security with the kings, and only saw the arrival of his Republican brother, ready to serve him as if the 18th of Brumaire had to be recommenced, or to impose a government in his own style.

Contradictions and misunderstandings were everywhere; and everything that combined to strengthen Bonaparte's position on his return from Egypt, now conspired, on his return from Elba, to weaken him. France desired peace, as always since 1798. She no longer believed that Napoleon

418

could secure peace by his victories. He had promised to make no war, and already the coalition was being renewed against him. He would at least take care not to be the aggressor. But here was Murat, once more his ally, betraying him a second time, and in a different way, by attacking the Austrians and attempting a conquest of Italy, and — what was worse — by letting himself be utterly defeated at Tolentino. After that, how could the fable of family alliance be upheld to the French people? Murat sought refuge in France, and his infuriated brother-in-law refused to see him. Napoleon was to hold the adventurous and versatile king of Naples responsible for the disaster of 1815, as he had already laid the blame for that of 1814 upon his shoulders.

War was inevitable. It was necessary, then, to revive the flame of the Revolution. In 1814 that had been dead. If it was rekindled in 1815 it would be against despotism. Napoleon's only support lay in men of Republican temper, who limited his powers at a moment when the safety of the commonwealth called for dictatorship. He was vexed by the shackles of the Additional Act. 'A muzzled bear who could still be heard growling,' said Mme de Staël, 'but still led as its leaders wished.' He had had to yield to repeated counsels and reinstate Fouché at the ministry of police. Fouché was convinced that two or three battles would end everything, and betrayed Napoleon with the Allies and with Louis XVIII at Ghent, at home and abroad. And it was Fouché who procured the election of the deputies, old comrades of the Convention, terrorists emerging from their retirement, men of '93, and — what was even worse for Bonaparte — men of '89, even La Fayette. Fouché's Chamber laughed when a representative proposed to bestow the title of 'saviour of the country' upon the Emperor. In ministerial councils, Napoleon flung insults at Fouché: 'I ought to have you shot!' And Fouché boasts of having retorted: 'Sire, I do not share your opinion.' The Emperor retained his insolent minister postponing everything until the day when he would be victorious, if he won a decisive victory. To recapture authority, he could now count only on the fortunes of arms, and he had lost faith and was overwhelmed by forebodings.

The strange ceremony of the Champ de Mai had to be postponed to June 1st, because it was impracticable in its promised form; but he had not countermanded it, because he firmly believed in the need for once more tempering the steel of his spirit in a popular demonstration, especially after the ratifying plebiscite had given him not half the former number of votes. The Additional Act satisfied nobody. The Champ de Mai was to repeat the festival of the Federation of 1790, and the distribution of the Eagles in 1804. It was at once depressing and fantastic, a parody of the Empire for the Emperor. Napoleon appeared in a theatrical costume, with a plumed cap, an embroidered cloak, which he flung back with a gesture learned from Talma, a sash, silk stockings, rosettes on his shoes; and under this disguise his face, says one witness, was 'anxious, drawn, severe, and Nero-like'. There was equal amazement at the sight of his three brothers beside him, clad in white velvet—Joseph, Lucien and Jerome, in the 'Spanish costume of French princes', who were still, between reconciliations, carrying on their rivalries and quarrels for a throne which had been re-erected for two months and would be capsized again in three weeks — hardly a longer time than was needed to clear away the platform of the Champ de Mai.

The costumes of Napoleon and his brothers reflected his uncertainties and embarrassment. This festival was both civil and military. It must not be predominantly military, to avoid talk of Napoleon as a war-maker. And in addressing 'the electors', he had also to appear before them with the majesty of Empire, though he now had only the accessories to enable him to do so. 'As Emperor, Consul, and soldier, I desire everything for the people.' But he hinted at a revision of the Additional Act after the unjust aggression had been repulsed. This ceremony was a mixture of everything.

It opened with an Archbishop and Mass, proceeded to the harangue of the representative of the electoral bodies, an oath based upon that of the coronation, and ended with the acclamations of the army and vows to go and bring back the Empress and his son, and to die for the throne and for France.

We have seen Napoleon at all times given over to wavering and perplexity; and now, during the Hundred Days, he drifted from one idea to another until at last he resolved upon staking his all. Furthermore, his physical vigour was lessened, his health undermined, and the poisoning of Fontainebleau had left its mark. He was still more sick in mind. He was obsessed by the downfall and the treacheries of 1814. The certainty that neither Marie Louise nor the King of Rome would return deprived him of much of his courage. What purpose could there be in restoring a monarchy when its heir was held captive? To free him, must he advance against a swarm of enemies, as far as Vienna, or even farther? Napoleon knew that war was inevitable, as he was under the ban of all Europe, and he had prepared war, as usual, in every detail. But he listened to everybody's advice, examined every side's views, weighing pros and cons, but adopting none. There were some who advised him to start out on a campaign instantly, forestalling the Allies, sounding the tocsin for all France to rally to arms. But he had been obliged to promise peace and renounce conquests: and how could Revolutionary enthusiasm be fired when solemn declarations had been made that neither Belgium not the left bank of the Rhine should be retaken. To call half a million men to arms in a patriotic uprising, he must have arms and horses to give them. Carnot, who lived upon memories and still believed that 1792 might repeat itself, was in favour of waiting for the enemy to invade. A spontaneous movement would then bring France solidly and eagerly behind her chief. But Napoleon gauged public opinion more accurately. He felt its weakness, its hostility to the conscriptions, and believed that an invasion of French soil would lead to a general break-up rather than to a spirit of energy. 'My policy calls for a gleaming flash,' he told Carnot.

He had thought of entering Belgium early in May, to surprise and forestall the English and Prussians. But he countermanded his orders. For information reached him that the enemy would not be ready before the end of July, whilst he himself was not yet ready in May; nor did he wish to appear as the aggressor, and he had to keep his Lyons promises and avoid all suspicion of dictatorship. Furthermore, according to some, he was in bad physical health, suffering from ailments which made it painful for him to be long in the saddle. Possibly he was apprehensive of fresh warfare. The fact remains that he did not set off until the Champ de Mai and the opening of the Chambers. Suddenly he made his decision and rejoined the army, leaving behind him a parliament which was manifestly ill-disposed towards him.

He left Paris in the early morning on June 11th. The day before, for the last time, he had heard Mass at the Tuileries, he had given audiences, he had been Emperor. He was anxiously scrutinized. And how changed men found him! He no longer showed that potent glance, that brazen profile, that domineering bearing of the head; his complexion had a 'greenish' tinge, his walk had become heavy and his movements uncertain; he gave a general impression of enfeebled power. At night he had dined in the family circle, and was almost cheerful, or affected to be so: 'more talkative than usual', said Hortense, and talking of his favourite subject, literature, for which he had unwittingly laboured so much, and which he was to enrich still further by the perfect rounding-off of his story. The name of Waterloo would enter into it like a knell. And at the close of the evening he murmured to Mme. Bertrand the right remark, the remark that 'Madame Mère' might well have uttered: 'If only we don't live to regret Elba!'

CHAPTER XXV

THE DARK PLAIN

Of all Napoleon's battles, the most famous is the one which he lost. Into his history Waterloo brought catastrophe, the last and crowning event of tragedies. An abrupt disaster, complete and resounding, the rounding-off of so many victories and strategic exploits by this military collapse — this was an element of legend and epic that was still lacking in Bonaparte's life. His life would soar higher than ever by martyrdom, and martyrdom did not linger.

In their mental reconstructions of the battle of Waterloo, hundreds of historians — the Emperor the first among them — have shown that it could have been won, and ought to have been won, without asking themselves the question of what would have happened the next day. Napoleon was beaten, and collapsed instantly. With Wellington and Blücher in retreat, the war would merely have continued, the same war that had lasted for twenty-three years. And on that Belgian plain the Emperor would still be risking the contest in which, essentially, Belgium had been the stake. With the subsiding wave of the Revolution militant, he had come to find his end here, near Fleurus and Jemmapes, before the gates of Brussels, for the places which Revolutionary France had conquered, and which, in spite of Europe, she had strained every nerve to preserve, even to the point of denying her own nature. The climax took place at the very starting-point. It brought about the final outcome, and provided the explanation of the unparalleled adventures that had gone before, closely linked though they were. The doleful sound of Waterloo in a Frenchman's ear depends not merely on the downfall of one man. To the French, it signified the shattering of a dream by harsh contact with the outer world.

It meant a renunciation, a turning inward of the spirit — in fact, a humiliation more cruel than the battle, which at least was lost honourably and with glamour.

In his ceaseless musing over the tragic hours on Mont Saint-Jean, Napoleon never tired of blaming everything and everybody — Grouchy, Ney, Soult, and fate. But he knew that chance was not enough to account for the failure. He was vanquished within himself before he came face to face with Wellington, and his soldiers were in the same plight. There was no confidence in their minds, and memories of 1814 weighed heavy on every heart. Carnot described that seven-day campaign in Belgium as 'a series of mistakes unworthy of the genius of Napoleon'. And all of these mistakes derived from a leader who lacked faith. His own sense of realism was too powerful to allow him to suppose that his successes would begin again after all that he had seen at Fontainebleau in 1814, and all that he had more recently seen in France and in Paris. The army was not under proper control, and an aftermath of enthusiasm, a lust for revenge, would not take the place of the discipline which had vanished. Cartridges were issued in which the men found flour instead of gunpowder, and one general, Bourmont, an opponent of the Additional Act, abandoned his corps when the frontier was reached. That was enough to send the word 'treason!' on its rounds. And it was all too easy to note the military chiefs who had not rejoined the colours, and likewise those, even marshals, who had followed Louis XVIII to Ghent. Others had worn the white cockade before they had resumed the tricolour, and were suspect. The Emperor had declined the services of Murat: his example might demoralize more men than he could have brought to his side. Ney had a command — but was he not the most deeply compromised of all? His 'iron cage' still hampered him in action. Napoleon was bereft of Berthier, and regretted not having Suchet instead of Soult as major-general. Grouchy was a political choice, and a bad one. It was convenient to attribute the failure to

Grouchy and to destiny. But already, at Ligny, d'Erlon had remained useless throughout the day, for lack of clear or repeated orders.

Lack of decision and activity, loss of time, carelessness, the hesitancy and perplexity which were heightened in Napoleon by the vastness of the risk and by anxiety, his 'fever of doubt', outwardly shown by a lamentable slowness, and a sort of indolent apathy — the same symptoms and reproaches rose at every step he took. When he gave orders capable of assuring victory, they were not carried out. On June 16th, the Prussians ought to have been shattered. Napoleon complained that Ney did not understand his idea, or was vacillating in its execution. 'Ney,' he said later, 'was not the same man.' And Ney, who had become so unwontedly circumspect, might have said the same of Napoleon, who was left in troubled surprise by the incidents of this engagement, and who, by too much thought, lost the fight on the following morning. When the Emperor decided to attack the English army, it was to be 'destroyed in a moment' — if it was still at Quatre-Bras. It was there no longer, having profited by the respite left to it to escape that destruction.

These men who had taken part in so many fights, who had traversed all Europe waging their wars, seem from a distance to have grown old, to be on the verge of senile collapse. Pages so crowded give an impression of long duration, whereas brevity is actually their most extraordinary characteristic. We do not remember sufficiently that Bonaparte himself was not even forty-six, none of his generals fifty, that Wellington was a few months older than he, and that the old man, the patriarch — seventy-six years of age — was Blücher. We tend to wish that the flame and energy should be extinguished in Napoleon, that he was already in the grip of cancer, that he was somnolent in the midst of action. We do not seek other and different explanations for the eclipsing of his genius. And yet Ligny and Quatre-Bras still showed the ideas of a god of battles, but a doubting god. His own inspira-

tions were no longer an illumination to him. He no longer
followed them; he was divided in mind, obsessed by other
than military concerns. On June 17th, when the English
were escaping him, he was talking with his generals about
public opinion in Paris, about the Chambers, about Fouché.
On the following night, at the Caillou farm, he dictated the
plan of battle for the morrow, the great and tragic battle,
and also letters 'necessitated', said Davout, 'by the cares and
embarrassments caused him by the Chamber of Representatives'. He was too much concerned with the rear, and
this weakened his will and darkened his thought. The immediate causes of the disaster at Waterloo are to be found
in a series of mishaps, the outcome of incredible omissions
and oversights, and of orders badly transmitted, insufficient,
or obscure. The general cause, in the supreme leader, was
mental vacillation and a secret despair.

And that despair became Napoleon's evil counsellor. On
the two days preceding the 18th of June he allowed precious
moments to go by. On the very morning of the 18th he
put back the hour for attack in order to wait for the ground
to dry after a violent downpour. Then he was seized by
haste. Suddenly he was in a hurry. He wanted an instant
result, a decisive battle, and wished to have it all over, for
better or worse. Long uncertainty was succeeded by rash
assurance. Soult, who knew the ground, pointed out that
Grouchy had a great many men, and that it might be well
to call for some of his troops. The Emperor replied that there
was no need to be concerned about the English, that it was
ten to one that he would beat them. Reille supported Soult.
He had known the English infantry in Spain, and Napoleon
had never measured his strength with Wellington. He got
the same answer: 'If my orders are properly carried out, we
shall sleep in Brussels to-night.' The Emperor was warned
that the Prussians were to effect their junction with the English at the entrance to the Forest of Soignes. He declared that
Blücher could not arrive for a couple of days yet, and that in

any case Grouchy had instructions to pursue them. When Ziethen's corps appeared on the field of battle, Napoleon still refused to believe that they were Prussians. Afterwards he was to blame Grouchy, who was always to be known as the general who did not advance to the guns, who was waited for and did not arrive, the general of whom Houssaye has justly remarked that he acted like a blind man, but one whom Napoleon did nothing to enlighten.

Discussion on Waterloo was to be endless; but it was a battle lost in advance. Nothing succeeded because there was nothing that was bound to succeed. Even prudence became baneful. If the engagement had been opened sooner, Wellington might have been beaten before Blücher joined him. But what if the horses and artillery became bogged? There was delay in capturing Hougoumont, at heavy sacrifice of men. But it was to harbour the artillery munitions. The Emperor, as usual, refused to give his Guard at a moment when their entry might have changed the outcome of the day. He threw them in too late. Too soon, and nothing would have remained for the supreme resistance. Might he not have ordered a retreat at seven in the evening, when the Prussians debouched? But it would have been hazardous in the actual confusion of the battle-field, and by then retreat and defeat were very much the same. Napoleon's dominating thought was that 1814 would repeat itself, if it were not something worse that was taking shape. In the last effort Ney called out the thought that was Napoleon's, and indeed everybody's — 'd'Erlon, if we get out of this, we'll be hanged, both of us!'

Those who had seen Napoleon on the morning of Waterloo were struck by his greasy pallor, and saw an ill augury therein. The English, for their part, were impressed by the French soldiers, especially by the cuirassiers and their desperate charges, and declared that they had never seen figures of such hostility. The general picture has lingered in men's imaginations and in history, a fit scene for the poetry that springs from catastrophe; it was doleful — that shout that the enemy were 'too many', the headlong flight, the last squares of the Guard, Cambronne, the twilight of heroes, the rout, the nocturnal retreat of the Emperor, whom some saw in tears.

He had left the battle-field slowly and regretfully. Then he left Belgium, the frontier, the army. It was a flight; and for that flight he was harshly condemned. Once again, the soldier mixing in politics! As in Egypt, as in Russia, he abandoned his soldiers, when they were not so grievously stricken that a leader could not have reformed them to stem the path of invasion. But he retorted that he no longer had an army, but only fugitives, blaming Ney, Grouchy, d'Erlon, 'in a chaos of ideas'. But underneath all his confusion of mind, which perhaps was simulated, Napoleon kept one fixed idea. His resolve had been taken as soon as he recognized defeat. He was haunted by the memory and experience of 1814. Was he to remain with his army and receive the summonses of the marshals while his deposition was decided upon by the Chambers in Paris? Was he to offer to continue the national war, and only to hear himself saying that he was no longer obeyed? Convinced that all that had befallen him in 1814 sprang from the fact of his absence from the capital, he returned without stopping to Paris, although he had announced that he would stop at Laon.

He told Las Cases that he had been mistaken in 1814, in his belief that France would make common cause with him when his danger was seen, but that in 1815, on his return from Waterloo, he was even more mistaken! If he ever supposed that he would recover power by a return to the Élysée, his illusion did not last for one day. On the morning of June 21st, worn out and harassed, he was back in Paris, whither the news of the catastrophe had preceded him. He later pleaded his fatigue, and the fact that he had eaten nothing for three days, as excuse for not going instantly to the Chamber in his uniform, his boots covered with mud. But when

Gourgaud told him that such an appearance would have swung over and galvanized the representatives, he answered frankly: 'My dear fellow, I was beaten, I had nothing more to hope for.' It is true, he gauged his position with an overwhelming clarity that filled him with a distaste for everything. He lingered in his bathroom, kept the ministers waiting, and at last held a council which deliberated without making any decision, and at which he intoxicated himself with words; he let hours go by, and meanwhile the Chamber of Representatives met, and, on a motion by La Fayette, declared itself in permanent session, adding that whosoever might seek to dissolve it would be guilty of high treason. Napoleon was overturned by La Fayette, who felled him with one motion and one speech.

Lucien advised Napoleon to appeal to the people, to use force and to break the Representatives. 'Be daring', he said to him. 'I have been daring too often,' answered Napoleon. The president of the 18th of Brumaire was there; but the general was not. Or rather, he was in the state that he had been in when he emerged from the assembly hall of the Five Hundred on the point of collapse, much as he would have been that day without his grenadiers, without Murat, Sieyès, and the propitious circumstances. After the defeat of Waterloo, Napoleon underwent a parliamentary defeat. He confided to Gourgaud that the action of the Chambers surprised him, that everything would have happened differently if only seven or eight deputies had been hanged, and Fouché before them. He had not even thought of it. In the *Memorial* he sought to convey that he would have gone off as a monarch who was a friend to his people, shrinking from blood, execution and civil war. In point of fact, he had less energy than ever with which to run a political risk. La Valette found him implacable of anything but exclamations — '*Ah! Mon Dieu!*' — with his eyes turned heavenward and a frightening, epileptic laugh. Houssaye describes him on that night of June 21st: 'his drifting thoughts seemed unable to settle down to make any decision whatever; at one moment he declared his readiness to use his constitutional rights against the revolting Chamber, at another he was talking of ending everything instantly by a second abdication.' Next day he was induced, after some fleeting ideas of dissolving the Chambers, to appeal to the army, the people, the *fédérés*. It would have meant leading a revolution, and leading the way into anarchy. 'The memories of my youth terrified me,' he confessed.

He remained inert. During the 22nd the Representatives gave him one hour to decide. In order to avoid dethronement pure and simple, and to preserve at least his character as a sovereign and the principle of his dynasty, he submitted.

He abdicated. And on what conditions! It was all worse than the year before at Fontainebleau, where he had still treated with the Allied sovereigns as equals, stipulating the place of his retirement, a sovereign status, a pension. Now he was naked and alone. He had neither his father-in-law nor the Tsar to shield him. The acclamation of the soldiers and workmen compromised him. The provisional government was impatient for his departure, and nobody was interested in his lot. Napoleon renounced the throne in favour of his son, and was the first to realize that Napoleon II would not reign – that it was all over. There were no farewells to the army, no flags to be kissed. Everything proceeded by motions and orders carried, votes, discussions in committees. He wanted at least to lend this procedure some tone and accent of nobility. He composed the document whereby he yielded his power to La Fayette and Lanjuinais, to the liberals and parliamentarians, with every attention to its words and phrasing. He read and reread it through, made corrections, and had it conveyed to the Chambers only when he was satisfied with its text. His power now lay only in style, in the art of coining formulas.

And now, having forsworn everything, having liquidated the adventure of the Hundred Days, and being perhaps, as Carnot opined, pleased at being relieved from all responsibility, the fallen Emperor's presence in Paris was merely a nuisance. People were anxious to see him gone. He lingered on at the Élysée, asking for safeguards, and permission to travel unmolested to America. As at Fontaine-bleau, it was a soldier, Davout, who came to inform him coldly that he must go and await his papers elsewhere. And meanwhile, in the eyes of the advancing Allies, he was merely an escaped convict, to be dealt with at the discretion of those who might recapture him. He would still have to escape from that desperate and humiliating position.

He had taken refuge at Malmaison, a place of many memories, leaving destiny to take its own course. Hortense, who spent those last days with him, was alarmed by his inactivity and apathy. If he was to embark for America and remain free, he was wasting time that he could not have again. He reviewed the course of his past life as in a dream. He thought of days gone by, of Josephine: 'I can still see her coming out of a garden-path there . . . Poor Josephine!' He saw Maria Walewska, his son, and his other natural son, the 'Count Léon', who was so like the King of Rome that he talked about him all one morning. And he had regrets: 'How lovely it is, Malmaison! How pleasant it would be to be able to stay here! Don't you think so, Hortense?' For a short time he accepted the idea of a retired existence in the United States, devoting the end of his life to science, and consulted Monge on the plan. Then came a fresh revolt against the idea of leaving everything and going into the void. The allied armies were advancing on Paris. He offered his sword to the provisional government, promising to leave as soon as he had repulsed the invaders. The Prussians were nearing Malmaison, and there was a fear lest Napoleon should be taken, and perhaps shot. Far from accepting the Emperor's proposal, the government begged him, on June 29th, to take the road.

This time he had no foreign commissioners to escort him. His custodian was General Beker, a liberal soldier who carried out his mission in a gallant spirit. His account shows the Emperor a prey to his uncertainties. At one moment Napoleon would be giving loquacious explanations of why he had left his army after Waterloo, where 'nobody, myself included, did his duty'; of how he had refused 'to nationalize the war', because he had always held civil wars and anarchy in horror; of how he had seen that everything was 'worn-out and demoralized'. The next moment he would be taciturn, exchanging only broken phrases with his travelling-companions, delaying on the road, and taking fresh hope from the cheers of those who recognized him on the way that he would not be abandoned, and would even be sent for and recalled.

Brief illusions. In his innermost self he had already envisaged the ending, the only ending that answered his sense of sublimity. The return from Elba had effaced the painful memories of the journey through Provence, his disguises and his tears. He had now to efface the flight from Waterloo and an abdication devoid of glory. This refuge in the United States would be a petty ending, a bourgeois retirement. He needed a last act that would be worthy of the rest, an epilogue that was not an ineffective exit. By the dominant interest in his destiny, by the artistic sense of his renown, by his instinct for greatness, he was compelled to place himself in the hands of England, so that his 'romance' might be concluded in the key of high tragedy. He had refused to seek asylum of his father-in-law, or to write to the Emperor Alexander. On June 24th, he had written to Caulaincourt: 'As for Austria, never. They have wounded me in the heart by keeping my wife and my son. As for Russia, that is giving oneself up to a man. With England, at least, one would be giving oneself up to a nation.' A matter of words. Actually, it was what he was bound to do. The step fascinated him by its historical turn. To place himself in the hands of his enemy, like Themistocles, whose name he had pensively murmured shortly before Waterloo, was a fine and lofty idea, conceived by the man of letters who dwelt within him. No doubt he gauged the risks. Once more, for a moment, his regrets at leaving everything by leaving France, his expectation of a miracle, his fears regarding the lot destined for him, struggled against the choice he had already resolved upon, as the spirit struggles with the body.

He spent four days at Rochefort, still apathetic, perplexed, inactive. He had to leave Rochefort in obedience to orders received from Paris. Fouché and the provisional government were anxious to know that he had gone. And Louis XVIII was even more so. Pushed off between the shoulders, Napoleon crossed to the Ile d'Aix, and wasted a few more days there. Joseph arrived, and vainly begged him to come to a decision, and to embark in his place for Bordeaux, whence he could reach the open sea. At the last moment he refused everything. He was 'the sole cause of his own loss, by his own uncertainties and hesitations', said General Beker. As a matter of fact, he disliked the idea of Mexico or the United States. He rebelled at the idea of hiding on board a foreign ship, and escaping like a bankrupt. What would happen if the English found the fugitive in the hold, behind the barrels? The more he thought of it, the more the project he had pondered since his abdication seemed to accord with Imperial majesty, and the more did it seem to be the only one worthy of him. Its very danger made it the noblest solution. All others made him look small.

Before placing himself in English hands, would he at least secure a discussion of the terms on which he would hand over his sword? Rovigo, Las Cases, and General Lallemand went as emissaries on board the *Bellerophon*, the chief English vessel cruising off the Ile d'Aix. Captain Maitland gave them no pledge. He had no safe-conduct for General Bonaparte, and his only mission was to convey him to England. True, he let it he understood, perhaps the better to induce the Emperor to board his vessel, that hospitality would be generous. When Napoleon at last made his decision, he surrendered unconditionally to his greatest adversary, to the foe whom he had been unable either to conquer or conciliate.

His sole concern now was with his figure in history; and he realized that all depended on his manner of taking this final step. He invested his surrender with as much solemnity as circumstances allowed. First there was his letter to the Prince Regent, in a memorable style: 'Exposed to the factions which distract my land, and to the hostility of the greatest powers of Europe . . . I come, like Themistocles, to throw myself upon the hospitality of the British people. I place myself under the protection of their laws, which I claim from Your Royal Highness as the most powerful, the most steadfast, and the most generous of my enemies.' Early on July 15th he embarked on the French brig *L'Epervier*, wearing the green uniform of the *chasseurs* of the Guard, with the legendary attributes — the legion of honour, the sword at his side, the small hat. Napoleon's farewell to France in the dawn, beside the tricolour, the weeping seamen, that last cry of 'Vive l'Empereur!' — how well grouped, how well painted it all is! And how well he answered General Beker! The general had asked whether he should accompany him over to the *Bellerophon*, and he answered with a few sentences which had only to be compressed to make the historic saying: 'No, general. It must not be made possible to say that France handed me over to the English.' An actor, but an actor who played only in the highest genre.

Captain Maitland saw a corpulent figure of a man coming on board, with small feet, pretty hands, and pale grey eyes. The man who had made Europe tremble was his prize, henceforth a prisoner for life. The English scrutinized him curiously. One of them wrote that his face was more like that of a Spanish or Portuguese monk than of the hero of modern times. He seemed to be heavy, somnolent, variable in temper. His companions made scenes, and quarrels, when his deportation to St. Helena was announced, Napoleon's face did not alter: his only emotion was at the departure of those who could not follow him into exile. Instantly he had grasped his role, and instantly he stepped into it. Henceforward he was a victim; and against the British government which had betrayed the trust of its vanquished enemy, he hurled a protest to the king, to the peoples, to the universe. At Plymouth the harbour was black with vessels trying to approach for a glimpse of him. If he did not know it before, he would learn that round his name and his person there already hovered, in pledge of immortality, a vast curiosity. To maintain interest and pity would be the task and the consolation of St. Helena.

During those cruel moments, the ideas that filled his mind were unexpected and strange. It seemed as if the most recent part of his memories had been wiped out. As the prisoner of England, he saw himself not so much Emperor of the French as the youthful general checkmated by Sydney Smith at Acre. 'If it hadn't been for you English,' he said to Maitland, 'I should have been Emperor of the Orient.' And when, after a long voyage on board the *Northumberland*, on October the 15th, 1815, the island that was to be his prison came into sight, he said to Gourgaud: 'It is not a pleasing habitation. I would rather have stayed in Egypt; I should now be Emperor of all the Orient.' Would that have been more fabulous than what he had been? He was the poet of his own life, the priest in charge of his own memory; and on his rock he was about to complete his fable, to build up images still more powerful, to offer the human race a potent nourishment. Really, he had already left this world. England, by her choice of this inaccessible island as the place of his captivity had raised him into regions of the ideal whence he could shine forth in all his glory.

CHAPTER XXVI

MARTYRDOM

NAPOLEON lived as a prisoner on St. Helena for five years, six months, and eighteen days. It was almost as long as the interval between Erfurt and his first abdication. He died there before completing his fifty-second year, and thus spent in captivity more than a tenth part of his life. Time enough to meditate upon his life, and shape it to his liking. Seclusion, the emptiness of his days, this isolation and idleness after having filled the world's stage, made up one last rich gift of fortune. His life became a perfected work of art, crowned by suffering and martyrdom. The greatest heroes need the rock of Prometheus, the stake of Hercules and Joan of Arc; the Napoleonic religion spoke of the Cross on Calvary.

And here too circumstances still aided the Emperor's fame. It had been a true inspiration to surrender to his enemies. By exiling him to the world's end, the English were not seeking vengeance, but only to get rid of an encumbering personage for whom there was no proper place. They were obliged to keep him; nobody claimed him. The other governments were delighted to let England have Napoleon. Every solution had its inconveniences of risks. The London Cabinet avoided the mistake of formal accusation and pompous passing of judgment. 'General Bonaparte' was relegated to an almost inaccessible island, with strict orders regarding his movements, and silence was organized round the prisoner. Napoleon retained only one right, but a valuable one — that of complaint. He had surrendered unconditionally, trusting to the generosity of the English people, who now made him undergo an inhuman treatment. He was becoming a victim. He systematically judged the conditions of his custody by the laws of hospitality. The petty spirit of

LONGWOOD, ST. HELENA

his gaolers did the rest. One of the occupations of the prisoner of St. Helena became the noting of their offences against the standards of correctness, and the exaggeration of his grievances; and he called the world and posterity to witness to the cruelty of his executioners and the outrages which they heaped upon him.

But he had not abandoned all hope. It was not only to future generations that he appealed. His name alone represented a force of opinion. The distant solitude of his captivity was evidence in itself that he was still an object of fear. He still counted for something. He had no thoughts of escape, for he knew that it was almost impossible and certainly futile. And in any case, what would he have done? Where would he have gone? But new combinations of events might take place — in England, a change of reign or of majority — in France a revolution — in Europe a great war. It might be useful to keep interest alive, and to excite pity. And even if he never emerged from this prison, what glamour would be lent by this long misfortune to the name of Napoleon in history! It would be an exaggeration to say that the fallen Emperor always looked on the favourable side of that misfortune. Sometimes he contrasted his lot with that of Ferdinand VII at Valençay, and let it be understood that he would not ask more of Louis XVIII. But whether resigned or not, he extracted all that was possible from his captivity. It might be added even, with admiration, not in irony, that he rose to this situation as he had risen to others, and that allowing for some impatience and some weakness, he played the role of martyr to perfection. For the idea of grandeur sustained him even more than the sense of his dignity. But it is nevertheless true that a distinction must be drawn between the facts of his life in exile and the picture of it that he bequeathed.

We should first picture the residence assigned to him by the liberality of the country into whose hands the new Themistocles had entrusted himself. Longwood was summed up in one phrase by Lord Rosebery, who sought the truth on behalf of England's honour: 'a collection of huts which had been constructed as a cattle-shed.' This wretched place had been hurriedly put in order to receive the exile. From royal palaces and noble bivouacs he passed to four constricted rooms, infested by rats, and quickly encumbered with papers and books. As ornaments, a few portraits, souvenirs of Josephine, the King of Rome, and Marie Louise; a few trophies, the alarm-clock of Frederick the Great; some poor relics of one-time splendour, the dinner service, the toilet articles. In this setting Napoleon was to end his days. He was guarded like a dangerous malefactor; his letters were opened, his walks so closely watched that he abandoned them. The place was bleak and lonely and windswept. The British government took pains to make the background of this last picture appropriate. With remarkable clumsiness they mustered every effect that would rouse sympathy for their prisoner. It was an enduring success. Napoleon at St. Helena still holds the boards. To make Longwood become in the world's eyes a place of torture, the hapless hero would only have to add one small touch to the picture.

We should then imagine the Emperor's suite, crowded into crannies and garrets, and subjected to all the exasperations of living on top of each other. The exile's faithful followers made up a circle highly favourable to the exaggeration of grievances. There were Montholon and his wife, models of devotion — he, a Frenchman of the old school, she, the Emperor's consolation. When she left the island, he was seen in tears. Las Cases was a former *émigré* who had become fervent in the Napoleonic cult, a gentleman and at the same time an active and skilful man of letters. He was the 'ideal biographer', and Napoleon's favourite companion, with whom it was possible to discuss literature. It seems, however, that Las Cases, who reconciled devotion with advertisement, left after he had completed his harvesting and assembled the materials for his book. Gourgaud, the former officer of artillery, the Emperor's aide-de-camp since 1811, had rallied to Louis XVIII in 1814, but returned during the Hundred Days: a 'fine young man', with a free tongue, but jealous, who provoked Montholon to a duel. His foible was for reminding Napoleon, who could not remember it, that he had saved his life at Brienne in 1814. Bertrand, who had already been 'grand-marshal of the palace' at Elba, was a former officer of the engineers, first and foremost a soldier, devoted to his Emperor and timid before his wife. Such was the court, as fruitful in jealousies and intrigue as if it had been at the Tuileries. Piontkowski, a Polish captain, arrived later on. And there were also the chief body-servant March-and, and the domestic staff. Then there was the Irish doctor O'Meara, who was succeeded by the Corsican Antommarchi, an irritating choice of Uncle Fesch. This doctor arrived before the end, with a pair of dull priests — whereupon the Emperor commented: 'My family send me nothing but brutes.'

These servants in adversity, who had sentenced themselves to deportation, made up the chorus of the tragedy. All except Bertrand kept diaries or scribbled memoirs, at least a few recollections. They all knew that they were entering immortality, and Napoleon was quite aware that notes were being made all round him. He made use of Las Cases, the ablest hand at editing, to spread abroad what he wanted to be believed. Las Cases added something of his own. And from this kind of collaboration sprang the *Memorial of St. Helena*, a book admirably contrived to arouse emotion and sympathy. Napoleon promised Las Cases that it would bring him plenty of money. But how much more glory it brought the Emperor!

But this plentiful literature does not in all ways lead to a knowledge of the truth. The accounts of the captivity do not accord, and the inaccuracy of some is obvious. O'Meara's is a pleasing romance. Antommarchi describes things which he neither saw nor heard, for Napoleon kept him at arm's length. Rosebery acutely points out that the first accounts to be published are the least worthy of credence. The veracity of Montholon, whose memoirs appeared in 1847, is greater than that of Las Cases, whose *Memorial* saw the light in 1823. Gourgaud, whose journal remained unpublished until 1898, is the man who told everything. In November, 1816, Las Cases was expelled from St. Helena for attempting correspondence with Europe, and may well have been anxious to return. Gourgaud, quarrelling or affecting to quarrel with Napoleon, went off in his turn in March 1818. Thereafter Montholon was too busy to keep a regular journal, and passed to recollections written at a later date. These circumstances, coupled with suppressions made for family reasons, give rise to many uncertainties. The last three years of the Emperor's life are cloaked in obscurity and silence. He can hardly be heard speaking. He was deprived of the chatter of Las Cases, the stimulation of Gourgaud. He wrote no letters, as he refused to have them read by the governor. Gradually his voice fades away. As Rosebery said, it was the period of his 'mouldering'. He was also suffering from the cruel malady of his father. Slowly he would grow weaker and weaker, to gutter out at last in silence and the dark.

We must, then, resign ourselves to seeing the captive Emperor only through the mists, and, above all, to seeing him in the somewhat romanticized version which survived from St. Helena. But fortune refused Napoleon nothing. To lend his tragedy the twist of popular melodrama, it provided him with a jailer. Sir Hudson Lowe seems to have been chosen by decree of Providence. Without him an essential theme in the lament would be missing. The governor was narrow-minded, a stickler for form, and weak. He was overweighed by a sense of his responsibilities, obsessed by fears of escape, tormented by the memory of Campbell returning to Elba to find his bird flown. He made the island bristle with guns and sentries, and took the strictest precautions. Sometimes he would rise in the middle of the night and gallop to Longwood to make sure that his prisoner was still there. He was comically suspicious, and would not allow the French, Austrian and Russian commissioners to fulfil their duties and make certain for themselves of the captive's presence. Hudson Lowe was hallucinated. It was not hard for Napoleon to drive him half-mad, while the Longwood diarists took all pains to paint him as an executioner. They succeeded brilliantly. The 'hired assassin of the British oligarchy' inscribed his name amongst the most cruel torturers known to history, and when he returned home even his compatriots turned their backs on him.

But the governor did not invent a new punishment every day, and if Napoleon sought to blacken him it was not only with the idea of making his own woes more pathetic in the eyes of posterity. Towards the end his relations with Husdon Lowe became less strained, through mutual weariness, and because the Emperor no longer had the same interest in the episodes and conflicts. He had obtained the essential in forcing respect for his person and his name. One point on which he never yielded was his title. The English insisted on calling him 'General Bonaparte'. 'The last time I heard of him was at the battle of the Pyramids and Mount Tabor,' he retorted once and for all. He was the Emperor Napoleon, and remained so. His invariable argument was that the Imperial title belonged to the nation and the dynasty, and that, consecrated by the voice of the people and by the Church, it had entered into the glorious heritage of the French nation. It followed that the man who had received it had neither the right nor the power to abandon it. For his own part, he would never admit that he was a usurper. At the most, he would admit an incognito, like a travelling monarch, and suggested being styled Duroc or Muiron, the names of the only two men, perhaps, whom he had ever loved. The English refused. They would not in any way recognize that he had ever reigned, and Napoleon attached the utmost importance to standing firm. He submitted to endless unpleasantness in his daily life in order to maintain that he was not merely 'a distinguished officer', as Admiral Cockburn's formula had it — the officer who said that he had never known of an Emperor having been on board the *Northumberland*. This, the dynastic idea, was kept intact. And it may be that the Second Empire would never have come into being had it not been for the orders given at Longwood to know nothing about a 'General Bonaparte' being there.

With equal tenacity Napoleon barred his door against domiciliary visits. He shut himself indoors rather than allow himself to be followed on his walks, and reduced Hudson Lowe to making spies observe his movements. Rather theatrically he offered his silver for sale — other pieces had been brought to him later — in order that it might be known how grudgingly England provided for his needs. One day he even ordered his bed to be broken up for firewood. He was untiring in accusing his 'executioners' of having condemned him to slow death, of killing him by pin-pricks. He blamed the 'deadly' climate for his state of health, although it was a tumour of the pylorus, the schirrus of his father, as he quite well knew. But it was essential that the English should seem to be murdering him: 'it is only through martyrdom', he said, 'that the crown can be restored to my dynasty'.

It was in this spirit of a political policy that Napoleon, ably assisted by Sir Hudson Lowe and seconded by the memoir-writers, magnified sufferings of which the greatest were of a moral kind. To secure the effect he aimed at, he had perforce to be persecuted; and his obstinate resistance aggravated the persecution. On any hypothesis, it was well calculated. Submissive resignation would have earned him a few conveniences and amenities. But how much he would have lost! Two sayings throw light on his ideas: 'My career was lacking in adversity,' and :'If I die upon the cross and my son lives, he will succeed.'

The written word was his other weapon. He had promised 'to write the great things we have done together'. During the voyage he had already begun dictating his memoirs. St. Helena became an active centre of literary production, and, true or false, whatever came from St. Helena was devoured in Paris and in Europe.

As a man of letters, Napoleon had fully realized that he had the opportunity of composing his own history, and so of stamping it with the character that he chose. Not only did he offer his own apologia, but he also gave his narrative the right touch to act upon men's imaginations, giving the facts a form which could not easily be reshaped. He gave a specific tone to his life, to his reign, and to his wars. He even re-fashioned his historic remarks, writing them as they ought to have been uttered; and they were thereafter repeated as he wrote them. He was like an author revising his writings when he has achieved the full power of his style. He thus contributed in large measure to giving his story the epic note; and to him that meant more than his defensive pleas. His careful shifting of blame on to other shoulders is too natural to deceive one. It is very hard to efface the accent of his *Commentaires*, and to narrate, for instance, the Italian campaign without being under the spell of the magnificence of his own version.

This literature is marked out by its character as propaganda, a genre in which Napoleon had become a master. It was no great matter to appeal to sensibility by painting the sufferings of the captive. The writer had a longer aim. He worked for the future. In the course of his reign, with its torrential rapidity, he had taken every idea in turn, according to the needs of the moment, according to the circumstances which always enslaved him. Of general design he had none. And how often had he changed his plan! At St. Helena he meditated. In the newly pacified Europe he discerned the transformations which he had produced by traversing it and disturbing it throughout ten years. Thereupon he conceived a doctrine. He attributed purpose to what he had done, and laid claim to the results. He had roused national passions against France. He became the father of the principle of nationality. He had purposely roused the peoples from their former lethargy. And what of his conquests and annexations? He had wished to form one single Italy, one single Germany, the basis for the Europe of the future, and for a League of Nations — free nations — in place of the Holy Alliance of the kings. His soldiers and administrators had spread abroad, beyond the boundaries of France, the ideas of the Revolution, and done so that these ideas might turn back against him. He took possession of this outcome of his wars. Everywhere they had conveyed progress and light, liberty and the destruction of abuses and fanaticism. He remembered that he had been a Republican from his youth, that he had penned the *Lettres sur la Corse*, that he had been the chief servant of the ideas of 1789. He no longer said that he had 'cleaned up' the Revolution; no, he had 'consecrated it and infused it into the laws'; thrice he had saved it, in Vendémiaire, in Fructidor, and in the Hundred Days. It was consubstantial with himself. It was inseparably joined with himself, and he was 'the victim of the ostracism of the kings'. How many months had passed since that monologue in Dresden, before the icy Metternich, when he had declared that every throne would be dragged down in his fall! But the role which he now offered himself was that of Napoleon the democrat, the representative of 'modern ideas'. And that role he seized. 'Every day strips me a little more of my tyrant's skin,' he said one day, as if he had been looking at his own bust. He was carving the figure of a humanitarian Napoleon, who was at the same time an incarnation of glory and *la patrie*. He was equalitarian, and free from clericalism. But he gave due distinction to merit, and, like most Frenchmen, even at loggerheads with the Church, he would die in the Catholic religion. Finally, he would leave for Napoleon II a liberal constitution and sage advice in government. He himself had been a dictator only 'through force of circumstances'. He had not been able 'to slacken the bow'. But the 'peril' had always been the same, 'the struggle terrible, the crisis imminent'. And that was his excuse . . . That seed flung into the future took root. The Napoleonic throne would not be raised again by his son. But the founder of the dynasty had at least worked for his nephew. The Empire of Napoleon III was born at St. Helena.

Michelet wrote angrily of the Bonaparte Prometheus, whose name was thus being relaunched into new destinies: 'With singular clumsiness he was lodged in St. Helena, in such a way that the cheating fellow was able to make a Caucasus out of his lofty platform.' St. Helena was a laboratory of legends, to some extent a manufactory of forgeries. One feels as it were 'an atmosphere of falsehood'. Napoleon was made complete by the fact that he was able to make his place of exile, not only a Caucasian rock, but also a prophet's tripod. He became the prophet and spokesman of the new age. His spirit animated even his rock. It was his last great work, and he accomplished it by the same means which had already so powerfully aided his policy. He had said that one secret of his government had been 'endlessly to kindle ambition, curiosity, and hope'. From St. Helena he resuscitated the hope of a happier world. Faithful to the Emperor's testament, the heirs of Napoleon would resolve all the problems of the century. His nephew, the son of Louis and Hortense, would be believed when he appeared pledging himself to settle every question, whether of order, of pauperism, or of Europe. And curiosity was redoubled by that voice announcing a gospel from the far distances of ocean.

The same man, the same artist, always capable of doubling his roles, was now turning to contemplate himself in the part of a Messiah. At moments he became prophetic. He wrote strange words: 'A new Prometheus, I am nailed to a rock where a vulture is gnawing me. Yes, I have stolen fire from heaven as a gift for France: the fire turned back whence it came — and here I am!' Then he became natural again, and with that became contradictory. Gourgaud's journal shows him to have been then as he had always been, with a full and merciless knowledge of men and life, adopting contrary opinions one after another; and it was impossible to declare that he was not sincere in each. He told La Cases that he did not regret his lost greatness; and at that moment it was probably true. But he also said: 'Ah, things were fine in those days! I could distribute power and place,' — and that is too human for Gourgaud not to be believed. When he was told of the condemnation and execution of Ney, the Emperor, according to Montholon, declared it a crime, and said that the judges had stained themselves with blood that was sacred to France, that the bravest of the brave had not been a traitor, that Louis XVIII had sullied his own honour. But according to Gourgaud he said: 'Ney has only had his deserts.'

And what of doctrine? Here, too, the Emperor's views were no less variable. The official programme of St. Helena was for the democratic and liberal Empire, tinged with a Republican spirit. But Napoleon would also say that authority was the greatest of benefits, that deliberating assemblies were a scourge — as Louis XVIII would find out — that executions were better than charters for consolidating a throne. The Additional Act was invoked as proof that the Emperor did not aspire to dictatorship. But he told Gourgaud: 'It was my intention to send the Chambers packing, as soon as I found myself victorious and with a free hand.' Similarly with everything. He declared his belief in the existence of God. When he heard atheism being criticized, he retorted that the most learned members of the Institute were atheists. He believed in the immortality of the soul, and then would maintain that anatomy could show no difference between man and calf. We are bound to feel that with Gourgaud, himself rather cynical, he spoke as he felt, whilst

446

he reserved his loftier sentiments for Las Cases and Montholon. It is clear that Las Cases and Montholon retained from the St. Helena conversations only the noble and generous sayings, those which would certainly enhance the fair fame of the Emperor. It is not surprising to find, through Gourgaud, his old lack of pity for the human race, stern towards all, holding no man in esteem, shattering the most illustrious with a phrase, with kindness neither towards his brothers nor even towards either of his wives. And what scorn for the peoples themselves! He had wished his body to lie on the banks of the Seine, in the midst of the French nation whom he had loved so well; yet France 'was now merely a dishonoured nation of cowards', who 'only got what they deserved', like Ney and Murat. Napoleon was sinking into misanthropy. He made life at Longwood difficult for even the most devoted. He wanted not one of his family to be with him, not even his mother or sister; and, perhaps to avoid his heart being made less hard, he barely read the letters that came from them.

Reading was perhaps his chief distraction. His exile, like his youth, was a debauch of reading. He never had enough newspapers, enough books; and the English were as sparing with these as with other things. One of his griefs was that he had not a Polybius. In the evening he would take a tragedy — the occasion was dreaded by his entourage — and recite the lines, as he used to do with Joseph on that other island long ago, giving comments and criticisms. He refashioned Voltaire's play, *Mahomet*, with his own hand. He was ingenious in time-killing. And then, as day followed day, came boredom, and bodily suffering as well. His death was perhaps hastened more surely by the dejection of St. Helena than by the climate, if it be true that an incurable cancer gnaws the flesh of one whose soul is sorrowful. He became shapeless and slovenly, and forgetful of the etiquette on which he had insisted, as on his title, to keep alive the Imperial idea through its prestige; he was listless and pros-

447

trate, or else, wearing a fantastic planter's costume, he would busy himself with gardening.

The prisoner became invisible, his illness more severe. In a kind of last review of the glories of his reign, he dictated his political testament, which was also in a way prophetic. Its cadenced sentences set forth his supreme recommendations to his son and to the French people, an appeal to time, his avenger, and his forgiveness of those whose 'treacheries' had been the undoing of the Empire and of France; he named Marmont, Augereau, Talleyrand, La Fayette — to the further execration of their memory. His 'dearly loved spouse', Marie Louise, was named with honour, as if 'that rascal Neipperg' did not exist. In that solemn declaration, Napoleon made a point of adding that he, and he alone, was responsible for the arrest and condemnation of the Duc d'Enghien.

He died on May 5th, 1821. 'Head . . . army . . .' were said to be the last two words he uttered. In his agony he flung himself out of bed with terrific violence. A storm was raging over the island when he died. The faithful Marchand wrapped him in the cloak he had worn at Marengo. Abandonment, simplicity, mystery — everything was still coming to the aid of Napoleon's legend. He was granted the end that best matched his glory. Death itself, by one more touch of grandeur, completed the unique composition of his life.

Hudson Lowe did even better. That jack-in-office raised formality to the pitch of genius. Montholon and Bertrand wanted one word to be carved upon the Emperor's tomb: 'Napoleon'. The governor would only recognize 'Napoleon Bonaparte'. He was obstinate. So were the Frenchmen. And the stone remained blank. 'Here lies . . . no name'. A poet seized the idea, and wrote some ringing elegiac lines. The lover of tragedies, whose taste had remained with the classic school, was thus borne forward into the lyric current of the new century. Ever constant in its zealous renewal of the themes of his history, his star, by one supreme act of favour, led him into the Romantic camp.

CHAPTER XXVII

TRANSFIGURATION

THE incomparable meteor had ended its earthly passage. But precautions had been taken that it should not stop. Once dead, Napoleon took on the animation of a new life. After all his metamorphoses, he now became an image and an idea.

Marvels had piled up, on the only head strong enough to bear them, the only one capable of making use of them. Humble beginnings, triumphs, disasters, built up the illuminated pattern with their violent ·colours. Not even adversity was now lacking. Enduring luck, the jealousy of his star, eager to bring this heroic existence to the peak of perfection, contrived to give Bonaparte the highest prize of glory. And glory herself rewarded him for having given her his only real love. He had always aimed high, always reckoned on the grand scale. And he was rewarded by having the greatest measure of posthumous existence, of subjective immortality, that a man can possibly have.

The immense popularity of Napoleon, the causes of which are easily visible, is nevertheless surprising in certain aspects. Firstly, he was an intellectual, a man shaped by books and reading. He did not believe in intuition, except in that acquired by study and knowledge. These are not vulgar qualities, nor apt to attract the vulgar. No spell-binding gifts are to be seen in this staunch logician, this military and political astronomer, this disdainful philosopher, an almost Oriental despot, a devourer of flesh and blood. He himself did not like crowds. He dreaded them. His Versailles was at Saint-Cloud, out of reach of the turbulence of Paris. As a ruler, he enjoyed prestige rather than affection. When he fell, devotion was hardly to be found anywhere. The magic of his name had wrought miracles, but produced no Bonapartist Vendée. He perished, perhaps, chiefly through the doubts of common-sense men. For some years average opinion had viewed him as a wild megalomaniac.

And yet the return from Elba had already proved how the appeal of memories could overcome the hatred of war and conscription, the revulsion from extravagant enterprises. Soon after Waterloo men began again to feel the humiliation of defeat. It heightened the glamour of past victories. The golden days of the Consulate, the glorious days of the Empire — 'men looked only at one side of those times'. With Napoleon, the sun seemed to be quenched. And then literature, wherein his trust had not been in vain, gave back to him a hundredfold the elements and material with which he had furnished it. Verse and prose, novels and plays — the 'man of the century' invaded them all. Anybody who had memories to offer — soldiers, officers, sergeants, valets — set them down on paper. The booksellers solicited memoirs, and provided scribes for the more illiterate authors. It was an exceptionally flourishing industry. The Napoleonic bibliography waxed greater and greater. It was destined to become a mountain. Every day the Emperor rose higher on this pedestal of printed matter.

And similarly, in a spoken propaganda, the 'people's Napoleon' lived on. Balzac showed an old soldier telling the whole legend in the barn. He lived on in the stories told by grandmothers, following the songs of Béranger. And through this literature of the humble, more potent than that of the great lyricists, the Emperor retained his hold over the minds of men.

The Restoration grew weary in the struggle against this phantom. Louis-Philippe tried to exorcize it, and the magician was disinterred from beneath the willow tree in that lonely valley of St. Helena. The return of the ashes seemed to be a political idea, a satisfaction offered to the national honour, an act of placation. The King of Rome, Austria's hostage, who had become Duke of Reichstadt, was dead.

THE EXILE
From a drawing made at Longwood, 1820

What further incarnation was to be feared? December 15th, 1840 beheld the funeral of the Emperor. He was laid to rest with great pomp in the Invalides, among the military heroes of France, near the banks of the Seine, as if to declare that his supreme wish had been granted, and that all was ended. But in his sarcophagus he lived on.

Then appeared the nephew, the son of Louis and Hortense, who as a child had been present at the Champ de Mai. A conspirator under the July monarchy, he was elected by popular vote under the Republic of 1848. The work of St. Helena had been successful. The legend was made incarnate. Those who had helped to spread it abroad, in prose and in verse, incredulous that literature could wield so much power, were stupefied. The sober and sensible men who had laughed at Louis-Napoleon Bonaparte were covered with shame. The thing which they had declared absurd and impossible had come to pass. Could words be thus powerful? Away on his rock, Napoleon had known that they could. The *Memorial*, the testament, the rhythmic sentences, had enabled him to restore his dynasty.

The Second Empire was a repetition of the First, without the genius; and like the First, it collapsed through an invasion. Sedan did not injure Austerlitz, nor even Waterloo. The invective which bruised and battered Napoleon the Small still drew its strength from Napoleon the Great.

Cæsarism stood condemned. The figure of the Cæsar himself, vanquished and overturned a third time in this pale heir of his, only glowed the brighter. Henceforth his power was spiritual. He became the high-priest of war, the high-priest of energy. Examples, lessons, a doctrine were sought at his feet. He gave them. And even when his disciples were beaten, it was not his fault, nor the fault of his teaching, but their own fault.

The time came when Europe staged battles which made those of Napoleon seem small in scale. It was doubtful whether even his genius would have been equal to these armed masses and gigantic fronts; but still men said: 'If *he* had been there . . .' That war was followed by unparalleled upheavals. And again men thought of Napoleon. Had not that scourage of God already been the instrument of the great transformations in Europe? Was he not credited with effects of which his wars had been the cause? War is a revolution, just as revolutions are war. Sixty battles fought by Bonaparte left behind them a new world, and he appeared to have fathered a society of which he had really only been the midwife. And the work of St. Helena bore fruit. Every people regarded him as their tyrant and their liberator in one. He stood out as one of the greatest revolutionary forces of history, a *primum movens* of humanity. Books and arguments had a fresh theme. The memory of Napoleon took on fresh life through sociology.

At bottom, men admire themselves in admiring Napoleon, just as his soldiers, in loving him, loved their own glory and their own sufferings. Forgetful of the events which enabled him to rise so high, and of the consummate skill with which he seized hold of circumstance, men marvel that any mortal should have succeeded in such a climb. If he had been merely the lucky soldier who becomes a king, he would be one among many. The Roman Empire, the history of Asia, are both packed with such instances. But his own case was unique in modern times and in the western world. Here was an artillery officer who, within a few years, acquired greater power than Louis XIV and assumed the crown of Charlemagne, never stopping on his headlong course: the phenomenon was justifiably viewed as prodigious in the century of 'enlightenment', in a rationalistic Europe, and above all in France, where the beginnings of other royal dynasties had been so slow, so modest, and so difficult, and where their establishment had required several generations. Napoleon's contemporaries were dazzled by the swiftness of his rise no less than by its height. And we still are. He himself expressed a slightly bourgeois amazement at it all when he told Las

Cases that it would need 'thousands of centuries' for the same spectacle to be repeated.

A spectacle which he also watched, when he had time. He had no vanity in being a great captain. War was 'a vast art which includes all others', and he could wage it as a man can play chess – 'a peculiar gift which was inborn in me'; and he flattered himself that it was not his sole faculty. Power he loved; but he loved it 'as an artist', and added: 'I love it as a musician loves his fiddle.' It is curious that he is still blamed for not having shown moderation, for not having been reasonable. Men persist in holding such a superhuman idea of Napoleon that they come to believe that it was within his own power to make the sun stand still, to halt the spectacle and the spectator at the most splendid moment.

And what was the man himself? One on whom life bestowed everything, beyond all measure, and one whom it also battered unmercifully. His first wife deceived him, his second deserted him. He was severed from his son. His brothers and sisters always disappointed him. Of any ordinary man, it would be said that he was unhappy. There was nothing which he did not wear out prematurely, even his own will. And how many days, in his most brilliant epoch, did he save from the cares that dogged him, from that sense that everything was brittle and entrusted to him only for a little while? 'You grow great joylessly,' said Lamartine, very truly. Always hurrying, consuming his days, he was led logically on and on, straight for the reefs which his imagination told him of; and he hastened ahead of his downfall as if eager to have it over.

His reign, as he knew, was precarious. He saw no sure refuge but a leading place in history, an unrivalled prominence amongst the world's greatest men. Analysing the causes of his fall, he always came back to the same point: 'And above all, a dynasty that was not old enough . . .' That was where he was helpless. Doubtful of preserving this miraculous throne, at the same time doing everything to strengthen it, he based his thought upon different images. Daru denied that his vast intelligence suffered any illusions: 'he never seemed to me to have any aim except that of gathering, during his blazing and headlong course upon earth, more glory, more greatness, and more power than any man had ever acquired'. Mme de Rémusat confirms in the religious aspect what Daru declared of the practical: 'I would venture to say that the immortality of his name appeared to him in a very different order of importance from that of the immortality of his soul.'

A thousand portraits have been drawn of Napoleon, psychological, intellectual, moral; a thousand judgments have been passed. But he always escapes, by a line or two, from the pages that seek to hold him enclosed. He is elusive, not because he is infinite, but because he varied with the situations into which fate thrust him. He was himself as shifting as his successive positions. His mental power, though vast, was above all else supple and plastic. But it had limitations. It has not perhaps been sufficiently noted that, for all his fruitfulness in prophecy — contradictory it is true — Napoleon did not foresee machinery or a mechanical age. His forecasts took no account of the development of the applied sciences. He did not even think of new engines of war; he waged war with the methods and weapons of Gribeauval and Suffren. Neither Jouffroy's nor Fulton's steamboat caught his attention. With his fondness for Ossian, and a memory packed with poetic lines which he applied to himself at moments of pathos, his turn of mind was perhaps mainly literary, and thereby somewhat Neronian. And yet he was unmatched in his care for detail. He knew the exact number of ammunition waggons in his artillery parks just as he knew the value of money. He was fanatical about audits and statistics, and insistent upon accuracy. But serious witnesses report that he was quite ready to declare figures out of the blue. Thus every one of his portraits diverges from the true at one place or another, and he can be made to say everything because he actually did say nearly everything. He has been styled 'Jupiter-Scapin', and 'the tragi-comedian', till one is weary. But he said of himself that it is not far from the sublime to the ridiculous, and that he could not be fully apprehended from that side. Nor could it be through his Italian or Corsican origins. If he waged a vendetta with the Duc d'Enghien, he waged none with Fouché, nor with many others whom he spared, even Bourbons. If it be admitted that, following the usage of his native isle, he was the slave of clan feeling, it has to be explained why he made exceptions of Louis and Lucien, and why Louis and Lucien, suckled at the same breast, should have stood clear of the tribe. In fact, the variety and plausibility of the interpretations of Napoleon are due to the way in which the diversity and mobility of his mind match the almost unexampled diversity in the circumstances of his life.

Except from the point of view of glory, or of 'art', it would probably be better that Napoleon should never have existed. All in all, his reign, which was meant to continue the Revolution, ended in dire failure. His genius prolonged a contest which he was foredoomed to lose. All these victories, all these conquests (which he had not begun himself) — to what end? To go back to just beyond the point from which the militant Revolution had started, where France had been left by Louis XVI, to abandon the natural frontiers to their place in the museum of derelict doctrines. It was not worth the cost of so much upheaval, unless to bequeath to history the legacy of some noble pictures. Bonaparte restored an order in Europe: but was it worth the disorder that he spread, the forces that he quickened only to bring them back upon the heads of Frenchmen? As for the Napoleonic state, which endured through four regimes and seemed to be built upon a base of bronze, it is in decadence. Gradually its laws are falling apart. Before long France will be further away from the Napoleonic Code than Napoleon was from Justinian and the Institutes, and the day is approaching when the impulse of new ideas will leave the work of the legislator as a thing outmoded.

A man of imagination, a potent maker of images, a poet, he had a strong sense of this flight of the centuries. Las Cases asked him once why he had not brought the sword of Frederick II to St. Helena along with the king's alarm-clock. 'I had my own,' he answered, pinching the ear of his biographer, with the smile that he could make so charming. He knew that in the imagination of the peoples he had eclipsed Frederick the Great, that his picture would hang upon their walls and his name upon signboards, until some other hero should arise to take his place. That other hero has not come. The fabulous adventurer, the Emperor with the Roman mask, the god of battles, the man who taught humanity that possibilities have no bounds, the demi-urge of politics and war, remains unique in his kind. It may be that, in the course of time, Ampère will count for more than Napoleon. The Napoleonic era may prove to be no more than a brief episode in what will be styled the Age of Electricity. In the end, perhaps, Napoleon will be but one of the figures of the solar myth, appearing in an island of the rising sun and fading out in an island of the sunset. He was hardly dead when men turned to such hypotheses and fancies. All men, all things, come to dust. Napoleon Bonaparte has no armour against oblivion. Nevertheless, after a hundred years, the glamour of his name remains intact, and his aptitude for survival is as extraordinary as his aptitude for ruling. When he left Malmaison for Rochefort, before delivering himself into the hands of his enemies, he lingered mournfully as he turned away from his memories and off the world's stage. From the memory of mankind he will pass no less slowly; and across the years, through revolutions and through strange rumour, the ears of men still catch the footsteps of the Emperor as he passes beyond the world's edge to reach new horizons.

SURVEY OF
NAPOLEONIC BIBLIOGRAPHY

SURVEY OF
NAPOLEONIC BIBLIOGRAPHY

I. GENERAL

Sources. The principal source is the *Correspondance* published by order of Napoleon III (28 vol. Paris 1857-59) followed by *Œuvres de Napoléon à Sainte-Hélène* (1870, 4 vol.). This publication is incomplete. In addition there are:

Lecestre: *Lettres inédites de Napoléon Ier* (1897, 2 vol.); de Brotonne: *Idem* . (1898) and *Dernières lettres inédites* (1903).

A. Chuquet: *Ordre et apostilles* (1911-12, 4 vol.).

Picard and Tuetay: *Correspondance inédite* (1912-13, 4 vol.).

The most complete itinerary has been given by Schuermans: *Itinéraire général de Napoléon Ier* (1908).

For legislative documents, see: *Bulletin des lois*, 3rd and 4th series.

Duvergier: *Collection* (vol. XII to XVIII).

Dalloz: *Répertoire* (1st edition 1865-70, 48 vol.).

Histories: There are innumerable histories of Napoleon. The older ones such as that of Walter Scott are only of interest as curiosities. The same cannot be said of:

Thiers: *Histoire du Consulat et de l'Empire* (1845-1862, 20 vol., index and atlas. Numerous editions in all languages).

Lanfrey: *Histoire de Napoléon Ier* (1867-75, 5 vol.).

Oncken: *Das Zeitalter der Revolution, des Kaiserreiches und der Befreiungskriege* (Berlin, 1880, 2 vol.).

Taine: *Les origines de la France contemporaine*: 3e partie: *le Régime moderne* (1891-94, 2 vol., unfinished).

A. Fournier: *Napoléon: Eine Biographie* (Vienna and Leipzig, 1886-93 3 vol.).

Lavisse and Rambaud: *Histoire générale* (vol. IX, 1893).

Masson : *Napoléon et sa famille* (10 vol. 1897-1913).

J. Holland Rose: *The Life of Napoleon I* (1905, 2 vol.).

The Cambridge Modern History, vol. IX. Napoleon (1906).

Lavisse: *Histoire de France contemporaine*, vol. II and III, by G. Pariset (1923, 2 vol.).

Madelin: *Histoire politique*, vol. IV of *l'Histoire de la nation française* edited by Gabriel Hanotaux.

NAPOLEONIC BIBLIOGRAPHY

II. YOUTH AND DEVELOPMENT

Sources. Youthful writings have been published by Masson and Biagi: *Napoléon inconnu* (1895, 2 vol.).

Histories. Gadobert: *La jeunesse de Napoléon Ier* (1897).
A. Chuquet: *La Jeunesse de Napoléon Ier* (3 vol. 1897-99).
P. Cottin: *Toulon et les Anglais en 1793* (1898).
C. J. Fox: *Napoleon Bonaparte and the Siege of Toulon* (1902).
J. Collin: *L'éducation militaire de Napoléon Ier* (1902).
O. Browning: *Napoleon, the First Phase* (1905)
H. F. Hall: *Napoleon's Notes on English History* (1905).
H. Zivy: *Le 13 vendémiaire* (1898).

III. FROM THE ITALIAN CAMPAIGN TO THE 18TH OF BRUMAIRE

Sources. The Memoirs of all the personages of that epoch must here be cited. In particular those of the Directors:
Barras, published by Duruy (1895-6, 4 vol.).
Barthélemy, published by Y. de Dampierre (1914).
Carnot, published by his grandson.
Gohier (1824, 2 vol.).
La Revellière (1895, 3 vol.).
See also the *Mémoires* of Masséna published by Koch (1849-50, 7 vol.).

For the Egyptian expedition:
Les Mémoires de Bourrienne (vol. II and III, 1829).
Lettres de Geoffroy Saint-Hilaire, Hamy (1901).
Vol. III of *Despatches and Letters* of Nelson.
Under the title: *Paris pendant la réaction thermidorienne et le Directoire*, Aulard published numerous police reports and extracts from the daily papers (5 vol. 1898-1902).

Histories. A Sorel: *L'Europe et la Révolution française*, vol. V, Bonaparte et le Directoire (1903).
Guyot: *Le Directoire et la paix de l'Europe* (1911).
Clausewitz: *Der Feldzug von 1796 in Italien* (Berlin, 1883).
Colin: *Étude sur la campagne de 1796-97* (1898).
Fabry: *Campagne d'Italie* (1900-1901, three volumes followed by *Mémoires*, 1905, and *Rapports*, 1905, the whole edited by the Section historique de L'Etat Major français).
Gaffarel: *Bonaparte et les Républiques italiennes, 1796-97* (1895).

G. Tivaroni: *Critica del Risorgimento italiano* (the first three volumes, Turin, 1888-97).

Bianchi: *Storia della monarchia piemontese* (Turin 1885, 4 vol., vol. II).

For Egypt the most recent and by far the best work is: La Jonquière: *L'Expédition d'Egypte* (1900-7, 5 vol., edited by the Section historique de l'Etat-Major).

For the coup d'Etat, Vandal: *L'avènement de Bonaparte*, t. I (1903), with critical indication of sources.

J. Bainville: *Le 18 brumaire* (1926).

Rocquain: *L'Etat de la France au 18 brumaire* (1874).

IV. PRIVATE LIFE

Sources. The chief *Mémoires* are those of: the Duchesse d'Abrantès (1831-37, 18 vol.).

Mme de Rémusat (1879-80, 3 vol.).

de Savary (1828, 8 vol.).

Considérations and *Les Dix Années d'Exil* of Mme de Staël.

Mémoires of the personnel of the Palais:

Beausset (1827-8, 4 vol.).

Constant (1830-1, 6 vol.).

Baron Fain (1908).

General Durand (1819, 2 vol.).

Meneval (1894, 3 vol.), etc. . . .

The book, *Mémoires et Correspondance de l'impératrice Joséphine*, (1820) is apocryphal.

Empress Marie-Louise: *Correspondance 1799-1847* (Vienna 1887).

Jérôme: *Mémoires et Correspondance*, du Casse (1861, 7 vol.).

Joseph: *Mémoires et Correspondance*, du Casse (1853-4, 10 vol.).

Queen Hortense: *Mémoires*, published by Prince Napoleon (1927, 3 vol.).

Histories. Frédéric Masson: *Napoléon et les femmes* (1893), *Napoléon chez lui* (1894).

Bouchot: *La toilette à la Cour de Napoléon* (1895).

A. Lévy: *Napoléon intime* (1893).

de Lescure: *Napoléon et sa famille* (1867).

Larrey: *Madame Mère* (1892, 2 vol.).

Masson: *Joséphine de Beauharnais, Madame Bonaparte, Joséphine impératrice, Joséphine repudiée* (1899-1919, 4 vol.).

Rocquain: *Napoléon Ier et le Roi Louis* (1875).

Welschinger: *Le Divorce de Napoléon* (1899), *Mariage de Napoléon* (Revue Revolutionnaire, 1888, 11).

Masson: *Marie Louise* (1902).

Masson: *Napoléon et son fils* (1904).

NAPOLEONIC BIBLIOGRAPHY

V. FOREIGN POLITICS AND WARS

Sources. Martens: *Recueil général des traités d'alliance et de paix*, with supplements and tables (Göttingen, 1817-76).

Talleyrand: *Lettres inédites à Napoléon*, p. by Pallain (1889) and *Mémoires*, p. by de Broglie (1891 and 2, 5 vol.).

Metternich: *Mémoires* (8 vol., vol. I and II).

Hardenberg: *Denkwürdigkeiten* (p. by Ranke, Leipzig, 1877, 5 vol.).

Nesselrode: *Lettres et papiers* (vol. III to V, 1905-7).

Castlereagh: *Memoirs and Correspondence* (1848-53, 12 vol.).

Tratchevski: *Documents diplomatiques*, concerning the relations between France and Russia (Petersburg, 1890-1, 2 vol. in Russian and French)

Bailleul: *Preussen und Frankreich, Dipl. Corr.* (Leipzig, 1881-87, 2 vol.).

For details of military events and the life of the combatants, refer to memoirs of the Generals and soldiers, especially:

Bernadotte: *Correspondance* (1819).

Davout: *Correspondance* (1887, 4 vol.).

Gille: *Mémoires d'un conscrit* (1892).

Lavallette: *Mémoires* (1831, 2 vol.).

Coignet: *Cahiers* (1883).

Marbot: *Mémoires* (1891, 3 vol.).

Marmont: *Mémoires* (1856-57, 9 vol.).

Murat: *Correspondance, Lettres et documents* (1899 and 1908-14).

Soult: *Mémoires* (1854, 3 vol.), etc. . . .

These memoirs are of unequal merit and should only be consulted subject to criticism.

Histories. Bourgeois: *Manuel historique de politique étrangère*, vol. II (1898).

Sorel: *L'Europe et la Révolution française*, vol. VI, VII and VIII with index (1903-4).

Tramond: *Manuel d'histoire maritime de la France* (1916).

A. T. Mahan: *Influence of Sea Power on the French Revolution and Empire* (1892, 2 vol.).

Driault: *Napoléon et l'Europe* (1910).

Pingaud: *Bonaparte, président de la République italienne*; *La domination française dans l'Italie du Nord* (1914, 2 vol.).

H. A. L. Fisher: *Napoleonic Statesmanship: Germany* (Oxford, 1903).

Froidevaux: *La politique coloniale de Napoléon* (Revue des questions historiques, 1901).

A. Lévy: *Napoléon et la paix* (1903).

Driault: *La Politique orientale de Napoléon* (1904).

NAPOLEONIC BIBLIOGRAPHY

Marshal Franchet d'Esperey and General Mangin:
Histoire Militaire et Navale, vol. VIII of the *Histoire de la nation française* of Hanotaux.

On the detail of military and diplomatic events:
Roberts: *The Negotiations preceding the Peace of Amiens* (Transact. of the Royal Hist. Soc., 1901, vol. XX).
H. M. Boxman: *Preliminary Stages of the Peace of Amiens* (Toronto, 1900).
Philipson: *La Paix d'Amiens* (Revue historique, 1901).
Driault: *Bonaparte et le recez germanique* (Revue historique, 1909).
O. Browning: *England and Napoleon in 1803* (London, 1887).
J. H. Rose: *Napoleon and English Commerce* (Eng. Hist. Rev., 1893).
Select Despatches relating to the Formation of the 3rd Coalition (London, 1904).
Coquelle: *Napoléon et l'Angleterre* (1904).
O. Brandt: *England und die napoleonische Weltpolitik 1800-03* (Heidelberg, 1916).
Yorck von Wartenburg: *Napoleon als Feldherr* (Berlin, 1885-6, 2 vol.).
Camon: *La guerre napoléonienne: Précis des campagnes* (1903), *les systèmes d'opérations* (1907), *les batailles* (1910), *la fortification* (1914). And also of interest:
Jomini: *Vie politique et militaire de Napoléon Ier* (1827, 4 vol. and atlas).
Mathieu Dumas: *Précis des événements militaires* (1817-26, 19 vol.).
Oman: *Hist. of the Peninsula War* (1902-11, 4 vol., Oxford).
Greillon: *Les Guerres d'Espagne* (1902).
Vandal: *Napoléon et Alexandre* (3 vol., 1891).
Fabry: *Campagne de Russie* (1900-3, 5 vol.).
Chuquet: *La guerre de Russie* (1912, 3 vol.).
Clément: *Campagne de 1813* (1904).
Houssaye: *1814* (1 vol., 1888), *1815* (3 vol., 1895-1905).
Fournier: *Der Kongress von Chatillon* (Leipzig, 1900).
P. Gruyer: *Napoléon, roi de l'île d'Elbe* (1906).

VI. INTERNAL POLITICS

Sources. The contemporary memoirs already cited.
Aulard: *Paris sous le consultat* (4 vol.). *Paris sous le premier Empire* vol. I and II (unfinished).
Selections from police bulletins and extracts from articles in the daily papers.
Gaudin de Gaëte: *Mémoires, Souvenirs, Opinions et Ecrits* (new edition in 3 vol., 1926).
Portalis: *Discours et travaux sur le code civil* (1844).
Pasquier: *Histoire de mon temps* (1893-95, 6 vol.).

NAPOLEONIC BIBLIOGRAPHY

Boulay de la Meurthe: *Documents sur la négociation du Concordat et sur les autres rapports de la France avec le Saint-Siège* (1891-1905, 6 vol.).

Villemain: *Rapport au roi sur l'instruction secondaire* (1843, in 4to).

Cousin: *Défense de l'Université* (Discours, 1844).

Pelet de la Lozère: *Opinions de Napoléon sur divers sujets de politique et d'administration* (Paris, 1833).

Histories. Vandal: *L'avènement de Bonaparte* (2 vol. 1905).

Esmein: *Précis élémentaire du droit français* (1908).

Ducoc: *Le conseil d'Etat* (1876).

L. Madelin: *Fouché* (1901, 2 vol.).

E. Mounet: *Histoire de l'Administration provinciale, départmentale et communale* (Paris, 1885).

Régnier: *Les préfets du Consultat et de l'Empire* (1907).

Passy: *Frochot, préfet de la Seine* (1867).

Dejean: *Beugnot* (1907).

Pingaud: *Jean de Bry* (1909).

Lévy-Schneider: *Jeanbon-Saint-André* (vol. II, 1901).

Stourm: *Les finances du Consulat* (1902).

Marion: *Histoire financière de la France* (vol. IV, 1797-1818) (1925: principal work).

A. Madelin: *Le premier Consul législateur* (1865).

Book of the *Centénaire de la Cour des Comptes*.

Schmidt: *L'organisation de l'Université Impériale* (Ecole des Hautes Etudes Sociales, 1912).

On the Concordat and religious policy:

Abbé Mounet: *Histoire générale de l'Eglise,* vol. VII (1912).

Debidour: *Histoire générale de l'Eglise et de l'Etat* (1898).

Rinieri: *La diplomazia pontificale nel secolo XIX,* vol. I (Rome, 1902), translated into French by Verdier (1903).

d'Haussonville: *L'Eglise romaine et le premier Empire* (1868-69, 5 vol.).

On the Opposition and conspiracies. E. Daudet: *Histoire de l'émigration* (3 vol., 1886-90 and 1904-05), and *La Police et les Chouans sous le premier Empire* (1898).

Chassin: *Les pacifications de l'Ouest* (vol. III, 1899).

G. de Cadoudal: *Georges Cadoudal et la Chouannerie* (1887).

E. Guillon: *Les complots militaires sous le Consulat et l'Empire* (1894).

H. Welschinger: *Le duc d'Enghien* (1888 and 1913).

Hamel: *Histoire des deux conspirations du Général Malet* (1873).

NAPOLEONIC BIBLIOGRAPHY

VII. ST. HELENA

Sources. Captain F. L. Maitland: *Narrative of the Surrender of Bonaparte* (London, 1826-1904).
Gourgaud: *Journal de Sainte-Hélène de 1815 à 1818* (2 vol., 1897).
Montholon: *Récit de la captivité de l'Empereur Napoléon* (2 vol., 1847).
Les Cases: *Mémorial de Sainte-Hélène* (4 vol., London and Paris, 1823).

Histories. Sir T. Ussher: *Napoleon's Last Voyages* (1895 and 1906).
Lady Malcolm: *A Diary of St. Helena* (1899).
W. Forsyth: *History of the Captivity of Napoleon at St. Helena* (3 vol., 1853).
Basil Jackson: *Notes and Reminiscences of a Staff Officer* (1903).
Earl of Rosebery: *Napoleon, the last Phase* (1900).
R. M. Seaton: *Napoleon's Captivity in relation to Sir Hudson Lowe* (1903).
J. H. Rose: *Napoleonic Studies* (1904).

INDEX

INDEX

INDEX

INDEX

INDEX

INDEX

INDEX

INDEX

Lightning Source UK Ltd.
Milton Keynes UK
10 March 2010